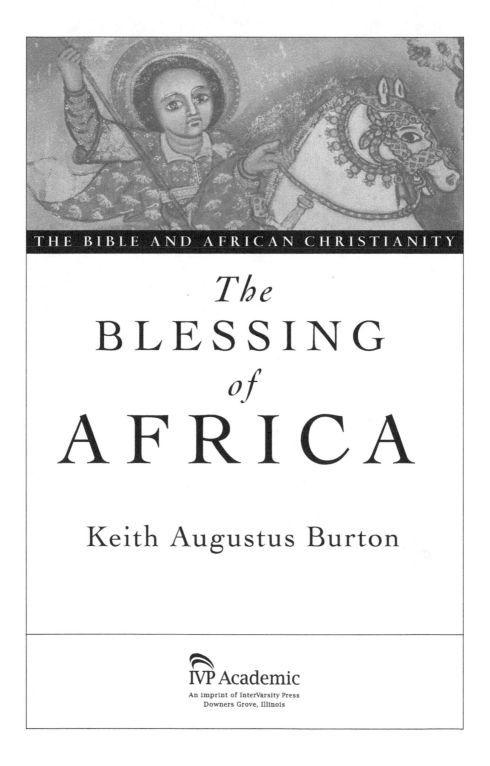

THE BIBLE AND AFRICAN CHRISTIANITY

The
BLESSING
of
AFRICA

Keith Augustus Burton

IVP Academic
An imprint of InterVarsity Press
Downers Grove, Illinois

InterVarsity Press
P.O. Box 1400, Downers Grove, IL 60515-1426
World Wide Web: www.ivpress.com
E-mail: email@ivpress.com

InterVarsity Press® is the book-publishing division of InterVarsity Christian Fellowship/USA®, a student movement active on campus at hundreds of universities, colleges and schools of nursing in the United States of America, and a member movement of the International Fellowship of Evangelical Students. For information about local and regional activities, write Public Relations Dept., InterVarsity Christian Fellowship/USA, 6400 Schroeder Rd., P.O. Box 7895, Madison, WI 53707-7895, or visit the IVCF website at <www.intervarsity.org>.

Scripture quotations, unless otherwise noted, are from the New Revised Standard Version of the Bible, *copyright 1989 by the Division of Christian Education of the National Council of the Churches of Christ in the USA. Used by permission. All rights reserved.*

Design: Cindy Kiple
Images: mural: J P De Manne/Getty Images
*   map: Joan Blaeu/Getty Images*

ISBN 978-0-8308-2762-6

Printed in the United States of America ∞

Library of Congress Cataloging-in-Publication Data

Burton, Keith Augustus.
  The blessing of Africa: the Bible and African Christianity/Keith
  Augustus Burton.
        p. cm.
  Includes bibliographical references and index.
  ISBN 978-0-8308-2762-6 (pbk.: alk. paper)
  1. Bible—History. 2. Africa—Church history. 3. Bible—Black
interpretations. 4. Blacks in the Bible. 5. Afrocentrism—Religious
aspects—Christianity. 6. Bible—Criticism, interpretation, etc. I.
Title.
  BS447.5.A35B87 2007
  276—dc22

                                                                                2007011184

P	21	20	19	18	17	16	15	14	13	12	11	10	9	8	7	6	5	4	3	2	1
Y	25	24	23	22	21	20	19	18	17	16	15	14	13	12	11	10	09	08	07			

To all of Africa's children who seek

peace in the midst of the storm.

"Blessed are the peacemakers,

for they will be called children of God."

MATTHEW 5:9

CONTENTS

Acknowledgments 9

Introduction 11

PART ONE: THE LAND OF HAM: *Defining Biblical Africa* 17
  1 The Table of Nations in Genesis 10 21
  2 Defining the Territory of Cush 30
  3 Defining the Territory of Misrayim 41
  4 Defining the Territory of Canaan 47

PART TWO: FAMILY REUNION: *Africans in the Bible* 57
  5 Identifying the Africans in Cush 61
  6 Identifying the Africans in Misrayim 73
  7 Identifying the Africans in Canaan 91

PART THREE: GROWING PAINS: *The Bible in Emerging
African Christianity* 111
  8 The Development of Christianity in Palestine 115
  9 The Development of Christianity in Egypt and North Africa . . . 123
  10 The Development of Christianity in Arabia and Ethiopia 135

PART FOUR: TOTAL ECLIPSE: *Islam's Distortion of the Biblical Message* . . 145
  11 The Influence of the Bible on the Qur'an 149
  12 The Growth of Islam in Biblical Africa 156

PART FIVE: HOSTILE TAKEOVER: *Europe's Manipulation
of the Biblical Message* 173
  13 The European Crusade Against Islam 175
  14 The Struggle for Control in the Ethiopian Church 186
  15 Mission and Colonization in Sub-Saharan Africa 196

PART SIX: FREE AT LAST: *The Bible and African Liberation* 207
  16 The Decline of Christianity in Islamic Africa 209
  17 The Shortcomings of Ethiopian Christianity 217
  18 The Impact of Christianity on Sub-Saharan Africa 227

Conclusion 245

Appendix 1: Descendants of Ham and the Modern Locations
              of Their Assigned Territories and Nations. 250
Appendix 2: Shared Blessings:
              Hamo-Semitic Africans in the Land of Cush 252

Works Cited 263

Author and Names Index. 280

Subject Index. 283

Scripture Index. 290

ACKNOWLEDGMENTS

A well-known African proverb states, "It takes a village to raise a child." Life experience has taught me that the "village" is an essential factor in every successful venture. Indeed, *The Blessing of Africa* could not have been completed had there not been selfless villagers whose varied and invaluable contributions helped to cheer me on to the finish line.

I would first like to express appreciation to the villagers who were instrumental in shaping the book. My editor, Al Hsu, has been a godsend. His patience, advice and constant encouragement helped to keep me on track. His fine work was complemented by other members of the proficient team at InterVarsity Press who helped to refine the manuscript and lent their creative talents to the cover design and maps. I am also grateful to the readers of the manuscript who exposed the fallible areas, which forced me to revisit, rethink and restructure.

Aiding the InterVarsity family were others who read and critiqued parts of the manuscript, particularly Doug Morgan and Hyacinth Burton. Further, how can I forget those who assisted me with different aspects of research during my wonderful years at Oakwood College—Roary Xavier Greene, Charles Bowie, Andrew Loiten and Wayne Moten. Additionally, I must mention my cousin, Marlon Reid, who also provided indispensable research assistance while writing term papers for his seminary classes. Most importantly are those villagers, both living and departed, who have taken the time to record and interact with history so that future generations can have the resources to dialogue with their past.

The second category of villagers include those who have been especially supportive of me and my family during the past three years. Their selflessness helped to preserve our faith in the family of God. These include George Ashley, Jeff Brown, Ernie Bursey, Marvin Carroll, Damian Chandler, Adean

Fearing, Cynthia Fearing, Edith Fraser, Trevor Fraser, Vince Goddard, Courtney Goulding, Daniel Hembree, Pamela Henry, Audrey James, Jeremiah Jasper, Robert Jewett, Ebenezer Jones-Lartey, Artie Melançon, James Melançon, Alphonso McCarthy, Pedrito Maynard-Reid, Belynda Mulzac, Kenneth Mulzac, Gregory Nelson, Hugh Page, Kingsley Palmer, David Person, Neil Reid, Russel Seay, Laura Shand, Lance Shand, David Taylor, Kenneth Vaux, Jerry Winslow, Robert Yee and Khiok Khng Yeo.

Finally, I am honored to acknowledge those villagers who know me most intimately—the members of my immediate family. Words cannot express how blessed I am to have my supportive wife, Cynthia, and two wonderful children, Sheereen and Kaleem, all of whom have expanded my concept of love. These are joined by my army of siblings whose unconditional love is exemplary: Courtney, Claudette, Dale, Rosey, Vanessa, Karen, Junior, Peter, Lincoln, Max and Ken. And where would I be without the love of my parents and parents-in-law, Nehemiah Augustus Burton, Cynthia Yvonne Morgan-Burton, Jose Shelton, and Petrenella Shelton—four blessed children of God, who have been a blessing to me and so many others.

Keith Augustus Burton
Sunday, March 25, 2007
Bicentennial Anniversary for the Abolition of Slavery

INTRODUCTION

Then Israel came to Egypt;

Jacob lived as an alien in the land of Ham.

PSALM 105:23

In Acts 10:9-16, the apostle Peter had a vision in which he was invited to partake of clean and unclean meat. Of course, as a law-observant Jew, Peter would never even think about eating from that spread. Even the clean meat that was on the sheet was considered taboo, simply because it was in the same geographical space as the unclean. The exact meaning of the vision was revealed to him when representatives from the Roman centurion Cornelius summoned him to come and minister to their master. After discovering that Cornelius had also been miraculously contacted by the same God, the meaning of the vision became clear to Peter, who declared, "Truly I understand that God shows no partiality, but in every nation anyone who fears him and does what is right is acceptable to him" (Acts 10:34-35).

The basic teaching of an inclusive God abounds in Scripture, yet some have used God's Word to perpetuate the myth of a cursed race—the dark-skinned sons of Ham. The myth has become so common that many have placed the text about the "curse of Ham" in their own imaginative Bibles next to verses like "cleanliness is next to godliness" or "God helps those who help themselves." Armed with a cadre of textual misinterpretations, allegations of a cursed race have been used to subjugate the peoples of Africa and other dark-skinned people for over a millennia. This book is written to join the growing battery of research that aims to set the record straight.

Working under the assumption that the author of the "Table of Nations" in Genesis 10 intended for it to convey an accurate geographical picture of Ham's descendants, this book defines "biblical Africa" as a territory that transcends our modern understanding of the continent and includes large portions of the Middle East. You will notice throughout the book that the term "biblical Africa" is often used interchangeably with the phrase "land of Ham." This is not to suggest that the ancients used these labels to refer to the region under observation. Only in the Psalms do we find a reference to the "land of Ham," and it would be centuries after the biblical world that a "continent" would be dubbed "Africa." However, I am using these terms *rhetorically* to reinforce the data of Genesis 10. Indeed, it is with the same rhetorical intention that I speak of Canaan, Misrayim, Cush and Put—terms that may not always corroborate the historically correct labels at certain points in history, but which are essential for defining the geographical area under consideration.

Although there are some who would probably prefer that I utilize the standard terms recognized by the scholarly majority, please understand that my use of nonconventional language is intentional. One of the purposes of this work is to encourage people to start thinking differently about history and the biblical world. It is often the conquerors who manipulate our understanding of history and influence the nuances of the dominant language of society. As a David in a sea of Goliaths, this work deliberately resists conforming to standard nomenclature. The stubborn stance is not for the purpose of forwarding a reactionary Afrocentric agenda, but serves to encourage all readers—in spite of ethnicity—to rethink the powerful implications of the language used to convey knowledge. As Cain Hope Felder proposed in his *Troubling Biblical Waters,* this book aims to agitate and educate, but is by no means intended to repudiate.

In developing the work, I am also aware that as victims of a racialized history of interpretation and nomenclature, when most people think about the biblical land of Ham their minds automatically scroll to "black" Africa. The legacy is so deep that few take the time to assess the territory covered by each of Noah's sons in the Table of Nations. Questions of pigmentation are apparently secondary to the recorder. This is not to say that the various tribes within each sector of Ham could not have exhibited unique ethnic characteristics. But from our vantage point, we will probably never know the original physical characteristics of all of Ham's progeny. It is for this reason that my primary emphasis in this study is on geography and not on our common understanding of "ethnicity."

While by no means exhaustive—and definitely not encyclopedic, this project is intended to offer a brief survey of the historical place of the Bible in the rhetorical "land of Ham." Its focus on the boundaries of Ham helps to enhance the ecumenical scope of the project, as contemporary black Africans are drawn into solidarity with their lighter-skinned Hamitic siblings in the northernmost sections of modern continental Africa and the Middle East. This book not only offers information about biblical "Africans" and significant "African" people and events throughout the history of humanity, but it places the story of the Bible and African Christianity in the wider global context.

Part one focuses on a definition of biblical Africa. It commences with a brief synopsis of the major studies on the Bible and Africa then establishes a case for the geographical boundaries of Ham. From a straight reading of the text, it is not difficult to reconstruct the modern geographical regions associated with Canaan, Misrayim and Cush. Put, on the other hand, is more difficult to locate. Notwithstanding, the study operates under the assumption that Put refers to sub-Saharan Africa, a conclusion that will no doubt be challenged, but one that—hopefully—will provide an alternative for those who wish to investigate further. Nonetheless, acceptance of my theory about Put's location is by no means essential to following the essential thrust of the study. Part one proceeds with chapters offering socio-political discussion on the biblical references to the three most referenced regions of Ham: Cush bears the honor of serving as the cradle for Eden (chapter two), Misrayim was a reliable place of refuge for God's people (chapter three), and the enigmatic Canaan is the cursed land of promised blessing (chapter four).

Organized like a "who's who in the land of Ham," part two beings with a brief discussion on ethnicity and geographical location. In order to appreciate the comprehensiveness of the study, it is important for the reader to move beyond the stereotypical depiction of how an African "looks." Archeological evidence from Egypt, Babylon and Assyria depicts a region that was inhabited by people of differing shades, facial features and hair texture. Having established a theory of ethnicity in Scripture, the chapters in part two discuss ethnic Africans in the three major regions of Ham. Each chapter places the Hamitic characters in distinct categories: political personalities, spouses and concubines, citizens and friends of Israel, and believers in Messiah.

Part three discusses the openness of Africans to receiving the biblical message of salvation in the Messiah. It commences with a brief discussion on the preparation of Africa for Christianity as it evaluates the impact of the Israelite/Jewish presence in Canaan, Misrayim and Cush. Many Africans were present on the day of Pentecost, and within two decades after the ascension of Christ, Christianity was entrenched in biblical Africa. This is not only evidenced by the fact that Jerusalem is located in the ancient land of Canaan, but references to African believers suggest a presence in the territories that sprawled from Misrayim and Cush. Providing the social setting for the early church, the Christianity of the former Canaan was the earliest in the land of Ham. In later Christian centuries, the Palestinian center appears to have moved from Jerusalem to Antioch in Syria. Christianity was probably introduced into Cush via Meroe by the eunuch, and it was the work of a Syrian monk that resulted in the Emperor Ezana establishing Christianity as the state religion of Ethiopia in the fourth century. There is no evidence of Ethiopian participation in the ecumenical councils of the church, which probably accounts for the strong Jewish flavor of Ethiopian Christianity. Probably influenced by the Greek legacy of scientific inquiry, the children of Misrayim produced many of the theologians for the early Christian church. It was also in Egypt that the allegorical method of biblical interpretation was born. It is safe to say that by the seventh century, Christianity was the dominant force in north and northeast Africa.

The fourth part of the book traces the growth of Islam in the biblical land of Ham. It starts with a discussion of the fact that as a product of Arabia, Islam was born in biblical Africa. After a brief evaluation of the religious influences on Muhammad, it is suggested that Islam actually started as a heretical Christian reform movement. The Qur'an is obviously based on stories from the Christian Bible and depicts Jesus in a positive light, attesting to his virgin birth, miracles, ascension, esteemed place with the Father and second coming. Some of the fanciful stories about Jesus were actually derived from spurious Christian literature like the *Infancy Gospel of Thomas*. Similar to some of the early Gnostic leaders, Muhammad saw himself as the comforter promised by Jesus. Part four will argue that although Islam obviously gained ground by wielding the sword, its success was strengthened by the centrality of the Bible in its doctrines. Christians faced with choosing between Islam and death probably felt that they were being forced to join a heretical Christian denomination. Having gained a stronghold in the Arabian section of Cush, Islam made great strides in North Africa (Misrayim) and Palestine (Canaan). It was not as successful in provincial Ethiopia, which held tenaciously to its Christian heritage. Although "orthodox" Christianity and Judaism survived in these regions, by the end of the Middle Ages, Islam was the dominant force.

Part five examines the impact of European colonialism on biblical Africa. It commences with a brief discussion on the effects of the crusade against Islam on the Orthodox churches in Palestine and Egypt. Chapter fourteen discusses the initial explorations into Ethiopia by the papacy and European monarchs who were fascinated by the legends of the mysterious Prester John. This was followed by an attempt to catholicize Ethiopia which led to civil war and the eventual expulsion of the Jesuit missionaries by King Fasilidas. With the establishment of the West African slave trade, Ham's fourth son, Put, began to move to the center stage of African Christianity (chapter fifteen). Let me hasten to comment that Put is the only son of Ham who does not have a prominent place in the biblical record, and it is almost impossible to determine the corresponding location from the biblical evidence. Nonetheless, in this work I suggest that the term can be applied to sub-Saharan Africa. Since the term "Put" is used rhetorically, I don't devote a lot of time to building a detailed case for its location, but I do elevate linguistic theories to make a case for a people with a common heritage. I also mention the prevalence of the culture of the Bible among the disparate tribes in sub-Saharan Africa as evidence of their exposure to the Bible before slavery. Written off as a totally pagan people by nations that claimed to be fulfilling God's will, the European invaders changed Put's name to Canaan and justified their oppressive actions with a twisted view of Scripture.

The final major section, part six, evaluates the place of the Bible in the land of Ham in the modern era. Following the consolidations of the Ottoman Empire and the birth of Islamic fundamentalism after the Second World War, Palestine (Canaan) and North Africa (Misrayim) are currently dominated by Islam (chapter sixteen). However, adherents to the Bible still have influence in the persons of repatriated Jews and the remnants of Eastern Orthodoxy. Chapter seventeen looks at the nations in the western areas of Hamitic Cush, which have also managed to maintain their grip on the Bible, although the witness has not always been strong. The most powerful witness to the Bible in recent ages comes from the nations of Put (chapter eighteen). Although introduced to an oppressive brand of Christianity, the sons of Put on the modern

African continent have embraced the biblical message of hope to such an extent that, according to estimates, Africa will soon have the highest concentration of Christians in the entire world. While the success of Christianity in Africa can be partially attributed to the missionary efforts of the colonizing powers, the real secret lies in the ability of the African to adapt Christianity to her own context. While the "mission" churches are still the majority, much of the explosive growth is taking place among the Independent African Christian Churches birthed during and since the colonial era with their own visionary leaders—and they continue to thrive in a land in which the Bible has discovered fertile soil.

PART ONE

THE LAND OF HAM
Defining Biblical Africa

These are the descendants of Ham,

by their families, their languages,

their lands, and their nations.

GENESIS 10:20

Africa rarely comes to mind when most people think about the lands of the Bible. The average person may recall Simon of Cyrene who carried Jesus' cross or the Ethiopian eunuch who was baptized by Philip, but for many the Bible is set in lands distant to Africa. Until recently, practically all books on biblical themes published in the West portrayed a biblical world that was exclusively European. Randomly leaf through any illustrated biblical book published before the last few decades and you will witness a world where Adam and Eve and the heavenly hosts of angels are all depicted as Scandinavian.[1] Africa's exclusion is also evident in the Bible maps that often include all of Italy and just the tip of the modern African continent when they feature the areas that were colonized by Greece or Rome.[2] Whether consciously or unconsciously, those

---

[1] See discussion in J. Daniel Hays, *From Every People and Nation: A Biblical Theology of Race* (Downers Grove, Ill.: InterVarsity Press, 2003), pp. 25-28.

[2] Notice even the following comment in the recent essay by Bruce M. Metzger, "Survey of the Geography, History, and Archaeology of the Bible Lands," in *The New Oxford Annotated Bible: New Revised Standard Version,* ed. Bruce M. Metzger and Roland E. Murphy (New York: Oxford University Press, 1991), p. 410: "Surrounded for the most part by desert, Egypt is bordered on the east by the Red Sea, and by Libya on the west." Nothing is mentioned about Ethiopia, Egypt's southern neighbor.

who assumed the responsibility to enhance the biblical message with pictorial aids failed to use all of the colors on the pallet.

Over the past century, several black scholars have sought to correct these unfortunate omissions. Starting with R. A. Morrisey's 1925 publication, *Colored People and Bible History*,[3] there have been a few attempts to investigate the real place of Africa in the biblical record. Influenced by the rise of black consciousness in the 1970s and the development of a liberation-oriented black theology, the last three decades of the twentieth century witnessed a new wave of resources dedicated to uncovering what the Bible really says about Africa. While there were several popular and scholarly contributions to the discussion,[4] it was Cain Hope Felder of Howard University who made the most significant impact with his groundbreaking monograph, *Troubling Biblical Waters*, and his two editorial works, *The Original African Heritage Bible* and *Stony the Road We Trod*.[5] The task of Biblical Africologists has also been assisted by several nonbiblical studies that highlight the African presence in the ancient world and contributions to historical culture.[6] While some of these works are written from secular humanist perspectives, the growing body of literature has definitely been helpful in sensitizing the reading community

---

[3]R. A. Morrisey, *Colored People and Bible History* (Hammond, Ind.: W. B. Conkey, 1925).

[4]Scholarly works include R. A. Bennet, "Africa in the Biblical Period," *Harvard Theological Review* 64 (1971): 483-500; Charles B. Copher, "The Black Man in the Biblical World," *The Journal of the Interdenominational Theological Center* 1, no. 2 (Spring 1974): 7-16; "Egypt and Ethiopia in the Old Testament," in *Nile Valley Civilizations*, ed. Ivan van Sertima (New Brunswick, N.J.: Journal of African Civilizations, 1985), pp. 163-78; "3,000 years of Biblical Interpretation with Reference to Black Peoples," *The Journal of the Interdenominational Theological Center* 13, no. 2 (Spring 1986): 225-46; *Black Biblical Studies: An Anthology of Charles B. Copher: Biblical and Theological Issues on the Black Presence in the Bible* (Chicago: Black Light Fellowship, 1993); David Tuesday Adamo, *Africa and the Africans in the Old Testament* (San Francisco: International Scholars Publications, 1997); "The Search for Africanness in the Bible," *African Journal of Biblical Studies* 15, no. 2 (2000): 20-40; and essays from Vincent Wimbush and Rosamond Rodman, eds., *African Americans and the Bible: Sacred Texts and Social Textures* (New York: Continuum, 2000). Among the many nonscholarly works are Ishakamusa Barashango, *God, the Bible and the Black Man's Destiny* (Washington, D.C.: IV Dynasty, 1982); Alfred Dunston, *The Black Man in the Old Testament and Its World* (Philadelphia: Dorrance, 1974; Trenton, N.J.: Africa World Press, 1992); and Latta Thomas, *Biblical Faith and the Black American* (Valley Forge, Penn.: Judson Press, 1986).

[5]Cain Hope Felder, *Troubling Biblical Waters* (Maryknoll, N.Y.: Orbis, 1989); and Cain Hope Felder, ed., *Stony the Road We Trod: African-American Biblical Interpretation* (Minneapolis: Fortress, 1991).

[6]E.g., Frank Snowden, *Blacks in Antiquity: Ethiopians in the Greco-Roman Experience* (Cambridge, Mass.: Belknap Press of Harvard University Press, 1970); Cheikh Anta Diop, *The African Origin of Civilization: Myth or Reality*, trans. Mercer Cook (New York: L. Hill, 1974); Ivan van Sertima, *Black Women in Antiquity* (New Brunswick, N.J.: Transaction Books, 1984); and Martin Bernal, *Black Athena: The Afroasiatic Roots of Classical Civilization* (New Brunswick, N.J.: Rutgers University Press, 1987).

to the issues of racism and exclusion in biblical interpretation.

The chapters of part one will examine the biblical data that address the enigmatic geographical location of biblical Africa. When used in a historical context, *Africa* must be understood adjectivally. In fact, the name *Africa* was only introduced to the region when the Romans gained entrance to the continent after defeating Hannibal's army in the Punic Wars. Even at that time, the term *Africa* only applied to the newly formed Roman province and to no other territory. At some time toward the end of the Middle Ages, the name was applied to the entire "continental" mass of land on which the original Roman colony was located. Some today would even want to separate Egypt from continental Africa. Given the complexity of the term, for the purpose of this work, it is necessary to move beyond the modern definition of Africa as the continent that borders the "Middle East." Modern terminology is only useful insomuch as that it provides a frame of reference with regards to ethnicity.

In light of the tenuous history of the term, it is necessary to define how "biblical Africa" is understood in this work. Later in part one biblical-historical reasons will be presented to justify the use of *Africa* as a synonym for the "land of Ham."[7] From a geographical perspective, the study will show that when applied to Ham and his descendants, "Africa" swells beyond its contemporary boundaries to include Saudi Arabia and the countries that share its peninsula; the western regions of the Middle East, including Israel, Iraq and Lebanon; and possibly the southernmost parts of modern Turkey. From the perspective of ethnicity, it will also be seen that the term *Africa* not only includes an expanded land mass but also a variety of people groups. With this in mind, this study will not allow theories of ethnicity to determine the extent of the investigation. Similar to studies on modern African history that include the accounts of the Boer Afrikaners in South Africa, the British in Zimbabwe and Kenya, the Indians in Uganda, the Italians in Somalia and Ethiopia, the French in Senegal, the Portuguese in Angola, the French in Sierra Leone and the Zulu in Matabeleland, this study on "biblical Africa" will include all sections of the land of Ham without regard to the ethnic shifts that resulted from migration and interracial marriages.

---

[7]This is not a novel concept; see Caroline Angenent, "About Ham and His Wicked Siblings," *Exchange* 24, no. 2 (June 1995): 137.

1

THE TABLE OF NATIONS
IN GENESIS 10

Genesis 10 contains what has traditionally been dubbed the "Table of Nations." The actual chapter contains the genealogy of Noah's three sons: Shem, Ham and Japheth. After the immediate descendants of each son is listed, the narrator writes, "These are the descendants . . . by their families, their languages, their lands, and their nations" (Gen 10:5, 20, 31).[1] Throughout the table, the narrator uses kinship language to emphasize the family ties between the three sets of descendants. The most common term in the passage is *b'nay* (sons [of]), which is used to identify prominent descendants, and probably should not be viewed as immediate offspring (Gen 10:1-4, 6, 7, 20, 22-23, 31). When the author wishes to identify a child of a specific person, he uses the word *yalad*—the famous "begat" of the King James Version, which is better translated "fathered" or "gave birth to" (Gen 10:8, 13, 15).[2] Relationships between the successive generations are also expressed by the less frequent term *yatsa'*, meaning "to come out of" (Gen 10:14).[3]

THE GEOGRAPHICAL BOUNDARIES OF HAM

Although the stated formula for identifying the respective descendants of Noah's sons appears pretty straightforward, some scholars have been challenged with organizing the names in the list into geographically coherent

---

[1]John H. Walton and Victor H. Matthews, eds., *The IVP Bible Background Commentary: Genesis—Deuteronomy* (Downers Grove, Ill.: InterVarsity Press, 1997), p. 31, reason, "This suggests the political division of the 'world' at the time the list was written."

[2]Some have correctly pointed out that the rendering of *yalad* in the qal perfect in these verses is different from those in the genealogical list of Genesis 5 which are structured as hiphil infinitives. However, in Genesis 4:18; 22:23; 25:3, the qal perfect verb is used for direct ancestry just as in this chapter.

[3]*yatsa'* conveys a genealogical meaning in Gen 46:26; Ex 1:5; Num 12:12; Jer 1:5 (although in these instances it is qualified by "thigh" and "womb").

groups,[4] and conclude that the list is determined more by political or socio-cultural factors than by genealogical reality.[5] While it is possible to find merit in some of the proposed theories, those who reject the reliability of the lists as genealogical tables are often influenced by presuppositions about the ethnic composition of the regions.[6] However, it must not be forgotten that the geographical nomenclature for the biblical world was radically different from the words *we* use to describe the area, and the literary cartographer of Genesis 10 was merely providing a formula that depicted his immediate world in *his* day.[7]

Judging from the formula, the table has two major purposes. First, it aims to show the interrelatedness among the various tribes through bloodline and language.[8] From the narrator's perspective, he has already established the major bloodline of the three subsections of the human family. Language provides a more objective method of establishing relationship. It is probably no surprise that as it relates to Ham, the descendants of Cush are tied together by the so-called Semitic or Afro-Asiatic language family, and those who probably

---

[4]Terrence E. Fretheim, "Genesis," in *New Interpreter's Bible* (Nashville: Abingdon, 1994), p. 408, reasons, "Many names in this list function epynomously, whereby the origin of a city/people/nation is explained by derivation from an individual progenitor."

[5]For instance, Gordon Wenham, *Genesis 1—15* (Waco, Tex.: Word, 1987), p. 215, writes, "So here, 'sons of' or 'fathered' might well be referring to a people's political or geographical affiliation, not its genealogical links." See also Bustenay Oded, "The Table of Nations (Genesis 10): A Socio-Cultural Approach," *Zeitschrift für die alttestamentliche Wissenschaft* 98 (1986): 14-31, who summarizes some of the major historical-critical explanations before forwarding his proposal that the table is a doublet to the one in Genesis 4, and it aims to portray Shem as "the father of the children of 'bene Eber,'" Ham as the "father of all the dwellers of the city and kingdom," and Japheth as "the father of all the isles of the Gentiles/Nations." See also brief comments by Jeffrey S. Rogers, "Table of Nations," in *Eerdmans Dictionary of the Bible* (Grand Rapids: Eerdmans, 2000), p. 1271.

[6]Oded, "Table of Nations," p. 14, asks, "Why would a scribe be tempted to link up Cush (an African people) with Nimrod, a hero belonging to the Mesopotamian world?" In no uncertain terms, he is denying the possibility that Nimrod could have been of African extraction. A more neutral assessment is offered by Victor P. Hamilton, *The Book of Genesis: Chapters 1—17* (Grand Rapids: Eerdmans, 1990), p. 332: "All writers on Genesis 10 continue to be perplexed by some of the peoples who are united in this chapter (e.g., Nimrod from Cush, or a Hamitic Canaan rather than a Shemitic Canaan), but such links testify to the ecumenic nature of civilization's beginnings. Internationalism precedes nationalism and provincialism."

[7]Also recognized by Knut Holter, "Africa in the Old Testament," in *The Bible in Africa: Transactions, Trajectories and Trends*, ed. Gerald O. West and Musa W. Dube (Boston/Leiden: Brill Academic, 2001), pp. 569-71. D. J. Wiseman, "Genesis 10: Some Archaeological Considerations," in *I Studied Inscriptions from Before the Flood: Ancient Near Eastern, Literary, and Linguistic Approaches to Genesis 1—11*, ed. Richard S. Hess and David Toshio Tsumura (Winona Lake, Ind.: Eisenbrauns, 1994), pp. 254-65, shows how archaeological discoveries have helped to explain some of the linkages between disparate ethnic groups in the table.

[8]Robert Brow, "The Curse of Ham—Capsule of Ancient History," *Christianity Today* 18 (October 26, 1973): 8-10, examines the linguistic commonalities among the various Hamitic groups.

sprang from the loins of Put are classified under the Bantu family group. The second and more important purpose of the Table of Nations—from the perspective of this study—is to provide an explanation for the geographical location of the various nations that comprised the narrator's world.[9] While scholars may wrestle over the theological agenda of the author, it is not hard to see that the author intended for these verses to serve as a written map that functioned both culturally and politically.

Although Japheth is the youngest son, his descendants are the first to be listed in the Table of Nations (Gen 10:2-5). Based on the names in the list, it appears that the nations associated with Japheth ranged from those southwestern sections of Eastern Europe that were a part of the former Soviet Union to the lower extreme of Western Europe on the Spanish coastline. Although the oldest brother, Shem and his descendants are listed last (Gen 10:21-31). This makes perfectly good rhetorical sense in light of the fact that from the following chapter to the end of the book of Genesis, the narrative concentrates on Yahweh's interaction with the Semitic patriarchs. The geographical territory occupied by Shem's descendants is harder to determine than Ham's or Japheth's. Judging by the names, the land mass occupied by Shem was the smallest of the three. Its eastern extremities occupied the territory of modern Iran towards the east, and its western borders apparently overlapped with Ham's, from its northern tip in the general vicinity of the Iraq-Turkey border to the Saudi Arabian south.

THE NATIONS OF HAM (GENESIS 10:6-20)

Ham's descendants are listed in the middle. While the exact etymology of the name Ham is disputed, it is probably no accident that it has the same root as the Hebrew terms *ḥam, ḥōm,* and *ḥammâ,* all of which denote warmth, heat or tanned.[10] If viewed ethnically, the term most likely reflects the probability that a significant number of Ham's descendants had a darker complexion than their Japhetic and Semitic cousins. However, it is probably meant to be under-

---

[9]Concerning Ham, Walton and Matthews, *Genesis—Deuteronomy,* p. 32, believe that "the common theme in the genealogy of the Hamites is their close geographical, political and economic importance to the people of Israel."

[10]See Leonard J. Coppes, "*ḥāmam, et al,*" in *Theological Wordbook of the Old Testament,* ed. R. Laird Harris, Gleason L. Archer, Bruce K. Waltke (Chicago: Moody Press, 1980), pp. 296-97; and Cheikh Anta Diop, *The African Origin of Civilization: Myth or Reality,* ed. and trans. Mercer Cook (Chicago: Lawrence Hill Books, 1974), pp. 246-47.

stood geographically, in which case the term would apply to those regions of
the globe that are generally warmer than others. According to Genesis 10:6-
20, the four prominent descendants of Ham were named Cush, Misrayim, Put
and Canaan.[11]

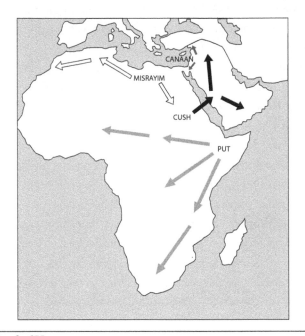

Map 1. The land of Ham

Of the four sons, Cush appears to have occupied the largest territory. The
Hebrew *Cush*, is probably derived from the Egyptian *kš*, which means "black."
The Greeks translated the word *Aethiopia*, literally meaning "burnt face"—an
indication of the dominant feature of those who inhabited the region known
to the Greeks. While the term *Cush* could be understood as a reference to ethnicity, it conveys a much broader meaning in the Table of Nations. The narrator is not so much concerned with ethnicity as he is with geography. Even as
it relates to the geography of Cush, one must be cautious in jumping to conclusions about precise locations based on modern classifications. Just as Rome
was used to identify both the capital of Italy and the entire empire, the term

---

[11]Fretheim, "Genesis," p. 408, proposes, "Ham serves as progenitor of the peoples (thirty in all) within
   the Egyptian political and commercial orbit, including sections of Africa, Arabia, and Mesopotamia."

Cush can be used in a primary sense to define the kingdom(s) lying south of Egypt and in a secondary sense as an organizing term for the many nations to which it gave birth. The kingdom(s) of Cush would have fallen within the modern nations of Sudan, Eritrea, Djibouti and Ethiopia. The power centers would have shifted throughout the years, with the earliest kingdom located along the eastern shores of the Red Sea, just above the horn of Africa, occupying the territory of modern Eritrea and Djibouti. The seat of power moved to Napata during the eighth century B.C.E., then to Meroe by the fourth century B.C.E.—a kingdom that lasted until the fourth century C.E.[12] For the purpose of our discussion, when referring to Cush as a kingdom, we will use the more recognizable term "Ethiopia."

In the context of Genesis 10, Cush takes on a much broader meaning as it identifies the geographical region occupied by his offspring. Interestingly, apart from Ethiopia itself, all the nations associated with Cush fall on the eastern side of the Red Sea, in the territory we know today as the Middle East. These nations are identified as Seba, Havilah, Sabtah, Raamah, Sabteca and Nimrod. With the exception of Nimrod, all of these nations occupied most of the territory of modern Saudi Arabia, Yemen, Oman and possibly the United Arab Emirates. Nimrod is featured as the most politically ambitious of the sons of Ethiopia. He is credited with establishing a presence in Babylon, Erech, Akkad, Calneh and Assyria (Gen 10:8-11). Nimrod's region of influence covered areas of modern Iraq, Jordan and parts of Syria and appears to overlap territory that some ascribe to Shem.[13] In this study, the term "Cush"

---

[12]For a history of Cush from the ninth century B.C.E. to the fourth century C.E. see Derek A. Welsby, *The Kingdom of Kush: The Napatan and Meroitic Empires* (London: British Museum Press, 1996). Welsby reminds his readers, "At the time when Rome was a small village on the banks of the Tiber and the Greek city-states held sway over minuscule territories, the Kushites ruled an empire stretching from the central Sudan to the borders of Palestine. The Kingdom of Kush outlived the Greek city-states and the period of Macedonian hegemony over vast tracts of the ancient world, and co-existed with the rise, heyday and much of the period of decline of the Roman Empire" (Ibid., p. 9). See also László Török, *The Kingdom of Kush: Handbook of the Napatan-Meroitic Civilization* (Leiden: Brill, 1997).

[13]Given the extent of Nimrod's empire *(mamlakah)* into northern territories (Gen 10:10-11), scholars tend to group the lands that originally fell under his jurisdiction with the nations associated with Shem. Hence, the Babylonians and Assyrians are labeled Semitics, and the language that they share with Arabia and Ethiopia is termed Semitic. However, apart from the fact that Asshur is listed as a son of Shem (Gen 10:22), there is nothing in the text to suggest that the narrator attributed the entire region exclusively to Shem. Notwithstanding, the text does suggest that some geopolitical entities could be classified as Hamo-Semitic, one of which would be Assyria (Asshur). Others would be Sheba and Dedan (cf. Gen 10:7; 25:3).

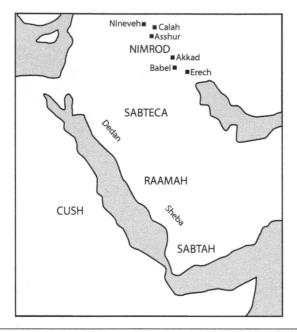

Map 2. Identified locations in the territory of Cush

will be used to denote the larger geographical area.[14]

Ham's second son was named Misrayim, a Hebrew term which probably has its roots in the word for "hardship" *(mesar)*, connoting the experience of the Israelites during the period of slavery. The inhabitants of the land that the Israelites called Misrayim referred to their country as *twy*, "two lands,"[15] or *kemi*, "black land."[16] Some believe that the self-designation *kemi* refers to the black fertile soil on the banks of the Nile. However, the assonance of *kemi* with the Hebrew *ham* is probably no coincidence. While ethnicity is not our major focus in this study, it is possible that similar to *ks/cush*, *kemi* may also have been used to refer to the skin color of the earliest inhabitants of the region. The Greeks named the land *Aegyptos*, plausibly derived from a local term meaning "house of the spirit of [the god] Ptah."[17]

---

[14]Hamilton, *Genesis: Chapters 1—17*, p. 336, refers to the region as "Ethiopian Cush, North Arabian Cush, and Kassite Cush."

[15]The reference to "two lands" probably influenced the Hebrew name for the region, which is actually in a dual form *(-ayim)*.

[16]Victor P. Hamilton, *"misrayim,"* in *Theological Wordbook of the Old Testament*, ed. R. Laird Harris, Gleason L. Archer, Bruce K. Waltke (Chicago: Moody Press, 1980), p. 523.

[17]Ibid.

Similar to Cush, the term *Misrayim* can also have a double connotation. On the basic level, it refers to the kingdom/country that has dominated the region for millennia. However, in the context of Genesis 10, Misrayim can also be used as a general designation for territory extending beyond the borders of both the ancient and modern lands bearing that name. The text shows that in addition to the kingdom, the territory of the descendants of Misrayim included the regions occupied by the Ludites, Anamites, Lehabites (Libyans), Naphtuhites, Pathrusites, Casluhites (forebears of the Philistines) and Caphtorites (Cretans). In twenty-first-century terminology, the lands associated with Misrayim extended from Sudan in the south to the northern and northwestern countries in modern Africa (Algeria, Tunisia, Morocco, Libya), and also included the island of Crete in the Mediterranean. In this study, the term "Egypt" will be used when referring to the nation or kingdom, and "Misrayim" will be used to designate the body of lands associated with Ham's second son.

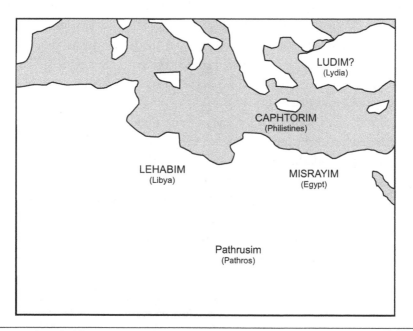

Map 3. Identified locations in the territory of Misrayim

The geographical location of the area occupied by Ham's third son, Put, remains an enigma. This is chiefly due to the fact that none of his descendants is named in the section reserved for him. Left to conjecture, many have positioned Put to the west of Egypt occupying the coastal areas of modern North Africa. Some aim for more specificity and identify it as Libya.[18] While acknowledging the lack of concrete data upon which to reconstruct the boundaries of ancient Put, the likelihood that the borders of his territory would have straddled those of one of his siblings must be taken into account when evaluating the scanty evidence. There is no way that Put could have bordered the nations of Canaan or Cush on the north, east or west, since they were surrounded by the Mediterranean Sea, the land of Japheth and the land of Shem.

The only other possible options would be the territory west of the kingdom of Egypt or south of Cush. Given the likelihood that Misrayim's offspring occupied all areas of the north to northwest African coast, it is hardly likely that Put is intended to be a part of this group. And those who wish to associate Put with Libya must find a way to dispose of the Lehabim. It is more probable that Put is an alternative spelling for the widely known Punt that was located immediately south of Cush and incorporated areas of modern Somalia.[19] Similar to Cush and Misrayim, Put probably referred to a kingdom as well as a broader geographical territory that may have covered the unknown expanse of sub-Saharan Africa. For reasons discussed later in the book, the enigmatic Put may very well have included the many tribes that currently inhabit central, western and maybe even southern Africa.

Ham's final son, Canaan, is the one most prominently featured in Scripture. Although an intricate part of the land of Ham, encased by Cush on the east and Misrayim on the south, Canaan is the fertile territory that Yahweh had promised to the descendants of Shem through Noah's prophecy and the blessings extended to Abraham, Isaac and Jacob. It is no wonder, then, that after the exodus from Egypt the majority of the biblical books from Exodus to the first third of Acts deal with events that occur within the boundaries of Canaan. Those indigenous to the region include the Sidonians, Hittites, Jebusites, Amorites, Girgashites, Hivites, Arkites, Sinites, Arvadites, Zemarites and Hamathites

---

[18]E.g., J. Simons, "The 'Table of Nations': Its General Structure and Meaning," in *I Studied Inscriptions from Before the Flood: Ancient Near Eastern, Literary, and Linguistic Approaches to Genesis 1—11*, ed. Richard S. Hess and David Toshio Tsumura (Winona Lake, Ind.: Eisenbrauns, 1994), pp. 250-53; and W. Creighton Marlowe, "Put," in *Eerdmans Dictionary of the Bible* (Grand Rapids: Eerdmans, 2000), pp. 1100-1101.

[19]See also David Tuesday Adamo, "The Place of Africa and Africans in the Old Testament and its Environment" (Ph.D. diss., Baylor University, 1986), pp. 99-100. For an interesting theory about Put, see Caroline Angenent, "About Ham and His Wicked Siblings," *Exchange* 24, no. 2 (June 1995): 152-53.

(Gen 10:15-19). Canaan's southern border straddled the Sinai peninsula while its northern front occupied the southeastern sections of modern Turkey.

If the intent of the narrator of Genesis 10 was to provide an explanation for the tri-sectional division of the earth at that time, then we have for our perusal

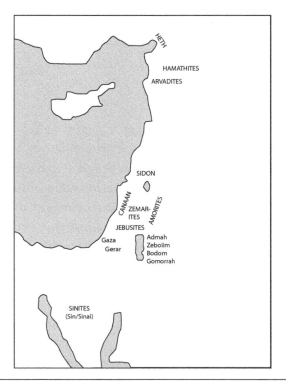

Map 4. Identified locations in the territory of Canaan

an ancient understanding of the major subsets of the human family. Writing from the perspective of his geographical location, the narrator carefully categorizes the various tribes according to their common ancestor. The descendants of Japheth settled in Turkey and migrated to several areas of Europe. Shem's progeny resided along the eastern border of the area known as the Middle East as well as portions of northwest Asia, but also had a significant presence in the land allotted to Ham. The vast region allotted to Ham's descendants stretched from the belly of Africa, through the majority of the Middle East, to the southernmost sections of modern-day Turkey. The next three chapters are devoted to a brief survey of the biblical references to the three most mentioned sections of the land of Ham.

2

Defining the
Territory of Cush

Influenced by modern stereotypes and governed by the geographical parameters established by the European academic establishment, Cush is probably
the only section of biblical Ham that most people associate with Africa. Programmed by a racist system that overemphasizes ethnic differences, people's
minds automatically veer toward black Africa whenever Cush is mentioned.
The effects of racialist programming are even seen in the work of modern Bible translators who are often ambiguous in their translation of the Hebrew
word *Kush*. For the most part, the translators of the King James Version were
careful to translate *Kush* with "Ethiopia," except for instances with proper
names and in Isaiah 11:11 and Habakkuk 3:7 where "Cush" is used.

The King James translation stands in stark contrast to some contemporary
Bible versions that demonstrate blatant racism in their translations. For instance, while referring to the man in David's army named *Cushi* as an "Ethiopian slave" (2 Sam 18:21), Today's English Version speaks of the river from
Eden being in the land of "Cush," and in brackets in the footnote adds "in Mesopotamia" (Gen 2:13). The New International Version only translates *Kush*
with Ethiopia once, and this is when it refers to a person's black skin (Jer
13:23). Even the widely celebrated New Revised Standard Version proves itself
ambivalent, translating every geographical reference of *Kush* as "Ethiopia,"
with the exception of Genesis 2:13, which it translates "Cush," and does not
even provide a footnote with an alternative reading. Modern Bible translators
can learn a lesson from those responsible for the Septuagint who, fully aware of
the geographical and ethnic implications of *Kush*, were careful to translate the
word with the commonly understood *Aethiopia*. It appears that they only made
exceptions with proper names, in which case the Hebrew is transliterated *Chous*
(cf. Gen 10:6-8; 2 Sam 18:21-32; 1 Chron 1:8-10; Ps 7:1; Zeph 1:1).

Readers of this work are challenged to expand their thinking when confronting geographical terms in Scripture. We have already seen that although "Cush" is the name associated with a specific kingdom, it can also be used to describe a family of nations. In this book, the decision has been made to refer to the kingdom of Cush as "Ethiopia" and the broader geographical territory as "Cush." However, were it not for the sake of distinguishing between the two, the more familiar term "Ethiopia" could very well have been used to identify both. Undoubtedly, those who have uncritically accepted the legacy of the European academic establishment would be flustered by an unauthorized renaming of historical regions currently recognized by the names given them by their scholarly forebears. However, utilizing Genesis 10 to rename the broader region "Cush" is probably more defensible than the imposition of the Greek term Mesopotamia or the English imperial phrase Ancient "Near" East.

It may be a little challenging to rethink the labels assigned to the geographical regions of the ancient world, but it must not be forgotten that with changes in world politics, borders change all the time. The Russia, Germany and Yugoslavia at the beginning of the twenty-first century are radically different than they were at the commencement of the last quarter of the twentieth-century. Similarly modern Israel, Greece, Rome and Ethiopia occupy radically different geographical areas than the vicinities that bore the same names in antiquity. Scholars have no problem referring to the ancient empires of Greece and Rome with the same names that designate significantly smaller modern locations, why is it so difficult to do the same for Cush? It is true that the Cush of the Bible was configured differently than it presently is, but the fact that its borders were considerably different than the modern state makes it no less Ethiopia than the Eritrean deprived Ethiopia that emerged after the Italian invasions of the nineteenth century. Having addressed the issue of geographical parameters, this section will now categorize the major references to Cush in Scripture.

THE LOCATION OF EDEN

Cush is the first identifiable geographical region mentioned in the Bible. When commenting on the location of Eden, the narrator of Genesis references a river that came out of Eden which had four major branches (Gen 2:10-14). He then provides significant details about the names of the tributaries and the lands with which the rivers were associated in his day. Gihon, the first river, is said to have encircled the land of Havilah "where there is gold" (Gen 2:11). The second river, Pishon, encircled the entire land of Ethiopia[1] (Gen 2:13). The third river, the Tigris, is located east of Assyria (Gen 2:14a). No area of land is associated with the fourth river, the Euphrates, but it is generally agreed that this is the river that ran through Babylon (Gen 2:14b). Based on the geographical locators provided, it is clear that all of the rivers associated with Eden were situated in regions of Ham linked to Cush's progeny (Gen 10:8-12). Given the prominent rivers that fell in its territory, there should be no surprise that the prophets referred to rivers as one of Cush's distinguishing characteristics (Is 18:1; Zeph 3:10).

In making their determinations about Eden's specific locale, most scholars are influenced by the two rivers that can still be identified: Tigris and Euphrates. Consequently, many have situated Eden in or around the vicinity of modern Iraq.[2] Some have even suggested that "Cush" in Genesis 2:13 is really a reference to the Cassite region of Mesopotamia,[3] and locate the garden north of Iraq in Armenia.[4] Apart from racist presuppositions, there is no real reason to ignore the testimony of the narrator who distinctly places two of the rivers in the regions of Saudi Arabia and modern Africa. When the whole testimony of Genesis 2:10-14 is taken into account, it would seem as if the location of the garden was south of the rivers rather than north.

Key to determining the location of Eden is the reference to the lone river that divides into four (Gen 2:10). The narrator is careful to number the rivers, which suggests that there was an order to them. The rivers developed in a complex pattern. The Pishon and Gihon are described as flowing "around" the lands of Havilah and Ethiopia. Given the fact that no rivers named Pishon and Gihon exist today or can be identified historically, scholars are forced to theorize about their locations.[5] The reference to Ethiopia makes it likely that

---

[1] Since Havilah and Assyria are regions in the broader territory of Cush, the Cush of Genesis 2:13 must refer to Ethiopia.

[2] John H. Walton and Victor H. Matthews, eds., *The IVP Bible Background Commentary: Genesis—Deuteronomy* (Downers Grove, Ill.: InterVarsity Press, 1997), p. 19, believe that Eden was located at the base of the Gulf.

[3] Victor P. Hamilton, *The Book of Genesis: Chapters 1—17* (Grand Rapids: Eerdmans, 1990), pp. 169-70, sees a "problem" with the Cush in Genesis 2 being the same as other references to Cush in the Bible, and opts for the Cassite reading. He also suggests a Mesopotamian location for Havilah.

[4] See Gordon Wenham, *Genesis 1—15* (Waco, Tex.: Word, 1987), p. 66.

[5] Ibid., p. 65, reports that the Pishon has been identified with the Indus, the Ganges, or another river in Mesopotamia or Arabia. W. F. Albright, "The Location of Eden," *The American Journal of Semitic Languages and Literatures* 39 (1922): 15-31, identifies both the Gihon and Pishon with the Nile.

the Gihon may be associated with the Nile.[6] However, the narrator describes it as "circling" Ethiopia. Since no circular river exists, it is possible that the narrator may have also had in mind the bodies of water that separate Ethiopia from Arabia. A part of the Gihon that made up the circle could very well be the Red Sea. If indeed the narrator had other bodies of water in mind when writing of the Gihon and Pishon, then the mystery of the Pishon may also be solved by the waters that surround the Arabian peninsula.[7] Nonetheless, even if the locations of the rivers cannot be determined, few would dispute the location of the lands associated with the rivers.[8] With this in mind, given the fact that the narrator mentions the southernmost rivers before those in the north, it is possible that the lone river from Eden originated in a land that was further south than provincial Ethiopia and Arabia. From this, one can extrapolate a location for Eden from either an extinct location situated in what is now the Indian Ocean before the flood, or an existing area in East or Central Africa.[9]

HOME FOR SHEM'S DISPLACED FAMILIES

During the early biblical period, Cush became the home to several clans with Semitic roots that had been birthed and nurtured on Hamitic soil. The first comprised the descendants of Abraham's eldest son, Ishmael, who was born in Canaan to Hagar, an Egyptian. After being evicted from Abraham's home, Ishmael and Hagar eventually ended up in the Arabian section of Cush to the east of the Red Sea where their descendants settled from Havilah northward to Shur (Gen 25:18). Of Ishmael's twelve sons, Kedar's descendants seem to have been the only ones to settle in a fixed area, and were known for their herding and craftsmanship (cf. Gen 25:13; Song 1:5; Is 60:7; Ezek 27:21).

---

[6]Although tending toward the Cassite theory, Wenham, *Genesis 1—15,* p. 65, admits, "It is the mention of the land of Cush which has led most ancient and modern commentators to identify this Gihon with the Nile."

[7]This theory is by no means novel. Wenham writes, "The Pishon must either be identified with an Arabian river, or with the Persian Gulf and Red Sea 'which goes round all the land of Havilah'" (Ibid.).

[8]Commenting on an early theory by Haupt who locates the Gihon and Pishon in Saudi Arabia and Ethiopia, John Skinner, *A Critical and Exegetical Commentary on Genesis,* 2nd ed. (Edinburgh: T & T Clark, 1930), p. 65, admits, "The theory perhaps combines more of the biblical data in an intelligible way than any other that has been proposed."

[9]For a similar discussion on the location of Eden, see David Tuesday Adamo, "The Place of Africa and Africans in the Old Testament and its Environment" (Ph.D. diss., Baylor University, 1986), pp. 79-94, who also points to recent topographical discoveries enabled by a NASA macroscope that provides evidence of an ancient river system in the southern Egyptian desert.

After Sarah's death, Abraham married Keturah, who bore him six sons: Zimran, Jokshan, Medan, Midian, Ishbak and Shuah (Gen 25:1-2). Keturah's place of origin is not mentioned, but it is probably no coincidence that her grandsons Sheba and Dedan are also listed as descendants of Cush through Raamah (cf. Gen 25:2; 10:7). While Abraham was still alive, he sent the sons of Keturah with their extended families "eastward to the east country" (Gen 25:6). More specifically, they settled southeast of Gerar in the Arabian region where Midian, Sheba and Dedan were located (Gen 25:2-6). Together with Ishmael, it is generally accepted that these non-Saranic sons of Abraham were the progenitors of the Arab people.

Of the sons that Abraham had with Keturah, Midian is the one most mentioned in Scripture. Indeed, it was Midian that provided refuge for Moses when he was a fugitive from Egypt (Ex 2:15—4:19). Unfortunately, the same Midianites launched an attack against the Israelites when they escaped Egypt (Num 22:1—25:18), and eventually Moses was forced to viciously subdue them (Num 31:1-11). Nonetheless, they did manage to bounce back, and during the period of the judges the Midianites controlled Israel for seven years (Judg 6:1—8:28). Over a thousand years later, the Arabian area of Cush would be the place where the apostle Paul—another displaced son of Abraham—found solace after he encountered the Lord on the road to Damascus (Gal 1:15-17). While the Bible does not stipulate it, some believe that Paul spent three years in Arabia being initiated into apostleship.[10]

Cush also provided a home for the Moabites and the Ammonites whose primogenitors were the two sons born from the incestuous sexual encounter between Lot and his daughters (Gen 19:36-38). Moab was situated east of the Dead Sea and Ammon lay above it. Both of these small kingdoms occupied territory that now falls within the borders of modern Jordan. Similar to the Israelites with Canaan, the descendants of Moab and Ammon had been given Hamitic land by divine decree (Deut 2:9-12, 19). In fact, although they would eventually become annexed into the Kingdom of Israel, Yahweh had given specific instructions to Moses that their land should never be confiscated.[11]

In spite of their blood ties with Israel, neither Ammon nor Moab offered humanitarian assistance to the battered refugees following their successful ex-

---

[10]E.g., John F. McArthur, *Galatians* (Chicago: Moody Press, 1987), p. 30.
[11]It was probably as a result of the conflict with the Ammonites that Moses gave half of the Ammonite kingdom to the tribe of Gad (Josh 13:25).

odus from Egypt. Their refusal to help would be the foundation of future hostilities between the three nations that lasted for centuries (cf. Num 22:1—24:25; Judg 10:11—11:33; 1 Sam 14:47; Zeph 2:8-9).[12] The extent of the enmity between them is enforced by the fact that Ammonites and Moabites were perpetually banned from joining "the assembly of the LORD" (Deut 23:3-4; Neh 13:1-2). This divine injunction did not stop Yahweh from subjecting Israel to the rule of both Ammon and Moab during the early settlement period (Judg 3:12-30; 10:6-9). In fact, the two were to remain a constant thorn in Israel's side until Saul defeated the menacing Ammonites just before he was inaugurated as the first official king of Israel (1 Sam 11:1-15). During this time, the Moabites were also showing a friendlier face and granted asylum to David's parents during his conflict with Saul (1 Sam 22:3-4). Unfortunately, after revived hostilities both Moab and Ammon were annexed into the kingdom after being subdued by David (2 Sam 8:2; 10:1—12:31; 1 Chron 18:2; 19:1—20:3). They were by no means willing subjects and attempted a revolution during the reign of Jehoshaphat; they also joined other disgruntled nations in guerilla raids against Israel (2 Kings 1:1; 3:5-27; 13:20; 2 Chron 20:1-30). Toward the end of the kingdom of Judah when its very existence was being threatened by Babylon, the Ammonites and Moabites apparently gained some independence and organized further raids against Israel (2 Kings 24:2). However, by this time the nations were so assimilated that a number of Jews had settled in Ammon and Moab as they sought security from their foes (Jer 40:11). During the Babylonian exile, there was mass intermarriage among the people, a taboo which enraged Ezra and Nehemiah to the point that they took drastic steps to force the Jews to divorce their foreign spouses (Ezra 9:1—10:44; Neh 13:23-30).

Edom was another Semitic nation residing in the extreme west of the northern regions of biblical Cush. Edom, meaning "ruddy" or "red," was named after Israel's brother, Esau, who had married several Canaanite women (Gen 36:1-5). Deeply embittered by his feud with his twin brother,[13] Esau had moved his entire family out of Canaan and settled around Mount Seir (Gen 36:6-8). Although there were already other inhabitants in the region (Gen

---

[12]They seemed to be more comfortable with their Canaanite and Ethiopian neighbors (see Ps 83:5-8).
[13]Interestingly, Esau's inferior blessing contained a clause that destined him to "serve" his brother Jacob (Gen 27:40). This is the verbal form of the same word used in conjunction to Canaan being a "servant" to his brethren (Gen 9:25-27).

36:20-30), Esau became the dominant influence (Gen 36:9-19; 31-42). Among his many descendants were the Amalekites, who established roots in the southernmost part of Canaan at the border of Egypt (Num 13:29; 14:25). They were the first to attack Israel after the exodus (Ex 17:8-16). Edom itself displayed hostilities against Moses and the Israelites by refusing them access through the land (Num 20:14-21; Judg 11:14-18). In spite of the cool reception, the Israelites were forbidden by law to exclude Edomites from joining their ranks (Deut 23:7-8).

Eventually under David, Edom became a part of the expanding Israelite kingdom (2 Sam 8:13-14; 1 Chron 18:12-13). Edom initiated a rebellion under Solomon (1 Kings 11:14-20), and it appears that it may have gained a level of independence after the Israelite kingdom divided, to the extent that it even formed an alliance with Judah and Israel to fight against the Moabites (2 Kings 3:1-27). At some point during the divided kingdom, Edom fell under the jurisdiction of Judah, but continuously fought for independence (2 Kings 8:20-22; 14:7-10; 2 Chron 21:8-10; 25:14-19; 28:16-17). With the eventual demise of Judah, Edom resumed a level of autonomy for several centuries until they were annexed into the Jewish Hasmonean Kingdom during the Hellenistic era. Ironically, by the time of the New Testament, it was the Edomite Herods who were the Roman-endorsed titular rulers of the Jewish people.[14]

CENTER OF COMMERCE

Many of the lands associated with Cush's descendants were known for commerce and industry, particularly in the area of luxury commodities. It is no accident that the first reference to Cushite territory in Genesis describes Havilah as a land of gold, bdellium and onyx (Gen 2:11-12). When searching for metaphors with which to compare wisdom, Job declares, "the topaz of Cush cannot compare with it; it cannot be bought with pure gold" (Job 28:19 NIV). Cush's reputation for manufacturing luxury items was probably enhanced by the trading efforts of merchants from Dedan, Sheba, Arabia and other territories in the region (Ezek 27:20-22; 38:13). Sheba had a strong reputation for producing frankincense, gold and other unnamed spices and precious stones (Ps 72:15; Is 60:6; Jer 6:20; Ezek 27:22), and her merchants were respectfully

---

[14]For a brief discussion on the Herods, see Everett Ferguson, *Backgrounds of Early Christianity*, 2nd ed. (Grand Rapids: Eerdmans, 1993), pp. 389-91.

known as the "travelers of Sheba" (Job 6:19). The Arabs were also known for their livestock trade (Ezek 27:21), and many Arabian and Seban kings showered Solomon with gifts (1 Kings 10:15; 2 Chron 9:14; Ps 72:10). One of the most intriguing stories of Solomon's reign involves the visit of the queen from Sheba who left him with many gifts (1 Kings 10:1-13; 2 Chron 9:1-12). In fact, Raamah is credited with contributing to the economic success of Tyre (Ezek 27:22). Another witness to Cush's reputation for luxury items appears in the story of Achan who, after the Israelite defeat of Ai in Canaan, couldn't resist stealing, among other things, the "beautiful Babylonian garment" (Josh 7:21).

MILITARY POWER

In addition to its reputation for wealth, Cush was also known for its military prowess and its participation in alliances with other African states during times of war. During the Israelite monarchy, configurations of these alliances included Egypt, Put, Lydia, Arabia and Libya—all nations descended from Ham (Ezek 29:10; 30:4-5, 9; Nahum 3:9). Jeremiah captures the dread of the army when he commands, "Charge, O horses! Drive furiously, O charioteers! March on, O warriors—men of Cush and Put who carry shields, men of Lydia who draw the bow" (Jer 46:9 NIV). Since African nations were often involved in alliances, their fate was intricately linked together (Ezek 29:10; 30:4-5, 9). When prophesying the embarrassing demise of Ethiopia with its partner, Yahweh warns the nations who held Ham's children in esteem, "those who trusted in Ethiopia and boasted in Egypt will be afraid and put to shame" (Is 20:5 NIV).

Interestingly, it was Assyria, the northernmost section of territorial Ethiopia that was appointed to shower divine vengeance on its parent (Is 20:1-6; 23:13). Assyria appears to have been a province shared by Semitic and Hamitic people, and was precariously perched on the border of the two territories. No substantive information is provided about Assyria until the final years of the Kingdom of Israel when Tiglath-pileser III attacked King Menahem (745-738/752-742 B.C.E.), and forced him to pay tribute (2 Kings 15:17-22). He also subjected Judah after Ahaz (735-715/732-716 B.C.E.) solicited his assistance to help in the fight against the Edomites (2 Chron 28:16-21; Is 7:10—8:8; Ezek 23:11-23). Under subsequent kings, Assyria continued its assaults against Israel until the kingdom was permanently obliterated and resettled with foreigners while Israelites were taken and dispersed in several foreign cities (2 Kings 15:29—17:41; 1 Chron 5:25-26; Jer 50:17; Ezek 23:5-10; Hosea passim). After Israel's defeat, Assyria's control of Judah was short-lived following Hezekiah's successful rebellion against Sennacherib (2 Kings 18:1—20:6; 2 Chron 32:1-33; Is 36:1—38:8).

Probably the mightiest military force in the history of Cush was the kingdom of Babylon. When Babylon is first introduced to the political world of the Bible, she is under the control of the mighty Assyria who had just brought an end to the northern kingdom of Israel (2 Kings 17:24-33). Soon after the demise of Israel in 722 B.C.E., the Babylonians sent goodwill envoys to the Judean king Hezekiah (2 Kings 20:12-19; 2 Chron 32:31; Is 39:1-8). However, by the end of the next century, Babylon had totally defeated Judah and had become the most powerful empire in the ancient world (2 Kings 24:1—25:30; 2 Chron 36:5-21).

Babylon grew so mighty that Yahweh even employed her as "his servant" (Jer 25:9) to be the instrument of his punishment against several nations, including Judah, Egypt and Tyre (cf. Is 47:6; Jer 20:3-6; Ezek 26:7; 29:17-20; 30:4-5, 10, 24; 32:11). As she executed divine judgment, Yahweh promised, "I will strengthen the arms of the king of Babylon, and put my sword in his hand" (Ezek 30:24). In return for all of her work, Yahweh rewarded the empire with the grand prize of Egypt as "his payment for which he labored, because they worked for me" (Ezek 29:20). Yahweh's employment of Babylon should not be mistaken as an indication of any special relationship. Like other nations, Babylon was merely employed to accomplish a divine task. In reality, she was despised to the point that of all the enemies of God's people, John the Revelator utilizes her name to epitomize the very nature of everything that is evil (cf. Rev 14:8; 16:19; 17:5; 18:2, 10, 21).

JUDGMENT AND RESTORATION OF THE NATIONS OF CUSH

Eventually, the individual Cushite nations would receive the judgment of God, though some of them will experience the joy of restoration. Many Cushite nations are listed among those who will eventually "drink the wine of God's wrath" (Jer 25:15-26). Yahweh is not arbitrary in his judgment, but provides the reason before executing justice. Ammon is judged for mocking the demise of the Israelites and taking pride in her strength (Ezek 25:1-7; Jer 49:4; Amos 1:13-15). Its territory is taken over by Cushites from Arabia and other foreigners (Ezek 25:4; Jer 49:5). The same Arabs were also destined to occupy the Moabite region (Ezek 25:8-11), which will also be ravaged by other calamities (Is 15:1—16:14; Jer 48:1-46). Not only did Moab refuse to acknowledge the elect status of Israel (Ezek 25:8), but she is also to be punished for her pride (Is 16:6; Jer 48:26-30; 42). Edom, the kingdom descended from Esau with mixed Hamitic and Semitic roots, was destined to be totally desolated because she acted vengefully towards Judah (Jer 49:7-22; Lam 4:21-22; Ezek 25:12-14; 32:29-30; 35:15; 36:5; Joel 3:19; Amos 1:11-12; Obad 1-21; Mal 1:2-5). Although Yahweh utilized Assyria for his purposes, she is also to be judged for her arrogance (Is 10:5-34; 14:24-27; 30:27-33; 31:8-9; Jer 50:18; Ezek 32:22-23; Nahum 1:1—3:19; Zeph 2:13-15), along with provincial Ethiopia (Zeph 2:12). Ultimate punishment for these Cushite nations is handed over to their sibling Babylon (Jer 27:2-11; Ezek 21:20).

Although Yahweh punished individual nations descended from Cush, some also had a similar place in his heart as his beloved Israel. In an impartial tone Yahweh asks Israel, "Are you not like the Ethiopians to me?" (Amos 9:7). And again in a Korahite psalm, he proclaims, "Among those who know me I mention Rahab [Egypt] and Babylon; Philistia too, and Tyre, with Ethiopia— 'this one was born there,' they say" (Ps 87:4). As evidence of his impartiality, he had already demonstrated his grace to Nineveh when he commissioned a Semitic prophet to call them to repentance, and was thrilled when the entire city repented and turned from their wicked ways. Jesus himself praises the people of Nineveh for their obedience to the prophetic word (Mt 12:41; Lk 11:32). Nonetheless, the fact that Nineveh and other Cushite nations had not remained consistent in their relationship with God meant that they too had to pay the same price for rebellion as the beloved Israel.

After the nations of Cush have reaped the rewards for their sins and idolatry, many will be restored to divine favor as the Messianic kingdom approaches. Indeed, at the inauguration of the Messianic kingdom, Yahweh promises to deliver his remnant "from Assyria, from Egypt, from Pathros, from Ethiopia, from Elam, from Shinar, from Hamath and from the coastlands of the sea" (Is 11:11; cf. Is 27:13). In Zephaniah, Yahweh envisions the day when he judges the nations and restores the faithful (Zeph 3:8-13). On this great day of restoration he declares, "From beyond the rivers of Ethiopia my suppliants, my scattered ones, shall bring my offering" (Zeph 3:10). In a powerful prophecy about the kings of the earth bringing gifts to the holy temple (Ps 68:28-35), the psalmist David affirms, "Envoys[15] will come out of Egypt, Ethiopia will quickly stretch out her hands to God" (Ps 68:31 NKJV).

In a not-so-glorious picture, Ethiopia and Egypt are subjected to Israel as they come to God's people in chains; however, their submission appears to be voluntary as a symbol of their acknowledgment that the God of Israel is the only true God (Is 45:14). Indeed, the Ethiopian eunuch who came to Jerusalem to worship at the inception of the Christian church is probably just a representative of the many sons of Cush who had embraced the religion of Yahweh (Acts 8:27).[16] Among the restored Cushite nations are Moab and Ammon, whose fortunes will be restored "in the latter days" (Jer 48:47; 49:6). Assyria will also be showered with honor. Isaiah prophecies that there will be a highway from Assyria to Israel (Is 11:16). Together with Egypt, Assyria, who Yahweh affectionately calls "the work of my hands," will comprise a third part of the special people of God (Is 19:23-25).

---

[15]Without providing an explanation for their decision, the RSV and NRSV read, "let *bronze* be brought from Egypt." This is probably due to the translators' belief that the word in the text for envoy/prince *(chashman)* contains a scribal error and should have been *chashmal* (bronze). However, there is no textual evidence that supports this theory.

[16]See Keith A. Burton, "Ethiopia," in *Eerdmans Dictionary of the Bible* (Grand Rapids: Eerdmans, 2000), p. 433. Glen Usry and Craig S. Keener, *Black Man's Religion: Can Christianity Be Afrocentric?* (Downers Grove, Ill.: InterVarsity Press, 1996), p. 35, assume that this was the first "Gentile" convert. However, he is identified as one of many Ethiopian adherents to the Israelite religion in chapter five of this study.

3

DEFINING THE
TERRITORY OF MISRAYIM

Misrayim's head nation, Egypt,[1] is the region of Ham most mentioned in Scripture. From the days of the patriarchs to the time of the Babylonian exile, Egypt was one of the most powerful kingdoms in the ancient world. For at least three thousand years during the periods ranging from the proto-dynastic era to the New Kingdom (c. 3000-1075 B.C.E.), Egypt could accurately be defined as the unrivaled global superpower. As a result of her magnificent architectural, commercial and literary achievements that have been preserved by the museum of time, more is known about Egypt than any of her siblings.

In an agricultural era that lacked the sophistication of modern irrigation systems, Egypt was blessed by the powerful Nile, which was a natural gift to her from different sources in ancient Cush and Put.[2] The Nile is actually formed by a merger of several rivers, the two most dominant being the White Nile, which is fed by what is known today as Lake Victoria in Kenya and Tanzania, and the Blue Nile, which connects with the White Nile at Khartoum but originates from Lake Tana in Ethiopia. The journey of the Nile from Lake Victoria—its furthest source—to the Mediterranean Sea—its depository—covers 4000 miles (6500 kilometers), and features a total of six impassable areas comprised of waterfalls and rapids, known as cataracts. The steady water source enabled the inhabitants of Egypt to find stability and nurtured the creative and entrepreneurial spirits of a people who probably found life relatively easier than those who lived in more barren areas of the world. When the writer of Genesis describes Egypt, he compares it to "the garden of the LORD" (Gen 13:10).

---

[1]As a reminder, I use "Misrayim" when referring to all the nations descended from Ham's second son and "Egypt" when speaking of the kingdom.

[2]See Lawrence A. Sinclair, "Nile," in *Eerdmans Dictionary of the Bible* (Grand Rapids: Eerdmans, 2000), p. 965.

PLACE OF REFUGE

From its first reference in Scripture, Egypt is portrayed as a place of sanctuary for God's chosen people (Gen 12:10—13:1). It was Abraham who first found refuge in Egypt during the era of the Middle Kingdom (1975-1640 B.C.E.). A descendant of Shem, Abraham was born in Ur of the Chaldeans (Gen 11:27-28), a Cushite territory. Following the death of Abraham's brother, his father planned to move the entire family to Canaan, but they eventually settled in Haran, a Semitic region that appears to have been named after Abraham's deceased brother (Gen 11:27-28). Eventually, Yahweh summoned Abraham from his father's estate in Haran and promised to fulfill the blessing of Genesis 9:26-27 in him (Gen 12:1-8).

After leaving the land of Shem, Abraham and his attendants passed through the promised land of Canaan and eventually arrived in Egypt during the time of a famine. His financial status would have probably been sufficient for him to have found sanctuary in Pharaoh's court, but in a bid to guarantee his life, Abraham asked his beautiful wife Sarah to pretend she was his sister. As he suspected, Pharaoh summoned her to his harem, totally ignorant that he was committing adultery with another man's wife. It was only when the Lord afflicted Pharaoh with plagues for his unwitting sin that Abraham's welcome was abruptly cut short and his entourage was asked to leave. From there they settled in the Negeb, a Canaanite region.

The final fifth of Genesis and the first quarter of Exodus is set almost exclusively in Egypt. As in the days of Abraham, Egypt was to again provide haven for Yahweh's chosen family. It is generally agreed that Jacob and his family initially entered Egypt during the period of the Middle Kingdom when Egypt had political, economic and military dominance of an area stretching from the northern parts of Ethiopia to the north-central areas of Canaan. Joseph was the first of Jacob's children to reside in Egypt after he had been sold into slavery by his brothers and miraculously elevated to the position of prime minister of the world's most powerful government. When famine plagued the lands within the sphere of Egyptian influence, Joseph persuaded the Pharaoh to provide sanctuary for his entire family, which moved to Egypt from Canaan. They were given permission to settle on the northern coast of Egypt in the land of Goshen (Gen 46:28—47:12).

Israel's descendants remained in Egypt for about 430 years (Ex 12:40). During their extended sojourn, Egypt made the transition from the Middle

Kingdom to the New Kingdom (c. 1539-1075 B.C.E.). The events in the opening chapters of Exodus appear to have taken place during the Nineteenth Dynasty when the capital was moved from Thebes to the Delta, in which the land of Goshen was located. By this time, the numbers of Israelites had increased from seventy to over one million (Ex 12:37). Threatened by the growth and success of the Israelites, one of the pharaohs, who apparently had no knowledge of the positive contribution Joseph had made to Egyptian history, initiated a program of forced labor that relegated all the descendants of Israel to the status of slaves. In fact, the oppressed Israelites were responsible for building the capitol city of Ramses (Ex 1:11). The prolonged slavery marked the end of Egyptian hospitality toward the people of the promise for several hundred years, and established an era of hostility in which Egypt was depicted as the epitome of bondage and oppression. However, even during the period of estrangement, Israelite law demanded that any Egyptian who desired could enter God's covenant people since it was Egypt's initial hospitality that helped to preserve Israel (Deut 23:7-8).

During the period of the Israelite monarchy, Egypt was still the place for exiles to find refuge. When Solomon in his evil years sought to kill Jeroboam after God had promised to give him the majority of the kingdom, Jeroboam sought and received sanctuary from Shishak, the Pharaoh who probably succeeded Solomon's father-in-law (1 Kings 11:26-40; 2 Chron 10:2). Uriah the prophet also fled to Egypt when King Jehoiakim issued a death sentence against him, but since Judah was under Egyptian rule he was not able to receive protection and was ultimately tracked down and killed (Jer 26:20-23). When Johanan intercepted Ishmael after the assassination of Gedaliah and rescued the hostages who were with him, he decided to continue on to Egypt rather than return to Jerusalem and face the Babylonians who may have blamed him for the dastardly deed (Jer 41:1—44:30). Although Yahweh through Jeremiah warned Johanan and his sizeable company not to go to Egypt, they went anyhow and settled in Tahpanhes, Migdol, Memphis and Pathros. Unfortunately, their presence in Egypt did not stop the Babylonian invasion, and they were destined to suffer with their hosts (Jer 44:27-30). Toward the end of the southern kingdom, Jeremiah spoke of a remnant of Judah residing in Egypt (Jer 24:8). When Judah came under full Babylonian rule, a number of people fled to Egypt for refuge (2 Kings 25:26). Isaiah envisions God's chosen in Egypt until God summons them in the Messianic age (Is

11:11; 27:13; see also Micah 7:12; Zech 10:10).

Egypt had earned its label as a place of refuge when Abraham and Sarah found sanctuary with a Pharaoh during a famine. The final person recorded in Scripture to have received sanctuary in Egypt is Abraham's promised seed, Jesus himself. Matthew is the sole Gospel writer who reports Herod's quest to kill Jesus and the angel Gabriel giving Joseph strict instructions to take Jesus and Mary to Egypt until Herod had died (Mt 2:13-15). Ever since the Babylonian conquest, the Jewish population in Egypt had been steadily growing. At one point, they had even garnered enough influence with the occupying powers to have a military colony and their own temple on the island of Elaphantine in the Nile.[3] Although meeting opposition at times, Jewish culture flourished in Egypt to such an extent that the first known translation of the Hebrew Bible into the Greek language took place in the land that once enslaved the translators' ancestors. By the time Joseph and the family arrived, Egypt had a sizeable Jewish population, rivaled outside of Palestine only by Syria.[4]

ISRAELITE ALLIES

Any lingering resentment that Israel may have had toward their former Egyptian oppressors was softened when Solomon sealed an alliance with an Egyptian Pharaoh by marrying his daughter (1 Kings 3:1). This was during Egypt's Third Intermediate Period (1075-715 B.C.E.) when her influence had waned and the united kingdom of Israel had become a major political force in the region (1 Kings 4:21, 30). Both governments had a military presence in the land of Canaan (1 Kings 9:16). Egypt also supplied military equipment to Israel (1 Kings 10:28-29). The alliance between the two nations was by no means steady. After the death of Solomon, when Israel had been ravaged by civil war, Shishak invaded the southern kingdom of Judah under Rehoboam and looted all of the treasures from the temple (1 Kings 14:25-28; 2 Chron 12:1-12). Rehoboam could not expect any help from the neighboring kingdom of Israel since not only were they rivals, but Shishak had provided sanctuary to Jeroboam when Solomon wanted to assassinate him. Although Egypt expressed hostility towards Judah, there appears to have been a continued alliance with Israel that lasted until Israel's demise in 721 B.C.E., when King Hoshea—al-

---

[3]See Everett Ferguson, *Backgrounds of Early Christianity*, 2nd ed. (Grand Rapids: Eerdmans, 1993), p. 377.
[4]See ibid., p. 403.

ready under siege from the Ethiopian kingdom of Assyria—made a desperate attempt to join with Egypt in an assault against his captors (2 Kings 17:1-4).

After Israel's demise, Judah also sought an alliance with Egypt. By this time, Egypt was waning in power as Assyria exercised dominance in the region. When Assyria attacked Judah, Hezekiah sent an envoy to Egypt to solicit support. Isaiah interpreted this as a lack of faith in God, and prophesied "the protection of Pharaoh shall become your shame, and the shelter in the shadow of Egypt your humiliation" (Is 30:3; cf. Is 31:1-3). Sennacherib's Rabshakeh also chastised Judah, taunting that Judah's reliance on Egypt was like a person relying on a broken staff for support (2 Kings 18:21; Is 36:6). Assyria's confidence did not frighten Egypt, and while Judah was under siege, Pharaoh Tirhakah assembled an army to fight Assyria (2 Kings 19:9; Is 37:9). Tirhakah ruled Egypt in the Late Period (c. 715-332 B.C.E.) during the Twenty-fifth Dynasty when the Ethiopians controlled Egypt. The politics of the region were extremely shaky, and by the time of Judah's King Josiah, Assyria and Egypt were allies and Judah had become one of Egypt's vassal kingdoms (2 Kings 23:28-35; 2 Chron 35:20—36:4). Toward the end of the southern kingdom, when Judah was besieged by the Babylonians, Zedekiah appealed to Pharaoh Hophra, who came to Judah's rescue, causing the Babylonians to temporarily retreat (Jer 37:3-10; Ezek 17:11-15). Not too long after, Egypt found itself at the mercy of the Babylonians (2 Kings 24:7).

JUDGMENT AND RESTORATION

Like other empires of antiquity, Egypt was the subject of many judgment prophecies. Yahweh provides several reasons for punishing Egypt, chief among them her prideful reliance on her natural resources and her idolatrous national narcissism (Ezek 32:12). The prophet characterizes Pharaoh as saying, "My Nile is my own, I made it for myself" (Ezek 29:3; 9). Elsewhere, Egypt is compared to the great Assyria which boasted in its military prowess and thought itself impregnable, but ended its days in disgrace (Ezek 31). Yahweh promises to punish Egypt for her pride and self-reliance. In graphic terms, Yahweh declares, "I have broken the arm of Pharaoh king of Egypt; it has not been bound up for healing or wrapped with a bandage, so that it may become strong and wield the sword" (Ezek 30:21).

As a result of her recalcitrant apostasy, Egypt's days of dominance had been diminished. The punishment was to extend from Migdol to Syene, a territory stretching from the Mediterranean coastline to the border of Ethiopia (Ezek 29:10; 30:6). Since Egypt had strong economic and political alliances with other nations and clans of Ham, the ramifications of her punishment extended beyond her borders. It appeared natural for her neighboring siblings to provide military assistance when necessary. However, since Yahweh had commissioned this sentence, the supporting nations of Ethiopia, Put, Lud, Arabia and Libya would have to suffer with her (Ezek 30:4-6; see also Nahum 3:8-10).

Egypt's judgment would come in several phases and would affect the entire land. Yahweh specifically mentions Memphis, Pathros, Pelusium, On, Pibeseth, Tehaphnehes and Thebes as the objects of his wrath (Ezek 30:13-18). The methods of judgment entail civil war, invasion and occupation, and natural calamities affecting the Nile and consequently the economy (Is 19:1-10). Like the Israelites, the Egyptians would also be dispersed among the nations (Ezek 29:12; 30:23, 26; 32:9). Egypt will also be forced to give up idolatry as they are stripped of their independence (Ezek 30:13). Egypt's punishment was entrusted to the armies of the Assyrians and Babylonians (Is 20:4; Jer 46:1-24).

Following the punishment and humiliation, Yahweh promises, "At the end of forty years I will gather the Egyptians from the peoples among whom they were scattered; and I will restore the fortunes of Egypt" (Ezek 29:13-14). However, the restored Egypt will not have the prestige of its glory days, but will be a "lowly kingdom" that will "never again exalt itself above the nations" (Ezek 29:14-15). Isaiah portrays the restored kingdom as one that learns humility and faithfully embraces the religion of Yahweh along with the remnant of Israel and the Assyrians (Is 19:18-25; 45:14; see also Zech 14:16-19).[5] In spite of its checkered history, this prominent son of Ham who both protected and oppressed God's chosen would eventually be blessed by God and included among his "people."

---

[5]This is in contrast to the picture in Joel 3:19: "Egypt shall become a desolation and Edom a desolate wilderness, because of the violence done to the people of Judah, in whose land they have shed innocent blood."

4

DEFINING THE
TERRITORY OF CANAAN

The Canaanite region of Ham provides the setting of the majority of the Bible. This may seem strange in light of the fact that the main people group featured in the Bible are the descendants of Shem. In fact, this apparent mismatch has caused many to unconsciously align Canaan among the Semitic regions as they confine biblical Africa to Egypt and Ethiopia.[1] However, a major presence of Semites on Cushite soil no more makes Canaan Semitic than Western European dominance on American soil makes America Europe. At this juncture, it is also necessary to chastise the European academic establishment for further obfuscating the Hamitic roots of Canaan by using the term "Semitic" to designate the language in the region.[2] With Akkadian, Arabic, Ethiopic and the languages of "almost all of Israel's [Canaanite] neighbors"[3] in the group, what—other than racist presuppositions—would justify the Semitic label?

Those unfamiliar with Scripture may well ask how so many descendants of Shem ended up establishing permanent roots on land that the Genesis cartographer obviously associates with Ham. From a strict socio-historical perspective, it could be reasoned that a tribe of foreigners invaded a strategically positioned nation and settled there in mass numbers. Indeed, historical sources,

---

[1]See J. Daniel Hays, *From Every People and Nation: A Biblical Theology of Race* (Downers Grove, Ill.: InterVarsity Press, 2003), pp. 30-34, who in his discussion of ethnicity in the Bible discusses Canaan under the heading, "The 'Asiatics': Israel and her 'Semitic' Cousins."

[2]For a brief study on the languages of the region, see Gonzalo Rubio, "The Languages of the Ancient Near East," in *A Companion to the Ancient Near East,* ed. Daniel C. Snell (Malden, Mass.: Blackwell, 2005), pp. 79-94.

[3]Although objecting to any association of Canaan with Ham, Hays lists "Canaanite, Moabite, Edomite, Ammonite, Ugaritic, Phoenician, Aramaic and Amorite" (*From Every People and Nation,* pp. 31-32).

including the Bible, provide a picture of an ancient world with fluid borders where people freely relocated to regions outside of their ethnic continent. However, from a biblical perspective, the presence of Shem's family in the land of Ham is nothing less than a supernatural fulfillment of one of the most significant—yet bizarre—prophecies in Scripture that catapulted Africa to the center of God's plan of universal salvation. It states: "Cursed be Canaan; lowest of slaves shall he be to his brothers. . . . Blessed by the LORD my God be Shem; and let Canaan be his slave. May God make space for Japheth, and let him live in the tents of Shem; and let Canaan be his slave" (Gen 9:25-27).

This prophecy was uttered by the freshly sobered Noah after he discovered that his youngest son Ham had seen him sleeping naked when he was in a drunken state.[4] Unfortunately, this powerful prophecy has often been obscured by racist spectacles that have led many to dub it "the Curse of Ham."[5] However, the text is indisputably clear that the prophetic curse was placed on Canaan—not his father. Had the curse been placed on Ham, then Ethiopia, Egypt and Put would have been implicated along with Canaan. Instead, Canaan was destined to be a servant even to his brothers.[6] The fulfillment of the blessed-curse is unveiled as one reads Scripture and witnesses the slow but miraculous movement of a small nomadic clan from relative insignificance to international prominence.

The unveiling of the prophecy also reveals two significant facts about its application. First, this was not a universal blessing for *all* of Shem's descendants. Of all the descendants of Shem, Abraham was the exclusive recipient of the blessing, and he was ten generations removed from Shem. Second, the prophecy is primarily about geographical territory, not people. When Israel would later engage in the conquest of Canaan, the leaders were given clear instructions to expunge the aboriginal inhabitants from the land, not to subjugate

---

[4]Some commentators make a lot out of Noah's drunkenness and question the legitimacy of a curse made by an intoxicated person. However, the text suggests that Noah was sober when he uttered these words (Gen 9:24). Moreover, attempts to paint Noah as an irresponsible drunkard are also unfair since the narrative implies that he was the first to experiment with wine (Gen 9:20-21). There is nothing to suggest that he was aware of the consequences of drinking his brew, or that he was ever inebriated again.

[5]For a study on the interpretation of the "Curse," see David M. Goldenberg, *The Curse of Ham: Race and Slavery in Early Judaism, Christianity and Islam* (Princeton, N.J.: Princeton University Press, 2003).

[6]See Robert Brow, "The Curse of Ham—Capsule of Ancient History," *Christianity Today* 18 (October 26, 1973): 10.

them (cf. Ex 23:31; Deut 7:2; Josh 13:1-6). It is clear then that while the ethno-tribal configuration of the region would eventually be altered when the descendants of Abraham inhabited the land, the geographical association of Canaan with Ham cannot be shaken.

CENTER OF COMMERCE

The smallest of the Hamitic regions, Canaan's western border straddled the Mediterranean. Its exposure to the sea opened it up to travelers from the European lands of Japheth as well as fellow Hamites from the north of the modern African continent and the islands of the sea. Tyre, one of the northernmost cities in Canaan, arose as the trading center for the region. It was a fortified city (Ezek 26:4) and was renowned among the nations for its naval dominance (Ezek 26:15-17). Ezekiel's description of the ships and their crews of Tyre is riveting (Ezek 27:4-11). Only the best material went into the Tyrian vessels: cedars from Lebanon, oaks from Bashan, pines from Cyprus, embroidered linen from Egypt, and blue and purple material from Elishah. The Tyrians even recruited the best crew members from foreign lands: rowers from neighboring Sidon and Arvad, pilots from Zemer, and experienced men from Gebal to caulk the seams. Since maritime travel was dangerous, ships often traveled with mercenary armies. Tyre solicited the notorious mercenaries from Paras, Lud, Put, Arvad and Helech.

Tyre used its strategic location as the platform for a very successful trading enterprise, and she was the "merchant of the peoples on many coastlands" (Ezek 27:3). So successful was Tyre that Yahweh himself praised her for her business acumen and ability to make a profit (Ezek 28:4-5). Its trading partners stretched as far west as Spain, through Greece and Turkey to the southern regions of Cush (Ezek 27:12-25). In fact, the merchants of Tyre had so much business that they had to contract some out to companies from Tarshish (Ezek 27:25). Given its reputation for trading with people near and far, Tyre must have been a cosmopolitan city hosting citizens from the places with which it conducted business. It was also a place of luxurious goods, high living and high culture (Ezek 26:12-13). This thriving port city was just a small portion of the land that Yahweh had promised to the descendants of Abraham.

LAND OF HOSPITALITY

The slow fulfillment of the bizarre blessing given to Shem commenced when

Yahweh entered into a covenant with Abraham while he resided in Haran (Gen 12:1-3). In the covenant, Yahweh promised to lead Abraham into a land that would serve as the foundation of a great nation. It soon becomes clear that the Promised Land was on territory that fell under the jurisdiction of Canaan, and was the natural heritage of Ham's descendants (cf. Gen 12:4-9; Ex 23:31). At first, Abraham moved rather tentatively through Canaan as he edged southward as if surveying the land that was his by promise but belonged to others by inheritance. It was not until Pharaoh expelled him from Egypt that Abraham and his nephew, Lot, settled in the Negeb—the southernmost territory of Canaan (Gen 13:1). From here, they moved to a location between Ai and Bethel (Gen 13:2-3).

As the two families expanded, they decided to separate, with Abraham staying in Canaan proper, and Lot moving to the already occupied town of Sodom. After the separation, Abraham made another move to Hebron, where he settled for a while. It appears that the Canaanite clans fully accepted Abraham and Lot into their territory. In fact, when Lot and others were kidnapped by hostile kings, Abraham assembled an army and managed to rescue his nephew and the other prisoners, as well as the spoils of war (Gen 14:1-16). Upon his return he was blessed by the king-priest of Salem, Melchizedek. Eventually, the cities of Sodom and Gomorrah were destroyed for their sinfulness (Gen 19:1-24). From there, Lot and his family settled in Zoar, immediately south of the Dead Sea.

Still living the life of a nomad, Abraham moved from Hebron back to the Negeb, where he settled in Gerar, between Kadesh and Shur (Gen 20:1). Here again he lied about his relationship with Sarah who was taken as a concubine by Abimelech, a Philistine king. Descendants of Misrayim through Casluhim (Gen 10:13-14), the Philistines had settled in Canaan and exercised a strong continuing influence in the region.[7] When Abimelech took Sarah to join his harem, God made a personal appearance in a night vision and told him to return her to Abraham. Coupled with this unfortunate incident, the consequent

---

[7]I am fully aware of the theories surrounding the origins of the Philistines (see Hays, *From Every People and Nation*, pp. 42-44), and am conscious that some see little validity in utilizing Genesis 10:13 to establish a genealogical connection between Philistia and Misrayim. However, in spite of efforts to associate the Philistines with the band among the sea peoples called *Peleset*, scholars have to admit that the "origin of the Philistines is not known with certainty" (ibid., p. 43). See also Neal Bierling, *Giving Goliath His Due: New Archaeological Light on the Philistines* (Grand Rapids: Baker, 1992), p. 51, who refers to the Philistines as "enigmatic people."

conversation between the two men reveals that Abimelech and his people were godfearing individuals.

Although deceived by Abraham, Abimelech allowed him to remain in Gerar (Gen 20:1-18). The strength of the relationship is portrayed in Genesis 21:22-34 when the two men made a covenant at Beersheba after their servants had been involved in a dispute over rights to a well. Although Abraham re-sided in Canaan, the circumstances surrounding the death of Sarah make it clear that he was living a nomadic lifestyle and did not own property (Gen 23:1-20). It was only after Sarah's death that he purchased the field and cave at Machpelah from Ephron the Hittite for use as a cemetery. Many years later, when Jacob was in Egypt, he specifically requested that his sons bury him in this location (Gen 49:29-33).

During the days of Isaac, there was another famine in the land (Gen 26:1). This time, Isaac was expressly forbidden to go to Egypt but went to Gerar where he sought sanctuary with King Abimelech of the Philistines. Similar to his father, Isaac also lied about the identity of his wife and was consequently chastised by Abimelech, who was concerned that one of his subjects could have been entrapped into an adulterous relationship with her. He then issued an edict that anyone who offended either Isaac or Rebekah would receive the death sentence (Gen 26:1-11). Receiving good favor, Isaac settled among the Philistines for a length of time and eventually evoked the anger of the locals due to his business success. Abimelech eventually asked him to leave the im-mediate vicinity, and consequently made a covenant with him as he settled in Beersheba—still a nomad (Gen 26:12-23).

The acceptance of the descendants of Abraham among the Canaanites is undoubtedly demonstrated with Esau's marriage to local women. He eventu-ally moved eastward into the Cushite region around Mt. Seir, which would be named after him (Edom), and where his descendants lived alongside the de-scendants of Seir the Horite (Gen 26:34; 36:1-43). Esau's younger twin, Ja-cob, lived among the Semites in Haran for a number of years, but eventually moved to Canaan where he purchased property in the vicinity of Shechem (Gen 33:18-20). Following a fatal conflict with the people of Shechem after the rape of Jacob's daughter, Dinah, Jacob was instructed to move to Bethel (Luz), another region of Canaan (Gen 35:6). Jacob, now Israel, later moved from Bethel to Eder, stopping briefly in Ephrath (Bethlehem), where his wife Rachel died while giving birth to Benjamin (Gen 35:16-21). It appears that

he finally found stability in Hebron (Mamre), the place where Isaac had settled (Gen 35:27; 37:14). The descendants of Abraham found a welcome place
in Canaan until famine hit the region and they voluntarily moved to Egypt
where they resided for 430 years.[8] When they returned to Canaan after the exodus, it was not for the purpose of continuing the legacy of peaceful coexistence, but to execute divinely mandated national eviction.

THE PROMISED LAND

The patriarchs had lived among the Canaanites, but only as long-term guests.
The situation would be much different when their descendants emerged from
Egyptian bondage. The descendants of the man whose grandson had left
Canaan for Egypt as an ally would return as avenging conquerors. For many
years, Yahweh had promised to fulfill the prophecy made first through Noah
in the blessed-curse, and repeated in covenant form to Abraham, Isaac and Jacob, but to this point their status had been that of sojourners. Now they were
about the business of permanent eviction as they followed divine providence
in the fulfillment of that peculiar blessing that was built on a curse.

Heretofore, the extent of the promised inheritance had not been provided.
The Egyptian Philistines had already secured a strategic section of Canaan on
the border of their parent land and straddling the Mediterranean (see Zeph
2:5). In all possibility, the Semitic Israelites could have been offered another
parcel of land. However, Yahweh's words were absolute and he had uttered
that *all* of Canaan would be surrendered to Shem's descendant. As if satisfying
the people's curiosity, when Moses led the children of Israel through the wilderness, Yahweh provided the geographical boundaries of the Promised Land:
"I will set your borders from the Red Sea to the sea of the Philistines, and from
the wilderness to the Euphrates" (Ex 23:31). The specific kingdoms and fief-
doms that had to be displaced in order for the promise to reach complete fulfillment are listed in Joshua 12:7—13:7.

Although the land of promise, Canaan was not handed to the Israelites on
a silver platter. The process of occupation took several hundred years from the
time Joshua seized Jericho to the conquest of Philistia under David. During
this time, the Israelites had to contend with the natives who ferociously fought

---

[8]When Joseph's brothers appeared before him in Egypt, they identified with the Canaanites (Gen
42:7-32).

to maintain their land. The first serious opposition Israel faced came from the Amorite kings Sihon and Og. By the time of Joshua's death, thirty-one Canaanite kings had been conquered—mainly from the west side of the Jordan (Joshua 12:7-24).

Although a number of potentates had been toppled, the majority of the Canaanite territory was still in the hands of local governments. Over the years of fighting for control, the Philistines proved to be the Israelites' most formidable foes. They were also transplants from a foreign soil, and they had no intention of allowing a band of homeless nomads to uproot them from their established settlements that they probably had to fight for themselves. In fact, Amos suggests that, similar to Israel, they were also enslaved by their Egyptian brethren in Caphtor (Crete) before Yahweh delivered them (Amos 9:7; see also Jer 47:4). Eventually, as a result of Israel's apostasy, the Philistines would gain the upper hand over Israel, and for many years during the period of the Israelite judges the people of promise would remain in servitude to Philistia (Judg 10:6-9; 13:1—16:31). Even when Israel regained some political power during the time of Samuel, the final judge of Israel (see 1 Sam 4:1—7:14), the fledgling nation was still not independent. In fact, elimination of the Philistines was the most pressing divine assignment given to Saul, the first official king of Israel (1 Sam 9:16). After a lifetime of warring against his arch enemies, David finally subdued the Philistines, and in doing so secured the Promised Land for his son Solomon, who "was sovereign over all the kingdoms from the Euphrates to the land of the Philistines, even to the border of Egypt" (1 Kings 4:21).

Scripture and history inform us that Israelite infidelity to Yahweh provided an obstacle to the ultimate fulfillment of the promise, and the nomad nation that had been miraculously delivered from a powerful empire would find itself in servitude less than a millennium after entering the land of promise. Israel's return to servitude provides an ironic twist to the original blessing that was given through Noah. Instead of Shem's descendants being served by Canaan, they found themselves serving a Cushite king in Babylon.

Israel's punishment did not release the inhabitants of Canaan from divine retribution, for they too had turned their backs from the God of their common ancestor, Noah. Hence, Yahweh's impartial justice is demonstrated in his judgment of the Canaanite nations—a judgment to eventually come at the hands of the Cushite Babylonians. Philistia was destined for destruction for her "unending hostilities" towards the Israelites (Ezek 25:15-17; Is 14:29-31; Jer 47:1-7). Tyre's biggest mistake was confusing her business savvy with natural ability and boasting about her economic position in the region (Ezek 28:5-6). For this prideful affront against the Creator, Yahweh contracts the neighboring Babylon to entirely eliminate this nation which had lost favor with God (Ezek 28:7-8; 26:7-14). The fact that Tyre was chastised for her unrighteous behavior means that she was expected to have an understanding of God's will. In fact, God uses language similar to the language he uses with Israel when he declares to Tyre, "You shall die the death of the uncircumcised by the hand of foreigners" (Ezek 28:10).

When the Greek empire gained prominence, the original tribes that occupied the Canaanite region had lost their individual identity and appear to have assimilated with the Jews. The only part of Canaan that was not classified as Jewish territory was the section under Syrian governance. Interestingly, it was also during this period that the full extent of Noah's peculiar prophecy was realized, for Canaan was not only the home of Shem's descendants through Abraham, but Japheth was being enlarged through the conquests of the Greeks and had established residence in the "tents of Shem" on the soil of Canaan (Gen 9:27). For a brief period during the time of the Hasmonean dynasty, the Jews had their final opportunity to enjoy the promise and remained sovereign until civil war infected the kingdom. However, by the time of the New Testament, it was the Japhetite Romans who controlled the land of Canaan's progeny, and who could also claim Egypt and portions of Cush as significant additions to their imperial portfolio.

THE LAND OF HAM: CONCLUSION

With the help of the cartographical template in Genesis 10, it is clear that practically all of the First Testament, the Gospels, and the first half of Acts were set in geographical regions associated with the offspring of Ham. The lands originating from Ham hosted the creation, the exodus, the Promised Land, and the birth, life and crucifixion of the Messiah. When the rhetorical force of the geographical term "Ham" is applied to the region, it encompasses a territory stretching from the heart of modern Africa to the borders of the so-called Middle East.

By concentrating on tribal configurations, the Table of Nations in Genesis 10 provides precise indicators that help to determine the specific area covered by three of Ham's sons. The largest territory was occupied by Cush and stretched from the sources of the Nile to the Assyrian home for the Tigris and Euphrates. Additionally, Cush played host to all four rivers of Eden and provided room for the Semitic kingdoms of Moab, Edom, Ammon and Midian, among others. Misrayim inhabited the second largest area, establishing a presence both on the northern border of the present African continent and in the middle of the Mediterranean. Unarguably the parent of the longest reigning superpower in the history of humanity, Misrayim provided refuge to the people of God on numerous occasions. And although the people of God suffered terribly in Egypt for many years, its kindness will eventually be rewarded when it is numbered among the elect of God. Although the son with the smallest territory, Canaan has impacted the Bible the most. The unfortunate scapegoat for his grandfather's prophetic curse, the disfranchised Canaan became the servant to Misrayim's rejected Philistines. He was further subject to assimilation by the Semitic Israelites, and he watched helplessly as the Greco-Roman Japhetites forcefully established their presence in the tents of Shem on territory that would have been his, had it not been for the curse.

FAMILY REUNION

Africans in the Bible

Can the Ethiopian change his skin?

JEREMIAH 13:23

Having established the parameters of biblical Africa based on the rhetorical rubric offered by Genesis 10, part two seeks to identify the characters in the Bible who—on the basis of heredity and location—can be identified as African. Previous attempts to identify biblical Africans have focused on the issue of race and ethnicity. These terms in themselves are fraught with ambiguity.[1] With so much amalgamation between groups of people with different physical characteristics, coupled with the common ancestry of all humans, how does one determine race? More importantly, what are the criteria for determining race and who makes the decision on the criteria?

Many people see ethnicity and race as synonyms, and the popular notion of ethnicity is usually determined by facial features, skin color and hair texture. It is believed that from these features one can extrapolate the probable origin of an individual's ancestors. This understanding takes seriously the fact that the term *ethnicity* is derived from the Greek word for nation, *ethnos*, and as such should refer to geographical origin. In some respects, this may be helpful

---

[1]See David Tuesday Adamo, "The Place of Africa and Africans in the Old Testament and its Environment" (Ph.D. diss., Baylor University, 1986), pp. 12-14. For studies on race and ethnicity, see Steve Fenton, *Ethnicity* (Cambridge, England: Polity Press, 2003); also Thomas Sowell, *Race and Culture: A World View* (New York: Basic Books, 1994).

in determining the macro-origin of the dominant contributor to a person's genes, but there are limitations if this method is used to pinpoint accuracy. The difficulty of using physical characteristics as the sole basis to determine ethnicity on the micro level is easily illustrated by looking at modern Africa. Africans in the extreme north tend to be lighter and have a different hair texture than those in Upper Egypt and the sub-Saharan regions. But even in Southern and Western Africa, the Zulu of South Africa and the Ebo of Nigeria tend to have more lighter-skinned members than other tribal groups.

Covering a much wider range than modern Africa, the biblical land associated with Ham's descendants presents more challenges when trying to determine ethnicity by modern standards. Based upon the pictographic evidence gleaned from archaeological finds in various parts of the land of Ham, it is safe to say that the inhabitants of Ham ranged from very dark-skinned individuals with curly hair to light-skinned individuals with straighter hair. This is further complicated by the fact of intermarriage and resettlement, as well as the apparently fluid borders with Shem and the obvious sharing of border territories (e.g., Assyria, Syria, Sheba and Dedan). In light of the difficulty in determining ethnicity, the goal of this section is not to identify the "blacks" in the Bible, but to name the biblical personalities who descended from the sons of Ham. Or to put it another way, since "Ham" is to be understood as a synonym to "Africa," our goal is to identify significant "Africans" in Scripture. The basis of the identification will not be physical appearance, but the genealogical table of Genesis 10.[2]

Some may reason that if most of the Bible was set in biblical Ham, then this chapter should cover practically everyone in Scripture. However, those personalities who do not have evident roots in the multiple families spawned from Ham will not be covered. Excluded from the discussion, therefore, will be nations in the region of Cush that have unquestionable Semitic roots, namely Ammon and Moab, the offspring of the incestuous relationship between Lot and his daughters. Conscious of the skepticism with which some

---

[2]This understanding of ethnicity is similar to the one proposed by Ann E. Killebrew, *Biblical Peoples and Ethnicity: An Archeological Study of Egyptians, Canaanites, Philistines and Early Israel: 1300-1100 BCE* (Atlanta: Society of Biblical Literature, 2005), pp. 8-10, who is also aware of the difficulties with precise definitions. Fenton, *Ethnicity,* p. 3, provides a basis for a definition when he writes, "ethnicity is about 'descent and culture.'" Charles Burney, *Historical Dictionary of the Hittites* (Lanham, Md.: Scarecrow Press, 2004), pp. xxi-xxii, speaks of the "disparate ethnic groups" that made up the Hittite population, and laments how an increase in archaeological knowledge has "merely complicated matters."

traditionalists will approach the overall thesis of this study, Hamo-Semitic personalities will also be excluded from this part of the book. These include the Edomite descendants of Esau and his Canaanite wives, the Arabian off-spring of Abraham and Keturah located in the tribes of Midian and Amalek, and the notable figures from Assyria which—as discussed in part one—is distinctly connected to Ham through Nimrod. Profiles on these Hamo-Semitics will occupy a fairly detailed appendix.

Some names in this section will no doubt be questioned. These include the few personalities associated with Philistia and Heth. However, in part one, we challenged the commonly accepted theories about the origins of the Philistines from among Indo-European sea peoples and asserted that there was no reason to omit the testimony of Genesis 10 as a probable record of Philistia's ties with Misrayim. Scholars have also been programmed to squeeze the Hittites into the Indo-European camp,[3] but here again the lack of an unimpeachable theory leaves room to assert the testimony from the Table of Nations which aligns Heth with the family of Canaan.

---

[3]In his concise yet exhaustive survey, O. R. Gurney, *The Hittites* (Baltimore: Penguin, 1962), p. 18, reports, "The Indo-European Hittite language was superimposed on the non-Indo-European Hattian by an invading people." See also Horst Klengel, "Problems in Hittite History, Solved and Unsolved," in *Recent Developments in Hittite Archaeology and History: Papers in Memory of Hans G. Güterbock*, ed. K. Aslihan Yener and Harry A. Hoffner Jr. (Winona Lake, Ind.: Eisenbrauns, 2002), p. 103.

5

IDENTIFYING THE
AFRICANS IN CUSH

Given the fact that most people automatically think of Ethiopia when the subject of the Bible and Africa arises, the discussion will commence with those personalities whose roots are firmly planted in the loins of Cush. The tendency to limit biblical Africa to Ethiopia is obviously due to the immediate association of Ethiopia with dark skin. Indeed, in the sole reference to ethnic characteristics in Scripture, Jeremiah asks, "can an Ethiopian change his skin?" (Jer 13:23). The dark pigmentation of Ethiopians appears to have been their most notable feature for a number of classical historians.[1] However, just like his siblings, the primordial Cush birthed a number of nations that exhibited a variety of "racial" features. Nonetheless, this study is not intended to uncover "racial" characteristics, but to capture the history of Ham's descendants in the wide region that has been categorized under the term "Africa."

In the previous part, we saw that the descendants of Cush annexed land on either side of the Red Sea extending far north into Mesopotamia. For organizing purposes, Cush's scattered clans can be categorized into three major groups. First are the Ethiopians who resided on the west of the Red Sea. Ethiopia, which is the genealogical center of Cush, encompasses a variety of nations in different periods of history.[2] Second are the Arabian Cushites who resided on the east of the Red Sea. A number of these were of mixed Semitic

---

[1]Cf. Diodorus Siculus *Library of History* 3.8.2-3; Strabo *Geography* 15.21; 17.2.1-3; Herodotus *History* 7.70.

[2]See J. Daniel Hays, *From Every People and Nation: A Biblical Theology of Race* (Downers Grove, Ill.: InterVarsity Press, 2003), pp. 34-35; Edward Ullendorff, *The Ethiopians: An Introduction to Country and People,* 4th ed. (Kingston, Jamaica: Headstart Printing and Publishing, 1998), pp. 44-92; Derek A. Welsby, *The Kingdom of Kush: The Napatan and Meroitic Empires* (London: British Museum Press, 1996); and László Török, *The Kingdom of Kush: Handbook of the Napatan-Meroitic Civilization* (Leiden: Brill, 1997).

heritage, but others appear to be pure representatives of their forebears. In addition to the Ethiopian and Arabian Cushites are those with roots in Mesopotamia. These Mesopotamian Cushites are mainly found in the people of Babylon and the Hamo-Semitic Assyrians.

POLITICAL PERSONALITIES

Nimrod's legacy in Mesopotamian Cush. Cush's son Nimrod is the only individual singled out with an abbreviated biography in the list of descendants of Noah's sons included in the Table of Nations in Genesis (Gen 10:8-12). Nimrod is the first politician mentioned in the postflood era and is described as a great warrior and hunter. Judging from the proverb that immortalized his name (Gen 10:9), he appears to have been a household name among the ancients, known for his standing before God as much as for his hunting skills. His reputation as a hunter and soldier probably betrays the charismatic personality of an individual who had natural industrial and leadership skills. Nimrod apparently utilized his influence to organize the first cities named in Scripture since Cain's city of Enoch (Gen 4:17). Indeed, it was he who had established the famed city of Babel upon which the notorious skyscraper was built (Gen 11:1-9). According to the Bible, this act was the catalyst for the division of humanity resulting in the diversification of languages which led to the establishment of geographically separated nations (Gen 11:8-9).

The longevity of Nimrod's name was probably guaranteed by the fact that he was responsible for laying the foundations for the mighty Babylonian and Assyrian kingdoms. When Micah prophecies to Israel, Assyria is still known as the "land of Nimrod" (Mic 5:6).[3] Several places in ancient Mesopotamia bore Nimrod's name, which also appears in various extrabiblical material. Some scholars believe Nimrod to be the biblical counterpart to the Babylonian and Assyrian god of war Ninurta (Nimurda) or the Sumerian hunter God Amarutu.[4] He has even been identified as Sargon of Agade who ruled Assyria around 2300 B.C.E.[5] or even Tukulti-Ninurta who reigned in the thirteenth

---

[3]E. A. Speiser, "In Search of Nimrod," in *I Studied Inscriptions from Before the Flood: Ancient Near Eastern, Literary, and Linguistic Approaches to Genesis 1—11,* ed. Richard S. Hess and David Toshio Tsumura (Winona Lake, Ind.: Eisenbrauns, 1994), p. 273, sees this as a fact that "should not be overlooked."

[4]See D. J. Wiseman, "Nimrod," in *New Bible Dictionary,* ed. D. R. W. Wood, 3rd ed. (Downers Grove, Ill.: InterVarsity Press, 1996), p. 825.

[5]Ibid.

century (1246-1206).[6] Whether or not he is the historical personality behind these figures, Nimrod, grandson of Cush, remains the inventor of the city-state political structure that has continued to this day.

In addition to Nimrod, a number of kings associated with Assyria and Babylon are mentioned in the Bible. For reasons stated in the introduction, discussion on the Assyrian kings has been reserved for appendix two. However, there should be no objection to the inclusion of the prominent kings of Babylon, the first of whom is Merodach-baladan. During the days of Assyrian dominance, King Hezekiah of Israel became deathly ill and was miraculously delivered with a divine promise that fifteen extra years would be added to his life (2 Kings 20:1-11). Since a number of the nations in the region were under the Assyrian yoke, a natural alliance was formed between sovereigns who were anxious for an opportunity to experience freedom. Therefore, it should not be surprising to see King Merodach-baladan of Babylon sending envoys with sympathy cards and a gift to Hezekiah (2 Kings 20:12-19).

Merodach-baladan was not necessarily a person with strong loyalties. He had earlier been an ally of Tiglath-pileser III whom he joined in fighting against another Babylonian leader, but took the opportunity to usurp the Babylonian throne when Sargon II assumed rulership over Assyria (721-710 B.C.E.).[7] Sargon quickly deposed the turncoat Merodach-baladan. Merodach-baladan remained quiet until Sargon's death, at which time he reclaimed the Babylonian throne by ousting the Assyrian appointee. In spite of his efforts to build alliances with Judah and other nations, Merodach-baladan was permanently ousted by Sennacherib and sought refuge in Elam.

The next prominent Babylonian king in Scripture is Nebuchadnezzar, who ruled over Babylon from 605 to 562 B.C.E. Nebuchadnezzar is perhaps the most renowned foreign potentate in Scripture.[8] Responsible for securing the demise of the mighty Assyrians, Nebuchadnezzar quickly sought to expand his empire while the nations were overwhelmed with trepidation. His expansion took him to Judah where he usurped control of the nation from Egypt (2 Kings 24:1-17). In fulfillment of Isaiah's prophecy to Hezekiah after he had

---

[6]So argues Speiser, "In Search of Nimrod."

[7]See Mark W. Chavalas, "Merodach-Baladan," in *Eerdmans Dictionary of the Bible* (Grand Rapids: Eerdmans, 2000), p. 887.

[8]For a concise study, see Ronald H. Sack, *Images of Nebuchadnezzar: The Emergence of a Legend* (Selinsgrove, Penn.: Susquehanna University Press, 2004).

shown Merodach-baladan the royal treasure, Nebuchadnezzar seized the king's wealth and the precious items from Solomon's temple, and he enslaved tens of thousands of the Judean elite who were deported to Babylon. The deportees included King Jehoiachin and his family. Nebuchadnezzar then selected Mattaniah—whom he renamed Zedekiah—to rule over Judah.

Nebuchadnezzar delivered the fatal blow to Judah when Zedekiah revolted (2 Kings 24:20b—25:7). In 587 B.C.E., he besieged Jerusalem and eventually overpowered the army. He captured Zedekiah and killed his sons in his presence, before blinding him and taking him in chains to Babylon. To add insult to injury, Nebuchadnezzar commissioned his commander, Nebuzaradan, to return to Jerusalem and burn the temple along with every grand estate (2 Kings 25:8-26). Following the destructive act of arson, Nebuzaradan ordered his men to plunder all the treasures from the Jerusalem temple. In a bid to instill fear and order in the newly vanquished land, Nebuchadnezzar executed the major religious leaders and installed Gedaliah as governor, thus ending the Israelite monarchy.

Nebuchadnezzar's treatment of the Jews who were deported to Babylon is described in the book of Daniel. Apparently, he not only desired to have the strongest world empire, but he also attempted to develop a Babylonian intelligentsia from among his captives. As we see with Daniel, Shadrach, Meshach and Abednego, the most promising candidates were rewarded with government positions. Although the captor of God's people, Nebuchadnezzar was divinely chosen as the repository of a prophetic dream that unveiled the future of the universe. This led him to proclaim the sovereignty of the God of Israel, and it appears that he eventually submitted to the Supreme God.

Nebuchadnezzar was succeeded by his son, Evil-merodach (562-560 B.C.E.). Possibly influenced by his father's recognition of Israel's God, Evil-merodach released King Jehoiachin from his thirty-seven years in custody (2 Kings 25:27-30; Jer 52:31-34). He elevated Jehoiachin above the other captive kings in Babylon and gave him a daily allowance until his death. His favorable treatment of Jehoiachin is also attested in extrabiblical material. Interestingly, Daniel does not mention this benevolent king. Evil-merodach was eventually killed by his brother-in-law, Neriglissar.[9]

---

[9]Ronald H. Sack, "Evil-Merodach," in *Eerdmans Dictionary of the Bible* (Grand Rapids: Eerdmans, 2000), p. 438. See also D. J. Wiseman, "Evil Merodach," in *New Bible Dictionary*, ed. D. R. W. Wood, 3rd ed. (Downers Grove, Ill.: InterVarsity Press, 1996), p. 349.

Belshazzar is the final Babylonian ruler mentioned in Scripture, and is also the last king of the Neo-Babylonian Empire. According to ancient sources, he was actually coregent with his father Nabonidus, who left him in charge of domestic affairs in Babylon while he sought to expand the kingdom in Asia (556-539 B.C.E.).[10] Although two of Daniel's major prophecies occurred during Belshazzar's reign (cf. Dan 7:1; 8:1), the Hebrew prophet who had once served as the empire's prime minister had apparently fallen from the political limelight. Daniel's influence had diminished to the point that Belshazzar did not even know who he was (Dan 5:11-13). Whether through ignorance or obstinance, Belshazzar did not share the same respect for the Hebrew faith as his ancestors. Indeed, according to the fifth chapter of Daniel, it was his flagrant disrespect for the vessels from the Jerusalem temple that triggered final judgment on Babylon. On the very night that he desecrated the holy emblems, the seemingly impregnable Babylon fell victim to the silver sword of the bear-like Darius the Mede and his Persian allies (Dan 5:1-31).

Sheba's mystery in Arabian Cush. Nebuchadnezzar, a Cushite king of Mesopotamia, had brought the remnant of Israel to their knees and led them into Babylonian captivity in chains. This shameful picture of a dispossessed people stands in stark contrast to the one portrayed centuries earlier when the newly established Israel demanded respect from its neighbors. In its early days, Cush's esteem for Israel was demonstrated by monarchs making extravagant deposits into the Israelite treasury. Perhaps the best known of these is the unnamed Arabian Cushite simply known as the Queen of Sheba.

The Queen of Sheba is probably the most enchanting Cushite politician in Scripture. Referred to as the Queen of the South by Jesus (Mt 12:42), she is first mentioned in association with her visit to Solomon during the early days of his reign (1 Kings 10:1-13; 2 Chron 9:1-12). The Bible states that the purpose of her visit was to "test him with hard questions" (1 Kings 10:1). The visit was successful, with Solomon answering all of her questions and the queen expressing how impressed she was at his accomplishments. In addition to presenting him with gifts—the quantity of which was greater than any that had ever been given to Israel—the Queen of Sheba also directed her praise to God. Solomon reciprocated by presenting gifts to the queen, responding to "every

---

[10]D. J. Wiseman, "Belshazzar," in *New Bible Dictionary*, ed. D. R. W. Wood, 3rd ed. (Downers Grove, Ill.: InterVarsity Press, 1996), p. 127.

desire that she expressed" (1 Kings 10:13). Ethiopian theologians interpret this phrase to mean that Solomon and the queen had a romantic relationship which resulted in the birth of a son, Menelek. The legend of Menelek is preserved in a thirteenth-century document known as the *Kebra Nagast*.[11]

The exact seat of this queen's power remains a mystery, due to the fact that two places in the Arabian peninsula bear the name Sheba. The more prominent Sheba was located in southwest Arabia in territory that falls within the borders of modern Yemen. This is also known as Saba,[12] the home of the Sabeans, whose descendants have preserved the stories of the mysterious queen whom they call Bilkis. The interaction of the Sabeans with the people of Israel is attested to both in the Bible and archaeology.[13] There was also a smaller region bearing the name in northern Arabia where queens are known to have ruled in the first half of the first millennium B.C.E.[14] Whatever region it was, both are located within the boundaries of ancient Cush.

Zerah's posterity in Ethiopian Cush. By the time of the division of the Kingdom of Israel, the Queen of Sheba's admiration for the people of God was obviously not shared by her Ethiopian siblings on the west of the Red Sea. The Bible reports that during the reign of Asa of Judah (911-870 B.C.E.), Zerah of Ethiopia launched an attack against Israel's 580,000 troops with an army of one million (2 Chron 14:9-15). Since no literature outside of this passage mentions Zerah, his exact identity remains a puzzle. Some suggest that he may have been the commander of an Egyptian army during the reign of Pharaoh Osorkon, or that he may have originated from the Arabian section of Ethiopia rather than Ethiopia proper.[15] Whatever the case, the Bible is clear that both Zerah and the vast army were readily identified as Ethiopians (2 Chron 14:12). Although Zerah's army outnumbered Asa's, they were utterly defeated.

---

[11]For a standard English translation, see E. A. Wallis Budge, trans., *The Queen of Sheba and Her Only Son Menyelek (I)* (Oxford: Oxford University Press, 1932). Going against traditional scholarship that sees the *Kebra Nagast* as a product of the thirteenth century, Bernard Leeman, *Queen of Sheba and Biblical Scholarship* (Queensland, Australia: Queensland Academic Press, 2005), suggests that the book is actually based on ancient documents that date to the time of Solomon.

[12]D. A. Hubbard, "Queen of Sheba," in *New Bible Dictionary,* ed. D. R. W. Wood, 3rd ed. (Downers Grove, Ill.: InterVarsity Press, 1996), p. 1088.

[13]See Wendell Phillips, *Qataban and Sheba: Exploring the Ancient Kingdoms on the Biblical Spice Routes of Arabia* (New York: Harcourt Brace, 1955), pp. 103-8.

[14]See Ibid., p. 106. See also Nabia Abbott, 'Pre-Islamic Queens,' *American Journal of Semitic Languages and Literatures* 58 (1941): 1-22.

[15]J. Daniel Hays, "Zerah," in *Eerdmans Dictionary of the Bible* (Grand Rapids: Eerdmans, 2000), pp. 1417-18.

Zerah's defeat by the relatively small Israelite army in no way hampered the imperial aspirations of Ethiopia. Less than two centuries after their embarrassment, as Sennacherib sought to quell internal disturbances in Assyria, Ethiopia saw an opportunity to attack (2 Kings 19:9; Is 37:9). This Ethiopian assault was led by Tirhakah (Taharka) and occurred around 701 B.C.E. Since the attack took place ten years before Tirhakah's ascent to the Egyptian throne when he became the sixth king of the Twenty-fifth (Ethiopian) Dynasty (c. 780-656),[16] most scholars assume that it was Egypt who affronted Assyria. However, in light of the fact that the biblical text explicitly states Tirhakah's origin, coupled with the reality that Shabako (c. 716-c. 702) was the Ethiopian ruler of Egypt at the time, there is no reason for excluding Ethiopia as the attacking power. In all probability, Tirhakah was the king of an Ethiopian province who was seeking to expand Ethiopia's sphere of political influence.[17] Given the fact that Ethiopia was governing Egypt at the time, it would only be natural for his army to consist of Egyptian soldiers who—based on the proximity of Egypt to Assyria—probably comprised the majority of the forces who went up against Assyria.

In the final biblical reference to Ethiopian royalty, the unnamed queen of Sheba's fascination with the religion of Israel is also shared by an unidentified official of another anonymous Ethiopian queen. We are briefly informed about the queen in Luke's account of the conversion of the man famously known as the "Ethiopian eunuch" (Acts 8:26-39). The Greek text refers to her as *kandakēs*, which some translations turn into a proper name, Candace. However, *kandakēs* appears to have been a title held by female rulers of the Ethiopian kingdom that was headquartered in Meroe.[18] Although some have suggested names for this anonymous queen, her identity cannot be confirmed with any degree of certainty.

While it is intriguing to learn of the presence of Ethiopian queens in antiquity, the real star of the story is the eunuch. Probably for his own theological

---

[16]For a discussion on the Cushite path to dominance over Egypt, see Donald B. Redford, *From Slave to Pharaoh: The Black Experience of Ancient Egypt* (Baltimore: Johns Hopkins University Press, 2004). Unfortunately, the subtitle implies that the other pharaohs of Egypt were not black. For a similarly biased philosophy, see also R. G. Morkot, *Black Pharaohs: Egypt's Nubian Rulers* (London: David Brown, 2000).

[17]Also suggested by William Shea, "The Murder of Sennacherib and Related Issues," *Near East Archaeological Society Bulletin* 46 (2001): 38.

[18]See Hays, *From Every People and Nation*, pp. 172-73.

reasons, Luke consistently refers to Philip's convert with a term that suggests his emasculation.[19] However, the Ethiopian was much more than a eunuch; he functioned as a powerful politician who served as the chief financial officer for the entire kingdom. As one who had gone to Jerusalem to worship (Acts 8:27), he was obviously an adherent to the religion of Israel. Given his Ethiopian extraction and his apparent physiological status that classified him as a eunuch, scholars are quick to assume that he could not have been a part of God's covenant people.[20] While it is true that he may not have been a "Jew" in the rabbinic sense, too little is known of the practice of Israel's religion in Ethiopia to disqualify him from the covenant people. Cushites on both sides of the Red Sea had been exposed to the Israelite faith for centuries,[21] and there is no reason to negate the possibility that this eunuch—even with his deficiencies—was following the faith of his fathers and mothers.

FRIENDS OF ISRAEL

The Ethiopian eunuch is just one of several Cushites whose life was intertwined with Jacob's descendants. The first mentioned in the Bible is Balaam, a prophet who resided in the Babylonian city of Pethor, which was located on the banks of the Euphrates. From the very outset, this Mesopotamian Cushite is described as an effective diviner with a stellar record of success (Num 22:6). When Moabite and Midianite delegates approached him with King Balak's request that he curse the Israelites, he let them know that he could only do it if Yahweh gave him specific instructions (Num 22:7-8). When Yahweh disclosed his special relationship with the Israelites to this foreign prophet (Num 22:12), Balaam let the delegates know that he could not fulfill the request and sent them back to Balak.

Some time later, Balaam received another visit from Balak's messengers, and this time he was offered a great reward to curse the Israelites (Num 22:16-17). He refused to accept the bribe, but then stated that he had to consult with Yahweh once more. Although it appears to have been his practice to consult with Yahweh before making any decision, the fact that he had already been

---

[19]See ibid., p. 173.

[20]D. A. Hubbard, "Ethiopian Eunuch," in *New Bible Dictionary*, ed. D. R. W. Wood, 3rd ed. (Downers Grove, Ill.: InterVarsity Press, 1996), p. 346. I'm not sure if Hubbard was aware of the implications of his statement that the Ethiopian was "barred from active participation in Jewish rites by his race."

[21]See Hays, *From Every People and Nation*, pp. 173-74; and Ullendorff, *Ethiopians*, pp. 49-50.

told that Israel was a special people suggests that the financial incentive presented a temptation for him (cf. 2 Pet 2:15; Jude 11). When Yahweh spoke to Balaam this time, he gave him permission to go, with the express instructions that he could only speak words that were divinely ordained.[22] Although God said that Balaam could go, when he actually saddled up his donkey and left, Yahweh was very angry and commissioned his special angel to take his life (Num 22:22, 33). Balaam was only saved by his donkey, who saw the angel of Yahweh standing in the middle of the road with a drawn sword and refused to pass him (Num 22:22-30). It was only when the donkey spoke after Balaam continued to beat him that Balaam's eyes were open to the theophany. Balaam immediately understood the living parable: the dumb animal was able to perceive that God did not desire anyone to take a path with the intention of cursing his people, yet the professed prophet was too blinded by selfish motives to discern God's will.

In spite of Yahweh's objection to Balaam's compliance, he ordered Balaam to meet with Balak. By this time in the narrative, it has become clear that Balaam is a whimsical character who nonetheless has a desire to follow God's will. Even when Balak barked at him in authoritative tones, Balaam let the nervous king know that he could only speak the words that God placed in his mouth (Num 22:36-38). His serious intent to fulfill the divine command in spite of powerful political pressure was audaciously manifest when instead of cursing the Israelites as Balak requested, he gave them a fourfold blessing before returning home (Num 22:41—24:25).

It is obvious that significant details in the story of Balaam are missing, for when his character is reintroduced in the account of the war against Midian, he is portrayed as an enemy of Israel (Num 31:8, 16). Apparently, after foiling Balak's vindictive agenda, Balaam met with Midianite and Moabite officials in Peor (cf. Num 25:16-18). In all appearances, Balaam was a "prophet for hire" who had no real allegiance to any people but simply fulfilled requests for spiritual advice. Evidently, he advised these enemies of Israel to have their women seduce the Israelite men and divert their allegiance from Yahweh to the Baal of Peor (Num 25:1-18; cf. Rev 2:14). Over twenty-four thousand Israelite men fell for this ploy, and the majority were consequently killed by

---

[22]Deuteronomy 23:5 and Joshua 24:9-10 give the impression that Balaam wanted Yahweh's approval to curse Israel.

tribal leaders (Num 25:4-9). Given his instrumental role in this terrible tragedy, when Israel attacked Midian, Balaam's name is listed among the Midianite kings[23] as one of the most significant fatalities of the battle (Num 31:8).
The same man who Yahweh used as an instrument of blessing became the victim of his own curse (cf. Num 24:17).

Balaam interacted with Israel as an outsider with questionable loyalty.
However, other sons of Cush were more intimately involved with the offspring of Jacob and appear to have fully identified with their Semitic cousins.
The first is featured in one of Israel's civil wars when Absalom revolted against
his father, David. Upon the request of his men, David did not accompany his
troops in the final battle against Absalom (2 Sam 18:2-4). The men were concerned about his safety, and may also have felt he was too emotionally attached
to the situation to remain alert and objective (cf. 2 Sam 18:5). Joab, one of
David's three commanders, did not have as much sympathy for Absalom, and
when he was told that the young long-haired delinquent was hanging on a
tree, he did not think twice about throwing three spears into his cousin's heart
(2 Sam 18:14). After Absalom's execution, Joab chose an unnamed Cushite to
carry the news of victory to David (2 Sam 18:19-23).

In a disturbingly racist tone, the commentators of the *New Oxford Annotated Bible* refer to the messenger as an "Ethiopian slave."[24] However, given the
nature of the conversation between Joab and Ahimaaz, it is obvious that this
man—though unnamed—held a position of respect and responsibility (2 Sam
18:19-21). The fact that Joab promised to give the blue-blooded Ahimaaz an
opportunity to carry news on another occasion is evidence enough that the
task of message bearing was too important to be entrusted to a mere slave. Envious of the Cushite, Ahimaaz defied Joab's order and made a dash to carry the
news to David himself. He took a shortcut and outran the Cushite, reaching
David first, but when the distraught king asked him about Absalom he
claimed he had no knowledge about the young rebel's fate. Eager for the complete story, David brushed Ahimaaz aside and waited for the Cushite's report
(2 Sam 18:22-31). The fearless soldier faithfully transmitted the full details to

---

[23]Evi, Rekem, Zur, Hur and Reba (Num 31:8).
[24]Bruce Metzger and Roland E. Murphy, eds., *The New Oxford Annotated Bible with the Apocryphal/
Deuterocanonical Books* (New York: Oxford University Press, 1991), p. 411. Although omitting the
Cushite from his list of examples, Roland Murphy, "'Nation' in the Old Testament," in *Ethnicity*, ed.
Andrew M. Greeley and Gregory Baum (New York: Seabury Press, 1977), pp. 75-76, notes that for-
eigners were fully accepted into Israelite society.

the king, and boldly endorsed Absalom's demise (2 Sam 18:32). Only one with authority would have dared add audacious comments to solemn news that had obviously disturbed the king (cf. 2 Sam 18:5).

Many years after the unnamed Cushite delivered the news of victory to David, the Bible provides the name of another courageous Cushite court official: Ebed-melech (Jer 38:7-13). Literally translated "servant of the king," Ebed-melech served King Zedekiah of Judah during the final days of the southern kingdom. Although his name suggests that he was a servant (*'ebed*), he should not be viewed as one who occupied the lower ranks of society, he was more like a public servant—a government official of sorts.[25] During his tenure Jeremiah was thrown in a pit by government officials who intended to permanently silence his prophetic voice. Knowing their evil motives, Ebed-melech could not stay silent, and he approached Zedekiah to appeal for Jeremiah's life. Judging from his brief conversation with Zedekiah, it appears that he was a man with authority who was able to persuade the king to reverse his earlier endorsement of Jeremiah's imprisonment (cf. Jer 38:4-5). After rescuing Jeremiah, he arranged for his protection by providing him accommodations in the court of the guard. In recognition of Ebed-melech's courage and fidelity, God commissioned Jeremiah to tell him that he would not be harmed or captured when the Babylonians launched their final assault against Judah (Jer 39:15-18).

Another personality of Cushite extraction whose life was intimately intertwined with Israel is the prophet Zephaniah, who introduces himself as the "son of Cushi" (Zeph 1:1). Given the three other names in his brief genealogy that ostensibly goes back to Hezekiah, king of Judah, it was probably his father's mother that hailed from one of the lands of Cush.[26] It may not be coincidental that Zephaniah's prophecies are careful to include information on the judgment and restoration of Cush. Cush's judgment is announced in Zephaniah 2:12, which most translators believe is really a judgment on Ethiopia. However, judging from the reference to the "north," Assyria, and Nineveh in Zephaniah 2:13, Nimrod's Cush is probably in the prophet's mind (cf.

---

[25]For discussion on the position that Ebed-melech probably held in government, see Hays, *From Every People and Nation*, pp. 132-38.

[26]Ibid., pp. 121-30, argues that "Cushi" was just a name and not an indicator of ethnicity. However, in his discussion on Ebed-melech, he appears to contradict himself when he states, "No doubt, to the inhabitants of Jerusalem, the term 'Cushite' would have elicited images of Black Africans" (ibid., p. 131).

Gen 10:11). Indeed, it would not be long before the Assyrians suffered defeat at the hands of the Babylonians. Cush's judgment would be followed by restoration. After being judged by the sword (Zeph 2:12), the remnant will be gathered from beyond the rivers of Cush to unite with other nations in an act of salvation that appears to symbolize a reversal of the confusion of Babel (Zeph 3:9-10).[27]

---

[27]Several other scholars have also noticed the allusions to Babel, see ibid., p. 129.

6

IDENTIFYING THE
AFRICANS IN MISRAYIM

Unlike Cush's scattered clans, the offspring of Misrayim did not stray too far from their ancestral homeland. With the exception of the Philistines, who eventually settled in the land of Canaan, the people of Misrayim remained in the geographical area known today as North Africa. Race is not the major emphasis of this study, but it must be noted that the progenitors of the clans of Misrayim who originally inhabited Egypt were probably similar in appearance to their Ethiopian neighbors. As late as the fifth century B.C.E., Herodotus provides a clue on the stereotypical appearance of Egyptians in his report on the inhabitants of Colchis, a region on the western banks of the Black Sea (located in modern Georgia). His belief that the inhabitants were originally from Egypt is deduced from their own testimony coupled by the fact that "they are dark-skinned and have curly hair."[1]

Although the earliest inhabitants of Misrayim resembled their Ethiopian brothers to the south, there was probably as much racial diversity as one would have found among the scattered clans of Cush.[2] Long before Herodotus re-

---

[1] See Herodotus *Histories* 2.103-105; also 2.57, where Egyptians are called "black."

[2] For a brief discussion on ethnic characteristics in ancient Egypt, see Frank J. Yurco, "Were the Ancient Egyptians Black or White?" *Biblical Archaeology Review* 15 (Sept./Oct. 1989): 24-29, 58. See also Anthony Leahy, "Ethnic Diversity in Ancient Egypt," in *Civilizations of the Ancient Near East,* ed. Jack M. Sasson, vols. 1-2 in 1 volume (Peabody, Mass.: Hendrickson, 2000), pp. 225-34 Donald B. Redford, *From Slave to Pharaoh: The Black Experience of Ancient Egypt* (Baltimore: Johns Hopkins University Press, 2004), pp. 5-6, points out the Egyptians' awareness of color differences. Kathryn A. Bard, "Ancient Egyptians and the Issue of Race," in *Black Athena Revisited,* ed. Mary R. Lefkowitz and Guy MacLean Rogers (Chapel Hill: University of North Carolina Press, 1996), pp. 103-11, warns against categorizing Egyptians in terms of black or white. After an interesting discussion on Egyptian and Israelite ethnicity, Usry and Keener, *Black Man's Religion,* p. 82, conclude, "To the extent that black is defined by skin complexion, nearly all Egyptians seem to have been dark enough that in [the United States of America] they could pass for the darker or lighter of us." For a full discussion, see ibid., pp. 60-82.

ported on the Egyptian settlers of Colchis, Egyptian art depicted a racially diverse society. Easily accessible via its long northern border that straddled the Mediterranean Sea, this diversity would increase as a result of continued trade with the sons of Japheth and subsequent conquests by the Romans and Greeks. Naturally, many of the European traders, soldiers and immigrants who settled in the lands of Misrayim chose spouses from among the locals. In some instances, particularly in Roman North Africa, there were even immigrant colonies that chose to remain segregated.

Most of the characters in Scripture who are descended from Misrayim were located in Egypt. We know of no Libyans—although the country is mentioned a number of times—and there are a handful of Philistines and Cyrenians. The preponderance of personalities from Misrayim—Egypt in particular—is obviously due to its geo-political relationship to the land where the people of promise eventually settled.

POLITICAL PERSONALITIES

Anonymous pharaohs from Abraham to Joseph. From very early on in the Old Testament narrative, we are introduced to the Egyptian political leaders who bore the title pharaoh. These form the majority of political personalities from Misrayim. The title "pharaoh" originally referred to the palace in which the sovereign of Egypt resided, and was eventually used to designate the ruler him/herself.[3] The first of many Egyptian pharaohs mentioned in the Bible is the one who governed Egypt at the time of Abraham and Sarah when Canaan was affected by a famine (Gen 12:10-20). According to the biblical record, Sarah was very beautiful, so before they entered Egypt, Abraham gave her the cowardly instruction to pretend she was not his wife. His selfish concern was self-preservation as he feared that another man would kill him just to take her as his wife. Being a person of relative wealth (Gen 12:4-5), Abraham and his entourage apparently sought sanctuary in the Pharaoh's estate, and must have thought his fears were justified when Pharaoh summoned Sarah into his royal harem.

Apparently, Pharaoh actually entered into a marriage with Sarah (Gen 12:19) and patronized Abraham with great honor and material goods. How-

---

[3]K. A. Kitchen, "Pharaoh," in *New Bible Dictionary*, ed. D. R. W. Wood, 3rd ed. (Downers Grove, Ill.: InterVarsity Press, 1996), p. 913.

ever, while Abraham was focusing on protecting himself, God was concerned about the violation of Sarah's virtue and the preservation of his holy standards, and so he afflicted Pharaoh's house with plagues. When Pharaoh discovered the cause of the plagues, he hastily chastised Abraham and sent him on his way. Pharaoh's actions demonstrated that he had a fear of God. Not only did he realize the sinful nature of adulterous relationships, but he extended grace to Abraham by allowing him to leave Egypt without punishment.

The probable identity of the pharaoh in this story is not too difficult to decipher. According to a dominant theory of biblical chronology, Abraham departed from Haran around the year 2083 B.C.E.[4] Not long after arriving in Canaan the famine struck, forcing him to move his caravan to Egypt. He would have arrived in Egypt during a divided kingdom with the Tenth Dynasty (ended c. 1986) holding its seat of power in southern Herakleopolis, and the Eleventh Dynasty (c. 2080-c. 1937) further north with administrative centers in Thebes and Memphis.[5] Since Abraham was on a quest for food, he probably would not have traveled the several hundred miles required to meet with a Tenth-Dynasty pharaoh, but more likely encountered one of the Theban pharaohs in Memphis. Given the dates, this would have either been Montjuhotep I (c. 2080-c. 2074), Inyotef I (c. 2074-c. 2064) or Inyotef II (c. 2064-c. 2015).

By the time Joseph arrived in Egypt around 1898 B.C.E., Egypt was once again a united kingdom with the Twelfth Dynasty (c. 1937-c. 1759) in power. The date of Joseph's arrival is estimated from the later arrival of Jacob, which took place around 1876 B.C.E. If this date is accurate, the reigning pharaoh would have either been Senusret I (c. 1917-c. 1872) or Amenemhat II (c. 1875-c. 1840).[6] Although briefly mentioned in the accounts of Potiphar and

---

[4]Here I follow the early chronology for the patriarchs and the exodus. See Norman Gottwald, *The Hebrew Bible: A Socio-Literary Introduction* (Philadelphia: Fortress, 1985), p. 16; and Andrew E. Hill and John H. Walton, *A Survey of the Old Testament* (Grand Rapids: Zondervan, 1991), p. 17. On the rationale for a shorter chronology, see discussion in S. J. De Vries, "Chronology of the OT," in *The Interpreters Dictionary of the Bible* (Nashville: Abingdon, 1962), 1:582-84.

[5]Egyptian dynasty information and names of kings are taken from Bill Manley, *The Penguin Historical Atlas of Ancient Egypt* (London: Penguin, 1996), pp. 132-35.

[6]Some scholars believe that Jacob's sojourn to Egypt took place at a different period of the Middle Kingdom when the Hyksos were in power. The Hyksos were a linguistically Semitic people who ruled Egypt for about two hundred years (c. 1720-c. 1550 B.C.E.). Of course, we have already seen that the language family termed "Semitic" appears to have more in common with the tribes of Ham than Shem. The Hyksos were actually from Canaan, and thus were Hamitic. See David O'Connor, "The Hyksos Period in Egypt," in *The Hyksos: New Historical and Archaeological Perspectives,* ed. Eliezer D. Oren (Philadelphia: University of Pennsylvania Museum, 1997), pp. 45-67.

his imprisoned royal stewards (Gen 37:36; 39:1; 40:1), Pharaoh's character is not developed until the text describes a perplexing dream he had about cows and grain (Gen 41:1-24). When his own magicians could not interpret the dream for him, he was introduced to the incarcerated Joseph who offered a full interpretation and provided advice on how the dream could provide Pharaoh with economic and political dominance in the region (Gen 41:25-36). Impressed by the wisdom of the innocent inmate, Pharaoh immediately elevated Joseph to the office of prime minister, and for the rest of his reign reaped the benefits of Joseph's efficient governance.

Pharaoh was obviously not familiar with Joseph's religious leanings, but he is portrayed as a pious individual who feared God. Not only was he chosen by God to receive a vision that really related to the preservation of Abraham's seed (cf. Gen 45:7; 50:20), but he was able to discern that it was God's spirit who was at work in Joseph (Gen 41:38). He was quick to extend benevolence to Joseph's family (Gen 45:16-20), and was moved to grant them prime land in the relatively luscious region of Goshen (Gen 47:1-6, 11). In return for his kindness, Pharaoh received a special blessing from Jacob (Gen 47:7-10). At the time of his death, Pharaoh was truly sovereign in Egypt, owning all the property and people in the kingdom.

Although not a Pharaoh, the unique role that Potiphar played in Israel's history merits him a mention in this chapter. Potiphar is first introduced as the captain of the royal guard who purchased the betrayed Joseph from the Midianite (Ishmaelite) traders (Gen 37:36; 39:1). He quickly recognized Joseph's organizational skills and appointed him as the chief administrator in his home (Gen 39:1-6). The biggest obstacle to Joseph was Potiphar's wife, who was fatally attracted to the good-looking and principled youngster and repeatedly tried to seduce him (Gen 39:7-10). After continued rejection, the frustrated spouse accused him of attempted rape, forcing Potiphar to place him in jail. In a society where adultery was punishable by death, the fact that Joseph was imprisoned suggests that Potiphar knew him to be innocent. However, in this honor and shame society where the social status of an individual determined one's legal rights, a slave was always wrong, and the captain of the guard's wife was always right.

Apparently, the jail in which Joseph was placed was actually located on Potiphar's estate. It did not take long for Joseph to gain the respect of the prison warden, and he was soon appointed chief trustee (Gen 39:21-23). It appears that Potiphar continued to communicate with Joseph, and placed him as the special caretaker for Pharaoh's butler and baker when they were imprisoned (Gen 40:4). It may or may not have been Potiphar's intention, but his special arrangement provided Joseph with an opportunity to make an impression on these two influential men, one of whom would eventually be instrumental in securing his release. While nothing more is said about the relationship between Joseph and Poitphar, some believe that this "captain of the guard" is the same Potiphera, priest of On, who later became Joseph's father-in-law (Gen 41:50).

Pharaohs during the exodus. Jacob's family did very well in Egypt. As a result of their ties with Joseph they enjoyed favored status, and although they did not totally insulate themselves from society, they managed to maintain their distinct identity. After four centuries in their adopted land, the children of Israel had greatly multiplied and were dispersed throughout the kingdom (Ex 1:7). Several dynasties had transpired during their Egyptian tenure, and the memory of their famous ancestor had disappeared from the nation's conscience. It is with this reality that the Bible reports the accession of a new Egyptian king who did not know Joseph (Ex 1:8). With xenophobic zeal this king initiated a campaign of oppression and genocide against his Israelite subjects (Ex 1:8-22). Like an eerie forerunner to Hitler, he was so paranoid about the Israelite's success that he was determined to halt their growth by ordering the murder of all babies born into their families.

The name of the pharaoh who initiated this atrocity is not given. However, if the early date for the exodus is accepted (c. 1446),[7] the events surrounding Israel's final days in Egypt would have occurred during the Eighteenth Dynasty (c. 1539-c. 1295).[8] For reasons given later in this section, the infanticidal pharaoh was probably Thutmose I (c. 1493-c. 1481). Even as the pharaoh carried out his dastardly scheme to annihilate the Hebrews, God was using his daughter to preserve the child who would eventually deliver God's people from Egyptian bondage (Ex 2:5-10). As the princess bathed in the Nile, she noticed a baby in a basket. The child had been placed there by his

---

[7]This date is approximate, and the way the evidence is portrayed in this section demands a later date.

[8]Some scholars date the exodus to the Nineteenth Dynasty (c. 1295-c. 1186 B.C.E.) during the reign of either Seti I (c. 1294-c. 1279 B.C.E.) or Ramses II (c. 1279-c. 1213 B.C.E.). The attractiveness of this date is enhanced by the fact that jointly, these two kings reigned for a period of eighty-one years, a length that neatly corresponds to the fact that the Bible only depicts two pharaohs over Egypt during the first eighty years of Moses' life.

mother, who wished to hide him from the Egyptian guards who had been charged with killing all Hebrew newborns. Moved with compassion, the princess decided to adopt him and hired his own mother to be his wet nurse and guardian. In a strange twist of destiny, the child's name was derived from that of his adoptive grandfather, Thut*mose*—the child who could have grown to be pharaoh was named Moses.

At an appropriate age, Moses was handed to the princess to be raised in royal splendor. If the estimated dates are correct, he would have seen the deaths of Thutmose I and the briefly reigning Thutmose II (c. 1481-c. 1479), who was succeeded by Thutmose III (c. 1479-c. 1425). The "princess" who adopted Moses could very well have been Hatshepsut, one of the two female "kings" in the Egyptian dynasties. If so, she would have been the stepmother of Thutmose III, who served as coregent from c. 1473 to c. 1458. Given the fact that Moses was her son, he would have been in line to the throne and probably would have succeeded Thutmose III. However, this son of slaves who was raised among Egyptian royalty could not forget his roots, and a series of dramatic events turned him into a fugitive from his stepbrother (Ex 2:11-15). His adopted mother must have been heartbroken by her son's decision (cf. Heb 11:24), and she died while he was exiled in Midian.

Thutmose III reigned for a good three decades after Hatshepsut's death (cf. Ex 2:23), and was succeeded by his son Amenhotep II (c. 1427-c. 1392). A cruel warmonger like his father, Amenhotep continued the oppression and exploitation of the Israelites.[9] Little did he know that while he raised havoc in Egypt his uncle had received a spectacular commission from the God of the Hebrews (Ex 3:1—4:20). Amenhotep was undoubtedly surprised when his father's stepbrother suddenly showed up in the royal court with his real brother Aaron, demanding that his nephew allow the Israelites a brief respite to celebrate a festival in the wilderness (Ex 5:1). Stunned by the audacious request, Amenhotep not only refused to accept the authority of the Hebrew God, but made things harder for the Israelite slaves by increasing their work load (Ex 5:2-21).

Amenhotep's obstinance set the stage for Yahweh's dreadful assault against the Egyptian people. In his consequent audiences with Moses and Aaron, his refusal to offer the Israelites freedom to worship was punished with terrible

---

[9]For a brief discussion on Amenhotep's cruelty, see Manley, *Historical Atlas*, p. 72.

plagues that affected the entire kingdom. At the outbreak of the second plague in which millions of frogs polluted the land, the beleaguered pharaoh appeared to soften his position and promised to grant Moses' request (Ex 8:8). However, as soon as the plague had abated he changed his mind (Ex 8:15). He appeared to concede again during the fourth plague, when flies covered the land, and even showed signs of recognizing Yahweh's sovereignty when he asked Moses to pray for him (Ex 8:25-28).

By the time of the seventh plague in which huge balls of hail pelted plant and animal life, Amenhotep again professed full repentance and acknowledged the righteousness of Yahweh (Ex 9:27-28). He also feigned repentance during the eighth plague when locusts consumed the vegetation (Ex 10:12-20). As thick darkness suffocated the land during the ninth plague, it appears that the harassed king resolved to let the people go and worship on the condition that they leave their livestock in Egypt (Ex 10:24). It was only after Moses insisted that it was necessary for them to take the entire inventory with them that the frustrated ruler reverted to his original position (Ex 10:25-29). Finally, with the tenth plague, when all the firstborn Egyptians and their firstborn animals were snatched in death like victims of a serial sniper, Amenhotep succumbed to all of Moses' demands and gave them permission for immediate departure (Ex 12:29-32).

It did not take long for the king to realize that Moses had deceived him, and he immediately assembled his forces and pursued the band of slaves upon whom the economy of Egypt depended (Ex 14:5-9). Amenhotep himself led the assault but would once more witness the mighty hand of Yahweh when his entire cavalry drowned in the depths of the same Red Sea through which the Israelites had walked on dry land only moments before (Ex 14:21—15:21). As Amenhotep stood on the shore watching his legions succumb to torrential asphyxiation, centuries of Egyptian history probably flashed through his mind. On the other side of the sea were a people that had been brought into the kingdom by a slave who had been elevated to the status of royalty. Now these same people had been taken from the kingdom by a member of the royal court who had abased himself to slave status in order to liberate his people.

Pharaohs during the monarchy. The liberated multitudes who escaped Egyptian bondage would eventually develop into a kingdom that gained the respect of its southern neighbor. By the time of Solomon's reign, Israel's prestige is evidenced by the king's marriage to Pharaoh's daughter (1 Kings 3:1).

Judging from the dates of Solomon's reign, she may have been the daughter of either Siamun (c. 978-c. 959) or Har-Psusennes II (c. 959-c. 945),[10] the final two kings of the Twenty-first Dynasty (c. 1069-c. 945).

Whichever one of the above-mentioned Pharaohs was Solomon's father-in-law, it is likely that Har-Psusennes was the one who provided sanctuary for Hadad the Edomite (1 Kings 11:14-22). Some interpret his kind actions toward Hadad as an indication of his antagonism towards Israel. However, there is nothing to suggest that Har-Psusennes had any controversy with Solomon. In fact, if indeed he were Solomon's father-in-law, his benevolence toward Hadad could be an indicator of his attempt to form alliances with neighboring kingdoms. This could explain why he gave Hadad his sister-in-law as a wife. In fact, Har-Psusennes' wife, Tahpenes, personally undertook the responsibility of rearing Genubath, her nephew from the union of Hadad and her sister. Har-Psusennes had become so attached to Hadad that he did not even want him to return home when the political climate had changed under Solomon (1 Kings 11:21-22).

Whereas Har-Psusennes did not pursue an adversarial relationship with Israel, his successor, Pharaoh Shishak, had other plans. Shishak is more than likely Shoshenk I (c. 945-c. 924), who was the first Pharaoh of the Twenty-second Dynasty (c. 945-c. 715).[11] Evidence of Shishak's indifference toward Israel is seen in the fact that he provided refuge for Jeroboam when Solomon, with Saul-like jealousy, sought to kill him after God had promised to give him the major part of the kingdom (1 Kings 11:26-40). When Jeroboam assumed sovereignty over the recently reshaped Israel, Shishak attacked the smaller sister kingdom of Judah with a pan-African army and robbed the temple of all its wealth, including the famous golden shields that Solomon had made (1 Kings 4:25-28; 2 Chron 12:2). Details of Shishak's assault against Judah have been preserved in the Karnak temple of Amon in Thebes.[12]

There does not appear to have been too much interaction between Egypt and the kingdoms of Israel during the divided monarchy. However, just before the demise of the northern kingdom by the Assyrians, King Hoshea sought the assistance of Pharaoh So, an alternative name for Osorkon IV of

---

[10]See Kitchen, "Pharaoh," p. 913.
[11]K. A. Kitchen, "Shishak," in *New Bible Dictionary*, ed. D. R. W. Wood, 3rd ed. (Downers Grove, Ill.: InterVarsity Press, 1996), p. 1097.
[12]Paul S. Ash, "Shishak," in *Eerdmans Dictionary of the Bible* (Grand Rapids: Eerdmans, 2000), p. 1215.

the Twenty-second Dynasty (2 Kings 17:4). Interestingly, Israel's first king, Jeroboam, was an ally of Pharaoh Shishak, the first king of the Twenty-second Dynasty. Now Hoshea, the final king of Israel, would seek an alliance with Osorkon, the last king of the Twenty-second Dynasty (c. 730-c. 715). There is no indication that So responded to Hoshea's requests—it appears that he wisely decided to stay out of a battle against a kingdom that had achieved impregnability.

After the fall of Israel, we see little interaction between Egypt and Judah. In fact, both nations were preoccupied with Assyria, their common enemy. The relationship between the nations was to change during the reign of Pharaoh Neco II, the second king of the Twenty-sixth Dynasty (c. 672-525).[13] The biblical account reports that Neco had received specific divine instruction to go against the Assyrians (2 Chron 35:20-24; 2 Kings 23:29-30). Probably in a bid to curry favor from the mighty Assyrians, King Josiah of Judah decided to join the battle in opposition to Egypt. The divinely appointed Neco prophetically warned the champion of Judean reformation that God would not allow Judah to prevail, but the stubborn Josiah persisted and met a violent death.

Following his victory, Neco subjected Judah to Egyptian rule and replaced the rightful heir to the throne, Jehoahaz, with his brother, Eliakim, whose name he changed to Jehoiakim (2 Kings 23:31-35; 2 Chron 36:1-4). Jehoahaz was taken into Egyptian captivity, and Judah was made to pay taxes to her new masters. Neco's reign over Judah did not last long. Shortly after his conquest, he was scared away by Nebuchadnezzar of Babylon, who had finally broken the yoke of the Assyrians and had begun his quest to establish the Neo-Babylonian empire (2 Kings 24:1-7; Jer 46:2).

Despite the fact that Egypt had attempted to annex Judah, many Jews felt comfortable establishing residence in the land of their former captors. Jeremiah informs us that many opted to remain in Egypt so that they could practice their pagan rituals to the "queen of heaven" (Jer 44:1-19). It appears as if they felt that Yahweh's anger was focused on the "land" of Judah, and they would escape judgment by shifting to another geographical region. In no uncertain terms, Jeremiah reminded them that God is not confined by geography. In fact, Hophra, the very Pharaoh who provided them sanctuary, would

---

[13]C. de Wit, "Neco, Necho," in *New Bible Dictionary*, ed. D. R. W. Wood, 3rd ed. (Downers Grove, Ill.: InterVarsity Press, 1996), p. 811.

also meet his demise by divine appointment, in the same way that King Zedekiah of Judah was handed over to Nebuchadrezzar of Babylon (Jer 44:30).

Hophra, whose Egyptian name was 'Wa'hibrē', was the fourth king of the Twenty-sixth Dynasty.[14] Referred to as Apries by Greek historian Herodotus, this Pharaoh is featured in a number of other places in Scripture. It is ironic that Jeremiah mentions Hophra's fate in the same breath as the fate of Zedekiah, since the latter had earlier sought military assistance from the Pharaoh against Babylon (Ezek 17:11-21). Apparently, Hophra experienced temporary success in repelling the Babylonians, but quickly retreated when the sons of Nimrod launched a counterattack (Jer 37:5-11). He was eventually killed in a revolt and was replaced by Amhose (Amasis II).[15]

OTHER PERSONALITIES

Friends and foes of David. The Pharaohs of Egypt are not the only offspring of Misrayim featured prominently in Scripture. Most students of the Bible are just as familiar with their Philistine cousins who had settled in the land of Canaan. Perhaps the most notorious nemesis in the Hebrew Bible is a Philistine named Goliath. Goliath is featured in the account of Israel's emerging monarchy when Saul's apostasy has resulted in Philistia's besiegement of Israel. He is described as a mighty warrior with an impressive arsenal, whose ten-foot frame towered over the frightened Israelites as he challenged the people of God to send him a worthy opponent (1 Sam 17:4-11). When the pubescent David responded to his challenge, Goliath was understandably insulted (1 Sam 17:42-44). The raging giant probably let down his guard as he rabidly ventured towards this insolent teenager. Before he knew what had happened he was knocked unconscious by a strategically placed stone from David's slingshot. The emboldened youth promptly decapitated the giant, and Philistia was ceded to Saul (1 Sam 17:48-53).

Ironically, it was a Philistine king named Achish who provided sanctuary for David when he was a fugitive from the same Saul he had saved (1 Sam 21:10-15). Although under Israelite control, Achish still maintained local autonomy over the province of Gath. Knowing that this Philistine king had no real allegiance to Saul, David sought and was granted asylum. For obvious rea-

---

[14]K. A. Kitchen, "Hophra," in *New Bible Dictionary*, ed. D. R. W. Wood, 3rd ed. (Downers Grove, Ill.: InterVarsity Press, 1996), p. 480.

[15]Ibid.

sons David wished to remain anonymous, but when Achish's attendants discovered that the man in their midst was the celebrated hero of Israel who had brought down Goliath, he feigned madness for fear that Achish would seek retribution.

Having succeeded with his deception, David quickly exited Gath and hid out in Adullam. However, after further encounters with Saul, he sought sanctuary with Achish again (1 Sam 27:1-4). This time, Achish extended a warm reception to David and even gave him the town of Ziglag (1 Sam 27:5-7). Over the year and four months that David stayed in Ziglag, Achish took a keen interest in his exploits. Apparently, his hospitality had conditions, and when he prepared to launch an attack against the Israelites, he naturally assumed that David and his soldiers would fight alongside his Philistine army (1 Sam 28:1-2). When the other Philistine leaders saw David's band integrated among the Gittites, they angrily ordered Achish to send him back, reasoning that he may turn against them in the heat of the battle (1 Sam 29:1-11). Achish had developed such a deep bond with David that it was difficult for him to deliver the news. However, David was probably relieved that he did not have to fight against his brethren. Achish and the Philistine alliance went on to soundly defeat Saul and the Israelite army, thus setting the stage for David's ascendancy to the throne.

When David and his army were released from the Philistine alliance, they returned to Ziglag to find that the town had been raided and pillaged by Amalekites (1 Sam 30:1-6). As he pursued the enemy, he encountered an unnamed son of Misrayim in the plain across the Wadi Besor. Not having eaten for three days, the man was at the point of exhaustion and had to be nurtured and refreshed. After he had eaten, he shared that he was the slave of one of the Amalekites who had raided David's town. When he fell sick during the journey back to Amalek, his master left him to fend for himself in the wilderness. Feeling no real loyalty for a group of people who had left him to die a slow and lonely death, the refreshed man agreed to lead David to the location of these bandits. As a result of his cooperation, David experienced a sound victory over the marauding Amalekites (1 Sam 30:7-20).

With the death of Saul, David had no reason to return to Ziglag and made his way to Jerusalem where he would eventually be coronated. One of the first projects he embarked on as king was the retrieval of the ark of the covenant, which had been captured by the Philistines when Eli still judged Israel (1 Sam

4:10-22). The ark had brought nothing but terror to the Philistines and they eventually returned it to Israel where it was installed in the house of Abinadab in Kiriath-jearim (1 Sam 5:1—7:1). Now that David was king, he ordered that the ark be taken from its current location in Baale-judah and established in Jerusalem with the sanctuary (2 Sam 6:1-19). Tragedy struck during transit when Uzzah, one of the attendants, tried to steady the shaking ark and was immediately struck dead (2 Sam 6:6-8). Gripped by fear, David cancelled the project and had the ark placed in the home of Obed-edom the Gittite (1 Chron 13:14).

Apparently, Obed-edom was not aware of the perils that had accompanied the moving of the ark, and was probably ignorant about the havoc it had caused in his native Gath about half a century before (1 Sam 5:8-9). He willingly agreed to house the ark for his ruler, and was soon the surprised recipient of unique blessings from Yahweh (2 Sam 6:11-12). When David heard about the Philistine's experience, his fear subsided and he assembled a new crew to move the ark to Jerusalem. Obed-edom moved to Jerusalem with the ark and, although not a Levite—much less an Israelite—he obtained the distinct privilege of joining the temple orchestra as a lyrist (1 Chron 15:18-21). He was also appointed as one of the two main gatekeepers for the ark (1 Chron 15:24).

David obviously had a strong affinity with the men of Gath. In fact, when he came out of exile to assume the crown of Israel, six hundred Gittites followed him (2 Sam 15:18). These loyal warriors also stuck with him when Absalom revolted and declared himself king—a rebellion that forced David into exile again. The Gittite Ittai was one of the many soldiers who formed David's bodyguard as he fled. Curious about Ittai's loyalty, David inquired of him why he chose to follow him when he could easily return to Jerusalem and align himself with Absalom's royal guard (2 Sam 15:19-20). The loyal Philistine took the opportunity to reveal his undying support for David and was granted permission to continue marching with the rest of the fleeing army (2 Sam 15:21-23). In the final battle against Absalom's rebel forces, Ittai was one of the three commanders David chose to quash the insurrection (2 Sam 18:2).

The presence of such a large contingency of Philistines in David's army in no way guaranteed his immunity from attacks by other Philistine kings. For the rest of his life David battled against Philistine opponents who wished to be the one to defeat the giant slayer. In fact, the record shows that David faced off with several other Philistine giants. On one occasion, the aging David was almost beaten by Ishbi-benob, but was rescued by Abishai, the brother of Joab (2 Sam 21:15-17). Other Philistine giants killed in battle included Saph, another Gittite named Goliath, and an unnamed man with twelve fingers and twelve toes (2 Sam 21:18-22).

Spouses and concubines. Other children of Misrayim mentioned in Scripture are not as fearful as the giants of Philistia. Several were actually espoused to notable men of God. The first was Hagar, the personal maid of Sarah (Gen 16:1-15), who was the unfortunate victim of an attempt to circumvent a divine promise. After several years of unsuccessfully trying to bear a child, Sarah suggested that her husband, Abraham, have intercourse with her maid. This was in full harmony with an ancient custom that allowed a woman to claim a child who her husband had fathered with a slave.[16] As a result of Abraham and Sarah's attempt to assist Yahweh in fulfilling his promise, Hagar gave birth to a son, Ishmael. Unfortunately, Hagar's successful pregnancy and boastful attitude incited the jealous Sarah to vengeful abuse of her maid, which led to Hagar running away.

As she sought refuge, Hagar became one of the few people in Scripture who were blessed with a personal appearance from Yahweh, who promised that she would be the mother of a great nation (Gen 16:10). The very name of her son, Ishmael, would be a testimony to the fact that God "heard" the desperate cries of this Egyptian slave woman (Gen 16:11). Hagar is also among the small list of worthies who provided a name for Yahweh when she dubbed him El-roi—the "God who sees" (Gen 16:13). After her divine affirmation, Hagar returned to Abraham's house and assisted in the raising of her son.

Fourteen years after Ishmael's birth, Sarah miraculously gave birth to Isaac at the ripe old age of ninety! However, the fact that she was now a mother did not alleviate her hatred for Hagar. She despised watching Ishmael play with his younger brother, Isaac. Eventually her jealousy drove her to order the banishment of the young boy and his mother (Gen 21:8-16). Hagar and her young son were dismissed with limited supplies and seemed to be facing certain death when their nourishment was depleted. However, she again received personal confirmation from the voice of God who reminded her of his promise

---

[16]For a discussion on the practice of surrogate motherhood, see Gordon J. Wenham, *Genesis 16—50* (Dallas: Word, 1994), p. 7. See also John H. Walton, Victor H. Matthews and Mark W. Chavalas, eds., *The IVP Bible Background Commentary: Old Testament* (Downers Grove, Ill.: InterVarsity Press, 2000), p. 48.

before miraculously supplying a well of water in the parched wilderness of Beersheba. She was blessed with the pleasure of watching her son mature, and personally picked a wife for him from her native Egypt (Gen 21:17-21).

Although Hagar is the obvious victim in Abraham and Sarah's impulsive scheme to assist the divine plan, Paul uses her character as a negative example in his allegory on freedom from the law (Gal 4:21-31). Focusing on her slave status, he categorizes all who desire to remain under the old covenant as children of slavery. Adversely, Sarah's children are compared to those under the new covenant who automatically receive the promises of God. While the allegory is effective in illustrating Paul's argument, it must not be forgotten that it is not intended to disparage either Hagar's character or cast disdain on her descendants through Ishmael. The innocent Hagar is simply the unfortunate vessel through which the unfaithfulness of Abraham and Sarah was made manifest.

The next woman of Misrayim espoused to a Semitic dignitary was from the opposite end of the social strata than Hagar. Asenath was the daughter of Potiphera, priest of On, who had been given to Joseph as a wife by Pharaoh (Gen 41:45). Not much is known about Asenath, but as the daughter of one of the leading priests, she must have been from the upper echelons of Egyptian society. Two children were born to her union with Joseph, Manasseh and Ephraim (Gen 41:50-52). These sons of Egypt would become the progenitors of Israel's only two "half tribes" (replacing the tribe of Joseph). One of the books in the Pseudepigrapha contains an embellished account of the relationship between Asenath and Joseph, and suggests that Asenath accepted the religion of Israel before entering into marriage.[17] This is more intended to exonerate Joseph for marrying a heathen than to portray Asenath as a righteous convert.

No list of famous couples in the Bible will omit the names of Samson and Delilah. For centuries, their tragic relationship has been used as an object lesson to warn those who are tempted to date outside the "faith"! The powerful draw of this didactic account often obscures the fact that this was actually Samson's second relationship with a woman of Philistia. Similar to many Israelite men of his day, Samson was attracted to foreign women, and when his

---

[17]For a full text and commentary, see Christoph Burchard, "Joseph and Aseneth: A New Translation and Introduction," in *The Old Testament Pseudepigrapha,* ed. James H. Charlesworth, vol. 2 (New York: Doubleday, 1985), pp. 177-247.

eyes encountered the woman of his dreams on an excursion to Timnah he compelled his parents to arrange a marriage (Judg 14:1-9). The marriage took place at a time when the Israelites were being ruled by the Philistines (Judg 14:4), but the fact that intermarriage was allowed suggests that the citizens of Israel still maintained a degree of autonomy.

Samson's marriage to the unnamed Timnite did not last very long. While the seven-day wedding feast was taking place, Samson posed a perplexing riddle to the Philistine guests that would have been impossible to solve (Judg 14:10-14). Feeling humiliated, the men approached Samson's wife and threatened to kill her and her family if she did not extract the solution to the riddle from her new husband (Judg 14:15). The intimidated bride utilized her womanly wiles and secured the answer from Samson, which she immediately passed on to her people (Judg 14:16-18). Incensed by the betrayal from the object of his passionate desire, Samson went on a killing rampage and returned to his father's house (Judg 14:19). Some time after when his anger had subsided, Samson decided to go back to his bride only to find that her father had married her off to the best man (Judg 14:20—15:2). His ex-father-in-law's offer of her prettier younger sister did not appease Samson, who was violently enraged to the point that he vandalized Philistine farmland and killed a thousand men with a donkey's jawbone (Judg 15:3-17). Needless to say, Samson and the woman to which he was fatally attracted were never reunited.

The testosterone-driven Samson did not learn his lesson from this unfortunate incident. He still sought sexual satisfaction from Philistine women (cf. Judg 16:1) and eventually became infatuated with a woman named Delilah (Judg 16:4). Although the text does not describe Delilah as a Philistine, there is general consensus that she was a citizen of Philistia.[18] When Philistine politicians discovered that Delilah was having an affair with Samson, they bribed her to uncover the secret of his unexplainable strength (Judg 16:5). Delilah quickly applied her seductive charms on this leader of Israel, and it did not take long for him to reveal his divine secret (Judg 16:6-19). The man with super-human strength who had eroded the authority of the Philistines and killed scores of men singlehandedly was finally conquered by a perceptive and deceptive woman who realized that in order to get to the source of his strength she first had to learn to manipulate his weakness.

---

[18]See Edward E. Hindson, *The Philistines and the Old Testament* (Grand Rapids: Baker, 1971), p. 130.

Another daughter of Misrayim to marry a leader of Israel was Solomon's Egyptian wife, mentioned earlier in the chapter. She appears to have been his exclusive wife for a number of years. Her special status is indicated by the fact that he built her a private home that was an exact duplicate of the one he had constructed for himself (1 Kings 7:8; 9:24; 2 Chron 8:11). The Egyptian princess was also the beneficiary of gifts from her doting father who gifted her with the city of Gezer after conquering it and killing the inhabitants (1 Kings 9:16). After a while, the unnamed princess would witness Solomon's harem increase as he added other Hamitic wives and concubines from Moab, Ammon, Edom, Sidon and Heth (1 Kings 11:1).

Believers in Messiah. Solomon's witness to the God of his ancestors was somewhat tainted, and rather than influencing his foreign wives to become partners in the covenant, he was drawn to their pagan practices. However, the testament of his most famous descendant was very different, and was influential in pulling many of Misrayim's offspring into the restructured covenant people. Of course, the descendant of whom I speak is none other than Jesus of Nazareth, the Messiah of prophecy. His ministry not only touched the populace of Palestine, but quickly spread to the surrounding lands. The New Testament mentions five people who can readily be defined as sons of Misrayim.

After Jesus had been sentenced to death he was made to take the ominous walk to the place of crucifixion. According to the synoptic Gospels (Matthew, Mark and Luke), the Roman authorities spared him the burden of carrying the cross, and instead forced a man named Simon from Cyrene to bear the wooded weight for our Lord (Mt 27:32; Mk 15:21; Lk 23:26). In New Testament times, Cyrene was a Roman province that had a significant Jewish population, which leads many to conclude that Simon must have been a member of the Jewish Diaspora.[19] As we learn from Acts 2:10 where both Jews and proselytes from Cyrene were present, adherents to Judaism did not have to trace their roots to Shem. Nonetheless, whatever his religious status, Simon's appearance was enough for the authorities to recognize that he was probably not a citizen, and was thus compelled to follow their orders.[20] With cross on shoulder, this son of Misrayim walked behind the Messiah and symbolically

---

[19]See J. H. Harrop, "Cyrene," in *New Bible Dictionary*, ed. D. R. W. Wood, 3rd ed. (Downers Grove, Ill.: InterVarsity Press, 1996), p. 250.

[20]For a discussion on the probable causes for Simon's forced recruitment, see Stephanie Buckhanon Crowder, *Simon of Cyrene: A Case of Roman Conscription* (New York: Peter Lang, 2002), pp. 49-50.

led the throng of mostly female mourners (Lk 23:27-31).

Apparently Simon was moved by the event and eventually accepted Jesus as Messiah. Mark's audience would have readily recognized him as the father of Alexander and Rufus (Mk 15:21), an obvious indicator that his sons had embraced the faith. It is highly likely that the Rufus Paul greets in his letter to the Romans (Rom 16:13) is the son of the famous cross-bearer. Evidence of Simon's physical appearance may be present in the reference to "Simeon who is called Niger" (Acts 13:1), a member of the church at Antioch who is assumed to be the same person identified by Mark.[21] Here, Simeon is listed among the prophets and teachers, along with Barnabas, Manaen, Saul (Paul), and another man of Cyrene named Lucius.

Famous early Christian leaders also included Apollos, a native of Alexandria in Egypt. Apollos was an itinerant evangelist who probably ministered in a number of places before working his way to Ephesus where he is first introduced to biblical writ (Acts 18:24-28).[22] He was obviously a powerful orator who had a firm knowledge of Scripture. He appears to have been influenced by the teaching of John the Baptist, and probably learned about Christ through the ministry of a layperson. Fortunately for him, while in Ephesus his preaching was assessed by Priscilla and Aquila, a missionary couple, who pulled him aside and helped him to refine his theology.

From Ephesus, Apollos left for Achaia with the full endorsement of the believers (Acts 18:27). While there he helped to strengthen the faith of the fledgling communities by engaging in public debates with Jewish scholars. Among other places, his ministry took him to Corinth where he also made a profound impact. In fact, his preaching was so effective that some preferred him over Peter and Paul (1 Cor 1:12). When Paul addresses the partisanship in Corinth, he does so with Apollos's knowledge (cf. 1 Cor 4:6). Not wishing to fan the partisan flames, Apollos rejected Paul's request to return to Corinth with the party that delivered the letter, choosing rather to return at a time that was more convenient for him (1 Cor 16:12). The eloquent Egyptian maintained friendly terms with Paul, and even benefited from his influence (cf. Titus 3:13).

---

[21]See F. S. Fitzsimmonds, "Simon," in *New Bible Dictionary*, ed. D. R. W. Wood, 3rd ed. (Downers Grove, Ill.: InterVarsity Press, 1996), p. 1104. But see also R. E. Nixon, "Simeon," in the same *New Bible Dictionary*, for a note of caution in associating these two.

[22]R. E. Nixon, "Apollos," in *New Bible Dictionary*, ed. D. R. W. Wood, 3rd ed. (Downers Grove, Ill.: InterVarsity Press, 1996), p. 57.

Apollos is the last son of Misrayim mentioned in Scripture, but the fact that his close associate was mistaken for a fellow countryman merits an explanation. By his own testimony we learn that Paul was born in Tarsus, a major city in the joint province of Cilicia-Syria. Although he was a Jew, as a native of Tarsus, Paul could very well have been a descendant of Ham through a Hittite ancestor who married a Jew. Nonetheless, in spite of the ethnic mixture that may have contributed to his lineage, we know he was not a converted Jew for he is able to trace his lineage to the tribe of Benjamin (Phil 3:4-6).

By his own testimony Paul was an "ethnic" Jew. However, when he was arrested in the temple on his final visit to Jerusalem (Acts 21:27-36), a Roman soldier confronted him with a very unusual question: "Do you know Greek? Then you are not the Egyptian who . . . ?" (Acts 21:37-38). The question could also be stated, "Do you know Greek? Are you not that Egyptian who . . . ?" The unusual nature of this question forces the Bible reader to ask the reason for this inquiry.[23] The first way in which the question can be read heavily suggests a racial reading. With this reading, Paul obviously did not *appear* to be someone who could speak Greek. Since Egyptians in Hellenized towns would have naturally spoken Greek, a similar conclusion could also be inherent in the second reading. In this instance, this would have been more of an accusation, which would have been the reason for Paul's immediate disclaimer and disclosure of his citizenship. Whatever way the question is read, it is still intriguing that the tribune would automatically identify Paul with a term reserved for natives. Paul must have looked like an ethnic Egyptian!

---

[23]Some may conclude that the query stemmed from Paul's evocative rhetoric which led the tribune to believe that he had apprehended an insurrectionist.

7

IDENTIFYING THE
AFRICANS IN CANAAN

Like many other Jews of antiquity, we will never know how Paul really looked. However, we do know that he was born and educated within the borders of territory that had been settled by Canaan's descendants. By Paul's day, there was probably little evidence of the aboriginal inhabitants of the land. The descendants of Heth had long been colonized by Indo-Europeans who changed their language, their genes and consequently their "ethnicity." Many of the other indigenous Canaanite clans had also been absorbed by foreign imperial powers from Mesopotamian Cush, Misrayim, Israel, and the European Greeks and Romans. After generations of intermingling with cultural groups from near and distant lands, the typical dweller within the borders of Canaan probably resembled his or her kin from the northern coasts of Misrayim.

Racist suppositions about skin pigmentation have led many to ignore the biblical linkage of Canaan to Ham as they align his descendants with Shem. Scholars have even programmed the masses into organizing the languages of Canaan under the "Semitic" category. It is difficult for them to conceive of the land most central to Bible history as an important quadrant of the "land of Ham." To accept this would mean acknowledging the Hamitic identities of Uriah, Melchizedek, Rahab, Abimelech, Jezebel and a number of other Canaanites. Nonetheless, in spite of scholarly bias, the biblical record is clear—Canaan is a son of Ham. This section discusses biblical characters who are descended from Canaan, especially as they relate to the people of the covenant.

POLITICAL PERSONALITIES

Political figures in the patriarchal period. After Abraham was deported from Egypt (Gen 12:20), he and his nephew Lot were compelled to part ways and settle in different parts of Canaan. Lot chose to set up his homestead among established cities situated around the Dead Sea. Unfortunately for Lot, the rulers of the city-states experienced conquest and ended up being vassal states in a fledgling empire that was presided over by the Semitic king Chedorlaomer of Elam (Gen 14:1-3; cf. Gen 10:22).[1] After twelve years of subjugation, King Bera of Sodom persuaded the kings of Gomorrah, Adma, Zeboiim and Bela (Zoar) to rise up against King Chedorlaomer. Sadly, they were stiffly defeated. Following the defeat, the twin cities of Sodom and Gomorrah were sacked, and Lot along with many of their subjects were taken into slavery. When Abraham heard of the assault, he assembled an army, swiftly defeated Chedorlaomer and consequently returned the spoils and the slaves to the fractured cities (Gen 14:13-24). Upon his return from the conquest, he was greeted by King Bera, who offered him all the spoils as a trophy. Abraham refused on the grounds that he did not want another person to take credit for making him rich.

When King Bera met Abraham after his victory over Cherdorlaomer, he was accompanied by another Canaanite king, Melchizedek of Salem. Melchizedek was not only a king, but he is also identified as a priest of God Most High (El Elyon). While some scholars believe that El Elyon was the name of the chief god of a Canaanite pantheon, the text is clear that this was just another name for the same indescribable Yahweh who had created all things (Gen 14:19-22).[2] Although located about sixty miles north of the cities named in the struggle against Chedorlaomer, it is generally agreed that Jerusalem is a later name for the territory of Salem over which Melchizedek ruled.[3]

On the surface, there is nothing spectacular about Melchizedek. He is merely described as a priest-king who provided Abraham with nourishment and blessed him. However, the biblical writers reveal that he was more than an ordinary person. The psalmist suggests that Melchizedek was associated with a mysterious priestly order to which the Messiah would belong (Ps

---

[1]For theories about the identity of this king, see D. J. Wiseman, "Chedorlaomer," in *New Bible Dictionary*, ed. D. R. W. Wood, 3rd ed. (Downers Grove, Ill.: InterVarsity Press, 1996), p. 182.

[2]Temba Mafico, "The Divine Name Yahweh *'Elōhim* from an African Perspective," in *Reading from this Place*, vol. 2: *Social Location and Biblical Interpretation in Global Perspective*, ed. Fernando F. Segovia and Mary Ann Tolbert (Minneapolis: Fortress, 1995), pp. 21-32, surmises that the various names for the divinity in the Hebrew Bible reflect a period when the disparate tribes that comprised Israel had localized gods that eventually were subsumed under Yahweh Elohim. However, the incident with Melchizedek demonstrates that the different names are simply attestations to the unlimited attributes of the same God.

[3]For discussion see J. A. Emerton, "The Site of Salem, the City of Melchizedek (Genesis xiv 18)," in *Studies in the Pentateuch*, ed. J. A. Emerton (Leiden: Brill, 1990), pp. 45-71. Jerusalem is also called Salem in Ps 76:2.

110:4). While some have speculated that this may be the indication of a secret priesthood, the reference is probably intended to distinguish between the Aaronic priesthood that is determined by levitical bloodline and an appointed priesthood where God unilaterally selects individuals for his purposes.

The New Testament book of Hebrews also makes reference to the mysterious Melchizedek and the priesthood to which he belonged (Heb 7:1-22). In his allegorical commentary about Melchizedek, the author of Hebrews depicts him as a type of Christ who by virtue of his name is both king of righteousness and king of peace (Heb 7:2). Another parallel is drawn from the fact that the parents of this important biblical figure are not mentioned in the commentary, which suggests that, like Jesus, he had no earthly biological parents (Heb 7:3). Although a Canaanite king who had no relationship to Abraham, Melchizedek is said to be the spiritual superior of the beneficiary of God's promise (Heb 7:7), and consequently superior to the levitical priesthood (Heb 7:9-10). The mystical Melchizedek is also featured in several extrabiblical writings.[4]

Soon after the destruction of Sodom and Gomorrah, Abraham left Mamre and moved southward toward Egypt, eventually settling in Gerar where Abimelech was king (Gen 20:1-18).[5] Here again, Abraham pretended that Sarah was his sister in order to protect himself from men who would kill him to get her (Gen 20:11; 12:10-20). Apparently confirming Abraham's suspicions, Abimelech, the local king, took Sarah into his harem. From our contemporary perspective, it's hard to imagine why anyone would want to be sexually involved with a ninety-year old woman to whom he was not married, however the fact that people obviously lived longer back then suggests that she may have had the appearance of an attractive middle-aged lady today. It appears that Sarah resided in Abimelech's house for a length of time, for soon none of the women in his household were able to bear children, and he himself was afflicted with an ailment—probably a sexual dysfunction (Gen 20:17-18). Eventually, God himself intervened in a night vision and warned Abimelech to stay away from Sarah.

---

[4]For further information, see Joseph A. Fitzmyer, "Melchizedek in the MT, LXX, and the New Testament," *Biblica* 81 (2000): 63-69.

[5]According to R. P. Gordon, "Abimelech," in *New Bible Dictionary,* ed. D. R. W. Wood, 3rd ed. (Downers Grove, Ill.: InterVarsity Press, 1996), p. 4, "Abimelech," meaning "servant of the king," may have been a cognomen of Philistine kings, similar to the title "Pharaoh" in Egypt.

Although polygamous like Abraham, Jacob and a number of other biblical characters, a close analysis of Abimelech's dialogue with God indicates that he was a man of integrity (Gen 20:4-5). His spiritual maturity is also evident in God's disclosure that it was he who had kept him from making sexual advances towards Sarah (Gen 20:6). Obviously he was a man with a conscience, or he would never have heeded God's voice. When Abimelech confronted Abraham, he expressed his disappointment that this man of God would deliberately deceive him and place him in a position where he could have sinned (Gen 20:9-10). Still, in submission to God's instructions (Gen 20:7), he allowed the fallible prophet to pray for the reversal of the infertility that plagued his household.[6] Even after this unfortunate experience, Abimelech extended benevolence to Abraham by presenting him with money, livestock and slaves, and allowing him to settle anywhere he desired within the territory of Gerar.

Abimelech maintained a distrust towards Abraham, but he still respected him as a man of God and treated him justly for the duration of the period in which he resided in Gerar. He even extended full citizenship rights to him, and when Abraham lodged a complaint against some of Abimelech's men who had seized one of his wells, Abimelech himself intervened and ensured that Abraham's newly dug well at Beersheba received government protection (Gen 21:22-34). Abimelech was probably relieved when Abraham and Sarah moved north to Hebron (Kiriath-arba), a Hittite stronghold. It was here that Sarah died (Gen 23:1-20).

Over the years, Abraham had accumulated a great deal of wealth in terms of commodities. However, he did not own any land or real estate, and consequently had nowhere to bury his wife. Sensing the need for stability, Abraham approached the Hittites for land to be used as a family cemetery (Gen 23:3-20). The Hittites were very receptive, and offered to share their own burial place with Abraham. Abraham had other plans and requested the city elders to persuade Ephron son of Zohar to sell him a plot of land in Machpelah. Initially, Ephron offered the field as a donation and declined any compensation. However, Abraham was probably aware that Ephron would have maintained rights to the land and insisted on paying the full price of four hundred shekels

---

[6]Interestingly, Sarah's infertility was reversed and she was soon to conceive and give birth to Isaac (Gen 21:1-3).

of silver in the presence of the city council.[7] Years after, Abraham himself was buried in that cemetery.

After burying his father, Isaac and his family were instructed to go to Gerar to find relief from a famine that had afflicted Hebron (Gen 26:1-11). As fate would have it, he would find sanctuary in the courts of Abimelech. Although Isaac was probably ignorant about Abraham's experience with the Canaanite king, he followed in his father's deceptive footsteps and claimed that his wife was his sister for fear that he would be killed by envious men (Gen 26:7). Fortunately for Isaac, Abimelech had learned his lesson from the experience with Sarah and was not as quick to summon beautiful female sojourners into his harem. When he eventually discovered Rebekah's true identity, he chastised Isaac and threatened capital punishment for anyone who assaulted either Isaac or Rebekah (Gen 26:9-11). This story drives home the consistency of Abimelech's integrity and compassionate concern for his citizens. Obviously a man who feared God, he understood he was also responsible for the spiritual welfare of his kingdom and subjects (Gen 26:10).

Abimelech's apparently liberal immigration policy afforded Isaac the opportunity to increase his wealth to the point that he became a political threat to his generous host (Gen 26:12-16). Abimelech ordered that Isaac relocate, and after several confrontations with the people of the land, he eventually settled in Beersheba. Soon after settling in Beersheba, Isaac received an official visit from Abimelech, Ahuzzah, his advisor, and Phicol, the commander of the Gerarite army (Gen 26:26). The purpose of the visit was to negotiate a peace treaty between the two peoples. This occasion provides another opportunity to witness Abimelech's political acumen. He was obviously a peace-loving leader who made preemptive alliances with potential political predators. This incident with Isaac is the last biblical exposure of this Canaanite monarch. However, all will probably agree that this African king exhibited godly traits that provide positive examples for government leaders throughout the ages.

Other Canaanite dignitaries were not as morally constrained as Abimelech. One of these was Shechem, after whom a city was named (Gen 33:18-19). Shechem's father was Hamor, a Hivite prince who sold a plot of land to Jacob as a homestead when he had reentered Canaan with his family. The suicidal

---

[7]This incident shows that Hittites had clearly established real estate laws and a systematic method of sealing transactions.

act that secured Shechem a permanent place in Scripture was the rape of Jacob's daughter, Dinah (Gen 34:1-31). After violating Jacob's innocent daughter, Shechem persuaded his father to secure her for a wife. When Dinah's twelve brothers found out what had happened, they were infuriated. Taking advantage of Shechem's desire to have Dinah for a wife, Jacob's sons pretended to agree to the union on the condition that all of Hamor's male subjects adopt the custom of the Hebrews and undergo circumcision. Although understanding that this would cause a painful inconvenience, Hamor reasoned that submitting to this rite of passage could have some financial benefits for his kingdom when the two clans merged (Gen 34:22-23). Apparently, Jacob's family demonstrated good faith by allowing Dinah to establish residence in Shechem's house (cf. Gen 34:26). Three days after the mass circumcision when the men were writhing in pain, Simeon and Levi initiated a merciless slaughter against Hamor, Shechem and their subjects, and plundered the city. Following this incident, Jacob was instructed to move his family to Bethel (Gen 35:1).

Political personalities in the settlement period. Jacob and his children resided peacefully in Canaan until they relocated to Goshen in Egypt. When they returned centuries later their numbers were much greater, and they were viewed as invaders by the descendants of their former allies. The first to confront them after the exodus was the king of Arad who easily defeated the inexperienced army and took several captives (Num 21:1-3). However, victory was short lived, and the Israelite counterattack resulted in the utter destruction of the towns of Arad, the devastated ruins of which were renamed Hormah (destruction).

Not long after their triumphant defeat of the king of Arad, the Israelites would be forced into battle again—this time with two Amorite kings: Sihon of Heshbon and Og of Bashan. Sihon was approached by Israelite messengers who requested permission to pass through his land (Num 21:21-32). He was probably aware that a similar request had earlier been denied by the Edomite king, who had assembled his army and intimidated the Israelites into taking an alternative route (Num 20:14-21). Bolstered by the belief that the untrained band of refugees posed no real threat, Sihon assembled an army and launched an attack against Israel. He must have been bemused and embarrassed by his bitter defeat that resulted in the confiscation of his entire kingdom.

Soon after Sihon's defeat, his colleague Og learned that Israel was on the warpath and rallied his troops to stop them (Num 21:33-35). Og was among the last of the Rephaim, a race of intimidating giants (Deut 3:11). To give an idea of his size, the narrator describes his bed as measuring nine cubits by four cubits (13' by 6'). With others in his army sharing his giant genes, few seasoned armies could have maintained their composure in their presence—much less the novice Israelites. Notwithstanding, Og's band of oversized bullies provided little challenge to the faith-filled Israelites, who totally massacred all the inhabitants of the kingdom and took pleasure in occupying the land. So significant was this conquest that whenever Israel repeated the story of the exodus, the conquest of the mighty Sihon and Og was recalled with great pride.[8]

Having garnered the courage to fulfill the divine agenda, Joshua led the Israelites to several more victories over Canaanite kings.[9] Another named king is Adoni-zedek of Jerusalem (Josh 10:1). Literally translated "my lord/master is righteous," his name is similar in meaning to the mysterious Melchizedek ("my king is righteous") who ruled Jerusalem during the time of Abraham. However, he was no friend of the people of God. Upon hearing of Joshua's successful defeat of Jericho and conquest of the king of Ai (Josh 8:1-29), Adoni-zedek decided to go on the offensive and formed an alliance with King Hoham of Hebron, King Piram of Jarmuth, King Japhia of Lachish and King Debir of Eglon (Josh 10:3-4). It did not take long for the Israelites to force the retreat of the Amorite coalition, and the five kings fled and hid in a cave at Makkedah (Josh 10:16-17). When Joshua discovered where Adoni-zedek and his allies were hiding, he had them arrested and publicly executed before disposing off their dead bodies in the same cave where they had earlier sought refuge (Josh 10:18-28).

After the execution of the Amorite alliance, Joshua continued his impregnable assault against the Canaanites (Josh 10:29-43).[10] When King Jabin of Hazor heard about Joshua's military success, he formed a coalition so large that it was difficult to count the number of men in the resultant army (Josh 11:4). In addition to securing the support of the neighboring King Jobab of Madon, the kings of Shimron, Achshaph and other close allies, the successful

---

[8]Cf. Deut 3:1-3; 29:7; Josh 2:10; 9:10; Ps 135:11; 136:17-22.

[9]For a candid discussion on the divine order to annihilate the Canaanites, see C. S. Cowles, Eugene H. Merrill, Daniel L. Gard and Tremper Longman III, *Show Them No Mercy: Four Views on God and Canaanite Genocide,* ed. Stanley N. Gundry (Grand Rapids: Zondervan, 2003).

[10]Joshua defeated the kings of Makkedah, Libnah, Debir and Lachish; King Horam of Gezer; and conquered the cities of Eglon and Hebron. The extent of his conquests covered Kadesh-barnea to Gaza and the territory of parts of Canaanite Goshen.

diplomat Jabin was also able to solicit the cooperation of the Amorites, the Hittites, the Perizzites and the Jebusites (Josh 11:1-3). Unfortunately for Jabin, his impressive coalition was not able to withstand the wrath of the Spirit-filled Israelites, and by the end of the battle they had experienced total annihilation (Josh 11:5-23).

Although Joshua had annexed significant portions of Canaan into the emerging Israelite kingdom, there were still vast amounts of territory to conquer after his death. Under new leadership, the anxious Israelites launched an assault against King Adoni-bezek of Bezek, who appears to have formed a coalition with other Canaanite and Perizzite city-states (Judg 1:4-7). Like all of the previous kings, Adoni-bezek experienced defeat and was publicly humiliated when his captors severed his thumbs and big toes. This undeniably cruel act was actually a brutal act of vengeance inflicted upon a king who himself had committed the same atrocity to seventy kings whom he had turned into his slaves. Following his painful abasement, Adoni-bezek was confined to Jerusalem where he lived out his days in misery (Judg 1:7).

In fulfillment of the curse uttered by the freshly sobered Noah, Israel's conquests were part of the divine plan to transfer the ethnic scape of the land inhabited by Canaan's progeny. While this military assignment was undeniably callous, the eradication of the enemy was intended as a means of alleviating temptation and preserving the holiness of Yahweh's special people. It soon became clear that the people of the covenant were not totally committed to the terms of the covenant, and as a result the act of total annihilation was never fully accomplished. In fact, Yahweh would often use the kings of Canaan to discipline his people. On one occasion, he even placed Cushan-rishathaim of Aramnaharaim as king over Israel for an eight-year period (Judg 3:7-8). It was not until the people repented and appealed to Yahweh that he appointed Othniel the nephew of Caleb to eliminate Cushan-rishathaim (Judg 3:9-11).

Not long after Othniel's success over Cushan-rishathaim, the Israelites fell into apostasy again—not once, but twice! The first time resulted in their subjugation to king Eglon of Moab (Judg 3:12-30). After the second repudiation of Yahweh's sovereignty, Israel was placed under King Jabin of Hazor, who apparently governed his kingdom through the might of his military, commandeered by the oppressive Sisera (Judg 4:1-3). Ironically, both Jabin and Sisera would eventually experience humiliating defeat at the hands of two women.

Extending his grace once more to his rebellious children, Yahweh ap-

pointed Deborah as judge over Israel. It did not take long for the female com-
mander-in-chief to commission Barak to lead the army that would liberate Israel from their Hamitic overlords. Barak closely followed Deborah's
instructions and was instrumental in securing Israelite victory over the tech-
nologically advanced Philistines (Judg 4:4-16). Sensing defeat, Sisera fled
from the scene of battle and was offered sanctuary in the home of Jael wife of
Heber, a descendant of Jethro (Judg 4:17-20). Since Heber's clan had a diplomatic relationship with King Jabin, Sisera was probably unaware that this
Cushite family had a close affinity with Israel. Believing he was in a safe place,
the unsuspecting Sisera slipped into a solemn slumber, and while he slept the
courageous Jael conducted a cruelly creative assassination by driving a tent peg
through his head (Judg 4:21-22). Following Sisera's death, Deborah continued the resistance against King Jabin until he was utterly defeated, thus securing the emancipation of Israel (Judg 4:23-24).

Political personalities in the monarchial period. By the time of the monarchy, Israel had gained the respect of her neighbors, and her presence in Canaan
was firmly established. After David had consolidated the tribes into a single
kingdom, Hiram of Tyre was the first named king to present him a gift (2 Sam
5:1-12; 1 Chron 14:1). With the Israelite empire increasing in strength and
influence, Hiram probably thought it wise to develop a cordial relationship
with his southern neighbor. It also appears that Hiram was a worshiper—or at
least an admirer—of Yahweh (cf. 2 Chron 2:11-12). Having some of the finest
artisans in antiquity among his subjects, the Tyrian king commissioned a construction team to build a house for David (2 Sam 5:11).

Hiram was still on the throne when Solomon succeeded David, and he immediately sent emissaries to the newly appointed Israelite king (1 Kings 5:1).
He was thrilled upon discovering that Solomon wanted to continue the
friendship between the two nations, and quickly agreed to a trade agreement
in which he would provide material for the building of the temple in exchange
for foodstuff (1 Kings 5:1-12; 2 Chron 2:3-16). Apparently, Hiram continued
to supply Solomon with material for the twenty years it took to build the temple and his palace. At the end of this period, Solomon appears to have been in
arrears to Hiram and offered him twenty cities in Galilee for compensation (1
Kings 9:10-14). Upon inspection of the sub-par cities, Hiram was insulted
and called the offering Cabul, meaning "a land good for nothing" (1 Kings
9:13). Nonetheless, he still gifted Solomon with a large amount of gold and

even gifted him with cities (1 Kings 9:14; 2 Chron 8:2), and the two kingdoms maintained close ties (cf. 1 Kings 10:22).

Given Israel's friendship with her northern neighbors, it was probably no big shock when King Ahab decided to marry Jezebel, daughter of Ethbaal the Sidonian king (1 Kings 16:31). This unfortunate union was ordained by hell itself, and Jezebel was to develop into the archetypal figure of feminine beast-liness. It did not take long for the unsanctified Jezebel to wrap her manipulating tentacles around the scepter of governance and set an agenda of unbridled apostasy for the gullible Israelites, to the extent that she ordered the execution of all the preachers in the land (1 Kings 18:4). She replaced Yahweh's messengers with hundreds of prophets devoted to Baal and Asherah (1 Kings 18:19). Jezebel was so brazenly evil that she even intimidated the apparently fearless Elijah who—after courageously killing hundreds of false prophets—ran for his life when he heard that this lone woman had ordered him killed (1 Kings 19:1-3). This strong-willed woman refused to tolerate weakness, and when Ahab sulked over Naboth's refusal to give him some land, Jezebel immediately plotted Naboth's speedy assassination and ordered her husband to take possession of the dead man's plot (1 Kings 21:1-16). This cruel act compelled Yahweh to urge Elijah to personally deliver the prophecy of Jezebel's and Ahab's gory demise (1 Kings 21:17-24).

The defiant Jezebel survived Ahab, and although her son Joram ascended to the throne, she continued to control the affairs of Israel (2 Kings 9:22). Jezebel's demise was orchestrated by the enraged warrior Jehu (2 Kings 9:14-37). After assassinating Joram on the very property that Ahab had extorted from Naboth, Jehu set his sights on Jezebel. Having received news about the plight of her son, Jezebel knew that the emboldened Jehu could not be intimidated by her strong-arm tactics. Competent at manipulative strategy, the aged woman had her beauticians provide her with an extreme make-over and as Jehu rode into the city she seductively looked out the window and feigned an offer of peace. Unmoved by her cosmetic facade, Jehu made his intentions known, and some of the very eunuchs who had fearfully attended to her every need mustered the courage to forcefully throw her out of the window. She hit the ground so hard that upon impact, her blood splattered on the surrounding wall and the stationed horses. Unfazed by this bloody mess, Jehu went inside for refreshments while neighborhood dogs ate her mangled corpse, leaving only her skull, feet and the palms of her hand. Although her remains had been mutilated beyond recognition, Jehu decided to show respect to her royal status and ordered that she receive a proper burial.

SPOUSES AND CONCUBINES

Jezebel's megalomaniac quest was definitely not shared by other Canaanite wives mentioned in Scripture. After Sarah's death, the aged Abraham fathered several other children with a woman named Keturah (Gen 25:1-4). Like the mysterious Melchizedek, no details are given about Keturah's pedigree. Initially, the text describes Keturah as Abraham's wife (Gen 25:1), however their offspring are later called sons of Abraham's "concubine[s]" (Gen 25:6). More than likely, in this male-dominated age where women had few rights, Keturah was a young slave in Abraham's house who was fulfilling a duty for her master. The absence of any reference to her heritage makes it reasonably safe to assume that like his former concubine, Hagar, Abraham had acquired her during his century-long sojourn in the African regions of Canaan and Misrayim. To the union of Keturah and Abraham, six sons were born: Zimran, Jokshan, Medan, Midian, Ishbak and Shuah. Like the other women in Abraham's life, Keturah was victimized by his insensitive decisions when he ordered that their sons relocate to the Arabian section of Ham. Jethro, one of Keturah's descendants, would later assist Moses in organizing the Israelites.

Since Abraham's immediate descendants were basically immigrant minorities in a foreign land, it is only natural that their first choice for spouses would come from among the people of the land. Indeed, when seeking a vessel through which the chosen seed would be born, it appears that the only option for Abraham was the Egyptian slave Hagar (Gen 16:2). Yet when Abraham and Sarah sought a wife for Isaac, they sent their trusted servant to the Semitic city of Nahor (Gen 24:2-10). Later, Isaac would send Jacob to Paddan-aram for a non-Cannanite wife (Gen 27:46—28:2). However, the ethnic heritage of the local women did not bother Esau, who took advantage of the polygamy allowances and married two of them: Judith daughter of Beeri the Hittite and Basemath daughter of Elon the Hittite (Gen 26:34).[11]

The Bible states that these two women made life "bitter" for Isaac and Rebekah (Gen 26:35). At first glance, it may seem as if these women were

---

[11]Different names are given in Gen 36:2: Adah daughter of Elon the Hittite, Oholibamah daughter of Anah son of Zibeon the Hivite, and Basemath, Ishmael's daughter. This may reflect different traditions from which the narrator tells the story or alternative names for the women.

crude, disrespectful and unruly to their parents-in-law. However, closer investigation shows that the "bitterness" was probably caused by prejudice and fear. Rebekah lamented her life would be over if Jacob married a Hittite woman (Gen 27:46), and even Abraham opined that the Canaanite women were not good enough for his favorite son, Isaac (Gen 24:3). When Esau discovered that his parents were not pleased with the ethnicity of his wives, he entered into a third marriage with his first cousin Mahalath, daughter of Ishmael (Gen 28:6-9). Her dominant genes were Egyptian, but she was a direct descendant of Abraham. Given the lessons that history has taught us about the depth of prejudice and racism, it is hardly likely that even this marriage made his parents happy. Eventually, Esau moved all three of his wives and their offspring and settled in Edom, a Cushite region of Ham that bordered Canaan on the east.[12]

Esau's love for Canaanite women was also shared by his nephew Judah, the fourth son of Jacob. After Joseph was sold into slavery, Judah moved away from his brothers and settled in the Canaanite city of Adullam, near Bethlehem (Gen 38:1-5). Here he married the daughter of Shua. The daughter is unnamed, but recent English translations of 1 Chronicles 2:3 have opted to translate her name with Bath-shua (e.g., NRSV). Bath-shua gave birth to three sons: Er, Onan and Shelah.

When Er reached marriageable age, his father arranged a wedding with a Canaanite women named Tamar (Gen 38:6-11). The text reports that Er was a wicked man and was eventually struck dead by God, leaving Tamar a widow. According to the ancient custom of levirate marriage, when a man died without a male descendant, it was his brother's duty to have intercourse with his widow with the sole purpose of producing a male offspring for his dead brother (cf. Deut 25:5-10; Ruth 4:1-12).[13] In the spirit of this law, Judah ordered his son Onan to fulfill his legal obligation. Unfortunately for Tamar, Onan only used this as an opportunity for self-gratification, and although he had several sexual encounters with her, he always withdrew before ejaculation (Gen 38:9). Appalled by his blatant disregard for the law, and probably in-

---

[12]The list of Esau's descendants through his Canaanite wives appears in Gen 36:1-43. One of the more notable descendants is his grandson via Elon, Amalek (Gen 36:16), father of the Amalekites.

[13]Some societies still have this practice. One of the contributors to the spread of HIV in parts of Africa today is that of brothers-in-law wanting to father a son with the widows of husbands who had died from AIDS.

censed by his selfish actions that amounted to sexual abuse of the innocent Tamar, the Lord eventually put Onan to death. Believing Tamar to be a bad omen, Judah asked her to move back to her father's house until his youngest son, Shelah, was old enough to fulfill the levirate duty.

After many years, Tamar recognized that Judah had no intention of allowing Shelah to fulfill her desire to mother a son, and so she decided to take things into her own hands. Following the death of her mother-in-law, Bathshua, Tamar disguised herself as a veiled prostitute and put herself in the path of Judah as he went to a sheep-shearing ceremony with his friend Hirah the Adullamite (Gen 38:12). The recently widowed Judah bit the bait and secured her services for temporary satisfaction. Not having any money, the testosterone-driven widower agreed to leave his signet ring, staff and cord with Tamar as surety for later payment. With a sense of victory, Tamar returned to her home and was nowhere to be found when Hirah returned to Enaim to deliver Judah's payment to her (Gen 38:13-23).

Months later, town gossips informed Judah of his daughter-in-law's pregnancy, and the enraged Judah made plans to have her burned alive for adultery (Gen 38:24-30; cf. Lev 21:9). When Tamar received the news of his intention, she sent a messenger with the tokens he had left with her, and he realized that he was the real culprit. Tamar's life was spared, and she eventually gave birth to twins, Perez and Zerah. Interestingly, from the line of Perez came the kings of the Davidic dynasty and eventually Joseph, the surrogate father of Jesus (Mt 1:3, 16), from whom he derived his kingly identity as the lion of the tribe of Judah. Although we are only informed of the ethnic identities of Judah's wives, it is only natural to assume that most of Jacob's sons would have married Canaanite women. Like Judah, they were miles away from their place of origin and probably were forbidden by social custom to marry the children of the slaves who had accompanied their father when he escaped from Laban's plantation.

FRIENDS OF THE COVENANT

Given the interdependency of the people of the covenant and their Canaanite neighbors, the forming of relationships that transcended ethnic boundaries was only natural. This was definitely true with Eliezer, one of the many slaves who were a part of Abraham's household. We are first introduced to Eliezer when Yahweh appears to Abraham in a vision to confirm his covenant with him (Gen 15:1-21). Abraham identifies Eliezer as originating from Damascus, the capital city of Syria. Although the northern parts of Syria (Aram) appear to be associated with Shem, the southern territories definitely fall under the region of Canaan. From the dialogue between Abraham and God, we learn that Eliezer was probably the chief steward in Abraham's house—similar to a butler. Although he was a slave, since Abraham had no biological children, Eliezer stood to inherit Abraham's estate.[14] Eliezer must have been deeply trusted and well treated, otherwise he could easily have plotted the demise of his master and hastened his change in social status. The birth of Ishmael, Isaac and the other sons through Keturah meant that Eliezer no longer qualified as heir. Nonetheless, he must have felt honored to be considered.

Another Canaanite with a place of prominence in biblical writ is Rahab, one of three Hamitic women listed in Matthew's record of Jesus' genealogy (Mt 1:5).[15] She is first introduced to the biblical saga as a Canaanite prostitute who resided in Jericho at the time when the new generation of Israelites began their conquest of the Promised Land (Josh 2:1). For some unexplained reason, the two Israelites whom Joshua had sent on a reconnaissance mission to Jericho ended up spending the night at her house. When the king of Jericho discovered the men's mission, he ordered Rahab to release them to him, but she hid them on her roof and deceived the pursuers into thinking they had already left. She later revealed to the men that she was aware of the divine favor that Yahweh had showered on the Israelites, and she voiced her desire to be spared with her family when the Israelites attacked Jericho. The spies gave her specific instructions on what she should do to escape the pending attack, and she and her household received amnesty while the entire city of Jericho was decimated (Josh 2:2-24; 6:17, 22-25). Rahab's family became an integrated and renowned part of Israel, and she gained a new respectability by uniting with Salmon from the tribe of Judah with whom she parented Boaz (Mt 1:5). In

---

[14]It was not unusual for men without sons to adopt an heir. See K. A. Kitchen, "Eliezer," in *New Bible Dictionary*, ed. D. R. W. Wood, 3rd ed. (Downers Grove, Ill.: InterVarsity Press, 1996), p. 310.

[15]Matthew's genealogy is not intended to provide every name in Jesus' ancestry. Unlike Luke's genealogy, which strives for accuracy, Matthew is more interested in creating a mnemonic device by shaping the list into three sets of fourteen names. Consequently, a number of names are excised, which may make it seem as if Rahab (who belongs to the early settlement period) is actually the grandmother of Jesse (who lived during the period of transition from the judges to the kings). Of course, this assumes that this is the same Rahab from Jericho. For commentary on Matthew 1:5, see Donald A. Hagner, *Matthew 1—13* (Dallas: Word Books, 1993), p. 11. For theories on the theological or literary intent of the genealogy, see Donald Senior, *Matthew* (Nashville: Abingdon, 1998), pp. 36-39; and R. T. France, *Matthew*, Tyndale New Testament Commentaries (Downers Grove, Ill.: InterVarsity Press, 1985), pp. 71-75.

the New Testament, she is also elevated as a paradigm of faith that works (Heb 11:31; Jas 2:25).

Rahab is one of many Canaanite women who married Israelite men, but there were also Canaanite men espoused to women of Israel. This was especially true for those who had chosen to become a part of the covenant people. One of the heart-rending stories in Scripture features Uriah the Hittite. Uriah was a faithful soldier in David's army who was fully committed to his adopted land and is listed among "the Thirty," David's exceptional warriors (2 Sam 23:39). He had married a native Israelite named Bathsheba, and lived in close proximity to the royal compound.

Uriah is introduced to the biblical narrative at a time when Israel was warring against Ammon (2 Sam 11:1-27). While this loyal soldier battled in the front lines, David had a sexual affair with Bathsheba, who became pregnant. In a desperate effort to cover up his sin, David sent for Uriah and cajoled him to spend a night with his wife. The diligent soldier refused to enjoy his conjugal rights while his fellow soldiers were engaged in battle. After learning that Uriah's commitment to duty prevented him from covering up the illicit pregnancy, David concocted a more devious plan. With an act that would embarrass a Mafioso, David had the trusted Uriah hand deliver a letter to Joab with orders for his own assassination (2 Sam 11:14-15). Joab followed David's instructions, and the faithful soldier who was a paradigm of loyalty was viciously murdered by the king of Israel via unwitting Ammonite assassins (2 Sam 11:16-21).

Uriah was not the only Canaanite to become an Israelite citizen during David's rule. Another was Hushai the Archite who provided assistance to David during Absalom's coup d'etat. Similar to Ittai, the Philistine mentioned earlier, Hushai wanted to join David's entourage. However, David persuaded him that he would be more useful if he returned to Jerusalem, infiltrated Absalom's inner circle and work as a spy along with the priests Zadok and Abiathar (2 Sam 15:32-37). It did not take long for Hushai to gain Absalom's confidence (2 Sam 16:15-19), and he was soon giving him persuasively damning advice while passing information to David (2 Sam 17:5-16). Hushai's forewarning helped David to avoid an ambush and readied his army for Absalom's final defeat (2 Sam 17:21-22; 18:1-18).

In addition to those who volunteered their services to the Israelite army were those Canaanites who chose to remain in certain regions even after they were conquered and controlled by Israel. One example is Araunah, one of the many Jebusites who remained in Jerusalem after the Israelite conquest. He is introduced to the biblical narrative at the time when Yahweh sent a plague upon Israel for David's presumptuous census (2 Sam 24:1-25). After the death of seventy thousand people, God was moved to compassion and commanded the destroying angel to cease the affliction. When Yahweh's special emissary received the command, he was in the vicinity of Araunah's threshing floor (2 Sam 24:16). The prophet Gad then ordered David to erect an altar at the spot where the angel was standing at the time the plague was halted. Araunah was oblivious to what had happened, and when he saw David and his team approaching his property he hurried to meet him and, after paying homage, inquired about the purpose of the visit. David informed the curious Jebusite that he wished to purchase the property for the purpose of building an altar. In a spirit of benevolent cooperation, Araunah offered the threshing floor to David as a gift. However, David insisted that the Jebusite accept payment, and only after the contract was sealed did the king build the altar and effected a stay of divine judgment. Several decades later, the humble location that hosted Araunah's threshing floor was to serve as the site for Solomon's magnificent temple (1 Chron 21:28—22:1; 2 Chron 3:1).

When Solomon eventually constructed the temple, he was greatly aided by Canaanite artisans, one of whom was Hiram of Tyre. Not to be mistaken for the king with the same name, Hiram was actually the son of a Naphtalite widow who had married a Tyrian and apparently resided in Tyre (1 Kings 7:13-14). His exposure to Tyrian craftsmanship and architectural acumen qualified him for the task of creating the interior decoration for Solomon's elaborate temple (1 Kings 7:15-47). Given the enormity of the project, he probably was responsible for the design and oversight of the meticulously detailed furnishings.

Other Canaanites featured in the Bible were not as high profile as Hiram of Tyre. Take for example the anonymously dubbed "widow of Zarephath," who was the exact opposite of Jezebel, her countrywoman. She had no ties to royalty and exhibited a selfless demeanor. Furthermore, she respected God's prophets and was a woman of great faith (1 Kings 17:8-15). When the biblical script first introduces this Zarephite, she was destitute and at the point of starvation. Apparently, the drought that Elijah had prophesied against Israel was also affecting her northern neighbors (cf. 1 Kings 17:1,

14). The hopeless widow was probably taken by surprise when the very Elijah who had prophesied the drought met her at the entrance of her city and requested a cup of water.

Although at the point of death, the unselfish woman looked beyond her own desperate need and sought to satisfy the stranger's thirst. As she went to the water source, Elijah must have evoked indescribable feelings of uneasiness within her when he asked for some bread to go with the water. At that time, the Zarephite woman was forced to share her grave situation with the man of God. She was probably surprised when Elijah instructed her to prepare bread for him first from her measly ration, and then prepare something for her two-person family. The Canaanite woman responded in faith, and found that not only was there enough to prepare a meal for her son and herself, but the Lord saw to it that her supplies did not run out until rain returned to the land.

God's miraculous intervention did not mean that the Zarephite would live "happily ever after." Some time after the miracle, her son became seriously ill and eventually died. Perplexed by the timing of his death, she questioned why God would spare him from starvation only to allow him to die from a terminal illness. She directed her frustration to her tenant Elijah, who was the closest symbol of God in her current reality. Feeling the depth of her pain, and appearing embarrassed about the tragedy, Elijah took the boy to his room and pleaded for God to restore him to life. The widow was ecstatic when her resuscitated son was returned to her, and voiced her revived confidence in the man of God (1 Kings 17:16-24). The Bible does not provide any more information about the woman or her son, but her example served as a paradigm of faith that Jesus used in his homecoming sermon in Nazareth many centuries later (Lk 4:25-26; cf. Heb 11:35).

Another woman of Canaan served as a living example of faith to Jesus and his disciples. Jesus encountered her during a brief excursion into the district of Tyre and Sidon (Mt 15:21-28 = Mk 7:24-30). Mark uses the politically correct term for the woman when he calls her Syrophoenician (Mk 7:26). However, writing to a Jewish audience and packing rhetorical power into the story, Matthew chooses the outdated—but charged—appellation Canaanite (Mt 15:22). This unnamed woman came to Jesus in desperation pleading that he exorcise her daughter. After a brief argument with Jesus—which was really pedagogy for the disciples—the woman's request was granted and her faith commended.

FAMILY REUNION: CONCLUSION

The disciples' attitude towards the woman of Canaan is somewhat paradigmatic of a long tradition of Western-dominated biblical interpretation that has omitted—and at times distorted—the significant contributions of the children of Ham to the biblical story. It stands to reason that if the majority of the events reported in the Bible took place in the lands associated with Ham's progeny, then a number of the featured personalities must have been descendants of Ham. This obvious deduction is often distorted by those who take the logic a couple of steps further and reason that if Ham is a synonym for Africa, then his descendants must have been black. This logic is consciously or unconsciously held by two opposing camps. On one side are Afrocentric apologists who charge those who reject the blackness of biblical characters with Eurocentric bias. The other camp consists of European traditionalists who accuse their opponents of revising history for political and sociological purposes.

Both camps have valid points, and they will only circumvent the impasse if they learn to listen to each other and reevaluate the evidence with the other's eyes.[16] When this is done, skeptical European scholars will see that they don't have to "throw out the baby with the bath water," and anxious Afro scholars will see that the baby is already clean and doesn't need another bath. Few can deny the logic that places the descendants of Ham in the lands occupied by his children. The more controversial deduction is the one that mandates distinct physical characteristics for these descendants. However, Hamitic or African origin should not presuppose predictable pigmentation. All descendants of Ham did not share the same "ethnic" traits. It is for this very reason that part two, "Family Reunion," has avoided jumping to conclusions about the "blackness" of the biblical characters and has focused on identifying the Hamites (Africans).

The resultant research has uncovered a host of Hamites in the biblical record. Ham has colored the pages of Scripture with a parade of politicians

---

[16]For a lively discussion that indirectly relates to this project, see the accusations made against Europe's distortion of history in Martin Bernal, *Black Athena: The Afroasiatic Roots of Classical Civilization*, 2 vols. (London: Free Association Books; New Brunswick, N.J.: Rutgers University Press, 1987, 1991); the critiques in Mary R. Lefkowitz and Guy MacLean Rogers, eds., *Black Athena Revisited* (Chapel Hill: University of North Carolina Press, 1996); and the responses in Martin Bernal, *Black Athena Writes Back* (Durham, N.C.: Duke University Press, 2001); and Jacques Berlinerblau, *Heresy in the University: The Black Athena Controversy and the Responsibilities of American Intellectuals* (New Brunswick, N.J.: Rutgers University Press, 1999).

picked from the pharaohs of Misrayim and the kings of Cush and Canaan, a supply of spouses selected from an array of women ranging from the obscure slaves of Egypt to the royal princesses of Sidon, and a family of friends found in people as diverse as the mercenaries of Ethiopia to the prostitutes of Jericho. As the biblical record makes clear, the gracious blessings of God have been shared with the scattered clans of Cush, the mixed multitudes of Misrayim and the colonized clans of Canaan.

PART THREE

GROWING PAINS
The Bible in Emerging African Christianity

Princes shall come out of Egypt,

Ethiopia shall soon stretch out her hands to God.

PSALM 68:31 (KJV)

Although the majority of the Bible was penned on African soil and the bulk of its stories were set in the land of Ham, its main characters were the descendants of the Semitic immigrants who had been placed there by divine command. Initially, the Bible was viewed as a sectarian book that contained the mysteries of the Jewish people. While the Jews engaged in successful evangelism and welcomed various ethnic groups into their ranks, the Bible seemed to function as a national biography with little relevance for those outside of the covenant. It was not until the aggressive missionary activities of the Christians that the treasures of the Bible were released from ethnic coffers and shared with the human family.

Given the geographical boundaries of Ham, it is safe to say that Christianity was born in biblical Africa. From the days of Abraham, the people of promise had established roots on African soil. Egypt was a favorite spot, and even after the exodus from slavery, Israel's descendants returned in droves to the "black" land of the Nile. They flourished in Egypt, establishing synagogues and schools and contributing to the philosophical volumes of the massive Alexandrian library.[1] Indeed, it was here that the Hebrew Bible was translated into Greek, making it accessible to an entire empire. The descendants of Israel also settled in Cush, and some sources suggest that Ethiopian royalty had fully embraced the religion of Abraham. However, among the sons of Ham, it was Canaan who was to bear the distinction of playing host to the Messiah and nurturing the fledgling Christian movement.

According to the Gospels, the land of Ham hosted Jesus' entire life and ministry. Of course, during the time in which he ministered, these regions bore the cosmopolitan flavor of Jewish nationals, Roman settlers and others from around the globe who had come to seek their fortune. Nonetheless, the multiethnic tapestry that contributed to the cultural wealth of the region did not change the fact that this was still biblical Africa. Only briefly interrupted by a sojourn in Egypt for an unspecified time, much of Jesus' earthly life was spent in Galilee and Judea with the occasional excursion into Syrophoenicia, Decapolis and Samaria.

After Jesus' ascension, his followers initially remained in the region. The beginning chapters of the book of Acts portray a church centered around Judea. Anticipating the imminent return of their Lord, many lived in kibbutz-type arrangements, sharing their wealth and resources. However, Jesus had commanded them to be witnesses in Jerusalem, Judea, Samaria and the ends of the earth (Acts 1:8). Rapidly fulfilling this command, the church quickly spread in all directions. Judging from the nations represented by those who accepted Jesus as Messiah on the Day of Pentecost, the Christian message was taken into Europe, Asia and Africa. By Acts 13, we read of an established congregation in Antioch of Syria and others throughout Asia Minor. Even as the messianic movement flourished with the addition of thousands of Jews and a growing number of Gentiles, the organization maintained headquarters in Jerusalem, where leaders of the church met to iron out doctrine and establish policy (cf. Acts 15).

Initially, the early Christians maintained identity with their Jewish siblings, and many continued worshiping at the temple and benefited from the special favors afforded Jews by the Roman Empire. However, the Jewish authorities were not very keen about associating with a sect that celebrated a crucified

---

[1]For information on the ancient library in Alexandria, see Luciano Canfora, *The Vanished Library*, trans. Martin Ryle (Berkeley: University of California Press, 1989).

Messiah and lowered the lofty standard of Judaism by admitting uncircumcised Gentiles into the covenant. It did not take many decades for the siblings to part ways as Christianity positioned itself as the true representatives of God's chosen.[2]

The Christianity that separated from Judaism was far from united.[3] The only rallying point for the numerous groups that were to evolve over the centuries was the common faith in Jesus as Messiah. Apart from this, there were marked differences on how the Bible should be theologically interpreted and applied. Interestingly, much of the debate centered around the very Jesus who was the focus of their faith. As the fragmented church developed throughout the regions that sprung from Ham, the dominant groups within Christianity emulated the intolerance of those among their spiritual forebears who questioned their right to be aligned with the people of God. This was sad, for the general Jewish legacy was one of tolerance. Even as they shunned their Messianic siblings, the rabbis encouraged a free-spirited dialogue that was eventually codified in the Talmud. However, many of the Christian "fathers" who sat in the seat of the rabbis were more concerned with ideological orthodoxy than dialogue. The result was a church more divided than the Judaism that had given it birth.

---

[2] See the collection of essays in James D. G. Dunn, ed., *Jews and Christians: The Parting of the Ways: A.D. 70-135* (Grand Rapids: Eerdmans, 1999). See also James D. G. Dunn, *The Partings of the Ways Between Christianity and Judaism and Their Significance for the Character of Christianity* (Philadelphia: Trinity Press International, 1991).

[3] For a lively discussion on the diversity in the earliest Christian communities, see Bart D. Ehrman, *Lost Christianities: The Battles for Scripture and the Faiths We Never Knew* (Oxford: Oxford University Press, 2003).

8

THE DEVELOPMENT OF CHRISTIANITY IN PALESTINE

It has already been mentioned that Christianity took root in the land that had originally been claimed by Canaan. Since it had been hundreds of years since the land was officially known as Canaan, most historians refer to the Canaan of the New Testament era as Palestine. This is somewhat misleading since it was not until the suppression of the Bar Kokhba revolt in 135 C.E. that the Roman Emperor Hadrian changed the name to *Syria Palaestina,* and not until the fourth century was the region exclusively known as Palaestina.[1] This was obviously meant to be an affront against the Jews, since *Palaestina* is the Latin word for Philistia—the ancient enemy of Israel. Correct terminology for the region in New Testament times would utilize the Roman provincial names of Judea, Galilee and Phoenicia. Judging from Jesus' confrontation with the Syrophoenician woman in Matthew 15, it is highly probable that some Jews still referred to the indigenous inhabitants as Canaanites. This alone should provide a basis—though admittedly a debateable one—to continue the use of the term "Canaan" with reference to this territory.

The Jesus movement that took root in the former environs of Canaan was to experience growing pains from the very start. Many of the obstacles it faced stemmed from its quest for identity. In close proximity to its Jewish roots, the religion of the Messiah started out as an aberrant Jewish denomination. The church in Jerusalem seemed intertwined with its Jewish sibling, and more than a decade after Jesus' ascension, some of the brethren were still faithfully attending services at the temple (Acts 21:17-26). The thousands who had initially embraced Jesus as Messiah never saw themselves as leaving one faith to

---

[1] Anson F. Rainey, "Palestine, Land of," in *Eerdmans Dictionary of the Bible* (Grand Rapids: Eerdmans), p. 998.

join another. They had simply received greater light and anticipated the glorious appearing of the conquering Messiah who would soon return in military might to rescue them from Roman oppression. Buoyed by the traditional First Testament view of Messiah, many of the early Christians probably did not even take the time to wrestle with such concepts as Jesus' preexistence and incarnation. These doctrines only became an issue as the New Testament canon developed and believers were forced to reevaluate their theological understandings of Messiah.

THE CHURCH OF THE JEWISH MESSIAH

Judging from the documents that have been preserved from the early days of Christianity, it is probably safe to say that there were two major divisions in the Jewish movement. The first can be termed "the church of the Jewish Messiah," and the second "the church of the Son of God." Each of these understood the parameters of the Bible and the teachings therein in radically different ways, some of which related to the closeness of the teachings to traditional Jewish doctrines. Those closest to their Jewish parent were Ebionites. Named from the Hebrew *Ebionim*, meaning "the poor ones,"[2] the Ebionites did not accept such "orthodox" teachings as the Trinity, original sin and the divinity of Jesus.[3] Some even rejected the notion of the virgin birth.[4] Instead they saw Jesus as the human son of Joseph and Mary who was adopted by God at baptism. As far as they understood the person of Jesus, it was not until his baptism when the Holy Spirit descended on him that he became the Son of God. Apparently, the group was in existence before the destruction of Jerusalem, and was still active in the fourth century when Epiphanius of Salamis listed them among the heretical.[5]

Some Jewish Christians also revered the surviving relatives of Jesus who collectively were known as the *desposyni* ("belonging to the master"). For the

[2]Hyam Maccoby, *The Mythmaker: Paul and the Invention of Christianity* (New York: Harper & Row, 1987), believes that the Ebionites, being led by the relatives of Jesus, probably were more faithful to the original and authentic teachings of Jesus than was Paul.
[3]For a concise synopsis of Ebionite beliefs, see Bart D. Ehrman, *Lost Christianities: The Battles for Scripture and the Faiths We Never Knew* (Oxford: Oxford University Press, 2003), p. 109.
[4]Jaraslov Pelikan, *The Christian Tradition: A History of the Development of Doctrine*, vol. 1: *The Emergence of the Catholic Tradition (100-600)* (Chicago: University of Chicago Press, 1971), p. 24, contrasts the two Ebionite camps.
[5]See Robert Eisenman, *James the Brother of Jesus: The Key to Unlocking the Secrets of Early Christianity and the Dead Sea Scrolls* (New York: Viking, 1996).

Ebionites, the *desposyni* included the relatives of Mary and Joseph, and the descendants of Jesus' sisters and brothers. Those who accepted Jesus as the actual Son of God only included the relatives of Mary and his siblings, whom they considered his half brothers and sisters. As a result of the elevation of the *desposyni*, the Ebionites reckoned the apostolic succession through James as opposed to Peter, support for which they gleaned from Galatians 2:9 and Acts 15:13-21. Each patriarch in the early communities was a *desposynos* who always bore the name of one of Jesus' brothers.

The core of the Ebionites' canon consisted of a high quality Greek Old Testament that had been translated by their faithful brother Symmachus. They did not recognize all of the books in the emerging New Testament canon, and Eusebius reports that they only possessed the *Gospel of the Hebrews* and did not recognize the authority of Paul's writings.[6] It is generally believed that the Gospel they possessed was the one Eusebius alleges was written by Matthew.[7] In addition to the Old Testament and their abridged New Testament, they held a wider body of theological literature in high esteem, including *The Recognitions of Clement* and *The Clementine Homilies*.

The Ebionites were not the only body of Christians to remain close to their Jewish roots. Members of another sect referred to themselves as the Nazarenes. Originally, *Nazarene* was one of several terms used to define the earliest followers of Jesus. It is derived from Nazareth, the village that nurtured Jesus, and is used to describe Christians by Tertullus, the attorney for the high priest Ananias (Acts 24:5). With the growing ecumenical flavor of Christianity, the term was applied to scattered communities that remained close to Judaism and held a similar theology. Epiphanius dates their inception to the time when Jewish Christians fled Jerusalem after the siege in 70. They were still in existence in the fourth century when Jerome speaks of their strong adherence to the Jewish law along with their belief in the virgin birth and other common Christian doctrines. While some scholars believe that the Nazarenes and Ebionites are one and the same,[8] Jerome makes a clear distinction between the two.[9]

---

[6] Eusebius *Ecclesiastical History* 3.27.
[7] Ibid., 5.8.
[8] E.g., Maccoby, *Mythmaker,* pp. 172-80.
[9] Jerome, *Commentary on Matthew 2* (12:13), reports, "In the Gospel which the Nazarenes and the Ebionites use, which we have recently translated out of Hebrew into Greek"; cited in Ron Cameron, *The Other Gospels: Non-Canonical Gospel Texts* (Philadelphia: Westminster Press, 1982), p. 100.

THE CHURCH OF THE SON OF GOD

The early Jewish Christians were content with accepting Jesus as the Messiah. However, as the faith became more intellectualized, interest began to grow about the person of Jesus. What made him the Messiah? What does it mean for him to be the "Son of God"? What is the relationship between Jesus and God? These questions formed the catalyst for a theological debate that would last for centuries as scholars began to apply logic, philosophy and allegorical mysticism to the study of the biblical teachings about the Son of God. For future generations of Christians, it was not merely enough to accept Jesus as the promised Messiah, but a person's standing before God depended on whether or not he or she embraced the decisions of the powerful majority and their orthodox theology.[10] The two places in Hamitic Canaan that nurtured the speculative theology were Caesarea and Antioch.

After the fall of Jerusalem, Caesarea quickly rose to prominence as the main center for Judean Christianity. Already in the second century it had hosted a very important church council that was held to discuss a controversy over Easter.[11] Notwithstanding, it was not for church councils that Caesarea gained renown, but for its famous theological school which was founded by the Egyptian theologian Origen during his temporary expulsion from Alexandria in 215. Some time after Origen's departure, the school apparently closed for a while, but was revived by Pamphilus, who had studied under Pierius at the catechetical school in Alexandria. A native of Palestine, Pamphilus sought to create a school that would surpass the scholarly stature of the Alexandrian seminary. His most impressive achievement was the creation of the earliest and most extensive Christian library of his day with a collection numbering 30,000 manuscripts.[12] The library was well staffed with a team of scribes who transcribed copies of Scripture along with the great theological works of the day.

---

[10]Edwin Hatch, *The Influence of Greek Ideas on Christianity* (New York: Harper & Brothers, 1957), p. 136, rightly notices that for the early Christians, "the inconsistency of one apparently true system with another did not vex their souls. Their beliefs reflected the variety of the world and of men's thoughts about the world. . . . But the result of the ascendancy of philosophy was that, in the fourth and fifth centuries, the majority of churches insisted not only upon a unity of belief in the fundamental facts of Christianity, but also upon a uniformity of speculations in regard to those facts."

[11]For a brief discussion on the Easter controversy, see Thomas M. Finn, "Pash, Paschal Controversy," in *Encyclopedia of Early Christianity,* ed. Everett Ferguson, 2nd ed., 2 vols. (New York: Garland, 1997), 1:876-77; and Henry Chadwick, *The Early Church* (New York: Penguin, 1967), pp. 84-85.

[12]The library was maintained by Eusebius. See Andrew Carriker, *The Library of Eusebius of Caesarea* (Leiden: Brill, 2003).

Among its holdings were the original copy of Origen's *Hexapla* and a copy of the Hebrew text of Matthew's Gospel. The library offered an indispensable service to early Christian thinkers, and helped in the theological development of a number of scholars including Gregory of Nazianzus, Basil the Great and Jerome. Unfortunately, the library was destroyed during the Muslim assaults of the seventh century. Pamphilus was martyred in 309 during the Great Persecution (303-313).

Pamphilus's most notable student was Eusebius of Caesarea (c. 260-c. 340).[13] The two worked so closely together and developed a deep bond of mutual respect that Eusebius referred to himself as Eusebius Pamphili (Pamphilus's son). He became the first to publish a comprehensive history of the early Christian church. His ten-volume work commenced during the Great Persecution and was completed when Christianity became the state religion. Eusebius was eventually elected bishop of Caesarea in 313, and continued to contribute to the field of knowledge. Among his works are a twenty-volume series on Old Testament prophecies about Christ *(Demonstration of the Gospel)*. As one who was fully aware of the challenges of biblical interpretation, Eusebius voiced his opposition to the hasty excommunication of Arius. For his honesty, he himself was excommunicated until he was given a hearing at the council of Nicaea and reinstated. Always a devoted churchman, Eusebius contributed to the theological thinking of the church until his death.

Antioch was home to the other theological center in the land associated with ancient Canaan. A prominent city in the Roman province of Syria where Antakya currently stands, Antioch was the first place in which the disciples were called Christian (Acts 11:26). According to Chrysostom, bishop of Constantinople, by the time of Emperor Theodosius I (379-395), there were 100,000 Christians in the region.[14] The growth of the church demanded formal organization, and organization needed theological justification. The rationale for structure was presented by Ignatius, the third bishop of Antioch. Dubbed one of the Apostolic Fathers, Ignatius was reportedly ordained to the bishopric by Peter himself, the alleged first bishop of Antioch. He succeeded

---

[13]For a biography of Eusebius see D. S. Wallace-Hadrill, *Eusebius of Caesarea* (Westminster: Canterbury Press, 1961).

[14]On intra-Christian relations in Antioch, see Magus Zetterholm, *The Formation of Christianity in Antioch: A Social-Scientific Approach to the Separation Between Judaism and Christianity* (London: Routledge, 2003).

Euodius. Apparently moving away from the congregational structure of the early church, Ignatius used Ephesians 6:1 to develop a theory of a monarchial episcopacy which held that a single ruling bishop was the representative of God for an entire geographical district.[15] This teaching eventually became standard throughout Christianity. In addition to his contributions to ecclesiology, Ignatius is also credited with moving Christianity further away from Judaism with his suggestion that sabbath had been replaced by the Lord's day.[16]

The theological school at Antioch is best known for its literal method of Scripture interpretation that differed from the allegorical method practiced in Alexandria.[17] After a period of obscurity, the school was revived by Diodore of Tarsus in the middle of the fourth century.[18] Diodore had trained in Athens and gained a reputation for holding the orthodox line against the nonorthodox bishops who controlled Antioch during his tenure. His fidelity was rewarded in 378 when he was promoted to Bishop of Tarsus. Two of his more notable students were John Chrysostom and Theodore.

A native of Antioch, John Chrysostom (347-407) lost his father early in life and was raised by his Christian mother.[19] After a period in secular education, he felt compelled to study theology under Diodore of Tarsus, who at that time was living as a monk. He was eventually ordained a priest in 386 and gained notoriety for his eloquent preaching abilities. Reading the Bible with the literalness associated with the Antiochene school, he placed a strong emphasis on the social gospel as he reminded the rich of their duty to the poor and spoke out against opulent lifestyles.[20] He was an influential evangelist, and in 397 held an evangelistic meeting that allegedly calmed a mob element in Antioch who had vandalized imperial property. He was elevated to Bishop of Constantinople in 398, in which position he continued to preach about the moral im-

---

[15]See Ignatius *Magnesians* 2:1; 6:1; 7:1; 13:2.

[16]Ibid. 9:1.

[17]For a discussion on early Christian strategies of biblical interpretation, see John J. O'Keefe and R. R. Reno, *Sanctified Vision: An Introduction to Early Christian Interpretation of the Bible* (Baltimore: Johns Hopkins University Press, 2005).

[18]Johannes Quasten, *Patrology*, vol. 3: *The Golden Age of Greek Patristic Literature from the Council of Nicaea to the Council of Chalcedon* (Utrecht: Spectrum Publishers, 1975), pp. 397-401.

[19]For a comprehensive biography, see Chrysostomus Baur, *John Chrysostom and His Time*, 2 vols. (Westminster, Md.: Newman Press, 1959). See also J. N. D. Kelly, *Golden Mouth: The Story of John Chrysostom: Ascetic, Preacher, Bishop* (Ithaca, N.Y.: Cornell University Press, 1996).

[20]On a discussion of the content of Chrysostom's preaching, particularly as it relates to gender and class, see Aideen M. Hartney, *John Chrysostom and the Transformation of the City* (London: Duckworth, 2004).

peratives of Scripture. His straight preaching upset politician and clergy alike, and he was eventually banished by his adversaries.

When Diodorus was called to the See of Tarsus, he left his student and associate Theodore to preside over the school.[21] Theodore was a native of Antioch and a close companion of Chrysostom, who had converted him to monasticism. In fact, it was while he was at the monastic school that he met Diodorus. The years in the monastery allowed him to immerse himself in the study of Scripture as he followed the literalistic interpretation of the Antiochene school, along with the unique understanding on the nature of Christ.[22] In the late 370s he launched his writing career with a commentary on the Psalms. In 383, he was ordained a priest in Antioch. It was during this period of his life that he wrote a treatise on the incarnation and penned additional Old Testament commentaries. Theodore left Antioch for Tarsus where he was consecrated Bishop of Mopsuestia, the town in which he spent the final decades of his life.

Theodore's most notable student was Nestorius (386-451), who later became Patriarch of Constantinople.[23] Like his teacher, he became embroiled in controversy when he opposed the catholic teaching that Mary was the mother of God *(theotokos)*, claiming that she should more correctly be referred to as the mother of Christ *(christotokos)*. In this christologically charged era, he was quickly denounced as a heretic. Although receiving support from fellow patriarch John of Antioch, he was condemned by the Council of Ephesus in 431. Repulsed by the anathema, a number of his sympathizers asserted their independence from the catholic church, a move which led to the development of the independent Nestorian churches.[24]

For some strange reason, the very Bible that heralded unity had become the tool that the disparate sides utilized to justify their orthodoxy and bolster their political agendas. This is not to say that there were no attempts to create a basis for unity. The scholars did not just involve themselves in internal conver-

---

[21]For a discussion on the life of Theodore, see Quasten, *Patrology,* 3:401-23.

[22]For a discussion on Theodore's proto-Nestorian views, see Ibid., 3:415-18.

[23]See ibid., 3:514-17.

[24]For a discussion on the Nestorian controversy, see Susan Ashbrook Harvey, "Nestorianism" and "Nestorius (ca. 381-451)," in *Encyclopedia of Early Christianity*, ed. Everett Ferguson, 2nd ed., 2 vols. (New York: Garland, 1997), 2:806-9; 809-10; and Philip Schaff, *History of the Christian Church*, vol. 3: *Nicene and Post Nicene Christianity from Constantine the Great to Gregory the Great, A.D. 311-600* (Grand Rapids: Eerdmans, 1910), pp. 714-22.

sations; they also made great strides to make the Scriptures—particularly the New Testament—available in the language of the people. As early as the third century, before any Latin translation, the scholars of Canaan produced the version known to theologians as the Old Syriac. This was followed by other versions: the Peshitta, Philoxeniana, Harklensis and Palestinian Syriac. Nonetheless, even with all these versions, the debate over how to apply the Word continued.

9

The Development of Christianity in Egypt and North Africa

Confusion over interpreting the content of Scripture was not limited to the newly named Roman province of Palestine. The brethren south of the border in lands descended from Misrayim were also involved in squabbles over how to rightly divide the word of truth. Seeing the value of accessing the Bible in a native tongue, Egyptian scholars had started translating the New Testament into the local Coptic language from as early as the third century. Over the years, various scribes produced the following versions: Sahidic, Bohairic, Proto-Bohairic, Middle Egyptian, Middle Egyptian Fayyumic, Fayyumic, Achmimic and Sub-Achmimic. However, as their brethren in Palestine were to discover, doctrinal unity is not gained by the mere act of producing a Bible version that people can understand in their own language. At the end of the day, the message on the pages must be *interpreted*.

The task of interpretation is never easy. Already in the New Testament we learn that the earliest Christians did not conform to a uniform orthodoxy, neither was there agreement on how to practice the emerging religion.[1] The problem was further complicated by the fact that Christians had inherited interpretive models from the rabbis who had long viewed the Old Testament as a dynamic book that could be interpreted in a number of ways. In addition to the issues raised by rabbinic methods,[2] those who studied the Bible in Egypt and North Africa would also have to wrestle with the influence of Greco-Roman philosophy in their interpretive endeavors. Jewish philosopher Philo of Alexandria had already applied Plato's philosophical principles

---

[1]For a discussion on heteropraxy in the early church, see Robert Jewett, *Christian Tolerance: Paul's Message to the Modern Church* (Philadelphia: Westminster Press, 1982).

[2]For a brief discussion on Jews in Egypt during the Hellenistic and Roman periods, see H. Idris Bell, *Cults and Creeds in Graeco-Roman Egypt* (Chicago: Ares Publishers, 1985), pp. 25-49.

to his study of the Old Testament, and it was only a matter of time before Christian scholars would follow suit. Added to the pluralistic heritage of Christian interpretation was the challenging reality that the religion was seeking to establish its identity at a time when the contents of the New Testament were still being debated.

FIELD OF HETERODOXY

By the second century, the brand of Christianity that had been transplanted in Egypt had assumed several identities. While most refer to these variant teachings as "heresy," I prefer the more neutral term "heterodoxy." Students of church history know that heretics are often labeled thus by those whose argument eventually prevails.[3] However, given the complexities involved with the interpretation of the biblical text, the term "heterodox" vindicates those who saw things differently from charges of rebellion against God and his Word.

The selective Bible: Gnosticism and Monasticism. Perhaps the most radical treatment of the Bible was manifest in the theology of the Egyptian movement that has become known as Gnosticism—a general term used to describe several Christian groups who adhered to a similar theological stance.[4] Some of the teachings associated with Gnosticism were already apparent in the New Testament. However, the systematization of the beliefs appears to have taken place in Egypt. While scholars have always had access to polemics against Gnosticism by various Christian apologists, a firsthand understanding was greatly enhanced by the discovery of the Nag Hammadi papyri in Egypt in 1945.[5] These forty-nine documents written in Coptic locate the inception of the teaching to the first quarter of the second century when Basilides (fl.125-155) and Isidore—a father and son team—suggested that Christianity be liberated from its Jewish parent.[6] Basilides was the chief architect of this teaching

---

[3]See Bart D. Ehrman, *Lost Christianities: The Battles for Scripture and the Faiths We Never Knew* (Oxford: Oxford University Press, 2003).

[4]For a concise introduction to Gnosticism, see Christoph Markschies, *Gnosis: An Introduction* (London: T & T Clark, 2003). See also Reimer Roukema and John Bowden, *Gnosis and Faith in Early Christianity: An Introduction to Gnosticism* (Harrisburg, Penn.: Trinity Press International, 1999). Since this study focuses on the Bible and Africa, it will not discuss Marcionite Gnosticism. Those who desire a discussion can consult Kurt Rudolph, *Gnosis: The Nature and History of Gnosticism* (San Francisco: Harper & Row, 1983), pp. 313-17.

[5]For an English translation of the documents, see J. M. Robinson, *The Nag Hammadi Library in English*, rev. ed. (San Francisco: Harper & Row, 1988).

[6]See Rudolph, *Gnosis*, pp. 309-13.

and despised Judaism to such an extent that he proposed a radical change in the very theological system upon which Christianity was built.

Basilides was obviously influenced by Platonic dualism and held that the spirit world was superior to the material world. According to Basilides, the supreme spirit God created several immaterial forces starting with Thought *(nous)* and Reason *(logos)*, and followed by a number of other spiritual entities, the lowest of whom was Yahweh of the Old Testament. Similar to the rebellious Yakub in Nation of Islam theology,[7] Yahweh created the evil material world and trapped some of the spiritual beings in human bodies. In a quest to rescue the entrapped spirits, the supreme God commissioned thought *(nous)* to enter the material world in the form of Jesus. Jesus' purpose was to inform the material-bound spirits about their true origins. Acceptance of this knowledge *(gnosis)* was sufficient to merit the individual's salvation. Since salvation was attained through knowledge, Basilides rejected the teaching of a crucified Christ, reasoning that a death can only be experienced by material flesh; hence spiritual entities can never die.

On the heels of Basilides was Valentinus, who rose to prominence in the middle of the second century (140-165).[8] Operating under a similar presupposition to Basilides regarding the spiritual and distant nature of God, Valentinus taught that the supreme Father God was the Deep *(bythos)*, from whom came Silence *(sigē)*, his bride. The offspring of their relationship was Thought *(nous)*. Eventually, twenty-four spiritual entities were produced and were collectively known as Aeons. Transgressing her assigned boundaries, the youngest Aeon, Sophia, gave birth by herself and produced a material anomaly known as the Demiurge. Associated with the creator, Yahweh, the Demiurge had a self-imposed mission to destroy the spiritual world. However, Sophia was able to instill spirit into some of the creatures created by Demiurge, and these became the "pneumatics" who can attain salvation by embracing the knowledge *(gnōsis)* of their true origin. Other humans fall under the category of the materialistic "hylics" and vacillating "psychics," for whom obtaining the knowledge necessary for salvation is much more difficult. So convinced was

---

[7]For an analysis of Elijah Muhammad's teaching on Yakub as creator of the white race, see Nathaniel Deutsch, "The Proximate Other: The Nation of Islam and Judaism," in *Black Zion: African American Religious Encounters with Judaism*, ed. Yvonne Chireau and Nathaniel Deutsch (New York: Oxford University Press, 2000), pp. 105-9.

[8]See Rudolph, *Gnosis*, pp. 317-26.

Valentinus about the evil nature of the First Testament that he encouraged his followers to openly violate the Ten Commandments. For these, the Bible had become a materialistic obstacle to discovering their true spiritual reality.

The Gnostics' libertarian attitude was by no means typical of Hamitic Egyptian Christianity. In fact, later generations took the Bible very seriously as is evident by the flourishing monastic movement that gained popularity in the late third century.[9] Egyptian monasticism apparently had its foundations in the southern non-Graecized regions of the country with the Coptic-speaking mystic known as Antony (d. 356). Upon inheriting his parents' wealth after their death, Antony was especially moved by Jesus' advice to the Jewish politician in Matthew 19:21, "go, sell your possessions, and give the money to the poor." He did just that and eventually moved into the wilderness where he had a supernatural experience. Following his cleansing, he inspired several monastic communities in the deserts and mountains as thousands left the villages and cities to engage in the study of Scripture and a contemplative life.

Also influential in the monastic movement was another Coptic native named Pakhom (Pachomius [290-346]).[10] Seeking a deeper spiritual experience after converting to Christianity in 313, Pakhom sought a life of solitude in Tabnessi along the Nile in 323. He was soon joined by thousands of disciples, and before his death had organized nine monasteries and two nunneries.[11] Those who devoted their life to the desert were totally unselfish and, in addition to spiritual exercises, spent their days in economic enterprises the profits of which were used for charity.[12] Egyptian monasticism became a model for other parts of Christendom, and the *Life of Antony*,[13] written by the Bishop Athanasius, became a manual for many.

The militant Bible: Donatism. Another significant religious movement

---

[9]For a brief discussion on the monastic movement in early Christianity, see James E. Goehring, "Monasticism," in *Encyclopedia of Early Christianity*, ed. Everett Ferguson, 2nd ed., 2 vols. (New York: Garland, 1997), 2:769-75; and Henry Chadwick, *The Early Church* (New York: Penguin, 1967), pp. 174-83.

[10]On the life of Pachomius, see Philip Schaff, *History of the Christian Church*, vol. 3: *Nicene and Post Nicene Christianity from Constantine the Great to Gregory the Great, A.D. 311-600* (Grand Rapids: Eerdmans, 1910), pp. 195-98.

[11]Mark Shaw, *The Kingdom of God in Africa: A Short History of African Christianity* (Grand Rapids: Baker, 1996), p. 34.

[12]Elizabeth Isichei, *A History of Christianity in Africa* (Grand Rapids: Eerdmans; Lawrenceville, N.J.: Africa World Press, 1995), p. 28.

[13]Athanasius, "Life of St. Anthony," in *Early Christian Biographies*, ed. Roy J. Deferrari, trans. Mary Emily Keenan (Washington, D.C.: Catholic University Press of America, 1952), pp. 127-216.

emerged after the Diocletian persecutions of 303-305, this time in the north-western regions of Misrayim, generally referred to as North Africa. During the persecutions, many church leaders sided with the state and—in what must have appeared to be the fulfillment of Jesus' prophecy in Matthew 24—they turned over Christian literature to be destroyed by the authorities. After the persecutions when the empire became more friendly towards Christians, many of the leaders who had assisted in the persecutions maintained their ecclesiastical positions. Indoctrinated into a high view of clergy, most of the members bowed to their authority, but a growing number were appalled that they were not held responsible for their actions. After Caecilian—who had been ordained by an alleged traitor—was elected Bishop of Carthage in 311, a council of opposing bishops met to discuss the issue, and in 312 elected a rival bishop in the person of Majorinus. Following Majorinus's death in 315, Donatus acceded to the bishopric. By this time Caecilian had launched an official complaint to the church—now under the auspices of the empire—which sided in his favor and attempted to force the secessionists into submission.

The Donatists were firm in their resistance and appealed to the Bible for their legitimacy.[14] As far as they were concerned, they were the faithful remnant represented by the wheat in Jesus' parable (Mt 13:24-30). Firm in their quest for reform based on Scripture, the Donatists stressed the need for individual holiness as they welcomed the manifestations of the Spirit in their worship services. The thirst for reform spread throughout the land, and Donatism soon became the majority faith in Roman North Africa. The rapid growth was accompanied by a radicalizing of the faith in certain rural areas where the teachings were adapted to a theology of liberation that resulted in adherents advocating the use of arms to overthrow the evil empire which was identified as the biblical antichrist. Known as Circumcellions, from their practice of encircling settlements before attacking *(circum cella)*,[15] these radical Donatists focused their zeal on the state-sympathetic catholics as they raped, killed, pillaged and confiscated "in the name of the Lord"! So willing were they to be martyrs for the Lord that many even committed violent suicide with the belief that they would receive a special place in paradise. Unlike the Gnostics who

---

[14]For a discussion on Donatist beliefs and society, see Maureen A. Tilley, *The Bible in Christian North Africa: The Donatist World* (Minneapolis: Fortress, 1997); and W. H. C. Frend, *The Donatist Church* (Oxford: Clarendon, 1952).

[15]See Schaff, *History of the Christian Church,* 3:362-63.

shunned the First Testament God, these radical Donatists appeared to have fully identified with Israel in its quest to rid Canaan of all pagan symbols. The Donatist extremists were outlived by their moderate siblings who survived until the time of the Islamic absorption into North Africa.

The unorthodox Bible: Arianism and Monophysitism. Undoubtedly, the arch-heresy for orthodox Christianity is the belief that garnered the name Arianism.[16] Named after its founder, Arius, Arianism is the belief that the Son of God had to be younger in time than the Father. Apparently, Arius was an Egyptian who was schooled in Antioch before returning to Alexandria. The theologians of Hamitic Antioch held to a more literal view of Scripture and shunned the allegorical interpretations that thrived in Egypt. In his attempt at a strict reading of the Bible, Arius reasoned that since Jesus is described as "begotten" there must have been a time when he did not exist. One of the prooftexts cited by Auxentius, a fourth-century Arian bishop of Milan was 1 Corinthians 8:6, which heralds "one God, the Father, *from (ek)* whom are all things and *unto (eis)* whom we exist, and one Lord, Jesus Christ, *through (dia)* whom are all things and *through (dia)* whom we exist" (my translation). Arius was not satisfied with merely discussing his differences with fellow theologians, but published simple ditties in a book titled *Thalia,* through which his view of the relationship between the Son and the Father was popularized among the masses.

Concerned about the impact of his teaching, the bishops of Alexandria held a synod in 321 C.E. in which Arius was denounced for his unorthodox teaching. Unhindered by the anathema, Arius continued to press forth, and his teachings soon spread through much of the eastern Mediterranean. The influence of Arianism became so great that in 325 C.E. the emperor, Constantine, summoned the First Ecumenical Council to deal with this and other issues. Arius's nemesis in the dispute was an Egyptian deacon named Athanasius.[17] Accompanying Alexander, the Bishop of Alexandria, Athanasius had written a theological treatise to establish that the Father and Son had the same origin and were thus inseparable. Athanasius's argument—along with other political factors—resulted in the emperor excommunicating Arius and his supporters and proclaiming that the Father and Son were of the same substance *(homoousios).* The decision was formulated into the Nicene Creed, which is still recited

---

[16]For a thematic introduction to Arianism, see Robert C. Gregg and Dennis Groh, *Early Arianism: A View of Salvation* (Philadelphia: Fortress, 1981).

[17]For a discussion on the Council of Nicaea and its aftermath, see Chadwick, *Early Church,* pp. 125-51.

in some Christian churches to this day.

Constantine's denunciation in no way quieted Arianism. By 335 C.E., Constantine had become sympathetic towards Arius's teaching, and the synod of Jerusalem welcomed him back into communion while anathematizing Athanasius, who had been the intermittent Bishop of Alexandria. Although defeated again in the Second Ecumenical Council held at Constantinople in 381 C.E., Arianism continued to spread throughout the Christian world and was the dominant Christology in Germanic Christianity until the eighth century, when the "heretics" were conquered by "Christian" kingdoms that held to the Nicene view. However, even as Nicene Christianity celebrated its apparent victory, they were to witness the survival of a more radicalized Arianism through Islam which acknowledged Jesus as the mysterious Son of God but believed it blasphemy to equate him with his Father.

The dispute over the relationship of the Father with the Son was not confined to Arianism. The theological discussions had introduced language that complicated the issue even more. Emperor Constantine had suggested that Jesus had the same nature as the Father *(homoousios)*, but there were many opponents of Arius who disagreed with this deduction. These taught that Jesus and the Father were of like nature *(homoiousios)*, and were dubbed "semi-Arians" by those who sided with the emperor. The Arian view was expressed by those who held that Jesus was unlike the Father *(aomoi)*. These questions became increasingly pertinent with the development of the doctrine of Mary as the god-bearer *(theotokos)*.[18] If Jesus was of the same or similar substance of God, then what was his nature like? Was he immutable like his father and thus restricted to one nature *(mono physis)*, or upon assuming a human identity did he add a second nature to his being?

Armed with an arsenal of texts and fueled by philosophical reasoning, the two sides argued vigorously. It did not take long for an Egypt that was familiar with the Isis-Horus-Osiris Trinity to embrace Monophysitism.[19] The champion of Monophysitism was the fifth-century monk Shenoute. Firmly convinced that this was the view of Athanasius—the bishop who countered Ari-

---

[18]For a concise discussion on the concept of Mary as *theotokos*, see Jaroslav Pelikan, *Mary Through the Centuries: Her Place in the History of Culture* (New Haven, Conn.: Yale University Press, 1996), pp. 55-65.

[19]For a discussion on Monophysitism, see W. H. C. Frend, *The Rise of the Monophysite Movement*, 2nd ed. (Cambridge: Cambridge University Press, 1979); and Schaff, *History of the Christian Church*, 3:762-83.

anism, Shenoute openly attacked Nestorius, Bishop of Constantinople, and rejected the ruling of the famed council of Chalcedon in 451 C.E. Following Chalcedon, the church in Egypt was split between the Melkites, who held to the dual nature of Christ, and the Jacobites, who maintained the Monophysite view. The antagonism between Melkite and Jacobite was still evident at the time of the Muslim invasion.

CENTER OF SYSTEMATIC THEOLOGY

The Bible and Alexandrian scholarship. Even as the various heterodox movements intersected in Hamitic Egypt, there was a deliberate attempt to establish an apparatus through which the Bible could be interpreted and doctrine formulated by able practitioners. The need for intellectual analyses of the Bible resulted in the formation of a catechetical school in Alexandria.[20] Although some credit the founding to Mark, the more likely founder is Pantaenus (d. 180), who later became a missionary to India.[21] Pantaenus was succeeded by his brilliant student Clement (c. 150-215), who holds the honor of being Christianity's first systematic theologian.[22] Following his conversion, Clement embarked on a quest to learn all he could about Christianity.[23] Trained in Greek philosophy, Clement sought to intellectualize Christianity with the hope that it would gain respectability and pass philosophical scrutiny. After brief spells with several Christian teachers, he finally attached himself to Pantaenus and was the natural successor following his departure.

Clement was succeeded by another bright mind named Origen (185-254), who was the most influential theologian of his time.[24] Origen's father, Leonidas, was martyred in 202 and Origen was so inspired by his fidelity that he committed his life to the study of God's Word. Reportedly, he immersed himself in the study of the Bible for many hours each day and committed much of it to memory. Skilled in Platonic philosophy, Origen contributed over 2000 treatises to the

---

[20] See Johannes Quasten, *Patrology,* vol. 2: *The Ante-Nicene Literature After Irenaeus* (Utrecht: Spectrum Publishers, 1953), pp. 2-4.

[21] See Ibid., 2:4-5.

[22] For an introduction to the life and times of Clement, see John Ferguson, *Clement of Alexandria* (New York: Twayne Publishers, 1974), pp. 13-43.

[23] Apparently, Clement was acquainted with a number of people who knew the apostles. See Eusebius *Ecclesiastical History* 5.11.

[24] For an introduction to his life and work, see Quasten, *Patrology,* 2:37-101; and Henry Chadwick, *The Church in Ancient Society: From Galilee to Gregory the Great* (Oxford: Oxford University Press, 2001), pp. 135-44.

field of Christian learning—mostly in the form of sermons and commentaries. He is also credited with compiling the *Hexapla*, an edition of the Bible containing six versions.[25] His lasting contribution is in the area of biblical hermeneutics, in which he proposed that there are three levels of meaning for each biblical passage: the literal, the moral and the spiritual. This paved the way for allegorical interpretation and provided a method to deal with the difficult texts of Scripture.

Among other leaders in the catechetical school in Alexandria was the remarkable Didymus the Blind (c. 309-c. 394).[26] Blinded from infancy, Didymus succeeded in amassing a wealth of knowledge. Not only is he credited with the invention of a script for the blind,[27] but he wrote several commentaries and influential scholarly treatises which contributed to the relevant theological debates of his time. Those who benefited from his wisdom included Tyrannius Rufinus, the Italian-born monk, and the famous Jerome, translator of the Latin Vulgate, who was privileged to sit at the feet of Didymus during an excursion to Egypt in 385.

Although not a teacher in the Alexandrian school, Athanasius (298-373) is another significant name in the history of the Bible and Africa.[28] As we saw in the previous section, he is best known for his defense of Trinitarian orthodoxy at the Council of Nicaea in 325. However, his most lasting influence on Christianity was the identification in 367 of the twenty-seven books that comprise the New Testament canon. In fact, many Protestant Christians see him as the father of the canon, although he did not include Esther among the inspired books of the First Testament.

The Bible and political theology in Carthage. The theological advances in Alexandria were mirrored by the strides of great theologians centered in Carthage, located in modern-day Tunis in Tunisia. The Carthaginian theological school was founded by Tertullian (c. 155-230),[29] a scholar who has prob-

---

[25]According to Quasten, *Patrology*, 2:44, Origen's groundbreaking work in textual criticism has earned him the title "the founder of biblical science." Origen's *Hexapla* contained (1) Tanak, (2) Greek Transliteration of the Tanak, (3) Aquila's Greek Translation of the Tanak, (4) Symmachus's Greek Translation of the Tanak, (5) Septuagint and (6) Theodotion's Greek translation of the Tanak.

[26]See Johannes Quasten, *Patrology*, vol. 3: *The Golden Age of Greek Patristic Literature from the Council of Nicaea to the Council of Chalcedon* (Utrecht: Spectrum Publishers, 1975), pp. 85-100.

[27]See John Lascaratos and Spyros Marketos, "Didymus the Blind: An Unknown Precursor of Louis Braille and Helen Keller," *Documenta Ophthalmologia* 86 (1994): 203-8.

[28]See Quasten, *Patrology*, 3:20-79.

[29]For a handy account of his life and works, see Timothy David Barnes, *Tertullian: A Historical and Literary Study* (Oxford: Clarendon, 1971), pp. 3-59.

ably influenced the shape of orthodox Christianity more than any other thinker in history.[30] Indeed, it was he who introduced the term "Trinity" *(trinitas)* into the Christian vocabulary, along with the teaching that the one God is revealed in three persons *(tres personae)*. Turned off by the hierarchical struc-

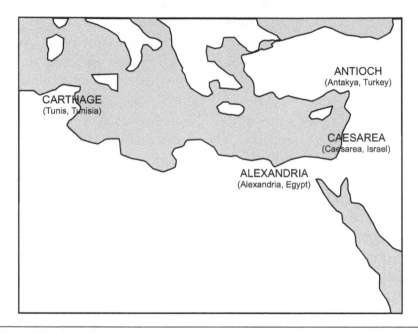

Map 5. Theological centers in emerging Christianity

ture and theological rigidity of the emerging Catholic church, Tertullian later joined the Montanists—a sect of Christianity that spoke in tongues and encouraged the gift of prophecy.[31] Interestingly, the Montanists rejected the Trinitarian formula devised by Tertullian, although he himself did not appear to have modified his teachings. Although distanced from the Catholic church, Tertullian continued to defend the faith and placed a strong emphasis on the biblical call to holy living, stressing his belief that the church as the "bride of Christ" should remain pure.

Cyprian (d. 258), Tertullian's theological successor, was not as rigid on the subject of holiness as his teacher.[32] He had accepted Christ while a supersti-

---

[30]For a brief glimpse into Tertullian's brilliance, see Chadwick, *Church in Ancient Society,* pp. 118-22.
[31]On Tertullian's involvement in the Montanist movement, see Barnes, *Tertullian,* pp. 130-42.
[32]See Quasten, *Patrology,* 2:340-83.

tious pagan rhetorician, and ascended to Bishop of Carthage just two years after conversion. Immediately upon Cyprian's embrace of the episcopacy, the emperor Decian began to persecute Christians, a two-year ordeal that transformed the former rhetor into a fugitive (249-251). When Cyprian returned to Carthage, he was faced with a divided church. Many had succumbed to imperial pressure and sacrificed to the emperor, and some who remained faithful felt that the apostatizers should be forever excommunicated from church fellowship. While Tertullian would have agreed with the position of those who had remained faithful, Cyprian believed that the backslider should be given the opportunity for restoration. Playing down the concept that would later be termed the "priesthood of all believers," Cyprian felt that the locus of holiness resided in the priesthood.[33] So serious was he about clergy holiness that he opposed the reinstatement of any lapsed priest—unless it was to the laity. As bishop, he felt it was his special role to battle against evil spirits.[34] Cyprian's fidelity survived the extreme test when he was martyred in 258. Several decades after Cyprian's death, the Diocletian persecutions once again upset the Carthaginian church. The theological disputes in the aftermath mirrored those that followed the Decian persecutions resulting in the Donatist split that was discussed in the previous section.

North Africa would not see its next influential theologian until Augustine (354-430), who later became the Bishop of Hippo, located in modern-day Annaba, Algeria.[35] Born in Tagaste and reared in Carthage, Augustine is heralded by Catholics as the preeminent theologian of Christianity. The son of a Christian mother and pagan father, in his youth Augustine embraced Manichaeism (a syncretistic blend of Christianity, Zoroastrianism and Buddhism).[36] While working in Milan as a professor of rhetoric, Augustine came into contact with the famous bishop Ambrose, whose preaching influenced him to reject Manichaeism. However, instead of embracing orthodox Christianity, he converted to Neo-Platonism. Eventually, Augustine converted to Christianity in 386 and returned to Tagaste in 388 where he founded a monastery.

---

[33]For a discussion on Cyprian's ecclesiology, see Ibid., 2:373-75.

[34]Shaw, *Kingdom of God in Africa*, p. 47.

[35]For a brief biography, see Garry Wills, *Saint Augustine* (New York: Penguin, 1999). See also Peter Lamont Brown, *Augustine of Hippo: A Biography* (Berkeley: University of California Press, 1967).

[36]For a critical discussion on Manichaeism, see Samuel N. C. Lieu, *Manichaeism in the Later Roman Empire and Medieval China: A Historical Survey* (Manchester: Manchester University Press, 1984). For a discussion on Augustine's dabbling with Manichaeism, see Brown, *Augustine*, pp. 46-60.

Augustine's philosophical positions strongly influenced his theology.[37] He is credited with refining the Catholic understanding of original sin and for arguing on the legitimacy of "just war"—even if the stated purpose was to stamp out heretics. Among his theological works is *The City of God*, in which he discusses the clash of ideologies between the church and the world. For Augustine, God was calling Christians to exemplify a radical God-centered love that surpassed narcissistic selfishness. Those called by God are to emulate Abraham, whose walk of faith would eventually be rewarded with the establishment of the eternal city.[38]

---

[37]For a discussion on Augustine's hermeneutics, see the collection of essays in Frederick Van Fleteren and Joseph C. Schnaubelt, eds., *Augustine: Biblical Exegete* (New York: Peter Lang, 2001).
[38]Augustine, *The City of God Against the Pagans*, trans. G. E. McCracken et al., 7 vols. Loeb Classical Library (Cambridge, Mass.: Harvard University Press, 1960-1981), 7:183 (22.3).

The Development of Christianity in Arabia and Ethiopia

The biblical scholarship that characterized Christianity in North Africa and Palestine does not appear to have lured the theologians of Cush. Although it borders both Canaan and Misrayim, parts of Cush sometimes seem far away from the centers of excitement. In spite of its isolation, there is much evidence of biblical faith in Cush that predates the New Testament era. Students of the Bible are well aware of the influence of Israel's faith in Babylon, Assyria, Midian, Edom, and other areas of Mesopotamian and Arabian Cush. However, few have considered the impact of God's revelation on the Ethiopian section of Cush. The fact that the Ethiopian eunuch came to Jerusalem to worship and possessed a Hebrew scroll of the prophet Isaiah clearly points to the existence of a Meroitic community familiar with the faith of Israel.[1] We have already seen that the prophets Isaiah and Zephaniah, as well as the psalmist, are well aware that God had established witnesses in the African kingdoms south of Egypt.

According to Ethiopian tradition, Israel's faith was introduced to the kingdom by Menelek I, the legendary son of Solomon and Sheba. However, the Bible is clear that even before the queen came to visit Solomon, she had heard of his fame (1 Kings 10:1). She even evidenced familiarity with the Israelite God and exhibited a fascination for the prosperous kingdom (1 Kings 10:9). Judging by the favor she bestowed on Solomon, even in the absence of the Menelek myth, it is clear that she would not have displayed any hostility to any of her subjects who chose to follow Israel's God. In addition to those who may have taken advantage of the queen's fascination with the Israelite faith, some believe that a number of Israelites from the tribe of Dan migrated to

---

[1]For a discussion on the likely origin of the Ethiopian eunuch, see the controversial discussion in Edwin M. Yamauchi, *Africa and the Bible* (Grand Rapids: Baker Academic, 2004), pp. 161-73.

Ethiopia during the civil war between Jeroboam and Rehoboam. These, they believe, formed the foundation of the Hebrew believers in Cush.

While none of these explanations can be objectively verified, it is true that by the early Christian centuries there were many in the land of Cush—particularly in Ethiopia—who lived by the precepts of the Bible. The roots in the Israelite faith were so deep in some parts of Ethiopia that even for Christians the Tanak was esteemed over the rest of the Bible. In fact, until recently, the Ethiopian church maintained such practices as seventh-day sabbath observance, circumcision and abstention from certain meats.[2] The isolated church also maintained control over its canon, and had translated the entire Bible into Ethiopic by the beginning of the sixth century. Longer than the Bibles of Catholic and Protestant Christianity, the Ethiopian Bible includes the entire Apocrypha and other books deemed pseudepigrapha.

ETHIOPIA'S ROYAL TREASURE

It would be difficult to ascertain the date from which the apocryphal and pseudepigraphical books were incorporated into the Ethiopian canon. Notwithstanding, it is clear that the book that convinced the eunuch of Jesus' messiahship was the canonical prophecy of Isaiah. In Acts 8:26-39, this government official was convinced by the Spirit's explanation through Philip and was the foreshadow of a trend of royal conversions in Cush. The historical record does not trace the activities of the official after his baptism, but it is safe to conclude that he would have shared his new discovery with his circle of colleagues. Eventually, Meroe would be joined by other kingdoms in Ethiopia whose citizens would join the eunuch in stretching their hands in warm acceptance of the biblical Word.

Apart from what can be inferred about the reception of Christianity in Meroe via the government official, nothing more is known about the interaction with the Christian Bible in other parts of Ethiopia until the fourth century.[3] Meropius, a Syrian philosopher, was traveling to India with an entourage and

---

[2]Cf. Archdeacon Dowling, *The Abyssinian Church* (London: Cope and Fenwick, 1909), pp. 20-24; J. Spencer Trimingham, *Islam in Ethiopia* (London: Oxford University Press, 1952), p. 29.

[3]The early history of Christianity in Ethiopia is recorded by the Roman monk Rufinus, who claims to have received information from Aedesius himself. (David Buxton, *The Abyssinians* [New York: Prager, 1970], p. 40.) Mark Shaw, *The Kingdom of God in Africa: A Short History of African Christianity* (Grand Rapids: Baker, 1996), p. 62, reports that Socrates Scholasticus would late utilize Rufinus's history for his own study.

decided to stop at a port on the Axumite coast. Unfortunately, some of the natives who were upset over a political dispute with Rome killed the philosopher and all of his company except for two young men, Frumentius and Aedesius. For some reason, they were sent to the capital and gained the favor of the king, who appointed Aedesius as his cupbearer and Frumentius as the royal secretary.

The king died soon after, and, at the request of his widow, the two privileged captives ended up serving as regents for the boy king Ezana. Grateful for their assistance, Ezana offered the men their freedom after he had assumed full regal responsibilities. Rather than return to Syria, Frumentius decided to visit Alexandria, where Athanasius had just been installed patriarch. Not long after their meeting, Athanasius ordained Frumentius a bishop, and by 350 the Syrian missionary had returned to his adopted nation. Fortified with his new ecclesiastical status, Frumentius shared his biblical faith with his former master, who promptly surrendered his life to Christ and submitted to the sovereignty of God. From the time of his conversion, the steles commemorating his conversion and the coins minted for the kingdom no longer gave homage to pagan gods. Instead, they spoke of the "Lord of All," "Lord of Heaven" and "Lord of Earth."[4]

Ezana's successors maintained the faith of their father, but for a long time Christianity remained a religion of the elite. Most of the citizens still held to the traditional beliefs that had gripped the nation for millennia. Things were to change in the fifth century when a group of Syrian monks known as the Nine Saints sought refuge in Ethiopia. Monophysite in theology, these monks quickly learned the local language and conducted vernacular translations of the Scriptures. They then set out to take the gospel to the people through the establishment of monasteries, and they experienced great success.[5] Unfortunately, these celebrated missionaries did not place a high emphasis on their catechumens learning the teachings of Scripture, and many of their "converts" maintained allegiance to their former superstitions while professing Christianity.

It appears that the eunuch's witness in Meroe did not take root for several

---

[4]Shaw, *Kingdom of God in Africa*, p. 63.

[5]Africologist William Leo Hansberry, *Pillars in Ethiopian History*, ed. Joseph E. Harris (Washington, D.C.: Howard University Press, 1974), p. 87, observes, "by the beginning of the sixth century, [Ethiopia] had attained a level of internal development and acquired a degree of external influence which placed it on a par with the Byzantine Empire as one of the greatest Christian powers of that age."

generations. In fact, unlike Axum, where Christianity was the treasure of the royal court, it was the commoners who popularized the gospel in the Nubian kingdoms that succeeded Meroe. These laypeople first received the faith from Egyptian missionaries, and it wasn't until the sixth century that Nubian royalty decided to give it a second look.[6] Interestingly, it was the Roman imperial family who commissioned the missionaries to Nubia, in response to a request from the Nubian monarch Silko, king of Nobatia. The Roman Justinian was married to Theodora, a native Egyptian who had escaped a life of prostitution after she was introduced to the gospel by Monophysite monks. Once a Christian, she lent her loyalties to the doctrinal positions of her rescuers. When she learned that her orthodox husband had dispatched a team of missionaries to catechize Silko's kingdom, she quickly assembled a Monophysite group led by the priest Julian and arranged for the delay of Justinian's team to ensure that the Nobatians embraced the Christianity that had established roots in Egypt. Influenced by Julian's presentation of the gospel, Silko was baptized and expelled the orthodox missionaries for their "heretical" views when they finally arrived!

Upon expulsion, the Orthodox missionaries set out for the second Nubian kingdom of Makuria and were successful in persuading the Makurian king to embrace their version of the faith. As orthodox Christianity flourished in Makuria, Julian's work was eclipsed by Longinus, an Egyptian missionary who possessed extraordinary administrative skills. In 575, Longinus set out to take the gospel to the third Nubian kingdom of Alwa. However, the most direct way to Alwa was through Makuria, and the orthodox Makurians refused him passage. Forced to remap his route, it took Longinus five years to reach Alwa. Fortunately, his efforts were not in vain and he received a warm reception from the royal court, the chief members of which received the Word and requested baptism. Although divided by a theological war that sprang from different readings of the Sacred Text, the scattered kings of Ethiopia entered the seventh century with the united consensus that Jesus the Christ was the *Negus Negasti* ("king of all kings").

ARABIA'S GROWTH CHALLENGES

Even as the Bible received a warm acceptance in the Axumite and Nubian sec-

---

[6]For a discussion on the Christianization of Nubia, see William Y. Adams, *Nubia: Corridor to Africa* (Princeton, N.J.: Princeton University Press, 1977), pp. 433-58. See also Yamauchi, *Africa and the Bible,* pp. 179-81.

tions of Cush, the various tribal groups that inhabited Arabian Cush on the east of the Red Sea were not as eager to forsake their gods for a faith rife with internal disputes. This is not to say that Christianity did not make any headway in the region, for already in the book of Acts we read of Arabian Jews among the audience of those who embraced the Messiah on the pivotal day of Pentecost (Acts 2:11). They must have established a Christian presence in their homeland, for several years later after Paul's supernatural encounter with the resurrected Christ, he spent a season in Arabia, possibly with Christian brethren (Gal 1:17-18). The influence of Christianity on the region continued after the biblical era, and a number of historians from the early church inform us of several missionary excursions into Arabia.

Given its proximity to Judea, it is safe to assume that the earliest Christian centers in the region were situated in the Arabian northwest.[7] At least by the third century the region had a significant Christian presence. Of course, Christian growth was accompanied with heterodox beliefs as people struggled to view the teachings of Scripture through the lenses of their own traditions. The heterodox nature of Arabian Christianity was so pronounced that the rigid orthodox were moved to condemn Arabia as "the mother of heresies." Origen himself had to be dispatched to the Arabian northwest in 250 to combat a set of teachers who refuted the orthodox teaching on the immortality of the soul. Although the Arabian church maintained its free-spiritedness, it cooperated with the global church and even sent a delegation of six bishops to the Council of Nicaea in 325.

The major missionaries to the Arabs were the many monks and hermits who sought reclusion in the Arabian desert and frequently encountered the nomadic Bedouins. Sozomenus, a fifth-century church historian, informs us of an Arab prince named Zocum who accepted Christianity along with his tribe after a Syrian hermit successfully prayed for him to have a son.[8] Simeon the Stylite, another noted hermit, was alleged to have miracle-working power, along with Euthymius, who allegedly converted the tribe of Aspebaetos after healing his paralytic son. Aspebaetos was later ordained bishop over his tribe

---

[7]For a detailed discussion of Arabian Christianity, see Gabriel Oussani, "Christianity in Arabia," in *The Catholic Encyclopedia* (New York: Robert Appleton, 1907), 1:666-74. See also Kenneth Scott Latourette, *A History of the Expansion of Christianity*, vol. 1: *The First Five Centuries* (New York: Harper & Brothers, 1937), pp. 233-35.

[8]Oussani, "Christianity in Arabia," p. 667.

by the patriarch of Jerusalem and attended the Council of Ephesus in 431. Monks and hermits were so revered that Rufinus writes of Mu'awiyah, a fourth-century Arabian queen who agreed to a peace treaty with Rome on the sole condition that a monk named Moses be assigned as bishop of her tribe.[9]

By the middle of the second century, Christianity had gained a firm footing in northeast Arabia and Babylonia.[10] By the end of the third century, these numbers included Christian slaves who had been relocated to Babylon from Syria and other parts of the Roman Empire. The biggest Christian success story appears to have taken place at the turn of the fifth century with a break-through in the Kingdom of Hira, under Nu'mân I (r. 390-418). Nu'mân at first persecuted Christians, and was infuriated when the ministry of Simeon the Stylite began to attract his subjects to the Arabian wilderness.[11] According to tradition, on the very night that he was about to issue a death decree for any-one who went to hear Simeon, he was visited by the hermit in a dream and threatened with death if the law was enforced. Needless to say, Nu'mân changed his mind and became a firm admirer of Christianity, eventually abdi-cating the throne and embracing an ascetic life himself. Some of his successors openly professed Christianity while others opposed it. It is probably safe to conclude that by the time of Islam, Christianity dominated in Hira. Interest-ingly, as in other parts of the Hamitic Christian world, the believers had an affinity to Nestorian and Monophysite theologies.

In addition to the progress in the northern sections of Arabia, the biblical message was also being impressed upon the people in the south. According to church tradition, the apostle Bartholomew was the first to bring the gospel to southern Arabia when he visited Yemen.[12] Eusebius informs us that Pantae-nus, the head of the catechetical school in Alexandria, provided further in-struction. Apparently Pantaenus followed the strategy of the apostle Paul and targeted his mission to the Jews who had sought sanctuary in Yemen after the destruction of the second temple. Jewish roots in the region went much deeper than the first century C.E., since the Himyarite rulers claimed to follow the Solomonic religion that had allegedly been introduced to the kingdom by the

---

[9]Ibid. After Moses refused ordination from the Arian bishop of Alexandria, the emperor Valens (374) chose a replacement.
[10]Oussani, "Christianity in Arabia," pp. 668-70.
[11]Ibid., p. 669.
[12]Ibid., p. 670.

Queen of Sheba. Appealing to the sensitivity of the Jewish regents, Emperor Constantius commissioned the Arian bishop Theophilus to conduct a diplomatic visit in order to request freedom of worship for Christian subjects in the Himyarite Kingdom. The success of the mission is judged by the fact that the Himyarite king himself commissioned the construction of three Christian churches. Arab historians report that Christianity flourished in the kingdom during the fourth and fifth centuries. By the time of Emperor Anastasius (491-518), the royal family had converted to Christianity and had been sent a bishop named Silvanus.

As Christianity spread, the Jews maintained a strong presence in southern Arabia, particularly Yemen, and had immense political and economic influence in Arabian society. Jewish dominance was not always a good thing for the fledgling Christians, who were often the objects of their persecutions. A most severe persecution took place under Dhu Nuwas who massacred thousands of believers and encouraged his Arab allies to do the same.[13] The massacre was so horrendous that it is recorded in both Christian and Arabic sources, including the Qur'an (Sura 85). When the Axumite King Elesbaan (Caleb) heard of the tragedy, he invaded Yemen and slaughtered thousands of Jews in retaliation.[14] Following his retributive act of vengeance, Christian churches were rebuilt and the church was refreshed. To seal his victory, Elesbaan installed his general Esimephaeus on the Himyarite throne. Esimephaeus was overthrown by another Ethiopian Christian named Abraha who immediately subjected himself to the Axumite king.[15] Under Abraha's reign many Jews and pagans joined the ranks of the church.

Abraha had an evangelistic spirit and was appalled to learn that thousands of pilgrims visited the Caaba, a popular heathen shrine in Mecca that housed many pagan gods. In a bid to lure them from their idolatry, he built a magnificent cathedral in Sanaa and rerouted the pilgrims to this place of worship. Abraha's pious act had serious political implications, for the Caaba was key to the economic survival of the Quraish tribe, who were the caretakers of the shrine. Knowing the fetishes of the Arabians, some Quraish leaders arranged for a hoodlum to desecrate the Christian church with feces,

---

[13]See Trimingham, *Islam in Ethiopia*, p. 41; and Kenneth Cragg, *The Arab Christian* (Louisville, Ky.: Westminster John Knox, 1991), p. 39.
[14]Details of the event are provided in Hansberry, *Pillars in Ethiopian History*, pp. 100-105.
[15]Oussani, "Christianity in Arabia," p. 672.

an act that was widely broadcast. This vile act of vandalism accomplished its purpose and affected attendance at the cathedral. In a zealous bid to vindicate his faith, Abraha assembled an army and marched against the Quraish and their allies the Kenanah.[16] He was so upset that he defeated every tribe that got in his way. As he neared Mecca, Abdul-Muttalib ibn Hashim, the Quraish chief, who was also the grandfather of Islam's founder Muhammad, offered a compromise with the enraged Christian king. When Abraha refused, Abdul-Muttalib arranged an ambush and utterly crushed the invading army.[17] The defeated Abraha hastily retreated to Yemen where he died in 550.

Abraha's sons, Yaksoum and Masrouq, succeeded him, but the Himyarite kingdom was significantly weakened. In 568, the Persians invaded and usurped control over Yemen and Oman.[18] Once they had settled, they expelled all Axumite nationals, which included a large number of Christians. Fortunately, the expulsion did not utterly destroy the Christian community, and many of the Himyarite nationals remained faithful to their creed. Even with the rise of Islam, the Christians in southern Arabia enjoyed freedom of worship, and Muhammad considered them brothers and allies. Muhammad even attended services at the church Abraha had built at Sanaa, and wrote about the times when he listened to the sermons of Bishop Quss ibn Sa'ida. Unfortunately, Muhammad's successors were not as tolerant toward those who had laid the foundation for their emerging faith, and during the reign of 'Umar (634-44), the second successor of Muhammad, all in the southern region were forced to embrace Islam or face expulsion from the region.[19] After centuries of Christian missionaries planting biblical seeds in an arid land, a new faith with a new book was preparing to harvest the fertile ground that had been sacrificially tilled and cultivated by selfless monks and hermits.

---

[16]For another version on the cause for the war, see Trimingham, *Islam in Ethiopia*, p. 41.

[17]For the Muslim account of the encounter, see Adil Salahi, *Muhammad: Man and Prophet* (Markfield, U.K.: The Islamic Foundation, 2002), pp. 18-22.

[18]Trimingham, *Islam in Ethiopia*, p. 42, purports that the Persians came at the invitation of Himyarite chiefs.

[19]The Sunna justifies 'Umar's actions by stating that Muhammad ordered the expulsion on his deathbed. However, as questioned by Youssef Courbage and Philippe Fargues, *Christians and Jews under Islam*, trans. Judy Mabro (London: I. B. Tauris, 1997), p. 7, "If the Prophet had actually ordained the expulsion of the Christians and the Jews, why was it not implemented by Abu Bakr, his immediate successor, and why did 'Umar wait until the end of his caliphate to execute it?"

GROWING PAINS: CONCLUSION

During the first seven centuries of Christian history, tens of millions had been exposed to the contents of Scripture. Furthermore, hundreds of tribes that had previously been divided by language and religion were provided with a basis for unity. Excited about the prospects of a borderless kingdom, scholars of the church poured their energies into systematizing a faith that would unite all siblings in Christ. Anxious to make the message available to the masses, linguists in Palestine, Egypt and Ethiopia painstakingly translated the words of the Bible, hundreds of years before the first English version was even conceived. It seemed as if gifted Christian intelligentsia in different parts of the land of Ham were all executing plans from the pages of a carefully constructed strategic plan.

Unfortunately, the systematic infrastructure did not create the type of unified body that was envisioned. Rather than celebrating the victory of Christ, these centuries were filled with theological and political wars, compromise and apostasy. In the territory that centuries before had been settled by Canaan, there was a marked divide between the church of the Jewish Messiah, whose Christianity resembled the religion of Israel, and the church of the Son of God, which had embraced the philosophical creeds of the ecumenical councils. And even as philosophical methodology dominated the instruction at its catechetical schools, the territories springing from Misrayim witnessed the flourishing of aberrant movements in the mold of Gnostics, Donatists and Monastics. Meanwhile, even as the western regions of Cush experienced minor setbacks, the Arabians in the east were fighting hard for their survival. Added to all this were the throngs of African Christians who had positioned themselves against their counterparts in the west by adopting Nestorian and Monophysite Christologies that struck at the heart of orthodoxy.

In spite of all the negatives, the widespread descendants of Ham could now claim the Bible as their own. No longer was it the sole property of the Semites who had been transplanted on the land of Ham, but it was a gift to the nations. With the translation of the Bible into the languages of the people, the stage was set for individuals to search the Word for themselves. Even those who could not read had the opportunity to hear the Word in their own tongue. Exposed to the message of Scripture, the children of Ham were provided with the opportunity to discover the hope that had inspired missionaries to risk life and limb in order to spread the gospel story.

In spite of the rapid advances of the early centuries, Christianity was to suffer a serious setback from which it has never recovered. While students of history may blame others for the assault against Christianity, an honest analysis shows that the initial wounds were definitely self-inflicted. Even as the throngs of believers dwelling in Africa were being exposed to the liberating words of the Bible, the cloistered elite who claimed to represent the masses were using God's book for their own political and philosophical purposes. They seemed to gain pleasure from complicating creeds and casting accusations against alleged heretics. For many, that which promised to be an easy yoke had become a heavy burden, and they yearned for a path that would insulate them from sectarian harassment. Millions were to find that path in the uncomplicated teaching of an illiterate Arabian tribesman.

TOTAL ECLIPSE

Islam's Distortion of the Biblical Message

And he sent them away from his son Isaac,

eastward to the east country.

GENESIS 25:6

The heterodox climate of emerging Christianity provided an arena for the nurturing of charismatic individuals with unique understandings of Scripture. In the previous part of this book, we saw how clerics like Nestorius and Shenuote influenced the emergence of splinter groups that eventually assumed identities apart from the one dominated by Byzantium orthodoxy. The chapters in part four cover the unimaginable evangelistic successes of Muhammad—a nontraditionalist who neither donned the garb of clergy nor claimed allegiance to any of the biblical religions that dotted the Hamitic-African landscape.

As far as we can gather, Muhammad was a self-trained Bible student who believed he was called to convert his fellow Arabians to the worship of the one true God[1] and to remind Jews and Christians of their religious responsibili-

---

[1]Some Christian commentators charge that the Muslim God is different than the Christian one. For instance, Timothy George, *Is the Father of Jesus the God of Muhammad?* (Grand Rapids: Zondervan, 2002), pp. 69-88, uses his trinitarian understanding of God to discredit the Muslim view. However, this logic would also discount the Jewish understanding of God—as well as the views of Unitarian Christians from antiquity to the present.

ties.[2] After overcoming heavy opposition, his simple message of submission to the one true God eventually captured the hearts of a people whose comprehension of the plain truth of Scripture had been obscured by the forest of philosophical jargon that had transformed Christianity and Judaism from practical faiths to intellectual fraternities. Unfortunately, Muhammad's straightforward approach was accompanied by his own interpretations of divine revelation that were codified in a book that claimed to illuminate, but eventually overshadowed, the Bible.[3]

Muhammad's religious outlook was shaped by his environment. Born in Mecca into the prominent Quraish clan—the guardians of the Caaba—Muhammad would have been exposed to the multitude of pilgrims who came to worship at the famous shrine. Among the pious worshipers were Jewish and Christian traders and missionaries who marketed their goods while telling stories from the Bible. They undoubtedly told the story of Abraham as they informed the Arabs of their common religious heritage (cf. Gen 25:1-18). Opportunities to expand one's religious outlook were also provided via the many Meccans who controlled the trade in the region and interacted with merchants from near and far. The adventurous Muhammad secured employment with one of the Meccan business people, a successful woman named Khadija, who eventually became his wife.[4] During his travels with Khadija's company, his religious horizons were greatly broadened as he came in contact with Jews and Christians in other parts of Hamitic Africa.

Reportedly illiterate, Muhammad would not have read the documents of the Abrahamic religions to which he was exposed, but it would not be far-fetched to say that he became a convert. Exactly to what he was converted can be debated. He obviously shared certain food taboos of the First Testament,

---

[2]On the universal scope of Muhammad's mission, see discussion in Jacques Jomier, *The Bible and the Qur'an* (San Francisco: Ignatius Press, 2002), pp. 7-16. According to Islamic tradition, Muhammad was not the first Meccan to reject polytheism in favor of biblical religion. Adil Salahi, *Muhammad: Man and Prophet* (Markfield, Leicestershire: The Islamic Foundation, 2002), pp. 58-59, records the story of four faithful men who preceded the Prophet: Waraqah ibn Nawfal, Abdullah ibn Jahsh, Uthman ibn al-Huwayrith and Zayd ibn 'Amr. The first three fully embraced Christianity, and Zayd, while sympathetic to Christianity, listened to two Christian priests who informed him that a prophet was to appear in Mecca. Salahi relates several accounts of Jewish and Christian theologians prophesying the coming of Muhammad (ibid., pp. 60-62).

[3]Muhammad's existential interpretation of biblical teachings could be attributed to the fact that there was no established Christian presence in Mecca. See Neal Robinson, *Christ in Islam and Christianity* (Albany: State University of New York Press, 1991), pp. 16-17.

[4]For commentary on their relationship, see Salahi, *Muhammad,* pp. 43-46.

and evidences awareness of sabbath sacredness[5] and circumcision, which would make it seem like he had embraced a form of Judaism. However, a number of Christian groups, including the church in Axum, adhered to these "Jewish" rites. Muhammad also accepted the divine inspiration of the prophets and apostles of God. These not only included the *tawrá's* Noah, Moses and Abraham, but also the *injíl's* John and Jesus, whom he recognized as Messiah. This fact alone suggests that his limited knowledge of the Bible directed him to embrace his own unique brand of Christianity. Although acknowledging Jesus as Messiah, Muhammad understood the core biblical teaching as centering on the oneness of God. As far as he was concerned, this meant that no other entity could rival the exclusive Divinity. It was with this monotheistic presupposition that he challenged the polytheistic practices of his own tribe.

Consistent with his understanding of monotheism, Muhammad also denounced the orthodox teaching of the Trinity—which he understood as the worship of God, Jesus and Mary.[6] He knew that the various Christian groups scattered around Arabia and Palestine were divided into two general camps. The Chalcedonians fully embraced the doctrinal position of the Catholic church regarding the nature of Jesus the Christ, and taught that he was fully God yet fully human at the same time. The Monophysites, on the other hand, believed that the Son of God possessed only one nature, which was fully divine. The very fact that these two opposing sides understood a human to be divine was blasphemous to the Arabian merchant. Fully embracing his self-professed role as God's appointed prophet, he was not willing to compromise in his efforts to reform the beliefs and behavior of the people who professed faith in God's written revelation. Within two decades after his death, Muhammad's interpretation of biblical religion had spread to every region of Hamitic Africa as the political mechanism of Arabian Islam expanded the borders of the empire to many of the nations that had sprung from the loins of Misrayim and Canaan. Over the next few centuries, the religious preference of the masses would shift from the various expressions of Christianity to the new Islamic revelation.

---

[5] Cf. Qur'an 2:65; 4:47, 154; 7:163; 16:124.
[6] For a discussion on Islam's problem with Nicene Christology, see Kenneth Cragg, *The Arab Christian: A History in the Middle East* (Louisville, Ky.: Westminster John Knox, 1991), pp. 18-19.

11

THE INFLUENCE OF THE BIBLE
ON THE QUR'AN

With the help of scribes, Muhammad's teachings were recorded in a volume called the Qur'an. The Qur'an is named after the Arabic word for "recite," which is the first thing that Gabriel allegedly uttered to Muhammad before giving him a revelation. The individual revelations, called suras, were eventually collated into a single volume and arranged from the longest to the shortest, without regard to chronology or content. Anyone reading the Qur'an would quickly see that Muhammad had high regard for the Bible. In his estimation, the Scriptures contained the authoritative word of God and should not be altered. He even condemned those who distorted the words of the Bible for their own gain.[1] As far as he was concerned, had Jews and Christians remained faithful to the revealed Word, they would not have needed another prophet. However, the fact that many had apostatized meant that God had to send another revelation. Like other founders of post-Christian movements who claim that their writings are in full harmony with Scripture, Muhammad declared that the Qur'an was a revelation that did not displace, but illuminated the Scriptures.[2] Similar to Paul, who maintained that God had not rejected the Jewish people (Rom 11:1-6), Muhammad recognized the place of his religious forebears in the scheme of salvation history, and affirmed that there are some godly people among them who will fare well in the judgment (Qur'an 2:62).

---

[1]"Those that suppress any part of the Scriptures which God has revealed in order to gain some paltry end shall swallow nothing but fire into their bellies" (2:174). "And there are some among [the People of the Book] who twist their tongues when quoting the Scriptures, so that you may think that what they say is from the Scriptures, whereas it is not from the Scriptures" (3:78).

[2]"And to you [Muhammad] We have revealed the Book with the truth. It confirms the Scriptures which came before it and stands as a guardian over them" (5:48). "This Qur'an could not have been devised by any but God. It confirms what was revealed before it and fully explains the Scriptures. It is beyond doubt from the Lord of the Universe" (10:37).

He even provided grounds for Muslim men to marry devout Christian and Jewish woman (Qur'an 5:5). However, the spiritual fulfillment of non-Muslims would not be complete until they embraced the newer revelation.

THE QUR'AN AND THE BIBLE

Muhammad's collection of revelations is built on stories from the Bible. So confident was he about his faithfulness to the original writings that he encouraged his potential converts, "If you are in doubt about what We have sent down to you, ask those who were reading scriptures before you" (Qur'an 10:94). Those who compare the Qur'an with the Bible quickly notice that Muhammad's understanding of Scripture differed from the accepted canons being used by the dominant segments of the fledgling Christian church. While he speaks of the *tawra* (torah) and the *injil* (gospel), he does not appear to have possessed manuscript copies of any book from the Old or New Testaments.

It is not hard to reconstruct the contents of Muhammad's *tawra* and *injil*. Judging from the names of those he considered to be prophets—for example, Moses, Aaron Abraham, Elijah and Isaiah —he must have been familiar with the major figures from the Tanak (Old Testament).[3] He is also aware of the biblical account of creation,[4] the flood,[5] the exodus[6] and other major events. Further, it is obvious that he was acquainted with Luke's version of the gospel story,[7] and the strong apocalyptic flavor in many of the suras indicate that he may have been familiar with the Apocalypse of John. He shows little sign of familiarity with the letters of Paul, Peter or James. In addition to the unquestionable biblical stories, Muhammad was obviously influenced by apocryphal gospel material.[8] He may also have been familiar with pseudepigraphical literature.

---

[3]For a synopsis of major studies on the Qur'an and the Bible, see Reuven Firestone, "The *Qur'ān* and the Bible: Some Modern Studies of Their Relationship," in *Bible and Qur'ān: Essays in Scriptural Intertextuality,* ed. John C. Reeves (Leiden: Brill, 2004), pp. 1-22.

[4]Cf. Qur'an 7:54; 10:3; 11:7; 25:59; 32:4; 50:38; 57:4.

[5]Cf. Qur'an 11:36-48; 25:37; 29:14; et al.

[6]Cf. Qur'an 2:47-74; 3:11; 7:103-55; 8:52-54; et al.

[7]E.g., Qur'an 19:1-22 = Lk 1:5-39.

[8]E.g., Qur'an 5:110 = *Infancy Gospel of Thomas* 2:3-5; 9:1-3. There are also parallels to the *Protoevangelium of James* and the *Gospel of Pseudo-Matthew.* On Muhammad's use of extrabiblical literature, see Jacques Jomier, *The Bible and the Qur'an* (San Francisco: Ignatius Press, 2002), pp. 48-52; and Suleiman A. Mourad, "On the Qur'anic Stories about Mary and Jesus," *Bulletin of the Royal Institute for Inter-Faith Studies* 1 (1999): 13-24.

THE ESTEEMED PLACE OF JESUS IN THE QUR'AN

With the strong biblical flavor of the Qur'an, it is not difficult to see how the Christian masses who had no real stake in the theological arguments embraced the new teaching. Their interest may have also been piqued by the importance the Qur'an places on Jesus; Jesus' prominence in the Qur'an is difficult to ignore. Although he is only mentioned in a few suras, he is an indispensable part of Muslim theology. According to the Qur'an, his major mission while on earth was to reveal the *injil* (Qur'an 57:27). An apparent transliteration of the Greek word *euangelion* (gospel), the term *injil* is used to define the major content of Jesus' message,[9] which—in Muhammad's estimation—involved the confirmation of the revealed *tawra* (torah) and an appeal for hearers to fully submit to Allah (Qur'an 5:44-47). As a reformer of Judaism, Jesus was also commissioned with providing divine answers to dissenting Jewish parties (Qur'an 43:63).

The Qur'an speaks of Jesus as one in a long line of prophets (apostles) that began with Abraham and ended with Muhammad.[10] Notwithstanding, few would deny that it portrays him in a unique light.[11] For Muhammad, Jesus was no ordinary prophet, he was a prophet par excellence. Muhammad—and the original audience—esteemed the Galilean prophet so highly that he placed words on the Messiah's lips to authenticate his own ministry: "I am sent forth to you from God to confirm the Torah already revealed and to give news of an apostle that will come after me whose name is Ahmad" (Qur'an 61:6).[12]

Jesus and the Holy Spirit. Unlike the other prophets, Jesus shared an unparalleled relationship with Allah. This relationship is unique because Jesus was empowered by the Holy Spirit of Allah which allowed him to heal the sick and raise the dead. In addition to the traditional Gospels, Muhammad's under-

---

[9]For a discussion on the meaning of *injil*, see Geoffrey Parrinder, *Jesus in the Quran* (Oxford: One World, 1995), pp. 142-51.

[10]"The Messiah, the son of Mary, was no more than an apostle: other apostles passed away before him. His mother was a saintly woman. They both ate earthly food" (5:75). In another place, Allah speaks of the covenants made with His prophets: "We made a covenant with you [Muhammad], as we did with the other prophets; with Noah and Abraham, with Moses and Jesus, the son of Mary" (33:7). And again, "He was no more than a mortal whom we favored and made an example to the Israelites" (43:59).

[11]See discussion in Jomier, *Bible and the Qur'an*, pp. 65-69.

[12]Neal Robinson, *Christ in Islam and Christianity* (Albany: State University of New York Press, 1991), pp. 36-38, notices that Jesus and Muhammad share a number of attributes and suggests that the intention may have been to legitimize Muhammad's ministry to those who believed in Jesus.

standing of the relationship between Jesus and Allah was informed by apocryphal works, particularly the second-century *Infancy Gospel of Thomas,* as is evident from the following Qur'anic verse: "Jesus, son of Mary, remember the
favor I have bestowed on you and your mother: how I strengthened you with
the Holy Spirit, so that you preached to men in your cradle and in prime of
manhood; how I instructed you in the Book and in wisdom, in the Torah and
in the Gospel; how by My leave you fashioned from clay the likeness of a bird
and breathed into it so that, by My leave, it became a living bird; how, by My
leave, you healed the blind man and the leper, and by My leave you restored
the dead to life" (Qur'an 5:110).[13] No other prophet in the Qur'an is attributed
with such miracle-working power. Neither is any other said to be strengthened
by the Holy Spirit. It is hard to deny that with the indwelling power of the
Holy Spirit the Qur'anic Jesus is exalted above all the other prophets: "To
some God spoke directly; others He raised to a lofty status. We gave Jesus the
son of Mary veritable signs and strengthened him with the Holy Spirit"
(Qur'an 2:253; see also 2:87).

Jesus and Mary. One who reads the Qur'an quickly notices that Jesus is frequently referred to as the "Son of Mary." This unique designation betrays Muhammad's knowledge of the debate in Christianity about the role of Mary as
theotokos, "bearer/mother of God." Nestorius and other Christian groups refused this Catholic appellation and preferred to refer to her as the *christotokos,*
"bearer/mother of Christ." Interestingly, Mary is the only woman who is
named in the Qur'an.[14] The Qur'an accepts the doctrine of the virgin birth and
suggests that Jesus was conceived after the Spirit breathed on Mary (Qur'an
21:91). While embracing the miraculous origins of Jesus, Muhammad rejected Catholic notions concerning devotion to Mary, although he was influenced by the doctrine of the immaculate conception.[15]

Muhammad believed the family of Imran—the biblical Amram who was
the father of Moses, Aaron and Miriam (Num 26:59)—held a special place in
the divine scheme (Qur'an 3:33-35). In fact, the first reference to the annunciation to Mary appears in a sura dedicated to the family of Imran (Qur'an

---

[13]See *Infancy Gospel of Thomas,* passim.
[14]For a discussion on Mary see Parrinder, *Jesus in the Quran,* pp. 60-74. For a Roman Catholic perspective, see also Fulton J. Sheen, "Mary and the Moslems," appendix in Jomier, *The Bible and the Qur'an,*
pp. 121-26.
[15]The Qur'an states that Mary's mother had consecrated her from the womb and received Allah's affirmation (3:35-37).

3:45-47). It has strong parallels to Luke's account, but has obviously been influenced by extrabiblical traditions. A more detailed account of the annunciation occurs in a sura devoted entirely to Mary,[16] and—like the one featuring the family of Imran—it also contains the annunciation to Zacharias concerning John the Baptist. Again in this sura, it is evident that Muhammad had access to some apocryphal material from which he built his account.[17] As far as he was concerned, this information was an authentic part of the "Book."

Jesus the Messiah. In the account of the annunciation recorded in the third chapter of the Qur'an, Jesus is called the Messiah who is "favored by God" (3:45). The use of the definite article makes it clear that Muhammad recognized the term as a title.[18] His exact concept of Messiah is not spelled out,[19] but Jesus is seen as one who will be honored in this world and eternity (3:45). In fact, all who follow him—even after he is taken to paradise—will be exalted above the unbelievers "until the Day of Resurrection" (3:55). On the day of resurrection, Jesus is assigned the role of "witness" (4:159), a significant assignment that is otherwise reserved for God himself (22:17). Given what we know about Jewish expectation for a Messiah and the radicalization of this expectation by Jesus who delayed the punitive aspect of the Messianic kingdom until his return, it appears that Muhammad had some concept of the second coming. While the exact nature of the *parousia* is not defined in Muhammad's eschatology,[20] the Qur'an portrays the Day of Resurrection as one when the wicked will be punished and the righteous rewarded.[21]

The crucifixion of Jesus. Although the Qur'an confirms the virgin birth and the Messiahship of Christ, it is ambiguous concerning the crucifixion.[22] Re-

---

[16]Mary is defined as the "sister of Aaron" (19:28). Muslim commentators suggest that the meaning is "virtuous woman." Robinson, *Christ in Islam*, p. 18, argues that Muhammad may have been influenced by the typological exegesis of the Syrian church that may have viewed the First Testament Miriam as a type of the New Testament Mary.

[17]Compare 19:16-36 with the accounts in Mt 1 and Lk 1.

[18]Cf. 4:157, 171, 172; 5:75; 9:31; et al.

[19]See suggestions by Parrinder, *Jesus in the Quran*, pp. 30-34.

[20]Although not explicit in the Qur'an, the second coming of Jesus is an important part of Muslim theology. See discussion in Robinson, *Christ in Islam*, pp. 78-105.

[21]The Qur'an continues the biblical teaching of a works-based judgment (3:161) and locates the place of reward and punishment as a "garden" and "fire" (3:185). Similar to the Bible, the Qur'an also states that a record of human actions is recorded in a book (17:13). There are scores of other texts relating the Day of Resurrection to the judgment (2:85, 113, 174, 212; 3:55, 77, 180, 194; 4:87, 109, 141, 159; et al.).

[22]See discussion in Robinson, *Christ in Islam*, pp. 106-41.

flecting the suspicion of Christian Gnosticism, in one place Muhammad writes that the person who the Jews crucified was one who was made to look like Jesus, and while the imposter hung on the cross Jesus had been miraculously taken up to God (Qur'an 4:157-58). This understanding of Jesus' death did not originate with Muhammad, but finds affinity in an early Christian teaching known as Docetism. Taking their name from the Greek verb *dokeō* meaning "to appear," the Docetists taught that Jesus only appeared to die on the cross, but since he was spirit it was impossible for him to experience death. In another place, Muhammad seems to contradict his assertion that Jesus escaped death. He writes, "[The Jews] plotted, and God plotted. God is the supreme Plotter. He said: 'Jesus, I am about to cause you to die and lift you up to Me. I shall take you away from the unbelievers and exalt your followers above them until the day of Resurrection'" (Qur'an 3:54-55). This text clearly states that Jesus not only experienced death, but has ascended into the presence of God—apparently after his resurrection.[23]

Jesus and divinity. According to the Qur'an, Jesus did not come into this world through natural means. His beginning is said to be similar to Adam's (Qur'an 3:59), which would naturally assume that they were both created beings who had no earthly parent. However, since the Qur'an teaches that Jesus came from the womb of the virgin Mary, he could not have been created in the same image as Adam. Further, since the Qur'an is adamant that God could never "father" a baby (Qur'an 4:171), that which was implanted in Mary would not have been a sperm, but a fertilized egg. Muhammad fully accepted his miraculous beginnings, but interpreted it in light of Adam's creation. Consequently, any attempt to elevate him to the status of divinity is condemned as idolatry (Qur'an 3:64). So repulsive is this transgression that Muhammad is instructed to plead with the "People of the Book" (Jews and Christians): "let us come to an agreement: that we will worship none but God, that we will associate none with Him, and that none of us shall set up mortals as deities beside God" (Qur'an 3:64). To validate his abhorrence, Muhammad invokes the words of Jesus himself as a witness to his full humanity: "For the Messiah him-

---

[23]Jesus' ascension is given further import when it is noted that most people who die stay dead until the judgment (3:185). Parrinder, *Jesus in the Quran*, pp. 105-21, attempts to reconcile these two passages and contends that the first does not deny the crucifixion of Jesus but shifts the actual act from the Jews to the Romans. See also discussion in Jane Dammen McAuliffe, "Followers of the *Qur'ān* Jesus," in *Qur'ān Christians: An Analysis of Classical and Modern Exegesis* (Cambridge: Cambridge University Press, 1991), pp. 129-59.

self said: 'Children of Israel, serve God, my Lord and your Lord'" (Qur'an 5:72; see also 5:117).

Although Muhammad highly respected the person of Jesus, he had a major problem with the doctrine of the Trinity,[24] which by the seventh century was an established pillar of orthodox theology. He does not appear to have fully understood the doctrine and identified the Trinity as Jesus, Allah and Mary (Qur'an 5:116).[25] However, even if he had a correct understanding, as one who had fought against Arabian polytheism, he would not have accepted a teaching that appeared to endorse a plurality of gods. In full agreement with the minority Christian sects that rejected the doctrine, Muhammad believed that the elevation of a human to divine status—even if it were the specially appointed Messiah—was tantamount to blasphemy (Qur'an 4:171). He condemns all Trinitarians and relegates them to the status of "unbelievers," claiming that they will receive their just punishment in the judgment (Qur'an 5:72-73). He desperately appeals to them to amend their ways as he points to a gracious God who is willing to forgive (Qur'an 5:74).

Islam's rejection of the Trinity is in no way a denial of the unique relationship that Jesus had with the Father. In fact, the Qur'an attributes some very interesting words to Jesus that depict him as a substitute for God while on earth: "I watched over them while living in their midst, and ever since You took me to Yourself, You have been watching them" (Qur'an 5:117). This statement is similar to a more expanded one that Jesus makes in the Gospel of John: "While I was with them, I protected them in your name that you have given me. . . . I am not asking you to take them out of the world, but I ask you to protect them from the evil one" (Jn 17:12, 15). The fact that Jesus and God assume a similar role is enough to show that Muhammad did not view him as a "regular" prophet. Although a human being, he was obviously one whom God had entrusted with unparalleled responsibilities.

---

[24]Although see Parrinder, *Jesus in the Quran*, pp. 133-41.
[25]Robinson, *Christ in Islam*, p. 20, suggests that Muhammad had been influenced by Nestorian arguments for rejecting Mary as the *theotokos*.

12

THE GROWTH OF ISLAM
IN BIBLICAL AFRICA

With the importance that Muhammad placed on Jesus, it is not difficult to understand why this new interpretation of biblical faith found fertile soil among so many Christians who inhabited the land of Ham. In all probability, most who professed Christianity did so on grounds other than spiritual conviction and had little knowledge of the biblical texts that informed their faith. This definitely appears to have been the case in Arabia, where there is no extant evidence to suggest that believers there even had a copy of the Scriptures in their native tongue. Like its Jewish parent, who reserved biblical studies for the rabbis, Christianity—in the main—had donned the garb of the hierarchical mystical religions of pagan antiquity and had surrendered the Bible to emperors and theologians. As a result, the masses were tossed to and fro as new interpretations were imposed upon them by warring bishops and imperial edicts. Scholars have long recognized that "the religious disputes which divided Christians in the Byzantine empire provided a fertile terrain for the new conquerors."[1] The largely uneducated masses were probably relieved to hear the simple message of the Muslim evangelists as they shared memorized portions of the Qur'an relating to the oneness of God, the judgment, charitable obligations and the godly Messiah.

Let me hasten to clarify that not all who embraced Islam did so on purely religious grounds. There were also those who converted for political and economic reasons. On the political realm, we have already noted that just decades after Muhammad's death, the Islamic empire had expanded beyond Arabia into Palestine and Egypt. Until recently, accepted Christian lore attributed Is-

---

[1]Youssef Courbage and Philippe Fargues, *Christians and Jews under Islam*, trans. Judy Mabro (London: I. B. Tauris, 1997), p. x.

lam's growth to forced conversions after conquest. This is far from the truth.[2]
Undoubtedly, there were cases where people were coerced to accept the new
faith—the same was true for Judaism and Christianity. However, many who
chose Islam did so to escape a state tax that was only levied on nonbelievers.
Furthermore, similar to Orthodox Christians who claim the soul of every
child born into a Christian home, Islamic growth came from the offspring of
marriages between Muslim men and non-Muslim women.

It is also necessary to elucidate that Islam did not grow as rapidly as some
have purported.[3] When the Islamic empire started to expand, the fundamen-
tals of the faith had not even been fully decided. Those who were initially entrusted with the task of evangelism only had portions of Muhammad's prophecies, which would not be collated until decades after his death.[4] It would
probably be safe to suggest that the earliest converts were drawn to an imperial
Islam that promoted an incipient theology that was more practical than the
ethereal dicta of philosophical Christianity. The fact that Islam positioned itself as the first-class carriage in the Judeo-Christian train also meant that
those already on the train who wished to upgrade could do so at their own
pace. This chapter will briefly cover the various Hamitic-African responses to
Islam in the first few centuries after its introduction.

RECEPTION AND RESISTANCE IN CUSH

Muhammad's association with Arabia is reason enough to commence our discussion with the spread of Islam in the lands originating with Cush. Couched
in the culture of Arabia and intricately linked to the unique identity of a particular tribe, it did not take long for this new understanding of the Abrahamic
faith to capture the hearts and minds of a people seeking authentic cultural
identity apart from the synagogue and cathedral. While contributing to the
success of Islam in Arabia, national identity may have also played a role in the
initial rejection of Islam by the Ethiopian kingdoms of Axum and Nubia. Not

---

[2]Mark Shaw, *The Kingdom of God in Africa: A Short History of African Christianity* (Grand Rapids:
Baker, 1996), pp. 75-78.
[3]Courbage and Fargues, *Christians and Jews*, p. 6, remind us that "Spiritual conquest did not . . . match
this frantic progress."
[4]Muslim tradition has it that the assembling of the Qur'an was authorized by Uthman, the third caliph
and former secretary to Muhammad. But see the controversial theory of John Wansbrough, *Quranic
Studies: Sources and Methods of Scriptural Interpretation* (Oxford: Oxford University Press, 1977), who
contends that the Qur'an was compiled from various sources no sooner than two centuries after Muhammad's death.

only had parts of Arabia served as vassals to their Cushite mother, but Christianity was much more organized and entrenched in that region. Before discussing the rejection of Muhammad's biblical interpretation by the Ethiopian nations west of the Red Sea, we will take a look at how his faith spread in the land of his birth.

Arabian and Mesopotamian reception. With the images of the bloody confrontation between Abraha's Christian army and the Caaban warriors still lingering in their minds,[5] the Meccans were not receptive to Muhammad's biblical message. They could understand an outsider like Abraha wanting to destroy their livelihood and centuries-old culture, but Muhammad was one of their own. Initially, he was simply viewed as a nuisance, who had only managed to convince his wife and his cousin Ali of his revelations. However, his tenacity and sincerity eventually yielded dividends, and a number of Meccans accepted his apostleship. He also directed his efforts towards Arabian pilgrims as they came to trade and worship.[6] With the zeal of the early Christian evangelists, these enlightened ones began to spread the message with so much success that they attracted the wrath of the tribal leaders. They were persecuted to such an extent that in 615 C.E. many sought refuge in the Axumite kingdom on the other side of the Red Sea.

Although targeted by his kinsmen, Muhammad courageously remained in Mecca where he continued to recruit seekers to the ranks of the faithful. His success at home was undoubtedly helped by a political maneuver that would safeguard the economic interests of the Quraish tribe. More specifically, Muhammad attempted to appease the tribal leaders with a vision supposedly from Gabriel that appeared to endorse the three major deities that were housed in the Caaba shrine.[7] These so-called Satanic verses had a temporary purpose and are not included in later versions of the Qur'an. Muhammad also cleverly reinterpreted the meaning of the Caaba, stating that God himself had ordained it as a place of worship to reflect the sanctuary in heaven. He also taught that it had been built by Abraham and Ishmael. By attaching such a

---

[5]See previous chapter.

[6]See Adil Salahi, *Muhammad: Man and Prophet* (Markfield, Leicestershire: The Islamic Foundation, 2002), pp. 191-200, for a description of Muhammad's evangelistic strategy.

[7]According to Ibn Ishaq, the earliest additions of the Qur'an had the following line appended to Qur'an 53:19-20, which discusses the goddesses al-Lat, al-ʿUzza and Manat: "These are the exalted Gharaniq, whose intercession is hoped for." Muhammad alleged that Satan whispered this line in his ear after Gabriel had given the recitation.

high significance to the Caaba, Muhammad ensured that it would maintain its status as a religious shrine and a center of commerce. In spite of these compromises, Muhammad was still not fully accepted in Mecca.

News of Muhammad's reforms spread to Yathrib (Medina) where some of the Jewish tribal leaders believed him to be the Messiah. Impressed by his reputation for fairness, the tribal federation of Medina sent a delegation to Mecca to persuade him to be their judge. He acquiesced and relocated to the new vicinity with a number of his followers in 622 C.E., an event known in Muslim circles as the *Hijra* (migration). While host to a strong Jewish contingency,[8] Medina was also home to a number of Christians and traditional worshipers. Muhammad did not seek to impose his religious understanding on the masses, but developed the "Medina Charter" which guaranteed freedom of religion for the multiple clans.[9] The political structure of Medina eventually gave rise to the *Umma,* a theocratic system in which all Muslims were expected to pay a poor tax *(zakat)* and declare allegiance to the one God.[10] The *Umma* would serve as the basic model for Islam as it spread to other areas of the world. Ever the politician, sensitive to the number of Jews under his charge, Muhammad mandated that his followers pray in the direction of Jerusalem. Relationships between Muhammad and the Jews eventually turned sour, and Muhammad decided to turn his back on Jerusalem and ordered his subjects to direct their prayers to his beloved Mecca.[11] The situation became so bad that the Jews of Medina joined the Meccan armies who were intent on the destruction of Muhammad. Muhammad's troops fought vigorously and, after staving of the assault, bought the Medinan Jews under subjection.[12] Following a period of conflict, Muhammad led an army of 10,000 men into Mecca in 630 C.E. and took control of the Caaba, thus solidifying his position as the main ruler in the Arabian region of Hamitic Cush.

As the undisputed chief of the most prominent Arabian clan, Muhammad was in the position to ensure the success of his message of reform. His effort to

---

[8]Moshe Gil, *A History of Palestine, 634-1099,* trans. Ethel Broido (Cambridge: Cambridge University Press, 1992), p. 11, calls Yathrib (Medina) a Jewish city.

[9]See Lewis M. Hopfe and Mark R. Woodward, *Religions of the World,* 9th ed. (Upper Saddle River, N.J.: Prentice Hall, 2005), p. 337.

[10]See Frederick M. Denny, *Islam and the Muslim Community* (Prospect Heights, Ill.: Waveland Press, 1987, 1998), pp. 30-31.

[11]Ed Hotaling, *Islam Without Illusions* (Syracuse, N.Y.: Syracuse University Press, 2003), p. 36, sees this as Muhammad's declaration of "spiritual independence."

[12]See Ibid., pp. 69-71, and Salahi, *Muhammad,* pp. 299-318.

unite the Arabian people was probably aided by a regional yearning for independence. Various clans had been under the hand of Axumite and Persian powers, and they had seen Jewish immigrants ascend to political prominence. Christianity had captured the imaginations of many, but it had been imported from Palestine, Egypt and Axum, and it had not even been contextualized by translation of the sacred writings into Arabic. This was their opportunity to unite under one umbrella and set the stage for empire. Taking advantage of the climate, Muhammad and his militant evangelists transmitted the faith throughout familiar territory and witnessed the masses embracing his interpretation of divine revelation—at least the snippets to which they were exposed.

The Muslim mission on the Arabian peninsula took on a different face after Muhammad's death. During his life, Muhammad was very clear that Jews and Christians were free to practice their faith—although they were subject to a tax. This favor was apparently continued under the reign of Abu Bakr, Muhammad's successor. However, the following caliph, 'Umar, started a program of religious cleansing and began expelling Jews and Christians from certain areas in 640.[13] Succeeding rulers do not appear to have enforced the rule with any seriousness, and while not too many Christians remained, a sizeable Jewish community could still be found in certain areas until the creation of the state of Israel.[14]

The successes in Arabia quickly spilled over to its northern Mesopotamian neighbor. Before the advent of Islam, the Iranian controlled region—known as Khvarvaran before taking the name Iraq (from the Persian *Eraq* meaning "lower Iran")—had been a stronghold of Nestorian Christianity. Indeed, during the First Caliphate (632-661), the Nestorians continued to flourish as they commissioned missionaries to establish the gospel in China and the Far East, and schooled their conquerors in Greek philosophy.[15] Southern Mesopotamia went the way of Arabia, and within fifty years of the initial conquest, an estimated two-thirds of the population were persuaded by the Qur'anic interpretation of Scripture.[16] By 750, the Abbasid Dynasty had transferred the capital of Islam from Damascus to Baghdad. Baghdad was a thriving economic and

---

[13]See Courbage and Fargues, *Christians and Jews,* pp. 6-7.
[14]Ibid., p. 7.
[15]Ibid., pp. 7-8.
[16]Courbage and Fargues estimate that by the year 700, the 9 million inhabitants of Mesopotamia consisted of 6 million Muslims and 3 million Christians (ibid., p. 8).

cultural center which quickly became the hub of Muslim missions. Indeed, it was from this cosmopolitan city that Arabic became the accepted language of the Islamic empire.[17] Similar to the way in which the pages of the New Testament were spread throughout the Greek-speaking Roman Empire, the Qur'an was taken to remote regions through an increasingly popular imperial vernacular. In northern Mesopotamia, it would be another five hundred years (1295) before Ghazan, the Mongol Ilkhan of Iraq and Iran, converted to Islam, a decision that led to the gradual erosion of Nestorian Christianity.

Axumite and Nubian resistance. While Islam gained popularity in Hamitic Arabia and its northern territories, the mother kingdom to the west of the Red Sea refused to embrace Muhammad's interpretation of inspired writ. Unlike its Arabian offspring, Christianity had become indigenized and was the formal religion of Axum and the Nubian states. The resistance to Islam may also have been influenced by the fact that the religion had been introduced to the region in its germinal stages. Islam first entered Axumite Ethiopia in 615 when several families of early converts sought sanctuary from persecution by the Quraish in Mecca. According to Islamic tradition, Muhammad himself advised them to go after recalling how the Axumites had come to the assistance of the persecuted Christians of Himyar decades earlier. Ibn Hisham, an early biographer of Muhammad, preserves his words: "If you go to Abyssinia you will find a king under whom none are persecuted. It is a land of righteousness where God will give you relief from what you are suffering."[18] The flight to Axum is often referred to as the first *Hijra.*[19]

The experiences of the Arabian exiles in Axum clearly demonstrate the early perception of Muhammad's teachings among Christians. Upon discovering that some of their clansmen had fled, the leaders of the Quraish sent an emissary requesting that Negus As'hamah, the Axumite king, deport the refugees. Before complying with the request, the justice-minded king decided to interview Jafar bin Abi Talin, one of the Muhammadan leaders. In his response, Jafar portrayed Islam as another version of Christianity, and the refugees were allowed to stay.[20] Given the various expressions of Christianity that

---

[17]Ibid., p. 9.

[18]Ibn Hisham, *Sira* (Cairo ed. 1937), 1.343; cited in J. Spencer Trimingham, *Islam in Ethiopia* (London: Oxford University Press, 1952), p. 44.

[19]Trimingham, *Islam in Ethiopia,* p. 44.

[20]Ibid., p. 45.

thrived in Hamitic Africa, it is not hard to see how Negus As'hama would have been persuaded by Jafar's arguments. After all, the fact that the Yemenite Christians subscribed to a version of Christianity contrary to Monophysitism did not stop his ancestor, Negus Elesbaan, from coming to their rescue when they were undergoing Jewish persecution. While it may seem to some that Jafar deliberately distorted the facts in order to protect the refugees, it could be equally true that he gave a sincere account of incipient Islam. This is further buttressed by the reality that when Muhammad rose to prominence in Mecca and arranged for the exiles to return to Arabia, many of them decided to stay, having adopted the Axumite brand of Christianity.[21]

As'hamah's kindness towards the Muhammadan refugees would reap future dividends for Axum. In gratitude for the king's benevolence, Muhammad decreed that Axum should be spared conquest—unless they attacked first. Given the tendency of the populations in Islamic states to eventually embrace the religion of Muhammad, this decree greatly aided in the preservation of Ethiopian Christianity. This is not to say that there were not attempts to convert the nation; Muhammad himself tried to convert the Negus to his understanding of Scripture. However, having resisted the pressures of the Chalcedonians for centuries, there was no reason for the Axumites to forsake their understanding of biblical religion for a theology that was still in process.

Throughout the centuries Axum exhibited an exemplary fidelity to Christianity while its neighbors became increasingly susceptible to the extrabiblical teachings of Islam. Muslim scholars warn against painting a picture of Abyssinia as an idyllic Christian island surrounded by a sea of Islamic infidels, and they correctly point out that in spite of the official state religion, Islam still thrived in this land of Monophysite orthodoxy.[22] However, this does not negate the fact that even as the seeds of Islam found fertile ground in other areas of Hamitic Africa, the land the emperor Ezana had led to Christianity maintained its biblical roots. By the tenth century, Axum had evaporated into the Abyssinian kingdom, but Christianity remained dominant. Sadly, in some areas of practice Abyssinian Christianity had followed its western siblings in ac-

---

[21]Working under the assumption that Islam was a developed faith at this time, Trimingham suggests that they were "the first converts from Islam to Christianity" (ibid., p. 45). See also Ulrich Braukämper, *Islamic History and Culture in Southern Ethiopia: Collected Essays* (Münster: Lit Verlag, 2004), p. 4.

[22]See Lidwien Kapteijns, "Ethiopia and the Horn of Africa," in *The History of Islam in Africa*, ed. Nehemia Letzvion and Randall L. Powels (Athens: Ohio University Press, 2002), p 227.

commodating itself to pagan rituals.[23] Nonetheless, on the main it had remained loyal to its understanding of biblical doctrines and had preserved its
unique Hebraic identity.[24] Undaunted by the Islamic expansion, the Abyssinian Christians maintained cordial relations with their Muslim neighbors and
subjects[25] as they did their part in recruiting entire people groups to their understanding of the biblical revelation.[26]

The treaty Muhammad made with Axum did not apply to its Nubian
neighbors. In a rabid effort to increase the territory of *dar al-Islam*, within
twelve years of the Prophet's death, the religion of Muhammad had established dominance in Arabia, Syria and Egypt. Fortified by a sense of impregnability after toppling Egypt in 641, the battle-hardened army set their
sights on Nubian Makuria in 652. By this time, Nobatia, the second of the
three Nubian kingdoms, had merged with Makuria. The Makurian army
proved themselves worthy opponents and soundly defeated the Islamic invaders.[27] Following the victory, the two sides agreed to a treaty in which Nubia would supply four hundred slaves to Muslim Egypt each year in exchange for goods.[28] Although this move guaranteed Nubia's security for a
number of centuries, it betrayed the true condition of a government that
professed allegiance to the Word of God but was more concerned with tem-
poral security.

During the period in which the treaty was in force, both Makurian and Alwan Nubia experienced a golden age of Christianity. Influenced by their Byzantium counterparts, the bishops in the region engaged in an ambitious
church-building spree. These churches were decorated with portraits of bibli-

---

[23]See Edward Ullendorff, *The Ethiopians: An Introduction to Country and People*, 4th ed. (Kingston, Jamaica: Headstart Printing and Publishing, 1998), p. 59.

[24]For a discussion on the nature of Abyssinian Christianity, see Trimingham, *Islam in Ethiopia*, pp. 49-
55.

[25]Seyyed Hossein Nasr, *Islam: Religion, History, and Civilization* (New York: HarperSanFrancisco,
2003), p. 141, informs us that Muslim kingdoms along the horn of Africa often paid tribute to the
Christian Ethiopian emperors.

[26]On the continued growth of Christianity under the Abyssinians, see Christine Chaillot, *The Ethiopian Orthodox Tewahedo Church Tradition: A Brief Introduction to Its Life and Spirituality* (Paris: Inter-
Orthodox Dialogue, 2002), p. 19: "Gradual Christian settlement began in Amhara (Wollo) from the
10th century, and in Shoa from the 13th century. Christianity spread to the parts south of the Amhara kingdom between the end of the 13th and the end of the 15th centuries. In the 14th and 15th
centuries the kingdom expanded, especially under King Amde Tseyon (1314-44)."

[27]Jay Spaulding, "Precolonial Islam in the Eastern Sudan," in *The History of Islam in Africa*, ed. Nehemia Letzvion and Randall L. Powels (Athens: Ohio University Press, 2002), p. 117.

[28]Shaw, *Kingdom of God in Africa*, p. 93.

cal scenes. Perhaps as a testimony to their continued resistance to Islamic pressure, practically all the Nubian churches include the theme of the three Hebrew captives whom Nebuchadnezaar had thrown in the fiery furnace when they refused to bow to the graven image.[29] This period in Nubian history also saw the elevation of the Nubian kings who were endowed with ecclesiastical authority and had the permission to serve as priests.[30] Although possessing this divine right, they were still subject to the bishops who could impeach them for abusing their power. Whether out of fashion or conviction, upon reaching old age a number of Nubian kings abdicated the throne and joined monasteries.

Nubia's ability to resist started to wane toward the end of the twelfth century when the Mamluk Turks began to rule in Egypt. By this time, the Crusades had started and the theological differences between Islam and Christianity were more pronounced. Nubian sovereignty came to an end in 1272, and the Mamluks installed a Nubian convert to Islam to the throne in 1315. Even before the conquest, a significant number of Muslims from Egypt and the mineral mines of Beja had settled in the area. By the end of the fourteenth century, the Christian presence in Makuria seems to have disintegrated.[31] The Nubian kingdom of Alwa came under the *dar al-Islam* in 1504, after which Christianity declined so drastically that by 1524 no Christian priests could be found in the entire diocese![32] So extensive was the disintegration of Christianity in the region that one Muslim historian exaggerates that Nubia had become "completely Islamic."[33]

IDENTITY AND INDEPENDENCE IN CANAAN

When Islam was first introduced to the body of nations that stemmed from Canaan, some historians assume that significant sectors of the region were "completely Christian."[34] It is probably more accurate to state that Christians formed a majority, and as in other parts of the Christian world, there would

---

[29]Ibid., p. 95.
[30]Ibid., p. 94.
[31]Ibid., p. 96.
[32]Ibid.
[33]Nasr, *Islam*, p. 140. Shaw, *Kingdom of God in Africa*, pp. 96-98, suggests that Nubia's failure to maintain a Christian identity was largely due to internal problems.
[34]Moshe Gil, *A History of Palestine, 634-1099*, trans. Ethel Broido (Cambridge: Cambridge University Press, 1992), p. 435, writes: "In 638, at the time of the Muslim conquest, Jerusalem was entirely a city of Christendom, and all its inhabitants were Christians."

have been a significant Jewish minority.[35] Chalcedonian Christianity dominated the region, although there was a Monophysite presence in Syria.[36] The
religious landscape was to change when 'Umar, the second caliph after Muhammad's death, conquered Damascus in 636 and Jerusalem in 637. The
120,000-strong Byzantine army tried to stave of the assault on Damascus, but
the 40,000 Muslim warriors did not see losing as an option. Likewise, after a
long siege, the citizens of Jerusalem decided to surrender to their southeastern
neighbors. This was a severe blow to the Palestinian Christians who had just
emerged from fourteen years of occupation under the Persian Sasanians (614-
628). However, they must have reasoned that occupation by forces that acknowledged sacred scriptures was a better option than being under the pagan
Zoroastrians from Persia. As far as they were concerned, the Arab forces were
just another Christian sect with some extreme views.

The Islam that was brought to Palestine was much different than the one
of later centuries. The official history of Islam makes it seem as if Muhammad
left an organized religion to continue his legacy. However, this is far from the
truth. As with any movement experiencing rapid growth, it was not until Islam caught up with itself that it began to take the shape of an organized religion. Like Christianity in its fledgling days, early Islam consisted of several independent communities known as *al-mu'minūn* (the faithful), each with its
own *amir* (chief). Moshe Sharon writes, "At this early stage, namely during
the first half of the seventh century, the term *Islam* did not yet denote a common defined faith for these *al-mu'minūn* communities. They derived their
initial monotheistic inspiration from the Prophet (or perhaps from more than
one Prophet), but under the influence of Jewish, Christian and classical envi-
ronments that developed along separate lines."[37]

It was in Palestine that Islam began to forge its own religious identity. The
seat of power had been transferred from Medina to Damascus after a series of
confrontations involving Ali bin Abi Talib, the fourth caliph to succeed Muhammad, and Muawiyah, a relative of the third caliph, Uthmar. Muawiyah
emerged as the first caliph of the Ummayad Dynasty (661-750), and contin-

---

[35]Robert Schick, *The Christian Communities of Palestine from Byzantine to Islamic Rule* (Princeton, N.J.:
    Darwin Press, 1995), p. 12, suggests that at the time of the Islamic conquest there were several mil-
    lion Christians in Palestine, and about 10-15 percent of the population were Jews.
[36]See ibid., pp. 10-11.
[37]Moshe Sharon, "The Birth of Islam in the Holy Land," in *The Holy Land in History and Thought,* ed.
    Moshe Sharon (Leiden: Brill, 1988), p. 227.

ued the work of expanding the *dar al-Islam*. During the period of expansion, the Muslim rulers were preoccupied with political power and had still not developed a complete theological identity that fully distinguished them from Christianity and Judaism. In many ways, the adherents were like the early Christians who took decades to sever ties with their Jewish parents and continued to worship in the temple and local synagogues. So comfortable were they in their relationships with Christians that the *mu'minūn* communities in Syria were engaged in a debate about the nature of Christ with the official church,[38] and some even worshiped in the same buildings as Christians.[39] As far as the followers of Muhammad were concerned, they worshiped the same God and revered the same Bible. In fact, they saw themselves as the true faithful who embraced the simple religion of Abraham and acknowledged all of God's messengers—including Muhammad.

After several decades, it became evident to the *mu'minūn* in Hamitic Canaan that they were not going to persuade the official church with their understanding of Scripture and God's revelation. They may also have experienced inner conflict as they became more familiar with the Christian canon and noticed that it was not in full harmony with the teachings of Muhammad to which they were being increasingly exposed in its oral form.[40] The official break came in 691 when Caliph 'Abd al-Malik (685-705) constructed the Dome on the Rock which had both political and religious purposes. Politically, his intent was to attract pilgrims away from Mecca. The religious purpose of the dome was spelled out on an inscription that established the three basic tenets of the new religion: (1) the acceptance of all God's prophets and their revelations, (2) the rejection of the divine sonship of Jesus (along with an affirmation that he possessed the Holy Spirit), and (3) the acceptance of Muhammad as the most important prophet and *Islam* as the name of the true re-

---

[38]Ibid., p. 228.

[39]Sharon (Ibid.) reveals: "Accepting the historical seniority of the Jewish and Christian revelations, the *mu'minūn* of Syria shared with the Jews and Christians not only their prophets and saints, but also their places of worship. Whichever way one looks at it, the fact is that *mu'minūn* and Christians shared the Cathedral of St. John in Damascus, and in all probability many other Christian houses of worship too." Courbage and Fargues, *Christians and Jews,* pp. 10-11, also inform us of a joint community at Homs, and report of the continued practice until the Crusades.

[40]Peter von Sivers, "Egypt and North Africa," in *The History of Islam in Africa,* ed. Nehemia Letzvion and Randall L. Powels (Athens: Ohio University Press, 2002), p. 22, reasons: "It appears that it was the still unsettled question of a Christian orthodoxy for the Byzantine Empire that inspired the rulers of the new Arab empire to search for their own, independent, religion."

ligion.[41] Although Christians have maintained a continuous—and ofttimes influential—presence in lands springing from Canaan until the present day,[42] under the name *Islam* the fragmented *mu'minūn* communities would finally forge their independent identity.

ACCOMMODATION AND ASSIMILATION IN HAMITIC EGYPT

When the armies of Muhammad invaded the Coptic lands of Hamitic Egypt, they found a nation embroiled in conflict with the Byzantine church. As far as Byzantium was concerned, the Coptic Monophysites were heretics who needed a strong hand to guide them to the "correct" understanding of Scripture. In order to contain them, they had appointed the Chalcedonian-minded Cyrus as patriarch and prefect over these rebellious wards. This imposition of a compliant leader did not change the thinking of the masses, and when the Arabian empire-builders arrived on Coptic territory, the natives offered little resistance. They had probably heard about this new aberration of biblical faith and figured it was just another sect in rebellion against the dominance of Byzantium.[43] It was only in Alexandria—the seat of Cyrus—that the invaders faced a challenge, and this was short-lived when the petrified patriarch surrendered after a brief struggle.

Inclusion in *dar al-Islam* had more political ramifications than religious ones. Unlike the intolerant patriarchs of Byzantine, the ambassadors of Muhammad did not mandate that their Christian and Jewish subjects embrace their version of truth. As far as they were concerned, they were all worshipers of the one true God in the great Abrahamic tradition. This is not to say that they believed the earlier revelations to be equal to Islam, but they allowed people to convert at their own pace. Some Copts did convert quickly, but the majority held on to their faith for some time. These were a resilient people who had suffered under the oppressive occupation of the Byzantines yet still refused to subscribe to the Chalcedonian creed. With such a history of courageous resistance, it is hard to imagine that they would have quickly relinquished their convictions as soon as the Arab forces came to town.[44]

---

[41]Sharon, "Birth of Islam," p. 229. See also von Sivers, "Egypt and North Africa," p. 22.

[42]Courbage and Fargues, *Christians and Jews,* pp. 13-14.

[43]Elizabeth Isichei, *A History of Christianity in Africa* (Grand Rapids: Eerdmans; Lawrenceville, N.J.: Africa World Press, 1995), p. 43, writes, "It was not clear at the time that Islam was a new religion; the 'Ishmaelites' were initially widely regarded as a Christian sect."

[44]See Courbage and Fargues, *Christians and Jews,* p. 15.

Under the Arabs, the Monophysite church regained its prominence and the champions of Chalcedon were forced to relinquish their grip. This left the environment open for religious freedom among the "people of the book." Judaism had been eclipsed by Christianity, which had drawn the allegiance of the vast majority. From all appearances, it would seem as if this institutional faith with its theological documents and well-defined management structure would have remained impregnable. However, the religion of Muhammad quickly became a worthy rival. Granted, there were some things that worked in its favor; the first of which was the tax levied on non-Muslims. For people who didn't really care to split hairs about intricate theological concepts, transferal to the new biblical interpretation espoused by the Arabian prophet only made sound financial sense.[45] In addition to the financial incentive, the formalization of Arabic as the official language of Egypt in 708 aided the promotion of Arab culture and consequently Arab faith. At one point, conversions to Islam were occurring so rapidly that the Muslim authorities had to encourage the Copts to maintain their loyalty to the church.[46] This decision may have been driven by economic expedience, but it also betrays Muslim acknowledgment of its religious roots. In fact, Christians worked side by side with Muslims on every level of public and political life. In this accommodating environment, it is no wonder that Christianity maintained its majority until the tenth century.[47] Nonetheless, by the time of the Crusades, the balance had shifted in favor of Islam and Christians became an increasingly distinct minority.

After their conquest of Egypt, the Arab invaders set their sights on her daughter kingdoms to the west, which they collectively termed *Bilad al-Mahgrib* ("Land of Sunset"). This was the North African territory that had nurtured Tertullian, Cyprian and Augustine, and was inhabited by the native Berbers and the descendants of Roman citizens. According to some estimates, of the two million inhabitants of North Africa at the time of the Islamic invasion, 1.5 million professed Christianity and 20,000 adhered to Judaism.[48] As in other parts of the Christian world, several interpretations of the Christian faith coexisted in North Africa. Most were loyal to the Donatist version of the Christian faith, which was the preferred religion of the Berbers who formed

---

[45]For discussion see ibid., pp. 22-25.
[46]See ibid., p. 16.
[47]Isichei, *A History of Christianity*, p. 43.
[48]Courbage and Fargues, *Christians and Jews*, p. 32.

the majority. These fiercely independent believers had successfully resisted the Arian onslaught of the Germanic Vandals, and had held strong against domination by Christian Rome—even when facing the threat of Emperor Justinian's sword.[49] These defiant patriots put up a stiffer resistance than their eastern parent, and it took the Arab armies from 670 to 705 to claim the North African provinces as subjects of *dar al-Islam*.

Apparently, Jews and Christians had joined forces in trying to ward off their rebellious offspring, and both traditions claim the feisty female Berber general, known simply by al-Kahina, "the prophetess."[50] Her clan appears to have been among the first to submit to the demands of Islam and had converted when they realized that resistance was futile. Following al-Kahina's surrender, Berber assimilation into Islam continued at a steady pace. Ironically, their absorption was a direct result of their desire to maintain independence. Unlike the intolerant Christian hierarchs from Rome and Byzantium, the Muslim power did not try to enforce a litany of creeds upon them, neither did they attempt to appoint religious leaders who reflected their political ideals. All the Berbers had to do was give lip service to Islam, and they would be free to follow their understanding of biblical faith according to the dictates of their own conscience.[51] Operating under the rubric of the new faith, the Berbers' unique Donatist identity soon disappeared. As Arab historian Abdullah Laraoui noted, "Developed away from all contact with the church, African Christianity slowly assumed the form of an abstract monotheism able to be satisfied with any dogma."[52]

Berber assimilation into Islam was also aided by the missionary efforts of the Kharijites. The Kharijites were a Muslim sect that had sided with the Shiites against the Sunnis in opposing the legitimacy of the Ummayad Dynasty in favor of a caliphate in the line of Ali.[53] A conservative movement, the Kharijites stressed the need for personal holiness which would have immediately endeared them to the pious Donatists in North Africa. Their zeal to enforce

---

[49]Ibid., p. 31.

[50]Isichei, *A History of Christianity*, p. 43.

[51]Courbage and Fargues, *Christians and Jews*, p. 34, surmise: "Hoping to free themselves from distant masters, first Rome, then Byzantium, the [Berber] tribes undoubtedly understood that Islam would preserve their autonomy and that a simple conversion would be sufficient for them to be accepted by the conquerors."

[52]Quoted in Courbage and Fargues, *Christians and Jews*, p. 32.

[53]Shaw, *Kingdom of God in Africa*, p. 77.

the religion of Muhammad was also aided by the fact that Islam was becoming a written religion,[54] which meant that their unique interpretations and embellishments of the Bible could continue to influence communities long after they had left.

As in other parts of the Arab world, the opportunity for tax relief and the opportunity to participate in all levels of civic life also provided incentives for North African Christians to convert to Islam.[55] The growing Muslim population was further aided by the intermarriage of Arab soldiers with native women, whose children—by law—were automatically expected to follow Islam. Although the religious demographics were slowly shifting, the three descendants of Abrahamic faith coexisted rather peacefully until the Crusades, at which time relationships became greatly strained. Although Christians under *dar al-Islam* were probably more sympathetic to their governments than the invading European armies, the fact that they shared the faith of the invaders did not help their survival. For example, after the Norman conquest of Sicily, Berber Christians were the objects of genocide.[56] The slaughter was so devastating that some believe that Christianity had almost disappeared from North Africa by the eleventh century.[57] While this view is probably exaggerated,[58] the new climate of suspicion resulted in mass conversions for the sake of survival. While Christians flocked to the faith of their rebellious daughter, their Jewish parent—though an apparently insignificant minority—managed to survive until recent decades.

TOTAL ECLIPSE: CONCLUSION

Had it not been for the Bible, it is hardly likely that Islam would have been so successful in captivating such a significant area of the land of Ham. In just a few short centuries, the Bible had gone through several changes with the people in the three regions of biblical Ham that have so far dominated this study. Initially, the majority had been isolated from the "Jewish" Bible which was viewed as the exclusive property of the descendants of Israel. With the expan-

---

[54]Ibid., pp. 77-78.
[55]Courbage and Fargues, *Christians and Jews*, p. 35.
[56]Ibid., p. 40.
[57]Isichei, *A History of Christianity*, p. 45.
[58]Shaw, *Kingdom of God in Africa*, p. 81, attests to the existence of Christian communities as late as the eighteenth century. Also, there were many Christian captives in North Africa during the Ottoman period.

sion of the "Christian" Bible following the advent of Messiah, the people of Ham enthusiastically embraced the message of hope as the sacred pages became a part of their reality. However, the priority of the Bible to Hamitic African faith would soon be replaced by other systems. In part three, we saw how this began with the philosophizing of the faith that resulted in a fragmented Christianity characterized by partisan creeds and warring clergy. Here in part four, in the previous chapter, we saw how the emphasis on heady theology over the less-controversial teachings of Scripture left the uneducated masses in a state of confusion and gullibility. Indeed, it was this environment that provided the fertile soil in which Islam would eventually flourish.

This chapter dispelled the myth that credits Islam's success to military conquests. This seems to be wishful thinking on the part of apologists who just can't imagine faithful Christians voluntarily switching allegiances to a new faith. This is not to say that there weren't cases where people were forced to convert. However, if we accept that Islam initially paraded itself as a Christian sect, it is not hard to see how the masses would have embraced a "heresy" that boasted the protection of a seemingly invincible army. The efforts of Muslim missionaries were further aided by the content of Muhammad's teaching that was primarily derived from the Bible. When those under *dar al-Islam* discovered their conquerors' reverence for Abraham, Noah, John and Jesus, their interest was naturally piqued. Further, the fact that they were allowed the freedom to worship God according to the dictates of their own conscience, and not in the mold of heavy theological creeds, enhanced Islam's attractiveness to a people seeking a less cumbersome way to practice their faith. All these factors contributed to the deception of Ham, and slowly but surely, a significant number of Christians in Hamitic Ethiopia, Egypt and Canaan would transfer their allegiance to a new faith. Although Abyssinia remained a Christian bedrock and the Copts maintained their independence, the biblical faith that had been nurtured in Africa would find a new identity in Christian Europe. Here it would don the garb of cultural imperialism that would eventually be used to launch an assault against the very parent that had given it birth.

PART FIVE

HOSTILE TAKEOVER

Europe's Manipulation of the Biblical Message

Do not gaze on me because I am dark,

because the sun has gazed on me.

SONG OF SOLOMON 1:6

After centuries of internal turmoil in the regions associated with the sons of Ham, Christianity had given way to Islam and the Bible was eclipsed by the Qur'an. It did not take long for the spiritual descendants of Augustine, Origen, Tertullian and Athanasius to forsake the faith of their fathers. The church in the West was experiencing its own struggles, but she did not appear to be too concerned about the conquest of her siblings in Orthodox Africa. After all, they promoted a different brand of Christianity and they did not recognize the authority of Rome.

The situation was to change when it became obvious that the Muslims were not content with their kingdom. They had already made inroads into southern Europe and desired to extend the territory of *dar al-Islam*. Like the ambitious Roman Empire in its heyday, they longed for the day when they could inscribe *orbis terranum* on their maritime maps. Not satisfied with the present borders, the Muslim imperialists sought to topple the Byzantine Empire—a move that would have firmly established them on European soil. This was hard for Christian Europe to ignore. If left unchallenged, the entire landscape of Western civilization would be altered.

Coupled with the very real threat of conquest was the idolatrous adulation for the places associated with holy writ. As long as the Muslim infidels maintained control of Palestine, Christians would be at their mercy during pilgrimages. The only solution appeared to be the total reclamation of the so-called Holy Land, which was the official rationale for the Crusades. Although unsuccessful, the Crusades appear to have whet Europe's appetite for the region, and soon vast armies were foraging into the lands descended from Misrayim, Cush and Put in a bid to absorb them into Europe. The imperial intentions became most clear in the dealings with the sons of Put who occupied much of sub-Saharan Africa. Armed with the Bible in one hand and a gun in the other, the wily invader sought to impose a version of Christianity that had no precedent in the Bible. With the full endorsement of the papal authorities, Europe assumed the role of a renewed Israel that had just received a divine command to capture the Promised Land from the cursed sons of Ham.

13

THE EUROPEAN CRUSADE
AGAINST ISLAM

The assault against Ham began with two centuries of European attacks against the lands that stemmed from Canaan. At the dawn of the twelfth century, the region appeared to be an unshakeable part of *dar al-Islam*. While Muslims formed the majority, they continued their policy of extending religious tolerance to the large populations of Christians and smaller groups of Jews. Christian places of worship were everywhere, and there was even a degree of freedom of expression that allowed the faiths to engage in verbal jousting.[1] This is not to say that relationships between the three Abrahamic faiths were excellent. Christian clerics, in particular, could not get used to the idea of an aberrant religion setting a political and cultural environment that made them feel like the Jews under the Roman Empire. They especially disliked the fact that although they were granted custody over the Christian shrines, ultimate control resided in the hands of their Muslim rulers who were not always consistent in their tolerance.[2] Their lack of autonomy was especially embarrassing for the many European pilgrims who viewed Jerusalem as the "Mecca" of Christianity and could not understand why the sacred lands of the Bible were being controlled by the people of the Qur'an. A pilgrimage that was supposed to be the pinnacle of their religious experience became cause for concern as they returned to their lands and appealed to their Christian kings to liberate the city of the Holy Sepulcher.

---

[1]See Ronald C. Funucane, *Soldiers of the Faith: Crusaders and Moslems at War* (New York: St. Martin's, 1983), pp. 147-57.

[2]Will Durant, *The Age of Faith: A History of Medieval Civilization—Christian, Islamic, and Judaic—from Constantine to Dante: A.D. 325-1300* (New York: Simon & Schuster, 1950), p. 585, mentions Al-Hakim, the "mad caliph of Cairo" who destroyed the Church of the Holy Sepulcher in 1010. However, it was Muslims in turn who helped to finance its restoration.

Even as the Christians residing under *dar al-Islam* were adjusting to their second-class status, those in Byzantium to the west were experiencing the scourge of the Muhammadan threat. The students of the Qur'an appeared to be growing invincible, and the Byzantine Emperor Alexius became concerned about his ability to protect the Christian lands under his jurisdiction. His fears heightened with the emergence of the Seljuk Turks who had grappled control of Jerusalem from the Fatamids in 1070. Within fifteen years they had annexed Antioch, and it was only a matter of time before they consumed other portions of the imperiled Byzantine Empire. Out of desperation, Alexius called for assistance from his enemies in Roman Catholic Europe, appealing to their common allegiance to the crucified Messiah. Emperor Alexius did not have to appeal for long. Already alerted by perturbed pilgrims, the leaders of Europe had long been watching the situation and knew that Islam had to be stopped. The Muslims had already become entrenched in the southern regions of Spain, and they could not afford to be hemmed in any further by these infidels.

Unknown to the desperate Byzantine emperor, Europe's offer of assistance was not as innocent as it seemed. He simply wanted reprieve from his enemies and the assurance of knowing that Christians could put aside differences and come to each others' aid in time of need. However, they had their sights set on expanding the realm of Roman Europe to the lands of the Bible located in Hamitic Canaan.[3] Conquest of these new lands would also open ports for Italian merchants who sought to globalize their markets. Armed with their own imperialist agenda, the armies of Europe would launch nine crusades against the dwellers of Palestine over a period of two centuries. Derived from the Spanish *cruzad* meaning "marked with the cross,"[4] the term *crusade* originally signified the cloth crosses sown on the garments of those who responded to the call to Christian jihad. As we will see, these wearers of the cross were unfamiliar with the biblical teachings of the one who hung on the cross, and rather than bring glory to the prince of peace, the crusaders would inflict irreparable damage to the body of Christ that has marred the church to this very day.

---

[3]For a discussion on the "motive" and "objective" for the First Crusade, see Carl Erdmann, *The Origin of the Idea of Crusade,* trans. Marshall W. Baldwin and Walter Goffart (Princeton, N.J.: Princeton University Press, 1977), pp. 355-71.

[4]Portuguese = *cruzada;* French = *croisade;* Italian = *crociata.*

THE FIRST CRUSADE

The first call to crusade came from Pope Urban II on November 27, 1095, at the Council of Clermont in France. The words with which he inspired his anxious audience set the tone for centuries of aggression against the land of Ham. With rhetoric befitting Moses himself, the pious pope transformed the European masses into the resurrected Israel: "Enter upon the road to the Holy Sepulcher; wrest that land from a wicked race, and subject it to yourselves. Jerusalem is a land fruitful above all others, a paradise of delights. That royal city, situated at the center of the earth, implores you to come to her aid. Undertake this journey eagerly for the remission of your sins, and be assured of the reward of imperishable glory in the Kingdom of Heaven."[5] This became a part of his stump speech as he traveled to other cities rallying the masses with promises of liberation for the serfs and economic protection for the lords.

Led by impromptu generals with telling names like Walter the Penniless and Peter the Hermit, tens of thousands responded to the call, and the First Crusade was launched (1095-1099).[6] Ill prepared, many died on the way, and the army that bore the cross soon took on the identity of wandering marauders as the desperate volunteers looted, pillaged and raped their way to Hamitic Canaan. Those who made it to Byzantium were cautiously received in Constantinople by Alexius who had been warned about some of the generals who wished to append the conquest of his empire to their task list. The lavish architecture and superior standard of living attracted the envy of those who had heretofore been accustomed to the primitive and practical European landscape. Alexius managed to keep them on track, and joined the command as they ventured into Nicaea—the hallowed city of Orthodox Christianity—and recaptured it for Byzantium.

The unified army then set out for Antioch, the coastal city in which the followers of Jesus were first called Christians. This was another Christian "holy" place that the Muslims had captured from Byzantium in 1085. Antioch provided a bigger challenge to the European army, which was forced into a prolonged siege of the city. During the eight months of besiegement the fidelity of the soldiers was tested to the utmost as they braved the elements of a harsh winter and remained alert just in case an army from one of the many Muslim

---

[5]Quoted in Durant, *Age of Faith*, p. 587.
[6]For an eyewitness account of the First Crusade, see Fulcher of Chartres, *A History of the Expedition to Jerusalem: 1095-1127*, trans. Frances Rita Ryan (Knoxville: University of Tennessee Press, 1969).

lands would come to the rescue of the Antiochenes. Their fears became reality in 1098 when Prince Karbogha of Mosul assembled a large army and set out to stave off the invaders.

When the crusaders received news that the Muslims had sent back-up forces to assist their endangered brethren, some of them felt defeated and decided to return home. On their return to Europe, they encountered Alexius and informed him that the Christian army in Antioch had experienced defeat. With no reason to doubt the deserters' story, the emperor of the East returned to Constantinople. Meanwhile, the faithful remnant who maintained the siege against Antioch felt that their host had let them down, and fear began to possess the hearts of these soldiers of fortune. The dark cloud was broken with shouts of joy when Peter Bartholomew, a French priest, claimed to have discovered the spear that pierced the side of Jesus.[7] Rejuvenated by this "divine" sign, the gullible faithful launched a successful assault against Antioch and claimed it for Europe.

In 1099, the refreshed army arrived at the gates of the final and finest trophy of the Crusade: the *holy* city of Jerusalem. Still hypnotized by the spell placed upon them by Urban II, the largely Italian and French army acted as if they were under the orders of Joshua as they went through the city slaughtering every man, woman and child. It mattered not whether the victim was Muslim, Jew or Orthodox Christian—all Jerusalemites comprised the enemy on this dreadful day. These dwellers of Muslim Palestine had been transformed into medieval Philistines, and as such were worthy of death. As if involved in a live reenactment from the pages of Scripture itself, the European warlords went forth with unrighteous indignation. Then after they had completed their bloody massacre, they entered the Church of the Holy Sepulcher, where they sang hymns of praise and offered prayers to their *god.*

For the next two hundred years, Palestine fell under the jurisdiction of the Papal See. After 465 years of Hamitic rule under Islam, Canaan would once again be subjected to his uncle's progeny as the tribes of Japheth set up house in the dwelling place that God had promised to the sons of Shem (cf. Gen 9:27). The newly formed Kingdom of Jerusalem was divided into four administrative sections: the Kingdom of Jerusalem, the County of Tripoli, the County of Edessa and the Principality of Antioch. The new rulers did not possess authority over all the land that comprised Syria and Palestine. Muslims

---

[7]For full account see ibid., pp. 99-101.

still controlled Aleppo, Damascus and Emesa; and Venice, Pisa and Genoa commandeered the port cities of Jaffa, Tyre, Acre, Beirut and Ascalon.[8] Notwithstanding, the limited authority they did possess was exercised with an iron hand. All former landowners—whether Muslim, Christian or Jew—were reduced to serfhood. The situation was so oppressive that "the native Christian population looked back to Muslim rule as a golden age."[9]

The majority of crusaders felt as if they had accomplished their purpose after the conquest of Jerusalem, and they returned to Europe. Those who stayed imagined themselves to be the new Israel as they conflated the teachings of the Old and New Testaments to justify their marriage of piety to violence. Among the settlers were two prominent orders of monks commonly known as the Hospitaliers and the Knights Templars.[10] The Hospitaliers had established a base in Jerusalem half a century before the commencement of the Crusades and had devoted themselves to medical and charitable works. With the changing politics in the region, their duties changed when in 1120 Raymond du Pay amended their job description to include the military protection of Palestinian Christians. Operating as a military brigade, whose full title was the Knights of the Hospital of St. John, the Hospitaliers donned black robes with white crosses on the left sleeve and became as proficient in the art of warfare as they were in deeds of charity.

The zeal of the Hospitaliers was rivaled by the Knights Templars, who distinguished themselves from the competition by wearing a white robe with a red cross on the mantle. New to Palestine, the Templars had been founded by Hugh de Payens in 1119, and resided in close proximity to Solomon's temple. These celibate soldiers of Rome took their task seriously as they defended the honor of the church with their martial arts and sophisticated weaponry. Unfortunately, their alienation from the biblical Messiah is evident in the words of their patron, Bernard of Clairvaux, who coaxed them on with the charge, "The Christian glories in the death of the pagan, because Christ is thereby glorified."[11]

---

[8] Durant, *Age of Faith*, p. 592.

[9] Ibid., p. 593.

[10] For discussion see Alan Forey, "The Military Orders: 1120-1312," in *The Oxford Illustrated History of the Crusades*, ed. Jonathan Riley Smith (Oxford: Oxford University Press, 1995), pp. 185-200.

[11] Quoted in Durant, *Age of Faith*, p. 593. For a concise discussion on St. Bernard's intricate relationship with the Templars, see Marie Luise Bulst-Thiele, "The Influence of St. Bernard of Clarivaux on the Formation of the Order of the Knights Templar," in *The Second Crusade and the Cistercians*, ed. Michael Gervers (New York: St. Martin's Press, 1992), pp. 57-65.

THE SECOND CRUSADE

While the remnant from the First Crusade settled in their millennial Kingdom
of Jerusalem, the stunned Muslims laid out a strategy to reclaim their land. Led
by Zangi, Prince of Mosul, the forces of Islam attacked from the north, and by
1144 the County of Adessa had reverted to Muslim hands. Sensing the beginning of the end of European rule in Palestine, Bernard of Clairvaux convinced
Pope Eugenius II to support the Second Crusade (1146-1148).[12] St. Bernard
quickly gained the support of King Louis VII of France and Emperor Conrad
III of Germany, and the masses were rallied to assault the forces of Islam. This
campaign was to prove disastrous, and the army suffered major losses before
they even reached the Promised Land. When Louis and Conrad finally
reached Jerusalem, only a handful of those who set out with them remained.
Still buoyed by the illusion of divine providence, they mustered an army from
among the fighting men in Jerusalem and sought to capture Damascus. Their
bravado was short lived when they learned that large Muslim armies from
Aleppo and Mosul were closing in on them. Sensing defeat, they chose to live
another day and sought safety in the closest Christian havens.[13]

It would be forty years before another Crusade would come to the land that
once housed Canaan. During this reprise, the Muslims had an opportunity to
regain more territory. In the regions that remained under the Kingdom of
Jerusalem, the European settlers had become more accustomed to the Muslim
majority and began to exercise the kind of tolerance that had been common of
their subjects under *dar al-Islam* before the tables had been turned. The European Christians slowly began to adopt Muslim culture, learning the Arabic
language and even marrying the women. In this period of relative peace, the
neighboring Islamic nations appeared content with leaving things as they
were. As far as they were concerned, in the past their faith had managed to
prevail in an environment that was predominantly Christian, and given time
it would prevail again.

---

[12]According to Hans-Dietrich Kahl, "Crusade Eschatology as Seen by St. Bernard in the Years 1146
to 1148," in *The Second Crusade and the Cistercians,* ed. Michael Gervers (New York: St. Martin's
Press, 1992), pp. 35-47, St. Bernard understood the Crusades to be the final eschatological show-
down between good and evil.

[13]For an analysis on the failure of the Second Crusade, see Martin Hoch, "The Price of Failure: The
Second Crusade as a Turning-point in the History of the Latin East," in *The Second Crusade: Scope
and Consequences,* ed. Jonathan Phillips and Martin Hoch (Manchester: Manchester University
Press, 2001), pp. 180-200.

Unfortunately, the antsy leaders of the Kingdom of Jerusalem were not sat-isfied with a peaceful coexistence. Brainwashed by intolerant clerics who were obviously unfamiliar with the gospel's message of peace, they were not pre-pared to rest until the followers of Muhammad were permanently put in their place. They repeatedly broke treaties with their Muslim counterparts and con-veyed an arrogant attitude of superiority. As they spurned Muslim offers of peace, they were continually embroiled in conflicts among themselves. So caught up were they in the jockeying for titles, positions and wealth that they did not realize that their Muslim neighbors were finding strength in unity. The Muslims would soon find a savior in the person of Saladin, a Kurd who had overseen the military conquest of Damascus and then merged it—and all other parts of Muslim-controlled Syria—into Egypt.[14] Having secured unity among his fellow believers, he sought regional stability by forming treaties with the Christian kings of Jerusalem. However, still drunk with arrogance, the Christian leaders continued to go back on their word, and things eventu-ally came to a head when Reginald of Châtillon led a band of soldiers to Mecca with the intention of demolishing the Caaba. An angry Egyptian army utterly defeated them and publicly executed a number of the zealot crusaders in Islam's holiest city. Reginald managed to escape and foolishly continued his impudent behavior, which ended when the long-suffering Saladin led his forces to a decisive victory over the seat of crusader power. By 1187, Jerusalem was once more under the jurisdiction of *dar al-Islam*.

THE THIRD CRUSADE

With European dominance diminishing in Hamitic Canaan, William, the Archbishop of Tyre, took a trip home to seek assistance in reversing the troubling trend in his adopted land. It did not take him long to convince the proud rulers of Europe to launch the Third Crusade (1187-1192).[15] This time it was the German Emperor Frederick Barbarossa—a veteran of the Second Crusade—who took the lead. Seizing the opportunity to prove their Christian piety, England's Richard the Lion Heart and France's Philip Au-

---

[14]For a summary of Saladin's ascent, see Hamilton A. R. Gibb, "The Rise of Saladin, 1169-1189," in Marshall W. Baldwin, ed. *A History of the Crusades*, vol. 1 (Madison: University of Wisconsin Press, 1969), pp. 563-89.

[15]For a concise synopsis of the Third Crusade, see Hans Eberhard Mayer, *The Crusades*, trans. John Gillingham, 2nd ed. (Oxford: Oxford University Press, 1988), pp. 137-51.

gustus joined their regal colleague. True to the script rehearsed in the first two Crusades, all armies suffered massive losses before embarking on Canaan's shore at the port of Acre. Philip had arrived first and held the city under siege for nineteen months before Richard's arrival in 1191. Richard joined Philip with an army reduced by shipwreck and the remnants of Frederick's troops, who—just a year earlier—had witnessed their monarch drown in a Cilician river. With the arrival of these anxious reinforcements, the besieged Muslims chose surrender over slaughter and ceded Acre once again to the wearers of the *crux*. After Saladin endorsed the agreement, Philip returned to France for medical treatment, leaving the English legend in command of what was left of the tri-state army.

Acre's conquest did not appease Richard; he had been bitten by the imperial bug and had set his sights on grander spoils. Undaunted by the decision of the German troops to return home and the lack of cooperation from the French, Richard added Arsuf and Darum to his military résumé before entering a truce with the beleaguered Saladin, who appeared to be losing the grip on his territories. In the predictable spirit of his Crusading predecessors, Richard took advantage of the dissent in Saladin's camp and turned his troops towards the grandest prize of all—Jerusalem. His plans were thwarted upon receiving news that Saladin had snatched Jaffa from under his nose. Refusing to accept such a public humiliation, the warrior king quickly changed direction and retrieved the city in lightning speed. This victory marked the final battle of a very strange Crusade which eventually ended in the halls of diplomacy. Before Richard left for England, Saladin agreed to European control of the sea ports and promised protection for Christian pilgrims to Jerusalem.

OTHER CRUSADES

With Jerusalem still in Muhammadan hands, the Christians of Europe continued to devise ways to permanently displace those who had usurped the Bible with the Qur'an. Incited by Pope Innocent III, an Italian army responded to the call for the Fourth Crusade (1202-1204).[16] Learning from the failures of the previous attempts to subjugate Hamitic Canaan, Pope Innocent suggested launching the attack from Egypt—which of course meant the initial conquest of Canaan's sibling. Fortunately for Egypt, the enterprising Italians

---

[16]See ibid., pp. 196-213.

were driven by their lust for the riches of Byzantine and, in blatant obstinance to Innocent, embarked on the tested route and were successful in subjugating Byzantium to Rome.

With the satisfaction of Europe's imperial ambitions, other Crusades were called. The depth of the religious deception around this time is seen in the attempted Children's Crusades of 1212.[17] Inspired independently by two young men, 30,000 youngsters from Germany and 20,000 from France responded to the call with cultic curiosity. Needless to say, many were displaced and others experienced death. The ones who came closest to the Promised Land were taken there by French merchants who sold them as slaves to North African Muslims. The children's tragedy did not dampen the Crusade craze, and Innocent III preached the Fifth Crusade in 1215. This time, the Germanic troops under Hungarian King Andrew followed his directions and successfully attacked the Egyptian city of Damietta.[18] Victory was short lived, and the invading army was forced to leave with nothing but the True Cross, the revered battle standard that Saladin had confiscated from Reginald in 1187.[19] Like the children before them, these troops never made it to Jerusalem.

These two failures were followed by the Sixth Crusade, which commenced in 1228 under the leadership of Frederick II, Emperor of Germany and Italy. Frederick had been excommunicated after failing to fulfill his promise to participate in the Fifth Crusade, and received little cooperation from other Christians. Interestingly however, he achieved more without lifting a sword than others who had shed the blood of countless innocents. Fortunately for him, Al Kamil—the leader of the Muslim army stationed at Nablus—was open to dialogue, and the two were able to look beyond the calls to holy war that could be justified by the manipulation of either of their sacred books and visioned the possibility of peace. Inculcating the pacifist teachings of Messiah, the two representatives of Islam and Christianity negotiated an agreement in 1229 that yielded several holy cities and practically all of Jerusalem to the Christians.[20] Prisoners were emancipated, and peace

---

[17]See ibid., pp. 214-16.
[18]On the crusade against Damietta, see ibid., pp. 216-27.
[19]Durant, *Age of Faith*, p. 597.
[20]Mayer, *The Crusades*, p. 236, writes, "The treaty meant that with a stroke of the pen Frederick II had achieved the objective sought for so long: Christian lordship over the Sepulchre of Christ, which all the military efforts of the years since 1187 had failed to attain."

reigned for a decade. Rather than celebrate the transformation of "spears into pruning hooks," however, the intolerant Pope Gregory IX refused to recognize the agreement, thus encouraging the militant Christian radicals to take Jerusalem on their own terms. After another example of abuse of power that typified European Christians on Hamitic soil, the Egyptian Sultan Baibars responded with violence, and by 1244 Jerusalem once more fell into the hands of Muhammad's spiritual heirs.

Still determined to claim biblical Africa for Europe, Louis IX of France recruited for the Seventh Crusade. In 1248 he led his armies into Egypt where they followed the plan of the Fifth Crusade and captured Damietta. Following a six-month hiatus in Damietta, they headed for Jerusalem, but were halted by a Muslim army in Mansura. In 1250, the defeated king was captured along with a number of his forces. He was treated kindly and nursed to health, but before he was released with the remnants of his army, he was forced to return Damietta and pay a ransom. The embarrassed Louis led his army to the Christian fortress at Acre where he stayed for four years before returning to France in 1254. Stubbornly clinging to his notion of divine appointment, King Louis preached the Eighth Crusade in 1267. This time he planned to attack Egypt from Tunisia before venturing to Jerusalem. He died before achieving the first phase of his plan. All crusading ambitions came to an end in 1291 when Sultan Khalil captured Acre and reclaimed the rest of Syria and Palestine for *dar al-Islam.*

Thanks to the Crusades, the Islam that emerged in Hamitic Canaan was more hostile to Christianity than the one the Europeans found. Bible and Qur'an were further separated as the roots of Muhammad's faith were severed by the negative witness of the Latin foreigners who lived the script of warring Israel in their attempt to purge the idolatrous Canaanites from the land of papal promise. Although eventual victors, the disciples of Islam had been raped and violated by a people who knew not what it meant to be merciful.[21] And the Muslims were not the only ones to learn from the experience; Orthodox Christians were forced to come to terms with the fact that they had more in common with their Muslim masters than their Catholic brethren. The biggest lesson was learned by the crusaders who had been defeated by a superior cul-

---

[21]According to Amin Maalouf, *The Crusades Through Arab Eyes,* trans. Jon Rothschild (New York: Schocken, 1985), p. 266, even in our modern age Muslims view the Crusades "as an act of rape."

ture.[22] However, this did not cause them to despair. On the contrary, it whetted the European taste for exotic adventure and expanding empire.[23] Their failed attempt to annex Canaan was just the beginning of a much more ambitious quest to control the larger part of the land of Ham.

---

[22]Maalouf suggests that the Crusades had a negative impact on Arab culture while positively affecting the culture of Europe (ibid., pp. 261-66).

[23]Aziz S. Atiya, *Crusade, Commerce and Culture* (Bloomington: Indiana University Press, 1962), p. 18, refers to economic historians who view the Crusades as "a form of colonialization and of medieval imperialism."

14

THE STRUGGLE FOR CONTROL IN
THE ETHIOPIAN CHURCH

Having failed in their attempt to create a European outpost in the Muslim lands of Palestine, the sons of Japheth now focused their energy on subduing other segments of Ham's progeny. They knew better than to turn on Egypt and North Africa where they had failed to get the Muhammadans to forsake their Qur'an and take up the Bible once more. Instead, they set their eyes on the territory of Cush, more specifically, Ethiopia, the mysterious abode of mythical Prester John—the Christian "priest-king" who had allegedly defended the faith against the Muslim apostates and pagan infidels[1] and had offered military help to Rome and Byzantium during the Crusades.[2] Nubian Christianity had been absorbed by Islam, and the heirs of Axum had managed to successfully defend the faith against those who had them edged in.

The version of Christianity the Europeans were to discover in Ethiopia was radically different from the one that had emerged in Europe. Through contact with the Alexandrian and Jerusalem patriarchs, they were probably aware that the Ethiopians had rejected Chalcedonian Christianity in favor of their own Monophysitism. They probably did not expect to find a version of Christianity that in many ways appeared to have just evolved from the earliest Christian communities that had rapidly spread throughout Judea. Although they had joined their Catholic counterparts in many aspects of religious syncretism, the Ethiopian Christians applied the Bible in a most literalistic way. In the tradition of those early Christians who fully identified with their Jewish roots, these sons of Cush adhered to the food laws, practiced circumcision, and ob-

---

[1]On the myths surrounding Prester John, see William Leo Hansberry, *Pillars in Ethiopian History,* ed. Joseph E. Harris (Washington, D.C.: Howard University Press, 1974), pp. 112-24.
[2]For a critical discussion on the authenticity of the alleged letter, see Ibid., pp. 115-24.

served the seventh-day sabbath.[3] Viewing the Ethiopians' interpretation of biblical faith as obviously primitive and heretical, for the next six centuries the Christian missionaries from the West would seek to fashion the Orthodox Church in the likeness of Rome.

INTERMITTENT INSURRECTION

While the European crusaders were ravaging Palestine, Ethiopia—which at this time was often referred to as Abyssinia—was faced with its own internal problems. Like many African empires, Ethiopia was actually comprised of a series of kingdoms, each with its own monarch. One of these kingdoms would often have prominence over the others, and the leader would bear the title "king of kings." The Axumite kingdom had maintained its preeminent position over Ethiopia from the first century B.C.E., and had remained unchallenged for at least a millennium. The kings of Axum had used their influence to persuade the other provinces to embrace Christianity, and a new national identity had been formed.

This is not to say that all Ethiopians welcomed the new faith. There were some tribes that preferred to remain loyal to ancestral traditions, and others—particularly among the coastal areas—did embrace Islam. There were also some who held on to the same Hebrew faith that had captured the hearts of many before Christianity was even born. It was probably in an attempt to restore the original faith that the Agaw peoples rebelled against the ruling dynasty in the tenth century.[4] The revolt was led by Judith[5] (Esat), the Queen of the Bani Hamuyah, who upon usurping the throne led a great persecution against Christians.[6] This period of discord provided an opportunity for the Muslims to successfully recruit among the abused and disenchanted. The church responded with diplomacy, and soon the formerly hostile Agaw were professing Christianity.

By the twelfth century, Agaw tribesmen had established the Zagwe Dynasty (1137-1270) and were the undisputed rulers of the Ethiopian empire. In

---

[3]See discussion in Aloys Grillmeier and Theresa Hainthaler, *Christ in Christian Tradition*, vol. 2.4 (Louisville, Ky.: Westminster John Knox, 1990), pp. 324-32.

[4]Some believe that these are the forerunners of the so-called *Falasha*.

[5]Wesley Curtwright, *The Hand of God in Ethiopia and Other Subjects* (New York: Vantage Press, 1974), p. 19, believes she was pagan.

[6]Edward Ullendorff, *The Ethiopians: An Introduction to Country and People*, 4th ed. (Kingston, Jamaica: Headstart Printing and Publishing, 1998), p. 58.

order to prove their legitimacy, the Zagwe contended to have roots even deeper than the Solomonic kings they replaced—they were descended from Moses and Zipporah![7] Although touting deep Hebrew roots, the Zagwe's embrace of the Ethiopian Orthodox faith led them to join in the efforts to restore Christianity throughout the land. A cultural revival was invoked, which led to the flourishing and refining of Ethiopic literature.[8] The most notable Zagwe king was Lalibala, the famed architect of the rock-hewn churches in Roha which later assumed his name. He envisioned Ethiopia as the renewed Jerusalem, as he attempted "to recreate the Holy Places in his own land."[9] Perhaps the most significant accomplishment of the Zagwe was their ability to persuade Saladin to grant the Orthodox Church permission to occupy a part of the Church of the Holy Sepulcher in Jerusalem and to set up a presence in the alleged place of the nativity in Bethlehem.[10] This not only speaks to the diplomatic astuteness of the Zagwe rulers, but suggests that the Muslims clearly differentiated between the crusading Christians from Europe and their dark-skinned siblings in the land of Ham.

SABBATH SHUFFLE

Although the Zagwe had made great progress in restoring the Orthodox faith, they were still viewed as usurpers by those who occupied the throne before the Agaw uprising. The end of the dynasty came in 1270, when Yekuno Amlak successfully reinstated the Solomonic dynasty. The alleged heirs of Solomon and Sheba once more regained their birthright. Upon assuming power, the Solomonids immediately sought to extinguish the growing influence of Islam, whose adherents now occupied the entire area of Ifat in the southeast. Amda Sion, the son of Yekuno Amlak, continued the suppression of the followers of Muhammad, and was so successful in his quest that a great many converted to Christianity.[11] The Muslim agenda appeared to preoccupy the next generation, and in his zeal to fight for the rights of Christians in all areas, Saida Ar'ad

---

[7]Curtwright, *Hand of God in Ethiopia*, p. 20.

[8]Ullendorff, *Ethiopians*, p. 62.

[9]Elizabeth Isichei, *A History of Christianity in Africa* (Grand Rapids: Eerdmans; Lawrenceville, N.J.: Africa World Press, 1995), p. 47.

[10]Curtwright, *Hand of God in Ethiopia*, p. 20. To this day, the Ethiopian Orthodox Church is one of several Orthodox churches that have retained administrative and domicile rights to the Church of the Holy Sepulcher (the Roman Catholic Church also has rights).

[11]Ullendorff, *Ethiopians*, pp. 64-65.

even began persecuting Egyptian merchants in retaliation for the way in which Christians were being treated in Egypt. Of course, this created a rift between Ethiopia and Egypt, one that was wisely mended by Saida Ar'ad's successor, King Dawit.

The Christianity that the newly invigorated Solomonids so desperately wanted to establish was different than the one to which Ethiopians had historically adhered. This "new" version of Christianity had been imposed on the Ethiopian Orthodox Church by its Coptic superiors in Egypt. The chasm between the Egyptian and Ethiopian versions of Christianity had been developing for a long time, as Egypt slowly departed from the Jewish practices that had been characteristic of Hamitic adherents to the Bible. Some Ethiopian Christians even recorded their lament over Egypt's apostasy when they heard that some Coptics were no longer eating kosher food: "we have heard that [the people of] Egypt have changed their faith. They eat what is forbidden in the law."[12] With Egypt's adoption of Western Christian practices, the episcopacy was concerned that Ethiopian Christianity had too much of a Jewish flavor. In fact, as early as the eleventh century, the Egyptian Patriarch Cyril II had warned the Ethiopians about their "Old Testament" observances.[13]

At the center of the controversy was the observance of the seventh-day sabbath. Before this time, it appears that the Coptic church had no problem with the sabbath. Indeed, it is no secret that for the Egyptian church, "the Sabbath seems to be held with a great deal of honour in its Coptic and Arabic literature."[14] However, as Egypt interacted more with the West, there appears to have been a growing disdain for the Judaic practices that characterized Christian culture in the region. Although the sabbath eventually became the major point of contention, "it is . . . apparent that the controversy over the Sabbath was only symptomatic of the divergences in religious practice that had developed between the Alexandrian and the Ethiopian Churches over the centuries."[15] Nonetheless, as the "mother" church, Egypt wielded tremendous au-

---

[12]Cited in Taddesse Tamrat, *Church and State in Ethiopia: 1270-1527* (Oxford: Clarendon, 1972), p. 246.

[13]Ibid., p. 209. We are also reminded that "As an essential part of the Christian tradition, the Old Testament had always had a great influence on the thinking and religious practice of the Ethiopians. In the absence of much literary development among them in the early Christian centuries, only the Bible provided the Ethiopians with the necessary guide-lines, and from it they drew not only their religion, but also much of their cultural and political inspiration" (Ibid., p. 218).

[14]Ibid., p. 209.

[15]Ibid., p. 219.

thority, and by the time of the Solomonid attempt to reestablish the supremacy of Christianity, a great number of Ethiopians had abandoned the observance of the seventh-day sabbath.[16]

While many Ethiopians went along with the Coptic edict, there were some for whom this amounted to heresy. The most notable opponent during this period was a clergyman named Ewostatewos (c. 1273-1352).[17] Citing the Ten Commandments and the Apostolic Canons, Ewostatewos argued strongly that sabbath observance was an integral teaching of Christianity.[18] Tired of being ignored by those to whom he made his case, he left Ethiopia for Egypt where he thought he might find a sympathetic ear. To his dismay, he found that the Coptic Church was not about to budge from its position. Nonetheless, with or without ecclesiastical endorsement, Ewostatewos and his followers remained firm in their belief, and their witness yielded great dividends as the supporters increased in numbers and influence.[19]

Fully intent on quashing the movement, the Egyptian Metropolitan Bartalomewos solicited the assistance of King Dawit. By now, the Ewostathians were under the leadership of Filipos. Feigning a desire to dialogue, Bartalomewos invited the leaders of the sabbath party to a conference, and when they refused to denounce sabbath observance he had Filipos imprisoned and exiled. Rather than suppressing the movement, Bartalomewos's treacherous act made a hero out of the man of faith, and many others joined the movement. Sensing the potential for civil unrest, Dawit ordered the release of Filipos and established a law that provided freedom of worship on the sabbath. This sparked a revival of religious nationalism throughout the country. "The observance of the Sabbath had long been deeply entrenched in the religious practice of the Ethiopians, and, when Dawit's protection of the 'house' of Ewostatewos removed their last fears of Alexandrian discipline, an increasing number of communities readopted the custom without any further inhibitions."[20]

Dawit was succeeded by three sons, the third of whom was Zara Yaqob (1399-1468). Ullendorff describes him as "the greatest ruler Ethiopia had

---

[16]Ibid.

[17]For a brief biography see "Ewostatewos," in *The Coptic Encyclopedia*, ed. Aziz S. Atiya (New York: Macmillan, 1991), 4:1050-51.

[18]Tamrat, *Church and State in Ethiopia*, p. 207.

[19]Ibid., pp. 210-19.

[20]Ibid., p. 224.

seen since Ezana."[21] Zara Yaqob had been trained by Ewostathian monks and was a great sympathizer of the sabbath cause. Upon acceding to the throne, he saw it as his sacred duty to reform and unify the Ethiopian Church. He found an unlikely supporter in the celebrated monk Giyorgis, who had initially been indoctrinated in the anti-sabbath teachings of the Egyptians, but had become one of the staunchest advocates of sabbath observance. With the people on his side and a growing number of clergy reverting to the ancient faith, the young monarch "believed that the only real opposition to the sabbath in the country came from the episcopal court. Once this was removed, the traditional affinity of the Ethiopians with the Old Testament would suffice to restore complete unanimity in Ethiopia."[22] Episcopal endorsement came at a specially called council in 1450, when the Egyptian bishops, Michael and Gabriel, agreed to the formalization of sabbath observance in the Ethiopian Church. Armed with ecclesiastical sanction and vested with political authority, Zara Yaqob reestablished sabbath observance as a universal obligation for Ethiopian Christians.

In addition to the revival of seventh-day sabbath observance, Zara Yaqob was responsible for other religious reforms. His most ambitious task was the commission to convert the "pagans." Although appearing to have great success, most who "converted" only became Christian in name. He also sought to provide religious education to the masses by assigning priests to certain districts for the purpose of instructing people in the Word. However, this in itself had mixed results in light of the fact that some priests were still sympathetic to the Coptic cause. In fact, it was during Zara Yaqob's reign that the Alexandrians sent a delegation to the Council of Florence in 1441, at which they signed a document of submission to the Catholic Church, effectively placing the Ethiopian Church under Rome. Of course, the Ethiopians refused to accept its validity.[23] Egyptian willingness to yield her identity to Rome would not be duplicated by a people who fought hard to maintain their own. Zara Yaqob's steadfastness resulted in the establishment of "ecclesiastical reforms which determined the special character of the Ethiopian Monophysite Church once and for all."[24]

---

[21]Ullendorff, *Ethiopians*, pp. 65-66.
[22]Tamrat, *Church and State in Ethiopia*, p. 228.
[23]Curtwright, *Hand of God in Ethiopia*, pp. 21-22.
[24]Ullendorff, *Ethiopians*, p. 66.

FEIGNED FRIENDSHIPS

The Western church had failed to absorb Ethiopia through its influence with Egypt. The next attempt would be more direct. The stage for Western infiltration was set after Zara Yaqob's passing when his son Ba'da Maryam ascended to the throne. Ba'da Maryam was not as firm as his father and was unable to effectively keep the kingdom together. As centralized power weakened, there was an upsurge in regionalism as the national unity that had been achieved through years of resilient struggle began to wane.

Events really took a drastic turn during the period of the Empress Helena, who was chief advisor to the Ethiopian kings. Concerned about the nagging presence of Muslims in the coastal areas, she solicited the help of the Portuguese navy to strengthen national security.[25] Finally seeing an opportunity to establish a presence in the mystical land of Prester John, the Portuguese quickly assented. By the time they arrived, Lebna Dengel was occupying the throne (1508-1540), and he did not share the empress's desire to form allegiances with European powers. In fact, he had just beaten back an army of Muslim invaders and felt that the major mission had already been accomplished. Nonetheless, in order to save national face, he allowed the Portuguese to stay.

The papacy decided to take advantage of the road into Ethiopia, and several teams of missionaries were sent to the kingdom. The most significant mission occurred in 1520, headed by Franzisco Alverez, who, together with the Coptic Abuna, convinced Lebna Dengel to submit to Rome.[26] Assuming their ultimate mission accomplished, the Portuguese forces headed home in 1526.[27] Unfortunately for Lebna Dengel, even as the triumphant Europeans were sailing home, the recouped Muslims had planned another attack, this time under the leadership of the dreaded Ahmad ibn Ibrahim (Gran). With ferocious determination they launched a devastating assault against the ruling powers, significantly decreasing the area under Christian control and destroying much of the rich theological literature that had only recently been developed.[28] Sensing his limitations while surrounded by a sea of Islam, Lebna Dengel wisely realized his need for outside help. Desperate times called for desperate methods,

---

[25]Ibid., p. 68.
[26]Curtwright, *Hand of God in Ethiopia,* p. 23.
[27]Ullendorff, *Ethiopians,* p. 69.
[28]Ibid., pp. 69-70.

and the proud and patriotic Ethiopian king placed the safety of his people before his own reputation and elevated the Portuguese priest Joao Bermudez to
the highest ecclesiastical position in the land. With the newly installed Roman
priest occupying the office of Abuna (Patriarch), Lebna Dengel cleverly announced that this bedrock of Monophysitism was ready to submit to the authority of Rome. This announcement was followed by a plea for European
military assistance in 1535.

By the time help arrived from Portugal, Lebna Dengel had passed away,
and his son, Claudius (Galawdewos), occupied the throne. The relatively small
Portuguese forces assisted in the final suppression of the Islamic threat. Ethiopia scarcely had time to breath before the kingdom experienced another serious uprising by the Oromo (formerly called Galla) who sought to take advantage of its weakened condition. The Oromo are believed to be the
primordial settlers in Cush, and they had resisted the pressure to accept Christianity. Bent on destruction, the Oromo ravaged the country as they indiscriminately killed Christians and burned churches. With gritty determination,
the Ethiopian crown endured the assault and rose from the smoke with renewed strength. It did not take long for Claudius to realize that he would need
every ounce of his newfound strength to wrestle with a new adversary: This
time, it was not indigenous tribes seeking their opportunity to dominate, but
the very Portuguese who had come to his nation's assistance.

Emboldened by a sense of entitlement for assisting in the liberation of
Ethiopia, a number of Portuguese decided to settle in this luscious and exotic
land and soon became an influential part of society. Apparently, their assimilation into Ethiopian society was an important part of a comprehensive plan
to Catholicize Ethiopia. The most prominent among the Portuguese immigrants was Joao Bermudez who—with good reason—claimed to be the official
Archbishop of the Ethiopian Church. Along with the priests aligned with
Bermudez were those commissioned by the Jesuits, who accompanied their
own bishop, Andrew de Oviedo. Fully aware that his father's elevation of Bermudez to Abuna was strictly a political move, and sensing the uneasiness of
the masses, Claudius moved quickly to set things straight. Although sympathetic to Catholicism, the emperor made it clear that the Coptic Archbishop
was the supreme head of the Ethiopian Church, and he let his guests know
that his nation had no intention of abdicating their Orthodox faith in favor of
Catholicism. Yet fully cognizant of his dependence on the West for military

assistance, Claudius skillfully played his political cards. After several carefully planned maneuvers, he positioned a Coptic Abuna as head of the church and announced his allegiance to the Alexandrian faith—which should have sufficed for Rome.

Although put in place by this move, the Catholics maintained a presence in Ethiopia through the Jesuits and continued their campaign for Ethiopia's permanent submission to Rome. Exercising the diplomacy of his forbears, Claudius politely engaged his guests in conversation, and eventually produced a document that outlined the theological positions of the Ethiopian faith. Known as the "Confessions of Claudius," this apology detailed the cardinal doctrines of the church and offered compromising explanations for the cultural practices that Catholicism deemed "Jewish." With this document, Claudius formalized his rejection of Rome's version of Christianity. Nonetheless, although entrenched in his beliefs, he permitted freedom of conscience in the realm of Christian denominationalism.

Claudius's son, Minas, did not learn the important lessons from his father, and when he ascended to power, this Ethiopian patriot initiated mass persecution of those who had converted to Catholicism, and expelled the Jesuits. Unfortunately, he appears to have underestimated the converts' loyalty to their newfound faith, and his intolerant zeal incited civil war. This intolerance was quickly reversed in 1563, when Sarsa Dengel succeeded his father and adopted his grandfather's gracious position. The Catholics embraced this new tolerance with evangelistic fervor and the missionaries began pouring back into the country.[29]

Among the Catholic missionaries was the Jesuit priest Pedro Paez. A shrewd and seasoned missionary, Paez had mastered the local language and managed to maneuver his way into the royal court. It did not take long for him to convert the reigning monarch, Za Dengel, who had succeeded his uncle Sarsa Dengel in 1597. Soon after conversion, Za Dengel convened an ecclesiastical council and announced the supremacy of Catholicism in Ethiopia. He then outlawed all practices of Ethiopian Christianity that did not conform to Roman Catholicism, and made it especially clear that he did not want any of his subjects to honor the seventh-day sabbath. The patriotic Ethiopians did

---

[29]Bairu Tafla, "Ethiopian Orthodox Church," in *The Coptic Encyclopedia*, ed. Aziz S. Atiya (New York: Macmillan, 1991), p. 996.

not take kindly to this decree, and a civil war erupted.[30]

In 1607, four years before the translation of the King James Version of the Bible, Za Dengel was murdered by his cousin Susenyos, who acceded to the throne. Undaunted by the violent resistance, Susenyos continued the opposition to seventh-day sabbath observance. During these years, Pedro Paez continued to control the religious direction of the kingdom. When Paez died in 1621, he was replaced by the bishop Alfonso Mendez, who assumed the position of head over the Ethiopian Orthodox Church. The people were incensed by this blatant abuse and a more violent civil war erupted in 1626. The resistance was so strong that Susenyos had to reverse the decision in 1632 and abdicate in favor of his son, Fasilidas.

Fasilidas did not intend on repeating the mistakes of his predecessors, and immediately restored the Orthodox faith. He was fully aware that the root of the problem was with those who had feigned friendship in order to indoctrinate the nation with a European version of Christianity, and in 1633 issued a decree announcing the permanent expulsion of all Jesuit missionaries,[31] a decree that stood until 1838![32] Once the troublemakers had been expelled, the Ethiopian church had the opportunity to flourish at its own pace. The theologians of the church continued their internal conversations as they utilized their own methods to interpret Scripture. Of note, the issue that occupied most of their contemplation concerned the nature of Christ—was he always divine or did he assume divinity at his baptism (a type of adoptionism)? The council of Boru Meda in 1878 endorsed the former view. The Ethiopians were proud of their Jewish roots, but were not prepared to further separate themselves from Chalcedon by adopting a Monophysite position that resembled the old Ebionite "heresy."

---

[30]Curtwright, *Hand of God in Ethiopia,* pp. 28-29.
[31]Ullendorff, *Ethiopians,* p. 75.
[32]Tafla, "Ethiopian Orthodox Church," p. 997.

15

MISSION AND COLONIZATION
IN SUB-SAHARAN AFRICA

Having failed at the quest to subdue Palestine, Egypt and Ethiopia, Christian Europe set her sights on the lands associated with Put, Ham's third son. The difficulty in determining the exact location of Put has already been discussed in the first chapter. The truth is, given the lack of genealogy for Put's offspring and the sparse references to him in the Bible, it is left to the interpreter to build a defendable theory. I have rejected those theories that equate Put with Libya, simply because the Libyans were the offspring of Egypt. It seems logical that since the writer of Genesis 10 uses the terms Canaan, Misrayim and Cush to describe tribes occupying large geographical regions, the same must be true for Put. For reasons given in chapter one, I equate Put with ancient Punt, which fell below Ethiopia. Some limit it to the horn of Africa, but I am working under the assumption that it encompasses a larger geographical area.

Based on what we know about the narrow and broader definitions for Misrayim and Cush, those who limit Punt/Put to a section in the horn of Africa should recognize that the territory probably only served as the provincial seat for the wider region. Consistency with the use of the primal ancestors' names in Genesis 10 necessitates a double definition. Is it possible that the descendants of Put can be located via linguistic analysis? Isn't the so-called Semitic language group one of the indicators of relationships between the tribes that comprise the Canaanites and those included among the Cushites? Since language has proven to be a solid indicator of familial ties between various ethnic groups, it cannot be overlooked that the nations below Ethiopia do have linguistic similarities. In fact, the Swahili spoken in Tanzania and Kenya is also a part of the wider Bantu family of languages. This alone should provide strong evidence for a common regional thread. Although home to hundreds of unique languages and dialects, the Bantu stamp suggests the interrelatedness of the numerous tribes that settled in the eastern, central, southern and western areas of the modern African continent. Indeed, it would be these undocumented descendants of Ham who would feel the brunt of Europe's pent-up wrath finally being unleashed after centuries of frustrated attempts to expand her borders.

Before we embark on our discussion on the evils of the European slave trade, it is necessary to remember that slavery had been taking place on African shores centuries before the unholy papal edicts. Aided by willing tribesmen who made a living out of kidnapping unsuspecting victims from rival tribes, Muslims from Arabia had already perfected the logistics of slave trading.[1] By the time the Europeans arrived, the renegade sons of Put who had sullied their hands with innocent blood with the help of their Cushite brethren were only too pleased to broaden their market and fatten their purses. Nonetheless, while a machine was already in place and mammon-driven Africans bore as much guilt as the capitalizing foreigners, European slavery appears especially heinous since it was conducted under the auspices of the Christ of peace, and was foreign to the New Testament teachings of equality.

PORTUGUESE POWER

The Portuguese had set their sights on Hamitic Put long before they had established a presence in Ethiopia. Pope Martin V had given permission for an African crusade in 1418, and the Portuguese—authorized by another papal decree—started trading in African slaves in 1441 (the same year that the Egyptian church pledged allegiance to Rome).[2] By 1452 Pope Nicholas V issued another edict that basically mandated the enslavement of all non-Christians encountered during the explorers' imperial quest. Covered by the Church's blessing and sanctioned by their commander in chief, Henry the Navigator, the colonizing sailors set sail with a large supply of ammunition and

---

[1]See John Hope Franklin, *From Slavery to Freedom: A History of Negro Americans*, 5th ed. (New York: Alfred A. Knopf, 1980), pp. 30-31.

[2]For a brief look at the arguments used to give theological support to the slave trade, see A. C. de C. M. Saunders, *A Social History of Black Slaves and Freedmen in Portugal, 1441-1555* (Cambridge: Cambridge University Press, 1982), pp. 36-40. For a balanced study of the Catholic involvement in slavery, see John Francis Maxwell, *Slavery and the Catholic Church: The History of Catholic Teaching Concerning the Moral Legitimacy of the Institution of Slavery* (Chichester: Barry Rose Publishers, 1975). For an attempt to vindicate the Catholic Church, see Joel S. Panzer, *The Popes and Slavery* (New York: Alba House, 1996).

specially appointed missionaries. Their simple plan called for the subduing of the natives through persuasion or force and the conversion of their victims through catechetical instruction. This strategy ensured the expansion of both kingdom and church. The missionaries operated under the policy of *padroado*, which meant that—although priests—they reported directly to the king.[3] As a part of this policy, they were to erect a stone cross called a *padrao* in every place in which they landed. The planting of the tainted symbol signified the transfer of ownership from the resident tribes of Africa to absent European landlords. The seriousness of their quest is demonstrated by the 1493 decree of Pope Alexander V that granted Portugal the right to incorporate all of Africa into its expanding empire.

The actual colonization of the land of Put commenced in 1456 when the Portuguese anchored on the uninhabited Cape Verde Islands. From this base, the beleaguering crusaders planted the *padrao* in Benin and the Congo, and by 1486, Bartholomew Diaz had reached the challenging Cape of Good Hope.[4] While not the southernmost tip of the continent, this was a significant accomplishment for the colonizing explorers. Building on Diaz's achievements, Vasco da Gama traversed the extreme south of the continent at Cape Agulhas and straddled the east coast, establishing outposts in Zambesi, Mobassa and finally the Kenyan coastal town of Malindi in 1498.[5] In less than half a century, the colonizing conquistadors had cast their capitalist net around the entire Bantu region that housed the ancient people of Put.

The "missionaries" followed closely behind the imperial mercenaries. By 1460, the Cape Verde Islands had developed into an unholy crossroads for African slaves being transported to the New World and for newly trained African priests who had finished seminary in Portugal and were awaiting assignment to their unsuspecting parishes on the mainland.[6] These programmed indigenous priests would not be the first to share the Catholic interpretation of biblical religion to their fellows. Adventurous European missionaries had already

---

[3]Mark Shaw, *The Kingdom of God in Africa: A Short History of African Christianity* (Grand Rapids: Baker, 1996), p. 108.

[4]Ibid., p. 110.

[5]Ibid.

[6]Apparently, after being acculturated into European mores, not many of the newly schooled Africans wished to evangelize among the natives. See Lamin Sanneh, *West African Christianity: The Religious Impact* (Maryknoll, N.Y.: Orbis, 1983), pp. 19-20; also Elizabeth Isichei, *A History of Christianity in Africa* (Grand Rapids: Eerdmans; Lawrenceville, N.J.: Africa World Press, 1995), pp. 55-56.

made their move, and Diogo Gomez could boast of the 1457 conversion of Nomimansa, a Malian king. He could also add the king of Efutu to his résumé, a local monarch who converted in 1503.[7]

Missionaries who ventured further inland into the central regions were also successful in baptizing the Congolese king, Mvemba Nzinga (Afonso), in 1491. While baptisms in other areas may have been politically motivated, Mvemba Nzinga was serious about his newfound faith and even renamed the capital São Salvador ("Holy Savior"). He encouraged his subjects to study for the priesthood and immersed the nation in Catholicism.[8] Other missionary success stories occurred in Angola, which the Portuguese colonized in 1575. Utilizing a new strategy, the Jesuits established villages comprised entirely of converts, with the hope that the practice would spread throughout the land.[9]

The Jesuits were also active on the eastern shores of the land of Put. From the base that Vasco da Gama left in Mozambique, the settlers heard of Mweme Mutapa (Monomotapa), the great emperor of Zimbabwe. The Jesuit priest Gonsalo da Silveira ventured to his court, and by 1561 had baptized the king and won the adulation of the citizens.[10] In the central areas of East Africa, it was the Augustinian Hermits who achieved success, and there was great rejoicing when Yusuf bin Hasan—who became sultan of Mombasa in 1625—became an ardent defender and evangelist of the faith.[11] From all appearances, it seemed as if the unholy alliance between church and state was working to the benefit of both institutions.

In reality, the missionary endeavors were cursed with complications and frequented by failure. Some potential converts saw right through the ruse and knew that pledging allegiance to the *padrao* equated to the surrender of sovereignty to the conquistadors. When Diogo da Azambuja introduced Catholic Christianity to Ghana in 1482, no argument possible could convince the local king Nana Caramansa to exchange his centuries-old beliefs for this foreign one. Many who had been seduced into baptism soon felt the true venom of the empire that had beguiled them. It did not take long for Mvemba Nzinga to discover the ruthless politics of church life, and he would have died three years ear-

---

[7]For background, see Sanneh, *West African Christianity,* 21-25.
[8]Shaw, *Kingdom of God in Africa,* pp. 112-14.
[9]Ibid., p. 115.
[10]Ibid., p. 116.
[11]Ibid., pp. 117-18.

lier than 1540 if the priest Alvaro had succeeded in his assassination attempt. Further, Mweme Mutapa would experience the wrath of an unforgiving "Christian" military after he was persuaded by some Muslim traders to execute Silvera for espionage.[12] And imperial intolerance would lead the promising sultan, Yusuf bin Hasan, to reject Christianity in favor of his original Muslim faith and become an ardent persecutor of those he once viewed as siblings.

Africans also came to discover that the "family of Christ" in Europe was engaged in some serious turf wars. The rest of Europe was not prepared to sit back while the Portuguese built a wall of *padraos* around the land of Put. At times the pioneering conquistadors chose to stake their claim with force, and in 1655, not too long after Spanish Jesuits had baptized the king of Benin, Portuguese soldiers forcefully claimed the land and immediately dismissed the priests, who to them were nothing but symbols of economic rivalry. The impression their warmongering made on the "souls" of the new converts was far from their minds. On other occasions, it was the Portuguese missionaries who had to retreat. Such was the case in Angola when the experimental Christian village project was fatally halted during the Dutch invasions of 1641-1647.

DUTCH DELUSIONS

The Dutch approached Africa with similar ambitions as the Portuguese. They were also engaged in empire building, which was conducted effectively through the Dutch East India Company. In true imperial style, they had set up outposts all along the West African coast, but it was the one they established in the Cape of Good Hope that changed the way Europeans related to the continent. The one commissioned to manage operations at the Cape was businessman Jan van Riebeeck, who landed in 1652 with five ships and more than one hundred workers.[13] When the Dutch supplanters began building a fort and planting crops, it was obvious that they had come to stay. This was not good news for the local Khoisans, who had become used to seeing Europeans come and go. Matters really got serious when the Dutch settlers started making unreasonable demands from the Khoisans and encroached upon their grazing land. Unwilling to allow the invaders to take advantage of them, the Khoisan tribes formed an alliance and launched several unsuccessful attacks

---

[12]See Isichei, *A History of Christianity*, p. 68; and Shaw, *Kingdom of God in Africa*, p. 118.
[13]For a discussion on the Dutch colonization of the Cape, see Leonard Thompson, *A History of South Africa* (New Haven, Conn.: Yale University Press, 1990), pp. 33-52.

against the fort between 1659 and 1677.[14] At the end of the struggle, they were forced to agree to a lopsided treaty with van Riebeeck, in which they ceded more land to their oppressors.

Jan van Riebeeck was to serve as the prototype of hundreds of thousands of misguided bigots who would follow him. He had been shaped in the mold of religious inflexibility and imbibed the intolerant chauvinism of the preconverted Saul. As chief administrator, he was the embodiment of the law—both political and religious—and he made sure that all in his sphere of influence ceased what they were doing on Sundays to attend service. He was willing to uphold the letter of the law, but was totally resistant to the spirit of the law. Puffed up by bigotry and a false sense of supremacy, this Dutch bureaucrat felt his people to be superior to the sons of Ham and vilified them with the most derogatory terms available.[15] Fueled by the sentiment of his Dutch Reformed brethren, he believed that his people were God's new chosen, and transferred the Noahic curse from Canaan to his older brother Put.[16] Somehow, his twisted view of Scripture justified his people's demonic delusions.

With the prevalence of this attitude, it is not surprising that the first "Christian" activities that Europe sponsored in the Cape were directed toward the Dutch settlers. Although there is documentation for the first Khosian baptism in 1662, missionary programs for the natives do not appear to have been high on the agenda; the spiritual needs of the insulated "chosen" were made the priority. In an effort to enforce the fidelity of the community, the first official Dutch Reformed congregation was organized in 1665. By 1745, there were five, as the number of settlers increased. The new arrivals not only consisted of Dutch natives, but also Huguenots who had sought refuge in Holland after being persecuted in France and who worshiped alongside their Protestant brethren. For these, the Bible was the property of the European elect and was too holy to be shared with the African infidel.

It was not until the Moravians established a presence in 1738 that an intentional effort to evangelize the natives commenced. In fact, when George Schmidt established his community at Genadendal, he specifically targeted

---

[14]William H. Worger, "Historical Setting," in *South Africa: A Country Study*, ed. Rita M. Byrnes (Washington, D.C.: Library of Congress Federal Research Division, 1997), pp. 13-14.

[15]Shaw, *Kingdom of God in Africa*, p. 120.

[16]For a discussion on the theological ideology of the Dutch settlers, see J. Alton Templin, *Ideology of a Frontier: The Theological Foundation of Afrikaner Nationalism, 1652-1910* (Westport, Conn.: Greenwood Press, 1984), pp. 3-9.

the natives. Rather than celebrate the spread of the gospel, the established church did everything in its power to shut the mission down—a move that was accomplished in 1748. More than anything, this dastardly deed demonstrated the bedeviled condition of those who claimed moral superiority. Blinded by their own misguided sense of worth, they were willing to allow their prejudices to obscure their ability to read and hear the clear egalitarian message of Scripture.

ENGLISH ENGAGEMENT

Of course, the Dutch attitude was no different than that of every other nation that sought to take advantage of the children of Put. While the Dutch had a strategy for permanent occupation, others were feverishly engaged in trading human cargo and mining the precious and plentiful minerals of Africa in order to pay for the luxuries of Europe. By 1800, the royal coffers of Europe's monarchs were bursting with symbols of stolen wealth, and millions of slaves had been amputated from their families and grafted in to the economic fabric of the so-called New World. At this stage in the game, the English had overtaken Portugal, Spain, France and Holland, and were the indisputable moguls of the international slave ring.[17] Slavery was so essential to the British economy that the government sought to protect it at all costs.[18]

The monarchs and pontiffs who profited from slavery would soon be confronted by ministers and prophets whose hearts had been touched by the liberating gospel. To be fair to the people of Europe, it must be noted that condemnation against ecclesiastically endorsed slavery had been voiced from the very beginning of the institution. When Spain decided to outlaw the enslavement of Amerindians, Spanish theologians reasoned that if it was wrong to enslave the aboriginals of the Americas, it was also wrong to enslave the African.[19] There had even been a voice of conscience among the Portuguese from as early as 1555, when Fernão de Oliveria denounced the slave trade in his *Arte da Guera no Mar*.[20] However, the fatal blow to the transatlantic slave trade was to come from the calculated conscience of England.

The one who brought momentum to the movement was Granville Sharp,

---

[17]On England's rise to slave trading prominence, see Franklin, *From Slavery to Freedom*, pp. 36-38.
[18]Shaw, *Kingdom of God in Africa*, p. 128.
[19]Saunders, *Social History of Black Slaves*, p. 42.
[20]Ibid., p. 43.

an evangelical who embraced the task of representing slaves on English soil who desired their freedom. Another notable abolitionist was William Wilberforce, an English member of Parliament who challenged the church with the publication *A Practical View of the Prevailing Religious System of Professed Christians* (1797).[21] Their voice was authenticated by Ottobah Cugoano and Olaudah Equiano, two emancipated Christian slaves with a heart for mission and equality. Equiano also published a bestselling book that introduced the masses to the rich cultural heritage from which many slaves had been snatched. These collective voices finally found strength in 1823, when Wilberforce and member of Parliament Thomas Buxton founded the British and Foreign Antislavery Society. It did not take long for churches to embrace the movement, and in 1807 the British Parliament passed a law criminalizing the slave trade. This was followed by a second law in 1833 that mandated the emancipation of all slaves on August 1, 1834.

While the abolition of slavery provides a reason to rejoice, it cannot be forgotten that the European exploitation of Africa went much deeper than the transatlantic slave trade. England committed her naval resources to policing the waters and even organized the establishment of colonies in Liberia and Sierra Leone where saved and former slaves could create a new life for themselves. However, the temptation to control the vast resources of Put's country was too great, and capitalist exploitation continued under the guise of empowering Africa through "commerce and Christianity." Few would deny that Africa needed economic empowerment, and the pure Christian gospel would definitely assist in the political, cultural and spiritual transformation of society. Nonetheless, the brand of Christianity introduced was still laden with Eurocentric chauvinism, and the commercial enterprises only served to laden the coffers of European banks at the expense of the exploited children of Put. By the end of the nineteenth century, the dominant powers of Europe sat in Europe and divided Africa amongst themselves as if it were an oversize Monopoly board, with England achieving the lion's share. And as recently as the twentieth century, Rwanda—the land that served as a paradigm for successful missions with its 95 percent Christian population—proved once more that it is hard for seed sown on shallow ground to take root.

---

[21]Shaw, *Kingdom of God in Africa*, p. 136.

AFRICAN AFFIRMATION

Many have attempted to justify the atrocities of Europe's militant zealots by suggesting that this was a way of getting the gospel to the people. However, possession of a Bible or regular attendance at lofty cathedrals does not equate with acceptance of the gospel. As the Moravian missionaries in Cape Town and the members of the British and Foreign Antislavery Society were to discover, God's Word calls Christians to practice the gospel of love. Chattel slavery and the exploitation of African resources have absolutely nothing to do with the propagation of the gospel. Actions speak louder than words, and no amount of catechetical classes could erase the image of slave ships transporting one's kin to unknown lands.

It is also important to remember that a knowledge of the biblical God preceded the European missionaries in the land of Put. While there is no direct evidence, it is not unreasonable to assume that Christians from Ethiopia, North Africa and Arabia shared the gospel message with trading partners from the ancient kingdoms of west and southeast Africa. And many who may not have had direct access to the Bible would have been familiar with the major biblical stories and characters through the work of Muslim missionaries. Names like Abraham, Moses, and Jesus would not have been foreign to them. Just by exposure to the Qur'an, they would have heard stories of the virgin birth and Jesus' miraculous healing ministry. They would have heard Jesus referred to as the Messiah and been familiar with his role on the day of judgment.

Neither can it be forgotten that even outside of Islamic influence, many African cultures that may not have possessed the documents of Scriptures still evidence familiarity with its contents. Interestingly, many of these cultures have a strong Hebraic flavor in their rituals and myths.[22] For instance, the East African Meru trace their origins to a deliverer who led them from bondage in Misri (Egypt) and established them in twelve tribes after God allowed them to pass through a body of water when they were being pursued by the enslaving army.[23] Similarly, the Lemba of southern Africa also speak of a long trek

---

[22]See Joseph J. Williams, *Hebrewisms of West Africa: From Nile to Niger with the Jews* (New York: Dial Press, 1930), who mostly focuses on the Akan, but covers some other tribes as well. See also Isaac Laudarji, "Ritual as Quest for Well Being in the Religious Universe of the Tangale People of Nigeria," Ph.D. dissertation, Northwestern University, 1994.

[23]See Daniel Nyaga, *Customs and Traditions of the Meru* (Nairobi: East African Educational Publishers, 1997).

from bondage and hail their ancestral home as Senna in the distant north (could this be Sinai?).[24] Then there are the Akan of Ghana, who have always had a seven-day calendar and who hail as their supreme being Onyamee Kwaame—the Saturday God.[25] These are joined by the Nigerian Yoruba, who—according to the autobiography of Olaudah Equiano—had many practices in common with the Jews long before the Europeans arrived.[26]

The sons of Put may not have been exposed to the interpretation of biblical faith that predominated the cathedrals of Europe, but they had already been provided with practical glimpses of God's Word. The foundation for the gospel had already been laid. One can't help but wonder how different things would have been in the territory of the Bantu if the European missionaries had entered the continent with pure motives.

HOSTILE TAKEOVER: CONCLUSION

Although initiated under the umbrella of the crusade against Islam, the European interference in the lands associated with Ham's progeny had very little to do with the promulgation of the gospel and everything to do with the propagation of a culture and acquisition of land. As they carried the cross as an ominous talisman, the sole purpose of those who fought in the name of Jesus was to impose their imperialistic interpretation of biblical writ on the children of Ham. Buoyed by notions of rightness, hundreds of thousands sowed the cross shaped patch on their garments and entered the lands of Canaan and Misrayim on a mission to slaughter Muslims and Orthodox for the sake of the kingdom. Rather than witnessing the triumph of the gospel, the bloodthirsty armies experienced defeat and the widening of the gulf between Islam and Christianity—a gulf that remains to this very day.

Seemingly unfazed by their failed mission, the crusading armies set their sights on the territories occupied by the descendants of Cush and Put. There were drastic differences in their strategies. Unable to justify an outright assault on the Hebraized Ethiopia, the Portuguese sent a covert missionary contingent to transform the church from the inside out. This approach was success-

---

[24]Tudor Parfitt, *Journey to the Vanished City: The Search for a Lost Tribe of Israel* (New York: Vantage Books, 2000).

[25]See Kofi Owusu-Mensa, *Saturday God and Adventism in Ghana* (Frankfurt: Peter Lang, 1993).

[26]Olaudah Equiano, "The Interesting Narrative of the Life of Olaudah Equiano, or, Gustavus Vassa, the African," in *The Classic Slave Narratives*, ed. Henry Louis Gates (New York: Penguin, 1987).

ful in converting a number of clergy and even some monarchs, but resulted in civil wars and the eventual expulsion of those who wished to transform the face of Ethiopian Christianity. The attack against Put was less diplomatic and more brazen in its intention. The inhabitants of the land and the land itself were placed on notice as millions were abducted and shipped to foreign lands and their precious minerals were disturbed from their millennial rest. Canaan, Misrayim and Cush had resisted the onslaught, but Put found himself trapped in an oppressive net. Even after the emancipation bell was rung, the people of Put had been beguiled into a trance induced by mental slavery.

In closing, the recent genocide in Rwanda demonstrates that enslavement is not only perpetrated by those who trap, chain and export unsuspecting innocents. The most powerful chains are those that bind the mind to a false ideology. When a newly baptized son of Put is ordered to reject his "pagan" name and adopt a European "Christian" name, he is being told that his culture is inferior. When the daughters of Put are told that the worship that God endorses cannot be accompanied with rhythmic dance and percussive instrumentation, they are being told that in order to be acceptable to God they must embrace the anthems and decorum of Europe. These efforts to strip God's children of their unique gifts have caused many to forsake Christianity and embrace other religions that are deemed culturally friendly. However, as we will see in the final chapter, in spite of the distortions, the Word of God continues to penetrate the hearts and minds of Ham's children, and although it has been abused as a tool to rape a people of their humanity, it has not been robbed of its potency and remains an indispensable vehicle of blessing.

PART SIX

FREE AT LAST

The Bible and African Liberation

I am the LORD your God,

who brought you out of the land of Egypt,

out of the house of slavery.

DEUTERONOMY 5:6

With the Bible being used to justify the enslavement, invasion and subjugation of African people, it's a divine miracle that any of Ham's ancestors still embrace it as an essential tool for spiritual growth. It is true that some have discarded it as a fabrication of European supremacy,[1] but many have been able to look beyond the atrocious acts of those who have effectively perpetrated a skewed hermeneutic, and have found liberation in its pages. After all, how could a book that was birthed in the land of Ham place an eternal curse on the very people who contributed to its message, preserved its content and deciphered mysterious theological teachings from its words? Moreover, how could a God who arbitrarily selected Ham's territory as the location of creation, redemption and re-creation hate the very people who—like the rest of human-

---

[1]The rejection of the Bible has resulted in the formation of new black religions that claim to be more relevant to the culture. For a study on the Kawaida faith, whose influence is still seen in the annual Kwanzaa observances, see Scot Brown, *Fighting for US: Maulana Karenga, the US Organization, and Black Cultural Nationalism* (New York: New York University Press, 2003). Some have discarded the Bible for other reasons; see Norm R. Allen, ed., *The Black Humanist Experience: An Alternative to Religion* (Amherst, N.Y.: Prometheus, 2003).

ity—are heirs to his divine image? Millions have come to terms with the fact that myth has no real power over truth, and they have usurped the racist lies that pit the Word of God against his Hamitic children. Indeed, even as we face the uncharted course of the twenty-first century, we hear the vast chorus of Ham's resilient progeny chanting anthems of liberation from their dispersed locations around the globe—anthems inspired by the biblical message of hope.

Of course, as the sons and daughters of Ham lift their voices in rapturous tones, the honest observer is forced to admit that they are not all singing the same tune. It is true that the Bible serves as the foundation for their hope, but even in the absence of the oppressor, they have been conditioned to read the pages through the lenses of religious interpreters. Nonetheless, in most cases the refrain is the same. They share a refrain that magnifies a God who has rescued humanity from the pit of perdition through the blood of his eternal Son, Jesus the Christ.

Part six begins with chapters on the echoes of the biblical anthem that still ring in the lands descended from Canaan, Misrayim and Cush. Although Islam has become a dominant force and the crescent moon of the Qur'an has threatened to eclipse the penetrating sunlight of the Bible, God's Word has proven indestructible. After listening for the echoes of Scripture in the aforementioned regions of Ham, chapter eighteen will revisit Put, who suffered great devastation in the previous chapter. Although plagued with warfare and pestilence, we will discover a land in which the stories of the Bible are being reenacted through mass baptisms, miraculous physical healings and marvelous acts of faith. Elijah, Peter, Moses and Paul would be no strangers to this world! The very tool the oppressor used to justify their padlocked chains has proven to be the key to their liberation. It will be seen that the same book that could have been discarded as a cruel curse has proven to be the source of bountiful blessings.

16

The Decline of Christianity in Islamic Africa

Touting its own interpretation of biblical writ, the keepers of the Qur'an first positioned it as a third testament that complemented the *tawra* and *injil,* and then promoted it to a position of dominance that negated the need for the earlier revelations held sacred by Jews and Christians. As discussed in previous chapters, Islam did not always display antagonism towards the two Abrahamic faiths that utilized various versions of the Bible for their doctrinal foundation. Unconsciously aware of the impact of Scripture on their prophet, they assigned the status of *dhimmi* to their Jewish and Christian kin. Although subject to intermittent acts of intolerance, the "people of the book" were blessed with the freedom to assemble and worship throughout *dar al-Islam.* The Crusades threatened to upset the status quo, but somehow the multifaith dwellers of the northern lands of Ham allowed their common ethnicity to transcend their rival confessions.

Following the victory over the crusading armies of Europe, Islamic power became more centralized with the founding of the powerful Ottoman Empire. Just three short centuries after its founding in 1299, the Turkish-based empire incorporated territory from Europe to North Africa. Ottoman land included all regions of biblical Canaan and major sections of biblical Cush and Misrayim. Determined to preserve and protect the realm of *dar al-Islam,* the Ottomans ensured that Islam was the official faith throughout the empire. However, in the tolerant spirit of their forebears, they also ordered the empire in a way that not only protected the religious status of the "people of the book," but gave them a powerful voice in government.

SMOOTH WATERS

The Ottomans were able to achieve religious equilibrium through the establishment of *millets*.[1] "Religion, language, community, ethnicity and the family made up the socio-cultural fabric of the millet,"[2] and in a way they were like borderless nations within the Ottoman Empire. The Ottomans defined four basic *millets* under *dar al-Islam:* Islam, Judaism, Greek Orthodox Christian and Armenian Christian. On the surface, these divisions appear rather neat, and would give the impression that the members of each *millet* all shared the same set of beliefs and standards. However, it is well known that Muslims were far from united with the deep rift between Sunni and Shia, and the cultural variations that expressed themselves in Sufism and would later birth radical groups like the Wahabbi. Further, Judaism was by no means uniform with its fragmented and independent synagogues scattered throughout Hamitic Canaan and Egypt. In addition, Christian denominations abounded in the various patriarchies. Nonetheless, the Ottomans made a move that led to a forced ecumenism, especially among the disparate Christian groups who had to align with the Chalcedonian Creed under the Greek Orthodox Church or with a Monophysite confession under the Armenians.[3]

While the Jewish and Christian *millets* did not have as high a standing as Islam, it is quite likely that the Ottoman compromise reflected the continued indebtedness of Muslims who recognized the essential place of the biblical faith in their own spiritual lineage. The *millets* provided the freedom for Jews and Christians to transmit their faith to consequent generations, and all religious matters were dealt with in-house.[4] Although the Patriarch of each *millet* was the ultimate authority in matters of religion and social welfare, the leader in each local community also wielded a certain amount of authority.[5] The only

---

[1]For a discussion on the establishing and development of the *millets,* see Kemal H. Karpat, "Millets and Nationality: The Roots of the Incongruity of Nation and State in the Post-Ottoman Era," in *Christians and Jews in the Ottoman Empire: The Functioning of a Plural Society,* ed. Benjamin Braude and Bernard Lewis (New York: Homes & Meier, 1982), pp. 141-69.

[2]Karpet, "Millets," p. 142.

[3]Kenneth Cragg, *The Arab Christian* (Louisville, Ky.: Westminster John Knox, 1991), p. 117, suggests that the consolidation of the various Christian sects may have been an expression of Islamic contempt for the great divisions among Christians.

[4]Apparently, Cragg (ibid., p. 118) understands the *millet* system to be a continuation of the *dhimmi:* "The Islamic *Sharīʿah* left all relationships within the *Dhimmah*—that is, matters of religious law, personal status, family, marriage, inheritance, and the like—to the law and custom of the community through the local church officials." For a discussion of Jews under the *millet* system, see Jacob Barnai, *The Jews in Palestine in the Eighteenth Century: Under the Patronage of the Istanbul Committee of Officials for Palestine,* trans. Naomi Goldblum (Tuscaloosa: University of Alabama Press, 1992), pp. 11-24.

[5]See Andrea Pacini, introduction to *Christian Communities in the Arab Middle East: The Challenge of the Future,* ed. Andrea Pacini (Oxford: Clarendon, 1998), p. 5.

limitation placed on the non-Islamic *millets* concerned proselytization. It was legal for a Christian or Jew to convert to Islam, but for a Muslim to cross the line was a capital offence.

Mutual cooperation may have worked for Muslims and Jews, but the other "people of the book" still had not learned the unifying message of the Savior, and rather than find a way to make the system work, priests from a number of denominations defected and joined the enemy of Eastern Orthodoxy: Roman Catholicism.[6] The new alliance with the West was further aided when, in the mid 1800s, the Ottomans declared that all citizens of the empire had equal rights regardless of religion.[7] This opened the doors for a season of missionary activity headed by European Catholics and American Evangelicals, who would focus their attention on their Eastern Orthodox siblings, as they invited them to embrace their version of biblical "truth."[8] These missionaries were accompanied by merchants who used the *millet* system to their advantage and reasoned that as Christians, they were automatically a part of the Christian *millets*. While the founders of the *millet* system never envisioned it to be a haven for foreigners, the manipulation of the system initiated a season of commercial exchange and social intercourse that provided great financial and social benefits for the Christian communities, especially those in Palestine and Egypt. The liberal civil rights laws also aided the growth of Christianity, and by the time the Ottoman Empire fell to the European powers at the end of World War I in 1914, Christians comprised about thirty percent of the population in Palestine.[9]

THE CHANGING TIDE

After the defeat of the Ottomans, the Hamitic portions of the empire were placed under the authority of European powers—particularly England. With

---

[6]Cragg, *Arab Christian,* p. 123, reports, "All the major groupings during the Ottoman centuries experienced the schisms in which erstwhile protégés threw in their lot completely with Latin Catholicism, bringing Arab Christianity into yet greater division. Greek Catholic, Coptic Catholic, Syrian Catholic, Chaldean Catholic, Armenian Catholic 'Uniates' all eventuated in the Ottoman period detaching from their parent churches and aligning with the papacy."

[7]Pacini, introduction, p. 6.

[8]For a discussion on the fragmenting of the churches in the region, see Jean Corbon, "The Churches in the Middle East: Their Origins and Identity from Their Roots in the Past to Their Openness to the Present," in *Christian Communities in the Arab Middle East: The Challenge of the Future,* ed. Andrea Pacini (Oxford: Clarendon, 1998), pp. 96-98.

[9]Pacini, introduction, p. 8.

their centuries-old kingdom diminished, the new Turkish leaders initiated a period of persecution against Christians under their jurisdiction.[10] While their siblings to the west experienced the anger of Muslim leaders, the Christians in Palestine were having a different experience. Probably emboldened by their numbers, coupled with the feeling of safety that naturally came from knowing that European "Christians" were now in charge, these Hamitic followers of Messiah delved into social activism. Interestingly, their agenda was not one that promoted the ideals of the imperial power, but was one that betrayed how deeply committed they were to their cultural roots.

Whether driven by the need to protest against Western occupation or the desire to minimize the role that religion often played in Islamic governments, Christian leaders rallied the masses to support the creation of socialist movements built on the foundation of the egalitarian policies of the later Ottomans. Indeed, it was a Syrian confessor of Greek Orthodoxy, Michel 'Aflaq, who founded the Ba'th Party that rose to prominence both in Syria and Iraq.[11] Meanwhile in Egypt, it was Christian Copts who were chiefly instrumental in founding the Wafd Nationalist Party.[12] If anything, the liberal social policies of the Ottomans engendered a collective pride among the citizens of Palestine and Egypt that would manifest itself in Arab nationalism.

Unfortunately, the very movement that sought to place nation over religion would eventually be manipulated to fuse religion with nation. It did not take long for the pro-Arabic movement to be hijacked by those who would eventually distort it into an unprecedented type of Islamic fundamentalism.[13] This growing resentment was chiefly fueled by the increasing influence of the European powers who had taken ownership of these ancient lands. The crusaders had finally achieved their prize, and some Muslims must have felt as if the promotion of the Arab cause by Hamitic Christians was merely a smokescreen behind which they could complete the work of political and religious domination.

---

[10]See ibid., pp. 10-11. For a discussion on the genocide, which affected mostly Armenian Christians, see Rouben Paul Adalian, "The Armenian Genocide," in *A Century of Genocide: Critical Essays and Eyewitness Accounts,* ed. Israel W. Charny, William S. Parsons and Samuel Totten (New York: Routledge, 2004), pp. 53-90.

[11]Pacini, introduction, p. 11.

[12]Ibid.

[13]For a discussion on the modern rise of Islamic fundamentalism, see Beverly Milton-Edwards, *Islamic Fundamentalism since 1945* (New York: Routledge, 2004).

Palestine was the epicenter of the seismic tremors that would eventually erupt into the decades-old religious rift that remains to this day. Somehow, the three spiritual branches of Abraham's seed have become so fixated with the arid and rocky terrain that they are deluded into thinking that possession of the land is the ultimate aim of their religious journey. The whole concept of a renewed kingdom being ushered in after the earth has been cleansed by God's antiseptic judgment, with God himself as the unrivaled monarch, has been replaced by a fragile desire to control a strip of land that has become synonymous with turmoil and strife. At the end of the day, it would be the smallest and most ancient clan among Abraham's seed that would hold the title deed, when the United Nations laid the foundation for the creation of the modern state of Israel in 1947.

Given the dominance of Christians and Muslims in the political history of Hamitic Canaan, some may be puzzled over how the Jews ended up with the envied prize. However, a brief recap of Jewish history in the region will provide an explanation. When the Ottomans ascended to power, the Jews in Hamitic Canaan were basically the remnants of the ancient Jews who—for whatever reason—did not participate in the global dispersion. The liberal Ottoman policies made it safe for Jews to visit their ancestral homeland.[14] By the sixteenth century, the indigenous Jewish population was joined by a number of Sephardim who had been displaced by the Catholic inquisitions.[15] At the dawn of the eighteenth century, Mizrachi Jews were in the habit of taking pilgrimages, and many of them decided to stay.[16] These were joined toward the end of the century by a large influx of Hasidic Ashkenazi.[17] By the turn of the century, a seemingly unstoppable stream of Ashkenazi Jews who had been victimized by so many European nations flooded into the Promised Land.

Jewish assimilation into Palestine was by no means easy. Many had come with messianic expectations,[18] and were surprised to see that the land of milk and honey was overrun by thorns and thistles.[19] In the pattern of some of their

---

[14]By the eighteenth century, the Ottomans were encouraging Jewish emigration into Palestine, and even chartered ships to transport them to their new home. See Barnai, *Jews in Palestine,* pp. 29-30.

[15]See ibid., p. 11.

[16]Ibid., p. 27.

[17]For a discussion on the Ashkenazi immigration, see ibid., pp. 37-39.

[18]In commenting on Jewish immigration in the mid-eighteenth century, Barnai writes, "There were three main reasons for [immigrating]: anticipation of the arrival of the Messiah, traditional motives, and economic and personal problems" (ibid., p. 29).

[19]See ibid., p. 32.

spiritual ancestors who returned to Egypt and Babylon after finding it difficult to resettle in Hamitic Canaan, some immigrants decided to find new shores for sanctuary. Those who stayed were the resilient remnant who were determined to hold on to their last hope of establishing a permanent *millet* in the biblical land of promise. By now the presence of the multinational Jewish contingency had become a constant source of discomfort to those who had been accustomed to a certain type of Jew. As far as Muslims and Christians were concerned, Jews were at the bottom of the social order, and although society had allowed some to succeed economically, they were expected to be aware of their subordinate place.[20] Somehow, after almost two millennia, it seemed that the reassembling of the scattered Jews had emboldened them to reclaim their prophetic voice.

The newly planted homesteaders were not about to bow to their prejudiced children, and responded to the hostility with an ideology called Zionism. The brainchild of Theodor Herzl, an Ashkenazi Jew from Austria, the Zionist movement was founded in 1896 with the stated purpose of establishing Israel as the homeland for all Jews.[21] Within twenty years, 40,000 Jews had "returned" to Israel. The Jewish cause was greatly aided in 1917 when the concept of statehood was endorsed by the Balfour Declaration, named after British Foreign Secretary, Arthur J. Balfour.[22] By 1920, the League of Nations placed Palestine under the direct authority of the British. The period that followed saw massive waves of immigration, especially by Ashkenazis fleeing Nazi persecution. By the end of World War II, over 600,000 Jews resided in Palestine, a shift in demographics that greatly infuriated Arab Christians and Muslims who felt they were being bullied and disenfranchised by the Western powers.

The frustration of the native Arabs manifested itself in spates of violence as

---

[20]For texts of primary documents depicting the life of Jews in Hamitic Canaan and Egypt in the nineteenth century, see Norman A. Stillman, *The Jews of Arab Lands: A History and Source Book* (Philadelphia: Jewish Publication Society of America, 1979), pp. 324-427. See also Bernard Lewis, *The Jews of Islam* (Princeton, N.J.: Princeton University Press, 1984), pp. 154-84. Lewis also discusses the problem with Christian and Muslim anti-Semitism: "a specific campaign against Jews, expressed in the unmistakable language of European Christian anti-Semitism, first appeared among Christians in the nineteenth century, and developed among Christians and then Muslims in the twentieth" (p. 185). See pp. 185-91, for a longer discussion on Arab anti-Semitism.

[21]For a discussion on the development of Zionism, see Ben Helper and Jihad Reinharz, *Zionism and the Creation of a New Society* (New York: Oxford University Press, 1998).

[22]Benjamin Blech, *Eyewitness to Jewish History* (Hoboken, N.J.: Wiley, 2004), pp. 268-70, suggests that the Balfour Declaration was actually a reward to Jewish scientist and Israel's first Prime Minister, Chaim Weizmann, whose invention of TNT helped England and the Allies to achieve victory.

Arabs and Jews formed rival paramilitary organizations in a violent bid to advance their diametrically opposed nationalist causes. Having fueled the flames with its obvious sympathies for the Zionist crusade, the culpable British sheepishly withdrew from the mandate in 1947, leaving the future of Palestine in the hands of the United Nations. Shortly after the UN General Assembly ordered an apartheid-like partition plan that granted 55 percent of Palestine to the Jews and the remaining 45 percent to the Arabs. The grand prize, Jerusalem, was to be Palestine's gift to the world, administered by the United Nations itself. This arrangement was quickly accepted by the Jews, but the Arabs interpreted it as strong-armed robbery of their rightful land. To nobody's amazement, a regional conflict erupted that resulted in the Jewish victors establishing the modern state of Israel in 1948.

The situation in Palestine has had wide reaching implications for Jews throughout the non-Put regions of the land of Ham. The anti-Jewish sentiment that had been brewing for decades unleashed itself in violent attacks against the dispersed children of Israel, resulting in mass emigrations and the total eradication of centuries-old Jewish communities.[23] It only stands to reason that the displaced victims who ended up in Jerusalem carried a hatred toward their persecutors that continues to manifest itself in the way Arabs are treated in Israel and the occupied territories. The alarming results of the backlash are demonstrated in the fact that whereas in 1945 there were over three quarter of a million Jews in Arab lands outside of the Palestinian mandate, less than eight thousand remain today.[24]

As a result of the Western role in the creation of the State of Israel, tolerance toward Christians in the region has also been affected. It should not be surprising to learn that the wave of Arab independence from colonial powers in the 1970s was accompanied by a rise in Islamic fundamentalism.[25] Although many Arab Christians have been influential leaders in the nationalist movements, extremist Muslims believe that their loyalty to Christianity automatically places them on the side of the Western oppressors. Notwithstand-

---

[23]For instance, Daniel J. Elazar, *The Other Jews: The Sephardim Today* (New York: Basic Books, 1989), p. 103, reports that between 1948 and 1970 approximately 40,000 Jews left Tunisia for Israel, and a similar number left for Europe. In Morocco, there were 265,000 Jewish residents in 1948, by 1968, only 22,000 were left. Recent figures show over 250,000 Jews of Moroccan origin in Israel (ibid., p. 109).

[24]See Lewis, *Jews of Islam*, pp. 190-91.

[25]Pacini, introduction, p. 13.

ing, while the adherents to the first book of the divine covenant are not wel-come in most parts of the Arab world, those who embrace both covenants have not fully fallen out of favor. In fact, though some oppose their participa-tion, Christians are woven into the political and economic fabric of Lebanese, Syrian, Egyptian and Jordanian society, and maintain a presence throughout the lands of Hamitic Canaan and Egypt. Having said this, as a result of the unrest in the region, the demographics have significantly changed since 1914 when Christians represented 24 percent of the regional population; today their numbers have dwindled to about 6 percent.

17

THE SHORTCOMINGS OF
ETHIOPIAN CHRISTIANITY

At the same time that the Bible was being challenged—and even re-
pressed—in Palestine, Egypt and North Africa, a significant majority in the
Ethiopian mainland continued to use it as a source of instruction. Members of
the Ethiopian Orthodox Church—in particular—had absorbed it into their
national identity and saw themselves as the continued embodiment of the
genuine people of God.[1] We have already seen how the rulers of the Zagwe
Dynasty engaged in a campaign to build the New Jerusalem on Ethiopian soil,
and national pride was further boosted by the well-timed appearance of the
Kebra Negast that "legitimized" the spiritual transference of divine election
from the Jews to the Ethiopians. As the self-proclaimed descendants of Solomon through Menelek I, the kings were also supposed to be blood relatives
of the Messiah himself. For the Ethiopian psyche, affinity with the house of
David was not just the mark of royalty, but the heritage of the entire nation.
This was a holy nation that had been marked by God.[2] The new identity was
so ingrained in the national psyche that "Ethiopian" became synonymous with
"Christian." In the mind of the church, there was no distinction between political and religious status, so if a person claimed to be Ethiopian he was expected to be Christian.[3]

Of course, not all Ethiopians were Christian. There was a prominent body
of Muslims who claimed to have received a greater light, and a small minority

---

[1] George A. Lipsky, *Ethiopia: Its People, Its Society, Its Culture* (New Haven, Conn.: HRAF Press,
1962), p. 100.

[2] See John W. Harbeson, *The Ethiopian Transformation: The Quest for the Post-imperial State* (Boulder,
Colo.: Westview Press, 1988), pp. 24-25.

[3] See Haile Mariam Larebo, "The Ethiopian Orthodox Church," in *Eastern Christianity and Politics in
the Twentieth Century*, ed. Pedro Ramet, vol. 1 (Durham, N.C.: Duke University Press, 1988), pp.
378-79.

that comprised the *Beta Israel*, "House of Israel,"[4] who held on to their claim to primacy. Nonetheless, the national ethos was regulated by the ecclesiastically influenced government whose actions were governed by the *Fetha Negast*, "Laws of the Kings." Written by Coptic Christian 'Abul Fada'il Ibn al-'Assal in 1240, the *Fetha Negast* assumed the status of constitution under Sarsa Dengel's reign in 1563. Based on Scripture, the writings of select church fathers and ecumenical canon law, this legal code-book served the empire until the Emperor Haile Sellassie introduced a modern constitution in 1931. As the supreme law of the land, the *Fetha Negast* also governed the actions of the Ethiopian kings, who were all expected to be faithful Christians. Indeed, it would serve as the basis for the deposing of Lij Iyasu in 1916 when he expressed an interest in Islam. And as late as 1960, Patriarch Basilios used the law to excommunicate insurgents whom his clergy had identified as "agents of the Devil."[5]

RESTORING THE THEOCRACY

Similar to ancient Israel, Ethiopia was to discover that possession of a law based on divine revelation does not guarantee national stability. There are spiritual forces at play whose sole intention is to create havoc and instability through the actions of frail human beings. The Ethiopian rulers had tried to create a theocracy after expelling the Catholic missionaries and isolating themselves from the "corruption" of the West, but by the nineteenth century, political affairs were in disarray.[6] The strong central government they had inherited from the celebrated Fasilidas had given way to the unstable *zamena mesafint*, "era of the princes," which was characterized by a breakdown in law and order.

Just when it seemed as if Ethiopia was headed toward anarchy, a line of emperors emerged who initiated an era of ecclesiastical and political reform. The work of reform commenced with Tewodros who acceded to the throne in 1855, after uniting the empire. The newly inaugurated emperor viewed spiri-

---

[4]It would be wrong to refer to the *Beta Israel* as Jews. Judaism implies acceptance of the Talmud and the inheritance of a tradition that is totally foreign to the Ethiopian followers of the religion of Israel. To refer to them as Jews is as condescending as the *Falasha* label that was placed on them.
[5]Larebo, "Ethiopian Orthodox Church," p. 380.
[6]Yohannis Abate and Mulatu Wubneh, *Ethiopia: Transition and Development in the Horn of Africa* (Boulder, Colo.: Westview Press, 1988), p. 12, report that the period of decline commenced in the period after Iyasus I (1682-1706).

tual revival as the key to national renewal. Probably influenced by the voices of the European abolitionists who challenged slavery by appealing to the gospel, he spoke out against Ethiopian slavery, which—as in ancient Israel—was legal. He also initiated a comprehensive campaign to convert the Muslims and attempted to enforce doctrinal unity in a church that was becoming more divided by theological wrangling over nonessentials.[7]

Upon his death in 1868, Tewodros was succeeded by the Emperor Johannes. Johannes was also committed to reform, but had a different approach than his predecessor. Tewodros had been extremely harsh on those whom the church hierarchy defined as "heretics" and meted out stiff punishments on all who strayed from the official version of the Orthodox faith. However, Johannes was much more conciliatory, and recognized the need for dialogue.[8] He also exercised tolerance towards the Catholics who had reentered the empire with the same missionary zeal with which they had been sent back to Europe two centuries earlier.[9] He recognized that they posed a danger to the theological unity of the church, but reasoned that objecting to their presence may be detrimental to Ethiopia's relationship with imperial-minded Europe.[10] While showing favor to Christians, Johannes was less tolerant to the Muslim populace, and entire villages were forced to convert to the Orthodox faith.[11] Notwithstanding, he did demonstrate a concern for human rights, and made tangible moves to end the slave trade.

Unfortunately, the successes of Johannes's era were marred by the imperial ambitions of Italy who wanted a piece of the African pie that was being parceled out to the European colonialists. The crafty Italians had legally purchased a section of an Ethiopian port in the province of Eritrea in 1869. By 1882, they had claimed ownership of the entire port and had begun to encroach upon the land. When Menelik II became emperor in 1889, he dealt with the situation by ceding Eritrea to Italy in the Treaty of Wichale. This must have been painful for the Eritreans in whose territory the Axumite king-

---

[7]See Harbeson, *Ethiopian Transformation*, p. 31.
[8]Ibid., p. 33.
[9]The Catholics were rivaled in Ethiopia by missionaries from the Church Missionary Society who entered Ethiopia in 1830. Mark Shaw, *The Kingdom of God in Africa: A Short History of African Christianity* (Grand Rapids: Baker, 1996), pp. 183-85.
[10]See Harbeson, *Ethiopian Transformation*, p. 33.
[11]See Haggai Erlich, *The Cross and the River: Ethiopia, Egypt, and the Nile* (Boulder, Colo.: L. Rienner, 2002), pp. 72-73.

dom had been headquartered. However, the namesake of the legendary love-child of Solomon and Sheba felt that by delivering Eritrea to the Italians, he had a chance to save the empire.

Menelik was wrong. Obtaining the Eritrean prize only whetted Italy's appetite, and in 1895 the purveyors of oppression attempted to aggressively seize more Ethiopian land. Italy had misinterpreted Menelik's sacrificial diplomacy as a sign of weakness and assumed that Ethiopia was theirs for the taking. The Italians had hoped that some of the provincial kings would join them in the assault against Menelik, but the Cushites stuck together until things came to a head at the Battle of Adowa on March 1, 1896. The Italians had planned an early morning surprise attack, which was foiled by the Ethiopians, who had risen even earlier for devotions and upon learning of the plan, decided to have their worship as they marched to meet the enemy. The remnant of Rome would soon experience the power of a nation armed with the presumption of divine providence, and were forced to raise the white flag of surrender. It would be several decades before they would muster the courage to attack again. The victory over the Italians gave the Ethiopians a huge morale boost and instant international prestige. Citizens and spectators around the globe witnessed the power of a resilient African nation at a time when the majority of Africans were confined to second-class citizenship. Having said this, the victory was somewhat marred by the fact that Italy was allowed to keep Eritrea,[12] a puzzling omission that has had devastating effects to this very day.

Menelik remained king until 1913, and not only witnessed the strengthening of the empire, but also the weakening of the church's power over people's lives. This was especially seen in the relaxing of ecclesiastical rules that prohibited the consumption of coffee, tobacco and alcohol.[13] In many ways, the ecclesiastical rules that had provided the foundation for government were hindering Ethiopia's transition to the modern age. After Menelik's death, the struggle between tradition and progress became more intense.[14] Facing death without a son, Menelik selected his grandson Lij Iyasu to be his successor. However, at the time of Menelik's death Iyasu was deemed too young to rule directly, so his authority was placed on hold until his twentieth birthday in 1916. The day of Iyasu's coronation never came. As he matured, he developed

---

[12]Abate and Wubneh, *Ethiopia*, p. 15; Harbeson, *Ethiopian Transformation*, pp. 35-36.
[13]See Harbeson, *Ethiopian Transformation*, pp. 36-37.
[14]See Harbeson, *Ethiopia*, pp. 38-41.

a fascination with Islam, an interest akin to heresy. This apostasy unleashed the fury of a number of provincial leaders and led to his excommunication and consequent dethroning. After a period of political wrangling, Menelik's daughter, Zawditu, was named empress, and the young and ambitious Ras Tafari Makonnen was elected crown prince.[15]

THE LAST OF THE PRIDE

From the very outset, the relationship between Zawditu and Ras Tafari Makonnen was shaky.[16] The empress was influenced by traditionalists who wanted to preserve the Ethiopian way of life, and the energetic Ras was eager to pull Ethiopia into the twentieth century. Following almost two decades of unrest and infighting, Ras Tafari was eventually coronated Haile Sellassie in 1930. Assuming the traditional title *Negus Negasti*, "king of kings," the emperor humbly sat in the throne of Solomon, determined to change the course of his nation. Probably the best-known Ethiopian king, Sellassie is seen by many as a king of biblical proportions. Not all assessments of Sellassie are positive, but his prophetic courage against the imperialist Western nations has made him an icon of African pride and liberation.

In the spirit of his ancient predecessors, Emperor Sellassie seriously embraced his position as a Christian king. Inspired by the biblical ideal of justice and equity and driven by the desire for national progress, he actively committed himself to the work of religious, societal and economic reform.[17] The work of reform had already commenced during his years as coregent with the empress, when he relieved the tax burden on the lower classes and championed a law that imposed penalties on those who worked on the seventh-day sabbath.[18] Now that he was emperor, Sellassie went a step further by introducing a new constitution in 1931.[19] To alleviate the concerns of those who may have seen the adoption of a constitution as a move away from ecclesiastical law, Sellassie uttered the following words in the speech given on

---

[15]For Haile Sellassie's account of events leading to the deposing of Lij Iyasu and his appointment to crown prince, see *My Life and Ethiopia's Progress, 1892-1937: The Autobiography of Emperor Haile Sellassie I*, trans. Edward Ullendorff (Chicago: Frontline Distribution International, 1999), pp. 41-62. See also Abate and Wubneh, *Ethiopia*, p. 15.

[16]Sellassie, *Autobiography*, pp. 62-64, attributes the schism to forces who were against his reforms.

[17]Abate and Wubneh, *Ethiopia*, p. 17.

[18]Sellassie, *Autobiography*, p. 40.

[19]For a summary of the process and Sellassie's commentary on the constitution, see Sellassie, *Autobiography*, pp. 178-201.

the day of ratification: "While God, being above every creature, would not find it difficult to issue orders by His word alone, yet His instituting law is because He knew that law should be the supreme ruler of the whole world."[20] He wanted to make it clear that the adoption of a constitution was in full harmony with the will of God.

Although the emperor firmly believed that laws originated from God, by limiting references to the church in the new constitution, he essentially weakened the political authority of the clergy. He recognized that the unbridled power traditionally vested in the church had presented a major obstacle to progress.[21] Notwithstanding, the constitution ensured that the church maintained its esteemed place in the empire, and even empowered the emperor with ecclesiastical authority. Other reforms focused specifically on the church and strove to liberate the Ethiopian Orthodox liturgy from its ritualistic formalism.[22] In order to make the service more relevant to the worshipers, mass was to be conducted in Amharic, the modern language of the people, and not in the ancient Geez that was only known to the priests. He also attempted to introduce sermonizing, but the stubborn clergy refused to acquiesce.[23]

Just when it seemed that Ethiopia was poised to make remarkable progress, the Italian enemy launched another attack in 1935. This time, the fascists came with heavy artillery and biological weapons. Like the biblical kings of old, Emperor Sellassie led his troops into battle, and the clergy responded to the call to arms like the tribe of Levi. Unfortunately, the ill-equipped Ethiopian army proved no match for the European superpower who had been stockpiling weapons and planning this assault for decades. On the advice of his counselors, Sellassie went into exile in England where he lobbied for assistance.

During the years of occupation, the Italians were intent on strengthening their grip on this ancient nation. Their first order of business was to punish the clergy who had participated in the resistance. Hundreds were indiscriminately slaughtered by Mussolini's purveyors of death. They also eased restrictions on Islam,[24] a move obviously intended to decimate the unique Christian identity that had fueled Ethiopian resilience. They further interfered in

---

[20]Ibid., p. 182.
[21]See Harbeson, *Ethiopian Transformation*, p. 40.
[22]For a summary of these reforms, see Sellassie, *Autobiography*, pp. 164-71.
[23]Lipsky, *Ethiopia*, p. 110.
[24]Erlich, *The Cross and the River*, p. 119.

church and regional affairs by declaring the Ethiopian Church independent from Egypt. Although the Ethiopians had desired independence for many centuries, they knew that liberty is never real when imposed upon a people by an occupying power. Enraged by this arrogant act, the Copts responded by excommunicating the newly appointed Abuna along with all of his appointed bishops.[25] Meanwhile, having been pulled into World War II, England finally decided to respond to Emperor Sellassie's plea for help. By 1941, the Italians were once again vanquished and expelled, and Eritrea was placed under British mandate before being ceded to Ethiopia.

Sellassie's reforms had suffered a major setback, but it did not take him long to get back on track. One of the first items on his agenda involved mending relations with the Egyptian Coptic Church. It's not so much that he wanted to be under the Copts, but he desired to gain autonomy independently.[26] He eventually negotiated an arrangement in which the Ethiopian Orthodox Church was granted independent status, while recognizing itself as an "extension" of the Egyptian Coptic Church.[27] This move toward ecclesiastical independence gave the nation the morale boost it needed to go forward after the hard years of oppressive occupation. Challenged to make bricks without straw, Sellassie pressed on in faith, even amending the constitution in 1955 to grant more power to parliament. Unfortunately, his inability to bring about expeditious reform incited displeasure among some of his officers who were curiously drawn to the Marxism that had captivated the Soviet Union and Cuba among others.[28] In 1974, several officers led a successful coup d'etat that led to the abolishing of the monarchy. After more than two millennia, the scepter that is alleged to have been passed down to generations of Ethiopian kings from Solomon's son Menelik was suddenly taken from the one who had so gallantly borne the title "Lion of Judah."

---

[25]For a recap of the events see ibid., pp. 112-17.

[26]See ibid., p. 119.

[27]For details see ibid., pp. 123-27.

[28]Although the emperor made significant progress, some have leveled severe criticism against his reform efforts, particularly as it relates to the related issues of slavery and economic disparity. (See Sellassie, *Autobiography*, pp. 78-81, for the Emperor's response to critics.) However it is often forgotten that his ability to effectively initiate all of his domestic reforms was greatly hampered by the looming threat of European imperialism. Despite attempts to play by the rules of the Western powers, the nation was repeatedly disrespected by racist imperialists who were desperate to break the back of Ethiopia—the final bastion of Hamitic independence. See Harbeson, *Ethiopian Transformation*, pp. 40-41; and Abate and Wubneh, *Ethiopia*, p. 14.

FAILED WITNESS

The 120-member military *Derg* ("committee") that assumed leadership of
Ethiopia sought to instantly bring about a socialist version of Jubilee. The
previous reforms had been too slow, and had not been friendly to the Muslim and "Israelite" segments of the population. Now armed with Marxist
ideology, this new regime—which would eventually be led by Mengistu
Haile Mariam—would show the followers of Scripture how to establish a
just society. Interestingly, the ones who welcomed the change in leadership
were the *Beta Israel*. Once treated as equals, the status of the *Beta Israel* had
been diminishing since the seventeenth century, when they were maligned
with the derogatory term *Falasha:* "a people without land."[29] Infected by the
same intolerant bug that had spread through Western Christianity, those
who claimed to be transformed by the gospel had learned to view their siblings with malignant contempt. Now with the socialist revolution, those
who had been deprived of land ownership for centuries were able to benefit
from the land redistribution program. It appeared that the secular *Derg* had
brought about the year of Jubilee.

Sadly for the *Beta Israel*, reality was to set in. Rather than relieve them from
scorn, they were scorned all the more. As far as the selfish masses were concerned, their rise from abject poverty to government-ordered land ownership
was unfair.[30] It soon became clear that the prejudiced Christians who prided
themselves in their Solomonic identity had no room in their heart to extend
unconditional love to the *Beta Israel* which represented the very root of their
Messianic faith. With the seemingly impenetrable incalcitrance of the Ethiopian Christians, those seeking parallels with ancient Israel may very well
blame the devastating famine of the 1980s on the rigid formalism of a people
who should have known better.

Fortunately for the *Beta Israel*, their plight had caught the attention of Jews
around the world. In fact, ever since the nineteenth century, European Jews
had made contact with the Israelite leaders in Ethiopia and had attempted to
better their situation with the establishing of a school and other types of aid.[31]

---

[29]For a description of the communal life of the *Beta Israel* in Ethiopia, see Gadi Benezer, *The Ethiopian
Jewish Exodus: Narratives of the Migration Journey to Israel 1977-1985* (London: Routledge, 2002),
pp. 16-26.
[30]See ibid., pp. 28-29.
[31]Ibid., pp. 27-32.

With the creation of the modern state of Israel, the religious leaders discussed the status of the *Beta Israel*, and in 1973 the Israeli government ruled that they were actual descendants of the tribe of Dan.[32] The *Beta Israel* were granted Israeli citizenship in 1975, and between 1977 and 1984, a number of them made the long trek from their Ethiopian homes to refugee camps in Sudan from where they would be processed and transported to Israel. Eventually in late 1984 and early 1985 the Israeli government airlifted 8,200 members of *Beta Israel* in Operation Moses and Operation Queen of Sheba.[33] Six years later, in May 1991, another spectacular airlift took place in Addis Ababa, when through Operation Solomon 14,500 Israelites were airlifted in thirty-six hours! This was their exodus, one which resulted in the eventual transferal of 85,000 Ethiopian children of Israel.[34] The Orthodox Christians may have viewed Ethiopia as the New Israel, but for the *Beta Israel* it was an experience worse than that of their spiritual forebears who endured captivity in Egypt and Babylon.

As the population of the *Beta Israel* dwindles, the challenge of shining the light of biblical truth is left to the several denominations of Christianity that remain in Ethiopia. Although a significant portion of the population have joined Catholic and Protestant communions, the Orthodox faith is still dominant. Unfortunately, the witness of the church is still somewhat weak. As one writer puts it, "Curiously, the Ethiopian rulers have used Christianity as a justification in their quest for empire while the Ethiopian Church itself appears to have been less aggressive in expanding its spiritual kingdom."[35] As recently as May of 1993, the Church missed a major opportunity to demonstrate the power of the gospel when, after a long and bloody struggle, Eritrea declared its independence from Ethiopia. Ideally, political differences should not have affected the relationships of the spiritual siblings in the church of God. However, by July of that same year, the bishops of Eritrea had petitioned the Egyptian Coptic leader, Pope Shenuoda III, for independent status, indicating their desire to separate from the Ethiopian Orthodox fellowship. The arrangement

---

[32]Ibid., p. 27.

[33]Earlier airlifts of descendants of Israel residing in Hamitic Ethiopia include Operation Magic Carpet, which took place between 1949 and 1951, and involved 45,000 Yemeni Jews. See Michael A. Weingarten, *Changing Health and Changing Culture: The Yemenite Jews in Israel* (Westport, Conn.: Praeger, 1992), p. 12.

[34]Benezer, *Ethiopian Jewish Exodus*, p. 33.

[35]Harbeson, *Ethiopian Transformation*, p. 25.

was finalized within two months, and the Eritrean Orthodox Tewahdo Church was born. Born in schism, the Eritrean Church has continued a policy of intolerance against other expressions of Christian faith—apart from Catholicism—and the state must approve any Protestant church before it can officially operate.

18

THE IMPACT OF CHRISTIANITY
ON SUB-SAHARAN AFRICA

Buoyed by the political realities of history, the vital center of biblical Ham has migrated from the narrow northern Canaanite territories to the southern expanses in the regions of Put.[1] The majority of the Bible's pages had been scripted in the biblical land of Canaan, which also served as the major backdrop for the ancient phases of salvation history. The lands descending from Misrayim had provided the academic apparatus for Bible translation and theological speculation. And while the eastern portions of the land aligned to biblical Cush had replaced the genuine Bible with Muhammad's faith-altering interpretation, those on the mainland held on to it as the foundation of their government. For thousands of years in the land of Ham, it appears as if the Bible had been migrating southward, seemingly in a quest for fertile ground. In a desperate bid for success, the Bible has traversed the arid Sahara and has shaken the remnant of its seed on the vast ranges of Hamitic Put. And now the divine reaper anticipates his harvest—the age of Put has finally arrived!

MISSION OMISSION

The triumph of the Bible in Put is nothing short of miraculous. In part five, we saw how sub-Saharan Africans were introduced to the Bible by warring clerics accompanied by musket-bearing mercenaries. Under the shadow of the looming *padrao*, these Europeans expanded the markets for the existing slave trade and claimed the land as their own. Even when the British—persuaded by the abolitionists—sought to replace the slave trade with "Christianity and

---

[1]Philip Jenkins, *The Next Christendom: The Coming of Global Christianity* (New York: Oxford University Press, 2002), pp. 1-6, writes of the general movement of global Christianity from northern Euro-American regions to southern African and Latin regions.

commerce," they did so with the expansion of the empire in mind. Somehow their apparent altruism was tainted by malevolent motives. Reflecting on the missionary movement, Kenyan liberator Jomo Kenyatta said, "When the missionaries came to Africa they had the Bible and we had the land. They said 'Let us pray.' We closed our eyes. When we opened them we had the Bible and they had the land."[2] The truth is, in many ways the missionary venture was more about commerce than Christianity. Nonetheless, the very missions that were tainted by the racist notions of cultural supremacy created the institutions that would invoke the spirit of freedom throughout the continent. Armed with the liberating message of Scripture, it would not be long before the sons of Put joined their Ethiopian brothers in the resounding chant of independence.

Slavery and freedom in East Africa. When the doors of opportunity reopened in Ethiopia in the early 1800s, Johann Ludwig Krapf was among the pioneers sent by the Christian Missionary Society to advance the Christian cause in Shoa. His interference in local affairs and constant urging for England to occupy the empire led to his team's expulsion.[3] Krapf ended up on the shores of Kenya with his pregnant wife, but tragically lost both her and their infant child soon after she gave birth in 1844.[4] Undeterred, he continued his work, utilizing his linguistic skills to translate the Bible into Swahili.[5] He was soon joined by other missionaries who assisted him in the challenging work of native evangelism. Twenty years and twelve converts later, he changed his strategy, opting instead to set up mission stations stretching from the east to the west, eventually linking to existing West African Christian settlements in Badagry and Abeokuta. Although his work as a missionary did not yield many converts, his Swahili translation of the Bible would serve as a lingering voice to the people of Put in Africa's horn.

In 1874, the work in East Africa got another boost with the arrival of Bartle Frere, who built on Krapf's concept and established a self-named town. Freretown housed a school and provided industry, and the citizens were restricted

---

[2]Quoted in Ibid., p. 40.
[3]Adrian Hastings, *The Church in Africa: 1450-1950* (Oxford: Oxford University Press, 1996), pp. 225-26.
[4]For an assessment of Krapf's life work, see Roland Oliver, *The Missionary Factor in East Africa* (London: Longmans Green, 1952), pp. 5-9.
[5]Mark Shaw, *The Kingdom of God in Africa: A Short History of African Christianity* (Grand Rapids: Baker, 1996), pp. 187-88.

from leaving. However, in spite of the penal colony type set up, the community sparked the creation of more Christian villages, which became sanctuaries for runaway slaves.[6] Upset by the interference to their trade, Arab slavers launched an attack against Freretown, but were not able to stop the flow of God's creatures who gravitated towards these strange oases of freedom. By 1888, the number of fugitive Christians had reached the two thousand mark, and a number of native leaders had arisen from among them. One of these leaders, William Jones, was ordained as a pastor for the community in 1895. While grateful for the sanctuary provided by these Christian villages, Jones quickly noticed that his liberators were still tainted by racism as evidenced by the way they treated their nonwhite colleagues.[7] His courage to protest the prejudice was rewarded by his being ousted from the Christian Missionary Society in 1897. By the end of the century, fugitive Christian communities were to disappear when the British colonized Kenya, effectively ending the slave trade. Ironically, the very nation that had profited the most from slavery and had ruled the masses in its dark-skinned empire with a heavy hand would become a symbol of freedom.

Even as Krapf and his companions sought to advance Christianity and commerce in Ethiopia's southernmost neighbor, the Arab rulers of Tanganyika and Zanzibar continued the African slave trade with cruel capitalist greed. According to reports, by the 1850s Zanzibar had become the most active slave center in the world, and the Muslim traders rivaled—if not surpassed—the evils of the Portuguese and Spanish, as infant children were stacked into vessels and made to travel for days without food.[8] Here again, it would be the separate but united work of Protestant and Catholic European missionaries that would halt the treacherous trade of Put's despised progeny.[9] At the end of the day, it was the Germans who cast the fatal blow on the horrendous slave trade in Tanzania when they defeated the Arabs in 1891 and claimed the land they had staked earlier at the 1885 Berlin Conference. In a strange way, chattel slavery in Eastern Africa had been halted by the General Act of the Berlin Conference—the very conference that initiated the so-called scramble for Africa

---

[6]Ibid., p. 190.
[7]Ibid., p. 191.
[8]Ibid., p. 193.
[9]Chiefly active were the Universities Mission to Central Africa, the Holy Ghost Fathers, the White Fathers and the London Missionary Society (Shaw, *Kingdom of God in Africa*, pp. 194-97).

and ceded ninety percent of the African continental portion of the land of Ham to insatiable European imperialists.

The mission to Buganda called for a different strategy. After acceding to the throne in 1856, Mutesa, the all-powerful Bugandan king, flirted for a while with Islam. In 1875 he was visited by a contingency that included the famous journalist Henry Morton Stanley ("Dr. Livingstone, I presume?"). Stanley tried his hand at sharing the gospel, and after evaluating his arguments Mutesa was persuaded to give Christianity a try.[10] The Christian Missionary Society responded to Stanley's call for assistance, and the Protestant understanding of Scripture was advanced in the royal court. Before the work of instruction was even completed, though, the White Fathers, a Catholic order, sought an audience and introduced the novitiates to the virulent division between Catholic and Protestant Christianity.[11] Needless to say, Mutesa never did embrace the Christian teachings, even after the groundbreaking efforts of Dallington Muftaa who painstakingly made portions of the Bible available to him in his native Lugandan tongue.

Biblical instructors of any ilk were definitely not welcome by the new king, Mwanga, who was an insatiable homosexual and was enraged that his courtiers who had embraced biblical morality refused his advances.[12] Mwanga engaged in a terrible campaign of persecution, burning missionaries alive. His reprobate mind underestimated the power of martyrdom, and his abject wickedness drew disgust from Catholic, Protestant *and* Muslim, who put their theological differences aside and executed judgment on the manic monarch whose immoral actions violated the teachings of both the Bible and the Qur'an. Following Mwanga's defeat in 1888, the Muslims claimed Buganda for *dar al-Islam* and expelled their Christian allies. However, England had already targeted the kingdom for Britannia at the Berlin Conference, and quickly snatched its catch before the Muslims got too settled. By 1894 Mutesa's kingdom was covered by the red, white and blue of the Union Jack.

Oppression and liberation in South Africa. Long before the Berlin Conference, or even the abolition of slavery, the British had already staked a claim on Dutch-colonized South Africa. Their quest for dominance was finalized in 1815. Two decades later as thousands of English immigrants took advantage

---

[10]Oliver, *Missionary Factor,* pp. 39-41.
[11]Shaw, *Kingdom of God in Africa,* p. 200.
[12]See Oliver, *Missionary Factor,* pp. 103-4.

of the home comforts that abounded in the established colony, the feisty Dutch embarked on a long march to distance themselves from their new over-lords. Known as the Great Trek, the march was undertaken with the dignity of destiny.[13] As far as these believers were concerned, this was just another nec-essary chapter in the life of God's chosen as they moved to their final destina-tion in the "promised" land of Canaan. After bloody—some say miraculous—victories over angry Zulu warriors, the Boers pitched their tents in Transvaal, determined to prosper again.

The English interference in Dutch affairs had begun decades before the Cape was added to the empire. Fueled by their desire to end slavery, the Lon-don Missionary Society had sent several missionaries to agitate the status quo and invite the natives to join the universal family of God. The first missionary to make his mark was Johannes Van der Kemp, himself a Dutchman who arrive at the Cape in 1799 with an able team of assistants.[14] It did not take long for him to start a work among indigenous Africans, a move that invoked the anath-ema of the Dutch Reformed Church. Unfazed by the racist opposition, Van der Kemp further infuriated his fellow countrymen when he married one of his pa-rishioners—a young African woman![15] This practical integrationist went on to establish a Christian community in Bethelsdorp, and was an outspoken critic of the racist system. The experiment at Bethelsdorp experienced marginal suc-cess, and was instrumental in developing indigenous missionary workers like Cupido Kakkerlak, from the Khoi people, and the Xhosan, Dyani.[16]

Other missionaries from the London Missionary Society followed Van der Kemp, each touting a similar message of equality. James Read is another ex-ample of a courageous man who defied convention and made a statement by marrying a Khoi. Fully immersed in his adopted culture, Read thrust himself into the fight against racial injustice. His success at endearing himself to the people is indicated by the fact that he was asked to serve as pastor for the first independent black church when it was established by natives in 1829.[17]

---

[13]For a comprehensive study, see Eric Anderson Walker, *The Great Trek* (London: A. & C. Black, 1934). See also Sheila Patterson, *The Last Trek: A Study of the Boer People and the Afrikaner Nation* (London: Routledge, 1957).
[14]Shaw, *Kingdom of God in Africa*, pp. 166-67.
[15]Given the fact that several missionaries from the London Missionary Society married natives (Eliz-abeth Isichei, *A History of Christianity in Africa* [Grand Rapids: Eerdmans; Lawrenceville, N.J.: Af-rica World Press, 1995], p. 107), this may have been a strategy for evangelism.
[16]Ibid.
[17]Hastings, *The Church in Africa*, p. 216; Isichei, *A History of Christianity*, pp. 107-8.

Not all whites went as deep into the culture as Read, but several more applied the prophetic message of Scripture to the situation in South Africa. Among these was the famous Bishop John Williams Colenso, an outspoken pluralist and proponent of the liberal historical criticism that was wreaking havoc in the seminary halls of Europe.[18] He directed his prophetic cry to the English, whose tactics were different than the Dutch, but whose objectives appeared to be the same. By appealing to the common brotherhood of all humanity, he became a major spokesperson for the rights of the Zulu nation.

Perhaps the most recognized missionary names from the nineteenth century are those of David Livingstone and his father-in-law, Robert Moffat. Moffat developed the concept of mission stations—centers of commerce that could be used for the advancement of Christianity. He was to devote fifty years of his life to Africa. Livingstone also devoted his life to Africa, but was more accomplished as an explorer than a missionary. The truth is, neither he nor his father-in-law experienced great success in evangelism, from a numerical perspective. After half a century in Africa, Moffat's converts only numbered around 200, and Livingstone is reported to only have baptized one person who later backslid![19]

Moffat and Livingstone's experience was all too familiar to the idealists who devoted their lives to enlightening the "heathen." Somehow, it was difficult for the natives to receive words of hope coming from the lips of those whose complexion resembled the very people who had weakened their collective spirit. What was so "good" about an apartheid gospel that favored those of a lighter hue? Given their experiences with their forceful visitors, it is not surprising that the major Ndebele, Zulu and Shona tribes were virtually impenetrable.[20] Added to the racist element—or maybe a part of it—was the problem of contextualization. Many of the missionaries found it difficult to translate the teachings of the Bible to the African culture. For instance, it wasn't difficult for them to explain the concept of a supreme God, but there was no parallel in traditional religions for a Chalcedonian Jesus. Further, having been catechized from Sunday school to seminary, they uncritically accepted the stories of the Bible. However, they were not prepared for the challenging questions that would come from those who, upon hearing the Bible

---

[18]Shaw, *Kingdom of God in Africa*, pp. 177-79.
[19]Ibid., p. 169.
[20]Isichei, *A History of Christianity*, pp. 113-16.

for the first time, would be naturally curious about the apparent contradictions between the Testaments.[21] After years of seeking a breakthrough, only the Tswana showed any interest.[22]

South African Christianity would not take life until the indigenous believers commandeered the reins. The platform for independent movements was already being constructed from the beginning of the nineteenth century. The *kairos* for the change was incited by the bloody British massacre of the Xhosa in 1811, which conjured several charismatic leaders who claimed to have experienced supernatural encounters with God. Nxele, a product of a Boer Christian environment, points to 1812 as the year of his divine visitation.[23] The voice that spoke to him denounced the staid formalism of European worship and encouraged traditional methods of praising God. In 1819, he rallied the Xhosa to pick up arms against the British, promising them victory. After the Xhosa defeat, Nxele was imprisoned on the infamous Robben Island, where he drowned while trying to escape. He must have died singing a similar song to his oppressed brethren in the American south: "Before I be a slave, I'll be buried in my grave, and go home to my Lord and be free." Thirty years later, another prophet, Mlanjeni, claimed that God had told him that the blacks would be victorious over the whites.[24] History reports that the Xhosa were once again beaten in battle.

Although defeated, Nxele and Mlanjeni became martyrs for African Christians who yearned for self-determination. In 1872, 158 Sotho Christians separated from the Paris Evangelical Mission in Hemon and declared themselves autonomous.[25] These were followed by Nehemiah Tile who broke from the Methodists in 1884 to found the Tembu National Church. Another Methodist, Mangane Mokone, formed the Ethiopian Church in 1892. In the spirit of the new Christian nationalism, the African Presbyterian Church was formed in 1898. In the main, the liturgy of these new churches was similar to the ones in the denominations from which they came. However, many of them made adjustments to items of doctrine, the most oft changed being the Western prohibition of plural marriages.[26] Independence meant that they did not have to

---

[21] See Ibid., pp. 121-24.
[22] See Hastings, *The Church in Africa*, pp. 311-12.
[23] Isichei, *A History of Christianity*, p. 109.
[24] Ibid., pp. 109-10.
[25] Ibid., p. 125.
[26] Ibid., p. 126.

endorse the countercultural missionary interpretation of Scripture, and were free to walk in the ways of Abraham, David and Solomon!

Colonization and independence in West Africa. In many ways, indigenous Christianity in West Africa was independent from its inception. As in the east and the south, the English were an important part of the missionary machinery. Already by the end of the eighteenth century, the English had gained significant influence in the region. In a strange twist of fate, even as the English economy was being fattened by the slave trade, Parliament responded to the demands of London abolitionists and in 1787 established a colony in Sierra Leone for free slaves.[27] Freetown, by name, was to be a Christian community populated by poor manumitted Africans from London, former slaves from the Caribbean and "recaptives" who the British navy rescued from slave ships bound for America. Patterned after the cities of Europe, Freetown was home to factories and academic institutions. The most notable building was the famous Fourah Bay College—the precursor to the University of Sierra Leone—which was the only European-style university in the region for almost a century.[28]

While some of the recaptives and repatriates followed the ways of Islam or traditional religions, the majority confessed Christianity, and a number involved themselves in Christian missions. Probably the most famous citizen of Freetown is the Anglican clergyman Samuel Ajayi Crowther. Crowther was a recaptive Yoruba who was the first student and later a professor at Fourah Bay College. Upon his ordination in London in 1843, he became the first Anglican priest in Sierra Leone. Obsessed with a passion for mission, Crowther was sent to Nigeria where he shared the teachings of Scripture with his native Yoruba, among others. His efforts were rewarded in 1864, when he became the first black bishop to Africa. Although elevated to a high ecclesiastical position, he was not immune from racism, and he spent his final days as a victim of church politics.[29] A letter written to the Archbishop of Canterbury in 1892 by his clergy colleagues attests to the success of his ministry.[30]

Inspired by the success of Freetown, other Christian communities were formed in West Africa. Notably, the catalyst for these was not abolitionists in

---

[27]Shaw, *Kingdom of God in Africa*, pp. 142-43.
[28]For a study on the institution, see Daniel J. Paracka, *The Athens of West Africa: A History of International Education at Fourah Bay College, Freetown, Sierra Leone* (New York: Routledge, 2003).
[29]See Shaw, *Kingdom of God in Africa*, pp. 155-56.
[30]For the text of the letter, see Thomas Hodgkin, *Nigerian Perspectives: An Historical Anthology* (London: Oxford University Press, 1960), pp. 309-11.

England, but freed Africans. Setting their sights on Badagry, a slave port on the Nigerian coast, two Hausa men who had been slaves in Trinidad persuaded a group of recaptives to purchase a ship, and soon a thriving community developed. The community was joined by Thomas Birch Freeman, a Methodist missionary. He used Badagry as a missionary base and was able to persuade the chief of Abeokuta to open up his community to recaptives. Empowered by these African Christian colonies, Crowther and Freeman achieved in a few short decades what the European missionaries thought impossible. Although still tainted by the culture of Europe, African Christianity would take root when it was nurtured by those who had experienced the liberating power of the gospel firsthand.

The success of the English-initiated communities attracted the attention of abolitionists in the United States. Under the auspices of the newly formed American Colonization Society, a team of eighty-eight freed slaves was commissioned to find a place on West African soil where an American version of Freetown could be duplicated. In 1820, the expedition came across a parcel of land south of Sierra Leone and—emulating the custom of the Europeans with the Native Americans—strong-armed the local king into giving them millions of dollars worth of land for goods worth only $300.[31] They called the place Liberia, and by 1866, 18,000 former slaves and recaptives had settled there.

Although claiming to be a Christian community, American apartheid had deeply infected the citizens of Liberia who viewed the indigenous population with contempt. Nonetheless, the call to evangelism was kept alive by Protestant and Catholic clergy who constructed permanent edifices to serve as bases for their regional missions. They also established educational institutions, among which was Liberia College. One of Liberia College's most famous personalities was Edward Wilmot Blyden, a gifted linguist and scholar from the West Indies.[32] Appointed to the faculty of Liberia College in 1862, Blyden went on to serve in several government positions, even placing an unsuccessful bid for president in 1885. He is best known for his theological contributions, and was probably the earliest black liberation theologian, calling for an authentic African Christianity that would unite all the children of Ham.

---

[31]Shaw, *Kingdom of God in Africa*, p. 150.
[32]See Hastings, *The Church in Africa*, p. 355. For a comprehensive study, see Edith Holden, *Blyden of Liberia: An Account of the Life and Labors of Edward Wilmot Blyden, LL.D., as recorded in letters and in print* (New York: Vantage Press, 1966).

MISSION POSSIBLE

The success of the indigenous evangelists provided a new boost to the missionary movement. Soon Protestant and Catholic alike recruited African evangelists and invested in the translation of the Bible into local languages. Some denominations experienced great success. The Methodists, for instance, made major inroads in Ghana through the work of Thomas Birch Freeman, who had founded the Christian community at Abeokuta. At the end of his fifty-year tenure in 1888, much had been accomplished. Mission agencies also recruited workers from the Caribbean and South America. In 1843, the Baptist Mission Society employed Jamaican missionaries to help start the work in Cameroon, and a black Brazilian served as the pastor of the six-thousand-member Catholic parish in Lagos in 1868. This was the beginning of a major breakthrough in Africa. Africans had shown that it *was* possible to get through to the so-called heathen.

Hijacked. The sons of Put had proven their worth on the mission field. They had not baptized great numbers, but had infused new life into the work. Given the purpose of evangelism, this should have been reason to celebrate— the Word of God was going forth, and the siblings of Ethiopia were stretching forth their hands to God. However, while the natives rejoiced at the power of the Spirit who had moistened the ground of the vast sub-Saharan plain, there was jealousy in the camp of some of their European colleagues. With the slow death of Christianity in the northern lands of Japheth, the challenge of Africa and Asia had given them a reason for existence. If enough qualified clergy were developed from among the sons of Put, there would be no real reason for their presence. Sam Crowther's experience with racism had already exposed the heavy glass ceiling that loomed over the heads of native workers, and it would be decades before ecclesiastical oppression would loosen its grip.

The situation was to intensify after the 1885 Berlin Conference, when the European powers devised their plan to partition Africa with total disregard to tribal borders. The colonizers entered Africa with plans to recreate it in its image. European-style governments were instituted and Romance and Germanic languages imposed on the people. The deliberate attempt to market Europe as a super-culture provided new missionary opportunities for eager adventurers from the northern lands. Capitalizing on the political *kairos*, thousands of missionaries poured in from Europe and America. The work of the indigenous missionaries had helped to alleviate some of the suspicion toward

Christianity, and the presence of the imperial powers provided protection and resources. This time around, failure was not an option.

A number of the independent churches had adopted Psalm 68:31 as a motto, but few would have imagined that the number of Ham's sub-Saharan sons who would "extend their hands to God" would grow from 4 million in 1900 to 34 million by 1950.[33] Most of the credit for this astounding growth goes to the colonial powers who created the infrastructure to enable speedy conversion.[34] Christians had easier access to government jobs and, in the new urban social system, were able to achieve higher status. Rural dwellers were seen as less threatening if they aligned with a denomination, a decision that also granted them access to economically empowering government programs. Construction of new roads and the development of mechanized transportation systems also meant that missionaries could establish posts in more places. It also helped both church and empire that the government often provided financial support to mission schools.

It was almost a fait accompli that students educated in the schools would submit to the pressure to convert, and their parents and other family members no doubt felt obligated. As the imperialist Romans provided the infrastructure for the spread of the gospel in the early church, so European colonialists would enable the Word of God to go forth—though often as a tainted witness. This is not to suggest that all the conversions during this period were influenced by expedience, it is simply highlighting a sociological reality. There must have been many who were convicted by the Spirit of God, but as the recent blood bath in Rwanda demonstrates, the gospel had not fully taken root. Notwithstanding, the European missionaries should be given due credit for their painstaking efforts in making the Bible accessible to the people. Indeed, it would be the words of the Bible that would stir up the spirit of freedom in the sons of Put and prepare the way for African independence.

Free at last. In the previous chapter, we saw how some Africans viewed the Bible as a living book that directly addressed the needs of their people. The supernatural experiences of the Xhosa prophets Nxeli and Mlanjeni laid the foundation for the birth of independent churches in South Africa. Jenkins locates the impetus for the independent church movement with the experiences

---

[33]Shaw, *Kingdom of God in Africa*, p. 207.
[34]See Jenkins, *Next Christendom*, pp. 42-43.

of Kimpa Vita in early eighteenth-century Congo.[35] Kimpa had been baptized by Capuchin missionaries who had given her the "Christian" name Beatrice. It did not take her long to realize that her name was not the only part of her identity that the missionaries wanted to change. When they began to degrade her culture, she revealed that she had received a vision from God who told her that the biblical characters were really black Africans, and there was nothing wrong with her culture. When she began sharing the revelation she was arrested and burned as a heretic and witch in 1706.

Two centuries later, William Wade Harris announced that he had been visited by the angel Gabriel.[36] With a message common to many leaders of independent movements, he was told to discard Western garb and don a white robe and turban. In 1913, he started his evangelistic outreach, taking his revelation to the eager masses in West Africa. His interpretation of the biblical message encouraged the keeping of the commandments including strict sabbath observance, and it endorsed polygamy.[37] He also promoted respect for certain traditional religious practices. During the course of his ministry, he personally converted over 100,000 to his understanding of biblical Christianity.

Not every prophet of independence was allowed the freedom of Harris. In 1918, Simon Kimbangu from Central Africa claimed to have received a call to a prophetic and healing ministry.[38] After a period of resistance, he finally submitted to the call in 1921. His message was well received, and he attracted the displeasure of his Belgian overlords, who had him tried and sentenced to death. His impending martyrdom only served to swell the ranks of followers, and in an effort to appease the masses, the authorities commuted his sentence to life in prison. When Kimbangu died in 1951, he left behind a church that has grown to several million members.

Some of the prophets of independence taught that God was calling them to more radical reforms that not only rejected imperial Christianity but also colonial structures. In 1915, John Chilembwe, a Baptist missionary stationed

---

[35]Ibid., pp. 47-48. Hastings, *The Church in Africa,* pp. 102-7, has a slightly different report and links her to the Antonian movement.

[36]For a study on the Harrist movement, see Sheila S. Walker, *The Religious Revolution in the Ivory Coast: The Prophet Harris and the Harrist Church* (Chapel Hill: University of North Carolina Press, 1983).

[37]For a synopsis of his beliefs see ibid., pp. 132-44.

[38]For a description of Kimbangu's ministry, see Wyatt MacGaffey, *Modern Kongo Prophets: Religion in a Plural Society* (Bloomington: Indiana University Press, 1983), pp. 33-41.

in what is now Malawi, claimed that God had ordered him to revolt against British domination and establish a National African Church.[39] Like Nat Turner and Paul Bogle who had received similar messages in America and Jamaica, his plan failed, and he was punished by the authorities.

Less confrontational was Alice Lenisha from the area known today as Zambia. In 1953, she shared her vision for cultural reform in the churches and started a movement named *Lumpa* ("better than all others").[40] Like the Millerites of the early 1800s, this apocalyptic sect believed that the second coming of Christ was imminent, and she along with hundreds and thousands of followers moved to a compound to prepare for his appearing. The movement was antiestablishment and refused to pay taxes or recognize the authority of the government. Surprisingly, it was the newly independent Zambian government that tried to use force to stop them, and the movement eventually dissipated after the prophet's death in 1978.

The independent church movement appears to be most active in southern Africa and has been especially vibrant in recent years. For this region of the land of Put, Jenkins reports four thousand independent churches in the 1990s with five million members.[41] Zimbabwe has a large independent movement, and only 30 percent of Christians in Botswana belong to "mission" churches. By far the most successful of these churches is the South African Zion Christian Church, which promotes a distinct dress and doctrine and has a membership of four million—according to government statistics.[42] It is highly probable that the explosion of the independent church movement in southern Africa is directly attributed to the continuation of Apartheid until recent decades.[43] By 2003, when the members of independent Christians were added to those in institutional churches, Africa boasted over 360 million Christians![44] Somehow, African Christians have examined the same book the oppressors used to justify their conquest, and have discovered encouraging words of freedom.

---

[39]See Hastings, *Church,* pp. 486-89.
[40]Jenkins, *Next Christendom,* pp. 50-51.
[41]Ibid., p. 68.
[42]If these statistics are correct, then Jenkin's estimate of five million total independent Christians in the southern Africa region needs to be revised.
[43]Jenkins, *Next Christendom,* p. 69.
[44]Based on current trends, Jenkins, *Next Christendom,* p. 3, reasons: "If we extrapolate these figures to the year 2025, and assume no great gains or losses through conversion, then there would be . . . 633 million . . . [Christians] in Africa."

By responding to the liberating mandates of Scripture, African Christianity has managed to rescue the Bible from the skeptical laboratory of the European academy. To be fair to Europe, the sons of Put have also helped to save the Word of God from the early philosophical speculation of the sons of Misrayim and the insular formality of the sons of Cush. And while some German and English theologians challenged the credibility of the stories of creation and resurrection, it was their believing brothers and sisters who boarded ships and planes to share the good news about the Resurrected One through whom the worlds were created. Indeed, it was in colonial mission schools that the liberators of Africa discovered God's plan for humanity.

It is no small wonder, then, that many of the leaders in the African liberation struggle were Christian:

> Zambian president Kenneth Kaunda was the son of a Presbyterian minister, while Senegal's leader Leopold Senghor had trained for the priesthood. Tanzanian Prime Minister Julius Nyerere and Ghanaian leader Kwame Nkrumah had both taught in mission schools. Nyerere was a Catholic who worked closely with the churches, and for all his radical nationalism, he praised the missionaries who, he felt, "had brought the best they knew to Africa, their church and way of life." He drew heavily on Christian thought and language in formulating his radical variant of African socialism, which he traced back to the early Christian communism described in the book of Acts.[45]

When it came to developing black leaders, the most effective mission school by far was Fort Hare University in South Africa, which was founded in 1916 specifically for the education of indigenous Africans.[46] The illustrious alumni roster includes Archibald Campbell Jordan, pioneer of African studies; Govan Mbeki, politician and father of South African President Thabo Mbeki; Yusuf Lule, interim president of Uganda; Oliver Tambo, revered member of the African National Congress; Joshua Nkomo, founder of the ZAPU and Zimbabwean statesman; Nelson Mandela, revered president of South Africa; Seretse Khama, first president of Botswana; Julius Nyere, president of Tanzania; Herbert Chitepo, ZANU leader; Robert Sobukwe, founder of the Pan Africanist

---

[45]Ibid., p. 148. For another list of names, see also Christopher Steed and Bengt Sundkler, *A History of the Church in Africa* (Cambridge: Cambridge University Press, 2000), p. 902.

[46]The brainchild of African leaders (Simphiwe A. Hlatshwayo, *Education and Independence: Education in South Africa, 1658-1988* [Westport, Conn.: Greenwood Press, 2000], 40), Fort Hare was cofounded by Scottish missionaries (Hastings, *Church*, p. 545).

Congress; Robert Mugabe, president of Zimbabwe; Kenneth Kaunda, first president of Zambia; Mangosuthu Buthelezi, leader of the Inkatha Freedom Party; Desmond Tutu, Anglican Archbishop and South African peace activist; and Chris Hani, leader of the South African Communist Party.

Thanks to an educational system that has produced African leaders who excel in the art of communication, the Bible has become a major instrument in changing the tide of colonial oppression. Indeed it is the Bible's teaching on the "brotherhood of man" that inspired Protestant and Catholic leaders in South Africa to put heady theological differences aside and develop the *Kairos* document in 1985. This prophetic statement challenged the churches to model the beloved community by integrating their congregations. Committed to the integrity of the Word, African Christians not only fought against the oppressor, but have served as prophetic voices to their own corrupt leaders during the postcolonial era. Indeed, it was Archbishop Luwum of Uganda and Cardinal Biayenda of the Republic of Congo who led the masses in protests against government corruption, and were silenced by government-endorsed assassins' bullets in 1977.[47] And in Mobutu Sese Seko's hellish Zaire, it was Roman Catholic Archbishop Christophe Munzihirwa who championed the rights of the persecuted and condemned all who perpetrated violence, whatever their tribal affiliation. This soldier of Christ met his bloody end when he was gunned down by Rwandan troops in 1996.[48] These modern martyrs who "loved not their lives unto death" (Rev 12:11 KJV) serve as a powerful reminder of the power of the gospel.

Perhaps the most radical demonstration of the success of God's Word in the land of Put occurred at the fall of Apartheid in 1994. The curse brought upon the land by Jan van Riebeeck and his European allies was finally broken. The spiritual descendants of Nxele and Mlanjeni could rejoice that their ancestors' blood was not shed in vain. Aware of the vengeful spirit that possessed the leader of neighboring Zimbabwe, the world watched in nervous anticipation to see how a people who had been imprisoned in their own land would respond. Surely the jubilant shrieks of those whose heavy chains had miraculously dissolved would be followed by the howls of the victims of retributive slaughter. Instead, humanity was humbled by the most amazing display of

---

[47]Steed and Sundkler, *History of the Church in Africa*, p. 904.
[48]Jenkins, *Next Christendom*, pp. 149-50.

biblical grace the world has ever seen, as Bishop Desmond Tutu assumed the chair of the Truth and Reconciliation Commission.[49] The captives who had been set free were now setting the captors free: "forgive us our debts, as we also have forgiven our debtors" (Mt 6:12).

THE BIBLE AND AFRICAN LIBERATION: CONCLUSION

As profound as the Truth and Reconciliation Commission may appear, on reflection, South Africa's gesture was simply a continuation of the same grace that the majority of African nations have extended to their captors after liberation. After all the atrocities that were wrought on the nations of Put in the name of religion, few would have been surprised if the new leadership had sanctioned revenge. Instead we saw leaders who had learned many lessons from their own experiences. Of course, those who have observed developments in Africa are well aware that the political climate has been far from ideal as the evil of tribalism continues to rear its ugly head. Nonetheless, the world is probably relieved that Idi Amin and Robert Mugabe are anomalies on the African political landscape. The miracle in Africa is witnessed by the fact that even after the official end of colonial structures, multitudes of expatriate whites who have pitched their tents in the land of Put are just as proud to call themselves African as their darker-skinned compatriots.

As the beacon of hope illuminates the land of Put, the potholes on the path that leads to his brethren in the north are shamefully exposed. Cush is still challenged with denominational rivalry and religious formality in the western areas of Ethiopia and Eritrea, while those in the eastern regions on the Arabian peninsula are still beguiled by the message of their seventh-century prophet. The followers of Muhammad are joined by the sons of Ham in the lands associated with ancient Misrayim and Canaan, where as a result of a tainted Christian witness, religious tolerance has long been forgotten. A small light still flickers among the faithful remnant who continue to practice their faith in adverse situations, but the crescent moon is threatening to eclipse the Son of Righteousness.

In spite of appearances, the Word of God *will* prevail in the land of Ham. Indeed, the same beacon of hope that exposed the religious tensions in the re-

---

[49]For an assessment of the process, see Andrew Rigby, *Justice and Reconciliation: After the Violence* (Boulder, Colo.: Lynne Rienner, 2001), pp. 123-45.

gion also illuminates another path. This is not a path frequented by the theologically embattled, but one filled with the millions who suffer in Africa. With the challenge of AIDS, poverty, starvation, government corruption and lingering tribalism, it is clear that many painful thorns and obstacles still blight this long and winding path. However, the same Bible refused by the Muslims and misused by the imperialists has demonstrated itself an able guide for all seekers of liberation. Those who suffer in the land of Ham do not need any more theological squabbles or ecumenical councils, they need to *see* the gospel at work as a witness. They need to experience the spiritually and socially transforming power of the gospel. They need to share the vision of the enlightened oppressed who have learned to look into the future and catch a glimpse of the promised land. They need to join voices with those of us who yearn for the day when all God's children can join the refrain of that old Negro spiritual: "Free at last, free at last, thank God almighty, we're free at last!"

CONCLUSION

Blessed be Egypt my people,

and Assyria the work of my hands,

and Israel my heritage.

ISAIAH 19:25

Students of Scripture should not be surprised to hear that the Bible preserves the story of Africa's blessing. Of all the places on the face of the earth, the Omnipotent One selected the lands associated with Ham's progeny to serve as the stage for the earthly phase of his salvation drama. From the rivers of Cush's Eden to the fertile banks of Misrayim's Nile and Canaan's Jordan, the divine hand executed the mighty works of creation, liberation and scriptural inspiration. Indeed, it was on the very soil settled by the children of Africa that inspired writers penned most of the books contained in the Christian canon. It is true that a part of the land was "cursed" by the sobered Noah—a much misunderstood curse that has been the source of countless woes. However, even the curse contained a blessing as the land of Canaan *served* as the location for the Messiah's birth, ministry and atoning sacrifice. When that most crucial moment in history arrived, although a representative from the most celebrated son of Ham bore the cross for our Savior, it was the "least" of Ham's sons who provided the platform for human redemption!

This study has not only highlighted the important place of the redefined Africa in biblical history, but it has also exposed the central role of *Africans* in the divine drama. Not only have the lands of Ham's children been blessed by election, but many of his offspring are listed among the expanded family of

God. In addition to the nameless multitudes from Misrayim that accompanied the Israelites in the exodus from Egypt, there are others who were woven into the very fabric of Israel's cloth. Through Joseph's marriage to Asenath, at least two of Israel's tribes could equally claim Egyptian identity, and it is no secret that Judah's seed was preserved though his illicit encounter with Tamar, his Canaanite daughter-in-law. Indeed, the seed of Judah that would eventually be merged with the divine Son of God would also have to pass through another Canaanite named Rahab—a prostitute from Jericho. Joining these women who have ensured Ham's permanent place in the people of promise are pious priests in the mold of the Canaanite Melchizedek and semi-Cushitic Jethro and royal personalities like Abimilech of Gerar, Pharaoh Neco and Nebuchadnezzar of Babylon, all of whom were addressed directly by God himself and were obedient to his directions.

Even after the biblical era, the Bible maintained its prominent place in the lands of Ham's descendants. Egypt had already gifted the ever-shrinking world with a Greek translation of the Hebrew Bible that made the scriptures available to many individuals throughout the scattered regions of the Roman Empire. Later, as the New Testament took shape, African scholars produced indigenous translations in Syriac, Coptic, Ethiopic and even Latin. The Bible translations were enhanced by the work of African theologians who devoted their lives to struggling with the meaning of the biblical texts. From theological centers in Antioch, Jerusalem, Alexandria and Carthage, these biblical scholars utilized various methods to devise ecclesiastical creeds and propose solutions to the mysteries of the incarnation and salvation. In their preoccupation with the preservation of the biblical message, it is obvious that Africa was not only prepared to *be blessed* but was eager to *be a blessing*.

Unfortunately, the fascination with biblical scholasticism was accompanied by an era of intolerance that resulted in a fragmented Christian community with each division claiming to have the correct understanding of biblical truth. The politically driven uncertainty of church leaders paved the way for a new religious movement that would use the Bible to its advantage. As African theologians joined their European counterparts in squabbling over issues that were more concerned with the philosophies of Aristotle and Plato than the teachings of Amos and Paul, the uneducated masses were drawn to the simple message of an Arabian merchant who claimed to possess the biblical gift of prophecy. This new teaching by the professed African prophet from the land of Cush was so dependent on the Bible that it initially appeared to be another attractive "heresy." The newly inducted adherents probably did not even realize that they were being moved further away from Christianity with the evolving teachings of this fledgling faith.

Muhammad capitalized on his unique manipulation of the biblical message to expand the *dar al Islam*—a global community where every citizen is obligated to submit to the will of Allah. Although Christianity and Judaism were included under Islam's tolerant umbrella, many Christians and Jews chose to join the youngest of the Abrahamic faiths for the tax breaks and other privileges that came with membership. With the rapid growth of Islam, it appeared as if the crescent moon was destined to eclipse the light of biblical truth in Ham's Africa. However, even as they watched their itchy-eared siblings transfer allegiance to this new faith, a resilient African remnant refused to embrace a third testament that in many ways contradicted the teachings of the two existing tried and tested testaments. Holding tenaciously to the faith of their fathers and mothers, Orthodox and Monophysite communities throughout Palestine, Egypt, North Africa and Ethiopia remembered the source of their blessing and refused to abandon God's Word.

The Christian children of Africa were still adjusting to the Islamic deception when they were forced to face the fury of their European "siblings" who used the Bible to justify their quest to control prime sections of the lands of Ham. Under the mandate of "crusade," the cross-wearing Europeans sought to replace the *dar al Islam* with their version of an imperial Christianity headquartered in the holy city of Jerusalem. Unfortunately, when the rabid armies assaulted Palestine, their zealous rage brought disrepute to the name of the peaceful Messiah. With misguided piety they engaged in a slaughter akin to ethnic cleansing. It mattered not that by the end of their carnage the dusty streets of Jerusalem were soaked with the mingled blood of indigenous Christians, Jews and Muslims. Eventually, the unified forces of Islam repelled the Crusaders from the regions of Canaan (Palestine) and Misrayim (North Africa). Fortunately, the Bible was so rooted in the soil of Ham that even after the Crusaders returned to their European bases, the light of Christ continued to shine in churches, cloisters, caves and cathedrals.

The faith of Africa's Christians would be further tested by their counterparts in Europe who had embraced strange methods of spreading their version of the biblical message. The Church of Rome was bent on changing the Hebraic nature of the Ethiopian church and sent Jesuit missionaries to infiltrate and indoctrinate the clergy. With so many Ethiopians committed to their ancestral faith, civil war erupted as the faithful resisted the pressure to conform to Rome. Eventually, the Catholic missionaries were expelled and unity restored. Skeptical of outside interference, the Monophysite church fiercely guarded her independence and preserved her understanding of the Bible unhindered for several centuries.

Having failed to significantly influence the nature of Christianity in the regions associated with the descendants of Canaan, Misrayim and Cush, the Europeans turned their attention to the "pagan" sons and daughters of Put. In addition to their exposure to Christianity from traders and missionaries from Ethiopia, Egypt and other parts of North Africa, a number of these dwellers of sub-Saharan Africa would have also been "missionized" by Muslim envoys who would have introduced them to Abraham, Moses, Noah, Jesus and other biblical characters. The Muslims were not only concerned with converting the natives, but sought a free labor force to support the industrialization and extravagances of their empire. Totally ignoring the biblical message of freedom and equality, the European capitalists competed with the Muslim Arabs for the enslavement of Put's children and introduced a centuries-long slave trade that further marred the image of Christianity. In addition to exporting humans from Africa to distant western lands, Europe annexed the territory of Put in the name of Christ and some—like the Dutch Boers—actually claimed the land as their divine birthright.

Miraculously, the very Bible that was used to justify the enslavement of Africa proved to be the very key that would unlock the chains of oppression and open the door to emancipation. This powerful book would plant the seed of the abolitionist movement in London and at the same time inspire African leaders to embrace the biblical mandate for liberation. Eventually, even those who were taken from the land of their ancestors and exposed to twisted interpretations of Scripture would find messages of liberty in a book that was used to justify their slavery. Throughout the Hamitic diaspora, children of Africa—most of whom originated from Put—have clung to the promise of hope that permeates the pages of holy writ and have gained renown for their piety and unique adaptations of Christian faith.

Put's experience has yielded many valuable lessons for his siblings *and* the offspring of his uncles, who populate the face of the earth. Imagine what would happen in Hamitic Canaan if the followers of Moses and Muhammad chose to utilize the *whole* Word of God as the arbiter for their disputes?[1] Imagine what would happen in Hamitic Ethiopia if the followers of the Messiah sought forgiveness from the *Beta Israel*, and strove for reconciliation between the Ethiopian Orthodox Tewahedo Church and the Eritrean Orthodox Tewahdo Church? After all, doesn't Tewahedo/Tewahdo mean "united"? Imagine what would happen in Hamitic Egypt if the Coptic Church chose to become a "no theological strings attached" parent to government-restricted evangelical churches, who in turn would learn the Coptic liturgy and hasten a revival in the land that not only helped to preserve the Bible but has so dutifully served the church? Imagine what would happen if the nations of the world that are populated by people who claim to follow the Book would renounce *all* violent acts of aggression and promote God's kingdom of peace? Imagine what would happen if all the world's *tribes* were prepared to emulate the love and forgiveness that a significant number of the sons of Put have extended to their former captors?

There are still some who believe that the Bible was the most heinous curse brought on the sons of Ham. Indeed, if the Bible were the spirit behind the Crusades, the slave trade, colonialism, the exploitation of resources and subjugation of natives, they would be right. However, the Bible tells a different story. It tells of a patient God who woos people by love, not violence (Jn 3:16). It tells of a just God who has prophesied against systems of inequity and calls his children to egalitarian community (Gal 3:28). It tells of a retributive God who is partial to the poor and oppressed and has already judged those who revel in exploitation (Lk 6:20-26). It tells of a restorative God who promises to make *all* things new (Rev 21:5). Let those who wish continue to argue over the applicability of the Bible to the black experience. It is true that many have twisted the Bible to justify their own bigotry. Nonetheless, few can deny that the same Bible that has erroneously been used to support a nonexistent curse has proven to be Africa's greatest blessing.

---

[1]For an interesting study on the challenges and possibilities of reconciliation, see Dan Bar-On, "Will the Parties Conciliate or Refuse? The Triangle of Jews, Germans, and Palestinians," in Yaacov Bar-Siman-Tov, ed., *From Conflict Resolution to Reconciliation* (Oxford: Oxford University Press, 2004), pp. 239-53.

Descendants of Ham and the Modern Locations of Their Assigned Territories and Nations (Genesis 10:6-20)

"These are the descendants of Ham by their clans and languages, in their territories and nations."
GENESIS 10:20

CUSH (Gen 10:7-12)	Modern Location
1. Ethiopia (41x)	Eritrea, Ethiopia, Sudan
2. Seba (Ps 72:10; Is 43:3)	Yemen/Saudi Arabia
3. Havilah (Gen 2:11; 25:18; 1 Sam 15:7; 1 Chron 1:9)	Saudi Arabia
4. Sabtah	Saudi Arabia (?)
5. Raamah[a] (Ezek 27:22)	Yemen
a. Sheba (1 Kings 10:1-13; 2 Chron 9:1-12; Job 6:19; Ps 72:10, 15; Is 60:6; Jer 6:20; Ezek 27:22-23; 38:13)	Yemen
b. Dedan (Jer 25:23; 49:8; Ezek 25:13; 27:20; 38:13)	Saudi Arabia
6. Sabteca	Saudi Arabia (?)
7. Nimrod (Mic 5:6)	Iraq (Nimrud)
a. Babylon (284x)	Iraq (Babylon)
b. Erech (Ezra 4:9)	Iraq (Warka)
c. Akkad	Iraq (near Baghdad)
d. Calneh (in Shinar) (Amos 6:2)	Iraq
e. Assyria (123x)	Iraq
I. Nineveh (2 Kings 19:31; Is 37:37; Jonah; Nahum; Zeph 2:13; Mt 12:41; Lk 11:32)	Iraq (Nineveh)
II. Rehoboth Ir	Iraq (near Mosul)
III. Calah	Iraq (near Mosul)
IV. Resen	Iraq (near Mosul)

[a]Jokshan, a descendant of Shem, also has two sons named Sheba and Dedan (Gen 25:3). They could possibly be the same people who either intermarried or occupied the same geographical territory.

MISRAYIM (Gen 10:13-14)   **Modern Location**

MISRAYIM (Gen 10:13-14)	Modern Location
1. Egypt (614x)	Egypt, Sudan
2. Ludites (Jer 46:9)	North Africa
3. Anamites	North Africa (?)
4. Lehabites/Libya (Nahum 3:9; Acts 3:10)	Libya
5. Naphtuhites	Egypt/North Africa
6. Pathrusites (Is 11:11; Jer 44:1, 15; Ezek 29:14; 30:14)	Egypt
7. Casluhites (Ancestor of Philistines [285x])	Egypt (?)
a. Philistines	Israel, Palestine
8. Caphtorites (Deut 2:23; Jer 47:4; Amos 9:7)	Crete

CANAAN (Gen 10:15-19)   **Modern Location**

CANAAN (Gen 10:15-19)	Modern Location
1. Canaan (163x)	Israel/Palestine
2. Sidon (49x)	Lebanon
3. Hittites (61x)	Turkey (south-central), Syria
4. Jebusites (45x)	Israel/Palestine
5. Amorites (86x)	Jordan
6. Girgashites (Gen 15:21; Deut 7:1; Josh 3:10; 24:11; Neh 9:8)	Israel (?)
7. Hivites (25x)	Lebanon
8. Arkites (Josh 16:2; 2 Sam 15:32; 16:16; 17:5, 14; 1 Chron 1:15; 1 Chron 27:33)	Lebanon (Tell 'Arqa)
9. Sinites	Egypt
10. Arvadites (Ezek 27:8, 11)	Syria
11. Zemarites (Josh 18:22; 2 Chron 13:4)	Israel/Palestine
12. Hamathites (39x)	Israel

SHARED BLESSINGS
Hamo-Semitic Africans in the Land of Cush

They shall rule the land of Assyria with the sword,
and the land of Nimrod with the drawn sword.

MICAH 5:6

Several of the major players in the biblical story had shared roots in both Shem and Ham. Scholars are often quick to emphasize their Semitic ancestry, and most totally ignore the fact that they are equally tied to Ham. The point at which all the families merged is not always clear. For instance, while we know that Assyria is related to Ham through Nimrod and is also a child of Shem, there is no record of the marriage that joined the two together. Other connections are much more evident. In the case of Ishmael both his mother and wife were Egyptian, which would have made his offspring more Hamitic than Semitic. The same was probably true for Esau, with his Canaanite wives, and their offspring who settled in Arabia. In this appendix, we will take a look at the names of significant Hamo-Semites whose characters play an important role in the divine script.

ABRAHAM'S OFFSPRING IN ARABIAN CUSH

The main players in the biblical story are the Semites who descended from Abraham, the father of the faithful. When Yahweh originally appeared to him in Haran, he promised to make him the primal ancestor of a "great nation" (Gen 12:2). However, when the covenant was renewed, Yahweh promised to make him the progenitor of "a multitude of nations" (Gen 17:5-8). In fact, the promise was reflected in his name change from Abram ("father of a nation"), to Abraham ("father of many nations"). The inclusion of others into the promise is by no means coincidental. God had a special plan for Abraham's son Isaac, but all who sprang from his loins would also receive blessings—even those with mixed ancestry.

Political personalities: Ishmael. As the son of a Semitic father and Egyptian mother, and having been raised in Canaan and Arabian Cush, Ishmael could easily be classified under any number of ethnic categories. Born into a hostile situation, Ishmael was the only son of Abraham for about fourteen years. Apparently, he was well-loved by Abraham who continued to view him as the son through whom the promised blessings would come (Gen 17:18). Although God had other plans about the vessel of the special blessings, Ishmael was also to be the recipient of God's gifts (Gen 17:20). Indeed, even before Isaac was born, Ishmael received the special sign of circumcision when he was thirteen years old (Gen 17:23-27). This indicated that he was as much a part of the covenant as Abraham and the generations of Abraham's offspring.

After the birth of Isaac, Ishmael apparently fulfilled his role as the attentive older brother (Gen 21:9). Unfortunately, Sarah's jealousy led to his dismissal from the only place he knew as home. Having such a strong relationship with Ishmael, it was not easy for Abraham to fulfill Sarah's request (Gen 21:11). However, after God's assurance that Ishmael was still to be a vessel of his blessings, Abraham expelled him and his mother from their home. As they ventured into the desert of Beersheba and it seemed as if they were going to die, Hagar hid the teenage Ishmael under a bush and went away so she would not have to watch her beloved son suffer (Gen 21:15-16). In this stressful moment, Ishmael apparently cried out to the God of his father, Abraham, and God responded to his plea by reaffirming the promise of blessing with Hagar and providing them nourishment (Gen 21:17-19).

Following this miraculous deliverance, Ishmael remained in the Arabian wilderness where he was raised by his mother. Here he learned hunting skills and eventually married an Egyptian woman. It appears that his unnamed wife was the mother of the twelve sons[1] God had promised him (Gen 25:13; cf.

---

[1]Ishmael's twelve sons are Nebaioth, Kedar, Abdeel, Mibsam, Mishma, Dumah, Massa, Hadad, Tema, Jetur, Naphish and Kedemah.

Gen 17:20). Ishmael's descendants settled in Arabia from "Havilah to Shur" (Gen 25:18), which is actually a part of the region that Yahweh had promised to Abraham (Gen 15:18-21). Although Abraham had other sons after the death of Sarah, when he died the funeral responsibilities were entrusted to Ishmael and Isaac who alone are identified as his "sons" (Gen 25:9). Ishmael was to live to be 137 (Gen 25:17).

Like his mother Hagar, Ishmael also features negatively in Paul's allegory of the two covenants. However, here again it must be emphasized that these verses comprise an allegory and are not intended to be used as a prophecy against Jews, Muslims or any other group of people. From all appearances, the biblical record depicts Ishmael as a faithful and beloved son who, like his better-known brother Isaac, was a fortunate recipient of God's bountiful blessings.

Political Personalities: Midianites. After the death of Sarah, Abraham married Keturah who bore him several sons, one of whom was named Midian (Gen 25:1-2). Not wishing for them to rival Isaac, he sent them away to Arabia where they settled. Years later when Moses fled Egypt, he found refuge in Midian. Jethro (Hobab) son of Reuel, the Midianite priest, offered him sanctuary and gave him one of his seven daughters as a wife (Ex 2:15-22). Although he had descended from a different Abrahamic line than Moses, we later learn that he served the same God and was fully aware of the system of sacrifices that Midian had undoubtedly transmitted to his offspring (Ex 18:10-12).

While Moses was facing his challenges in Egypt, he had apparently sent his wife and two sons back to his father-in-law. Now that they were liberated, Jethro returned his family to him (Ex 18:1-27). When Jethro arrived at the encampment, he manifested genuine concern in Moses' well-being. He listened attentively to the story of God's miraculous deliverance and offered a sacrifice of praise. The next day, he observed his son-in-law at work and noticed that he needed an effective administrative system to effectively govern the people. The concerned Jethro warned Moses that his current methods were damaging to his health, and devised a comprehensive program for him that both educated the people about the laws of the community and delegated administrative responsibilities to a significant number of trustworthy men (Ex 18:18-22). After sharing the plan, Jethro let Moses know that the implementation was not optional since the instructions had been given through this Ethiopian priest-prophet by God himself. Having faithfully delivered this helpful message, Jethro returned to Midian with the peace of mind that his daughter and grandchildren would not have to bear the frustration that comes when a father is never at home!

Evidently, this was not the last time that Jethro visited his daughter's family while they sojourned in the wilderness. On one of his visits, Moses pleaded with him to stay and provide navigational assistance for their wilderness sojourn (Num 10:29-32). He enticed his father-in-law with the argument that if Jethro remained around the Israelites, he would probably receive some of the many blessings that Yahweh was bestowing upon them. Moses' desire for Jethro to stay may also have been driven by his knowledge that Israel would one day fight against the Midianites, and Jethro's family would be protected if they stayed close to the Israelite camp. It appears that despite Jethro's initial refusal of Moses' offer (Num 10:30), he relocated his entire family among the Israelites (cf. Judg 1:16; 4:11, 17-22).

Heber, one of Jethro's descendants, belonged to the Kenite clan.[2] The Kenites had traveled with the Israelites for a period during their wilderness sojourn and entrance into Canaan, and most had settled in the Amalekite section of Cush. For some unexplained reason, Heber chose to live apart from his siblings and established his camp among the Canaanites where he secured a peace treaty with King Jabin of Hazor (Judg 4:11, 17). This was to prove providential for Israel when they were engaged in battle with King Jabin and his general Sisera. When Sisera realized that his army was about to experience defeat, he sought sanctuary in a tent belonging to Heber's wife, Jael (Judg 4:18). Jael's allegiance to Israel was far stronger than the diplomatic alliance with Hazor, and she assassinated Sisera as he slept (Judg 4:19-22). Jael became an instant hero in Israel, and she was prominently featured in a popular song that celebrated Israel's victory over her enemies (cf. Judg 5:6, 24-27).

The incident with Jael occurred at a time when the apostate Israelites were under subjugation to King Jabin of Hazor (Judg 4:1-3). The merciful Yahweh appointed Deborah to liberate Israel (Judg 4:4-24), and this time Israel managed to remain faithful for forty years before assuming old habits and losing the right of self-governance to the Midianites and Amalekites (Judg 5:31—6:6). Responding to Israel's plea for help, Yahweh then designated Gideon to emancipate his rebellious people (Judg 6:7—7:23). The highpoint of his tri-

---

[2]For a brief discussion on the Kenites and the theory that they were the ones who introduced the divine name Yahweh to Israel, see J. A. Motyer, "Kenites," in *New Bible Dictionary*, ed. D. R. W. Wood, 3rd ed. (Downers Grove, Ill.: InterVarsity Press, 1996), p. 643.

umph was the capture and execution of the two Midianite captains, Oreb and Zeeb (Judg 7:24-25). Although the characters of Oreb and Zeeb are not developed in the plot, it is obvious that their demise had significant implications throughout Israel (cf. Judg 8:1-3).

The death of Oreb and Zeeb marked only the beginning of the liberation struggle. These were just the captains of the army, and Gideon was not going to rest until he captured the two kings of Midian, Zebah and Zalmunna (Judg 8:5). After a thorough and eventful pursuit, he eventually launched a surprise ambush against the Midianite army in Karkor and arrested Zebah and Zalmunna (Judg 8:6-12). As the narrative unfolds, it soon becomes apparent that Gideon had a vendetta against these two kings who confessed to killing his brothers in Tabor (Judg 8:18-19). It was Gideon's wish that his oldest son Jether execute the Midianite kings, but Jether was too afraid so he carried out the deed himself (Judg 8:20-21). The victory over the Midianites led to another forty year era of peace for the Israelites (Judg 8:4-28).

Political personalities: Edomites and Amalekites. Other Hamo-Semitics residing in Arabian Cush traced their roots to Esau, Abraham's grandson. While Jacob's family continued the nomad life inherited from Abraham and Isaac, Esau's family settled in the place that was named after the color of his ruddy brown skin, Edom (cf. Gen 25:25).[3] Having established a permanent geographical location for consequent generations, it was only natural for the Edomites to install a system of government to maintain the social order. The administrative model that eventually evolved took the form of a monarchy that, according to some theories, was established 150 years before the one in Israel (Gen 36:31). The succession of kings named in this primary monarchy are Bela son of Beor, Jobab son of Zerah, Hushman the Temanite, Hadad son of Bedad, Samlah of Masrekah, Shaul of Rehoboth, Baal-hanan son of Achbor, and Hadar husband of Mehetabel and father of Matred (Gen 36:31-39). Given the names of these kings and their varied geographical provenances, it is obvious that the early Edomites did not have a dynasty that gave preference to a certain family. Instead, there appears to have been a revolving system in which the crown rotated among the chieftains of the various city-states when a ruling king died.

---

[3]The Hebrew word translated "red" is *'admoni.* But see Genesis 25:30, which traces the nickname Edom to the incident in which Esau surrendered his birthright to Jacob (Gen 25:29-34).

By virtue of proximity, it was only natural for Edomites to be involved in the political affairs of Israel. Their participation was not always positive. One example of an Edomite rabble rouser is Doeg, who served in Saul's army. Doeg is first introduced when David sought nourishment from the priest Ahimelech while fleeing for his life from Saul (1 Sam 21:1-6). Initially identified as the chief of Saul's shepherds (1 Sam 21:6), it is soon revealed that he had actually been commissioned to superintend all of Saul's servants (1 Sam 22:9). When Saul lamented that no one in his inner circle was willing to provide intelligence about the whereabouts of David, the treacherous Doeg revealed details about David's meeting with Ahimelech (1 Sam 22:6-10). The infuriated Saul sent for Ahimelech and accused him of conspiracy, before sentencing him to death. When none of his servants obeyed the impetuous command to execute the man of God, Saul ordered the eager Doeg to carry out the despicable deed (1 Sam 2:11-19).

Hadad was another man of Edom who features negatively in Israel's story (1 Kings 11:14-22). Hadad had been a member of the royal house when David conquered Edom and killed a sizeable number of its citizens. The fortunate prince escaped and found refuge in Egypt where the Pharaoh provided him with a house and an allowance. Hadad so endeared himself to the royal court that Pharaoh even gave him his sister-in-law in marriage. When Hadad learned that David had died, he begged Pharaoh leave so that he could re-establish his presence in Edom. No details are provided about his activities upon repatriation, but the text lets us know that he became a nagging adversary to Solomon (1 Kings 11:25).

Animosity between the seed of Jacob and Esau also appeared in Israel's relations with the Amalekites, descendants of Esau's grandson Amalek. The two nations faced off when Saul was king of Israel, and the Amalekites experienced a sound defeat (1 Sam 15:1-8). The prophet Samuel had given Saul specific instructions to kill every human and animal that remained from the battle. Unfortunately, Saul chose to disobey and spared the Amalekite king along with the premium livestock he had plundered (1 Sam 15:8-9, 17-21). When Samuel found out about Saul's disobedience, he was furious and ordered that Agag be brought to him. The petrified Agag realized that his end was in sight, and the man of God pronounced retributive sentence before cutting him into pieces (1 Sam 15:32-33).

Unbeknownst to Saul, his own end would come at the hand of an Amalekite. The initial account of Saul's death states that he committed suicide when his armor-bearer refused to kill him in a fierce battle between the Israelites and the Philistines (1 Sam 31:1-5). However, the young Amalekite—who described himself as a resident alien of Israel—gave a different story (2 Sam 1:1-10). He claimed that when he encountered Saul, he was at the point of death and was propped up by a spear that ran through him. He went on to say that after inquiring about his identity, the tortured king requested that the Amalekite take him out of his misery and he acquiesced out of compassion. Given the contrary details in the original account of Saul's death, it appears that the young Amalekite had lied to David in the hope of receiving honor and recognition. Unfortunately for him, David interpreted his assisted euthanasia as a treacherous act against God's anointed, and ordered the Amalekite killed for disrespect (2 Sam 1:11-16).

Arabian wives: Zipporah and Cozbi. Not all Abraham's offspring in Arabian Cush were men of war. Some women also contributed to the biblical cast. A significant name is Zipporah, one of the seven daughters of Jethro, priest of Midian. This fortunate woman was the beneficiary of Moses' chivalry when troublemakers harassed her and her sisters while they drew water from a well (Ex 2:16-22). Although the Midianites had descended from Abraham and Keturah, they had lived in the northern regions of Arabia for centuries and had become full-fledged Cushites (cf. Num 12:1). After meeting Moses, Zipporah's father offered her to him in marriage. According to the custom of the day, she had no say in the matter, and two sons were born to the union, Gershom and Eliezer (Ex 2:22; 18:3-4). Zipporah and the boys accompanied Moses when he received the call to return to Egypt (Ex 4:18-20). During the journey, Moses had a paranormal experience which was only resolved when Zipporah circumcised one of the sons and touched the foreskin on Moses' genitals—apparently a symbolic circumcision for the uncircumcised Moses (Ex 4:24-26). Her ability to perform this delicate surgical procedure indicates that the Midianites had been careful to preserve this special covenant ritual.

At some point during his adventures with Pharaoh in Egypt, Moses sent Zipporah and the boys back to Jethro in Midian. The family would not be reunited until Jethro accompanied the mother and sons to the Sinai peninsula where the Israelites were camping after the exodus (Ex 18:5). This was probably a big culture shock for Zipporah who had to try hard to blend in to a homo-

genous group who viewed her as an outsider. She was even despised by Moses'
siblings, Miriam and Aaron, who were upset that Moses had married an Ethiopian (Num 12:1). There are some who feel that Zipporah was alienated because of her dark skin color, and even suggest the leprosy that turned Miriam
as "white as snow" was a direct punishment for her color prejudice (Num
12:10). However there is nothing in the text to suggest that skin color was an
issue. In fact, for Miriam to be turned as "white as snow" meant that she herself must have had a darker complexion. More than likely, Miriam and Aaron
were jealous of Zipporah's access to Moses, and felt that they had more rights
than this alien foreigner. Nothing is said about Zipporah after this incident,
but we can assume that she continued to provide spiritual and emotional support for her special husband.

Unlike the dutiful Zipporah who had maintained her ancestral allegiances
to Yahweh, Cozbi was one of the thousands of Midianite women who joined
with the Moabites to seduce the Israelite men into sexual immorality and idolatry (Num 25:1-18). The only paramour mentioned by name, Cozbi's claim to
fame was gained when Phineas the grandson of Aaron thrust a spear through
her and her Israelite lover Zimri (Num 25:7-8). Although aware of the overall
plan (Num 25:17-18), Cozbi probably felt she was fulfilling her national duty
by doing her part to break down the barriers between the two nations, and was
probably oblivious to the fact that it was divinely forbidden for Israelite men to
cohabit with foreign women. Given the fact that both of the victims' fathers
were heads of their respective clans (Num 25:14-15), this relationship may have
even been an attempt to form an economic alliance between two families.
Whatever the motive behind her union with Zimri, the freshly executed Cozbi
was the antidote that halted the murderous plague that had claimed the lives of
24,000 apostate Israelites (Num 25:6-9).

THE ASSYRIAN CONNECTION IN MESOPOTAMIAN CUSH

The Hamo-Semites residing in Mesopotamian Cush were located in Assyria,
a kingdom founded by Ham's grandson Nimrod. Practically all of the Assyrians featured in the Bible were members of the royal court. One of the first
mentioned was Tiglath-pileser III who proved to be a thorn in Israel's side
(745-727 B.C.E.). Under his rulership, the Assyrian Empire experienced unprecedented expansion, and before his death it stretched westward to the borders of Egypt, eastward where he annexed Media and Namri, and southward

where he usurped the Babylonian throne two years before his death.[4] He is first introduced in biblical writ as "King Pul" who threatened an attack against Menahem of Israel (2 Kings 15:19-20). Menahem quickly used the incident for his political advantage, and agreed to pay Tiglath-pileser a huge sum of money in return for protection. With a pro-Assyrian king on Israel's throne, Tiglath-pileser did not have to stay in the region.

Apparently Menahem's successors did not continue to pay the protection money, and during Pekah's reign, Tiglath-pileser returned with a mission, capturing several Israelite towns and resettling the citizens in Assyria (2 Kings 15:29). Apparently afraid of the Assyrians, Pekah decided to take out his frustration by soliciting the help of King Rezin of Aram to attack Judah (2 Kings 16:5-20; 2 Chron 28:16-27). King Ahaz of Judah thought quickly and pledged his allegiance to Tiglath-pileser. Ahaz sealed his servitude to the Assyrian by stripping the treasures from the Jerusalem temple and sending them to his new master. Ahaz was so desperate to prove his fidelity to Tiglath-pileser that, after a state visit to Damascus, he had the high priest build an altar in Jerusalem that was the exact replica of the Assyrian one, and adopted the Assyrian religion.

Tiglath-pileser was succeeded by his son, Shalmaneser (727-722 B.C.E.).[5] When Shalmaneser acceded to the throne, Ahaz was still king of Judah, and Hoshea was the puppet king of Israel who had been appointed by his father. When Hoshea stopped paying tribute to Assyria and sought an alliance with King So of Egypt, Shalmaneser launched a three-year siege against Samaria (2 Kings 17:1-6; 18:9-12). By the end of the siege in 722 B.C.E., Assyrian accounts state that almost 30,000 Israelites were dispersed around the empire, marking the termination of the northern kingdom. To solidify the permanence of the dissolution of Israel, Shalmaneser relocated captives from other parts of the expanding kingdom to the former Israelite territory, thus creating the new province of Samaria (2 Kings 17:24-41). When tragedy began to afflict the new inhabitants, Shalmaneser demonstrated his religious sensitivities by commissioning an Israelite priest to induct the refugees in the ways of Yahweh. This effort resulted in the development of several hybrid religions that

---

[4]D. J. Wiseman, "Tiglath-Pileser," in *New Bible Dictionary*, ed. D. R. W. Wood, 3rd ed. (Downers Grove, Ill.: InterVarsity Press, 1996), pp. 1186-87.
[5]D. J. Wiseman, "Shalmaneser," in *New Bible Dictionary*, ed. D. R. W. Wood, 3rd ed. (Downers Grove, Ill.: InterVarsity Press, 1996), p. 1085.

fused the religion of Israel with various foreign superstitions.

Apparently, Shalmaneser died at the end of the siege of Samaria and was succeeded by Sargon II (722-705 B.C.E.). Isaiah is the only book in the Bible to mention him by name (Is 20:1), but he played a significant role in transforming the demographics of the region. A superior military strategist, Sargon completed the annexation of Samaria and achieved significant military victories over Egypt and Babylon.[6] Following Sargon's death, several of the nations that comprised the Assyrian Empire saw an opportunity to revolt. Hezekiah, king of Judah, appears to have been part of a regional alliance that was determined to gain independence. Unfortunately for the alliance, Sargon's son and heir, Sennacherib successfully quashed the rebellions and eventually arrived at Jerusalem (2 Kings 18:1—19:37).[7] The frightened Hezekiah apologized to Sennacherib and promised to pay him whatever was requested. Apparently, Hezekiah was not able to fulfill his promise, and Sennacherib sent a delegation threatening to demolish his waning kingdom if he did not pay up. Hezekiah sought divine assistance, and through the prophet Isaiah was told that the Lord would protect Jerusalem. This did not guarantee protection for other towns in Judea, and the historical record shows that a number of them fell to the Assyrian sword. Nonetheless, Jerusalem was spared when the Assyrian army experienced massive losses via supernatural intervention.

Following his failed attempt to subdue the people of God, Sennacherib returned to Nineveh where he was assassinated by his sons Adrammelech and Sharezer (2 Kings 19:36; Is 37:38). The younger son, Esarhaddon, stood up against his brothers and drove them into exile before assuming the throne (681-669 B.C.E.).[8] He continued the legacy of empire building and claimed to have extended his empire to Ethiopia after defeating Tirhaka, the Napatan king of the Twenty-fifth Dynasty. Apparently he continued the strategy of his forebears by resettling captives in different parts of the empire. A number who had been relocated to Samaria had adopted a hybrid version of the religion of Israel and were still holding firm at the time of the return from Babylonian captivity (cf. Ezra 4:1-2). Some believe that this group of refuges formed the catalyst for

---

[6]D. J. Wiseman, "Sargon," in *New Bible Dictionary*, ed. D. R. W. Wood, 3rd ed. (Downers Grove, Ill.: InterVarsity Press, 1996), p. 1063.

[7]D. J. Wiseman, "Sennacherib," in *New Bible Dictionary*, ed. D. R. W. Wood, 3rd ed. (Downers Grove, Ill.: InterVarsity Press, 1996), pp. 1075-76.

[8]D. J. Wiseman, "Esarhaddon," in *New Bible Dictionary*, ed. D. R. W. Wood, 3rd ed. (Downers Grove, Ill.: InterVarsity Press, 1996), p. 332.

the Samaritans—a religious community that exists to the present day.

With the passing of Esarhaddon, the Assyrian empire experienced the last of the great kings in the person of Ashurbanipal (668-630 B.C.E.).[9] He continued the humiliation of the "great" Egypt in a major campaign against Tandamane, another Cushite king of the Twenty-fifth Dynasty. The human spoils of war were once again dispersed throughout the empire, with Samaria receiving more foreign transplants (cf. Ezra 4:10). In addition to his military activities, Ashurbanipal had a love for the arts and was responsible for commissioning a library in Nineveh. While he worked on developing the culture of the empire, his opponents took the opportunity to pry open the fingers that held them in a tight grip. His own twin brother rose against him from Babylon, and Egypt and Judah slowly regained autonomy. The mighty Assyrian kingdom did not last much longer after his death.

CONCLUSION

In assessing the multiethnic scope of the biblical narrative, it is obvious that the Bible is not just concerned about the twelve clans that descended from Jacob. While they are central to the overall plot, many of the supporting players have significant roles. This is especially true for the descendants of Ham. Indeed it was Canaan who cultivated the Promised Land and transformed it into the place of milk and honey for the Israelite invaders. It was Misrayim who opened his breadbaskets to Jacob and his sons and spared them from the painful agony of famine. Finally, it was Hamo-Semites of Arabian Cush whom Yahweh included in the covenant with Abraham and used as an agent of discipline on the rebellious Israelites.

---

[9]D. J. Wiseman, "Ashurbanipal," in *New Bible Dictionary,* ed. D. R. W. Wood, 3rd ed. (Downers Grove, Ill.: InterVarsity Press, 1996), p. 94.

WORKS CITED

Abate, Yohannis, and Mulatu Wubneh. *Ethiopia: Transition and Development in the Horn of Africa.* Boulder, Colo.: Westview Press, 1988.

Abbott, Nabia. "Pre-Islamic Queens." *American Journal of Semitic Languages and Literatures* 58 (1941): 1-22.

Adalian, Rouben Paul. "The Armenian Genocide." In *A Century of Genocide: Critical Essays and Eyewitness Accounts,* edited by Israel W. Charny, William S. Parsons and Samuel Totten, pp. 53-90. New York: Routledge, 2004.

Adamo, David Tuesday. *Africa and the Africans in the Old Testament.* San Francisco: International Scholars Publications, 1997.

————. "The Place of Africa and Africans in the Old Testament and Its Environment." Ph.D. dissertation, Baylor University, 1986.

————. "The Search for Africanness in the Bible." *African Journal of Biblical Studies* 15, no. 2 (2000): 20-40.

Adams, William Y. *Nubia: Corridor to Africa.* Princeton, N.J.: Princeton University Press, 1977.

Albright, W. F. "The Location of Eden." *American Journal of Semitic Languages and Literatures* 39 (1922): 15-31.

Allen, Norm R., ed. *The Black Humanist Experience: An Alternative to Religion.* Amherst, N.Y.: Prometheus, 2003.

Angenent, Caroline. "About Ham and His Wicked Siblings." *Exchange* 24, no. 2 (June 1995): 137.

Ash, Paul S. "Shishak." In *Eerdmans Dictionary of the Bible,* edited by David Noel Freedman, p. 1215. Grand Rapids: Eerdmans, 2000.

Athanasius. "Life of St. Anthony." In *Early Christian Biographies,* edited by Roy J. Deferrari; translated by Mary Emily Keenan, pp. 127-216. Washington, D.C.: Catholic University Press of America, 1952.

Atiya, Aziz S. *Crusade, Commerce and Culture.* Bloomington: Indiana University Press, 1962.

————. "Ewostatewos." In *The Coptic Encyclopedia,* edited by Aziz S. Atiya,

4:1050-51. New York: Macmillan, 1991.

Augustine. *The City of God against the Pagans.* Translated by G. E. McCracken et al. 7 vols. Loeb Classical Library. Cambridge, Mass.: Harvard University Press, 1960-1981.

Barashango, Ishakamusa. *God, the Bible and the Black Man's Destiny.* Washington, D.C.: IV Dynasty Publishing, 1982.

Bard, Kathryn A. "Ancient Egyptians and the Issue of Race." In *Black Athena Revisited,* edited by Mary R. Lefkowitz and Guy MacLean Rogers, pp. 103-11. Chapel Hill: University of North Carolina Press, 1996.

Barnai, Jacob. *The Jews in Palestine in the Eighteenth Century: Under the Patronage of the Istanbul Committee of Officials for Palestine.* Translated by Naomi Goldblum. Tuscaloosa: University of Alabama Press, 1992.

Barnes, Timothy David. *Tertullian: A Historical and Literary Study.* Oxford: Clarendon, 1971.

Bar-On, Dan. "Will the Parties Conciliate or Refuse? The Triangle of Jews, Germans, and Palestinians." In *From Conflict Resolution to Reconciliation,* edited by Yaacov Bar-Siman-Tov, pp. 239-53. Oxford: Oxford University Press, 2004.

Baur, Chrysostomus. *John Chrysostom and His Time.* 2 vols. Westminster, Md.: Newman Press, 1959.

Bell, H. Idris. *Cults and Creeds in Graeco-Roman Egypt.* Chicago: Ares Publishers, 1985.

Benezer, Gadi. *The Ethiopian Jewish Exodus: Narratives of the Migration Journey to Israel, 1977-1985.* London: Routledge, 2002.

Bennet, R. A. "Africa in the Biblical Period." *Harvard Theological Review* 64 (1971): 483-500.

Berlinerblau, Jacques. *Heresy in the University: The Black Athena Controversy and the Responsibilities of American Intellectuals.* New Brunswick, N.J.: Rutgers University Press, 1999.

Bernal, Martin. *Black Athena: The Afroasiatic Roots of Classical Civilization.* 2 vols. London: Free Association Books; New Brunswick, N.J.: Rutgers University Press, 1987, 1991.

———. *Black Athena Writes Back.* Durham, N.C.: Duke University Press, 2001.

Bierling, Neal. *Giving Goliath His Due: New Archaeological Light on the Philistines.* Grand Rapids: Baker, 1992.

Blech, Benjamin. *Eyewitness to Jewish History.* Hoboken, N.J.: Wiley, 2004.

Braukämper, Ulrich. *Islamic History and Culture in Southern Ethiopia: Collected Essays.* Münster: Lit Verlag, 2004.

Brow, Robert. "The Curse of Ham—Capsule of Ancient History." *Christianity Today* 18 (October 26, 1973): 8-10.

Brown, Peter Lamont. *Augustine of Hippo: A Biography.* Berkeley: University of California Press, 1967.

Brown, Scot. *Fighting for US: Maulana Karenga, the US Organization, and Black Cultural Nationalism.* New York: New York University Press, 2003.

Budge, E. A. Wallis, trans. *The Queen of Sheba and Her Only Son Menyelek (I).* Oxford: Oxford University Press, 1932.

Bulst-Thiele, Marie Luise. "The Influence of St. Bernard of Clarivaux on the Formation of the Order of the Knights Templar." In *The Second Crusade and the Cistercians,* edited by Michael Gervers, pp. 57-65. New York: St. Martin's Press, 1992.

Burchard, Christoph. "Joseph and Aseneth: A New Translation and Introduction." In *The Old Testament Pseudepigrapha,* 2:177-247, edited by James H. Charlesworth. 2 vols. New York: Doubleday, 1985.

Burney, Charles. *Historical Dictionary of the Hittites.* Lanham, Md.: Scarecrow Press, 2004.

Burton, David. *The Abyssinians.* New York: Praeger Publications, 1970.

Burton, Keith A. "Ethiopia." In *Eerdmans Dictionary of the Bible,* edited by David Noel Freedman, pp. 432-33. Grand Rapids: Eerdmans, 2000.

Cameron, Ron. *The Other Gospels: Non-Canonical Gospel Texts.* Philadelphia: Westminster Press, 1982.

Canfora, Luciano. *The Vanished Library.* Translated by Martin Ryle. Berkeley: University of California Press, 1989.

Carriker, Andrew. *The Library of Eusebius of Caesarea.* Leiden: Brill, 2003.

Chadwick, Henry. *The Church in Ancient Society: From Galilee to Gregory the Great.* Oxford: Oxford University Press, 2001.

———. *The Early Church.* New York: Penguin, 1967.

Chaillot, Christine. *The Ethiopian Orthodox Tewahedo Church Tradition: A Brief Introduction to Its Life and Spirituality.* Paris: Inter-Orthodox Dialogue, 2002.

Chavalas, Mark W. "Merodach-Baladan." In *Eerdmans Dictionary of the Bible,* edited by David Noel Freedman, p. 887. Grand Rapids: Eerdmans, 2000.

Copher, Charles B. *Black Biblical Studies: An Anthology of Charles B. Copher: Biblical and Theological Issues on the Black Presence in the Bible.* Chicago: Black Light Fellowship, 1993.

———. "The Black Man in the Biblical World." *Journal of the Interdenominational Theological Center* 1, no. 2 (spring 1974): 7-16.

———. "Egypt and Ethiopia in the Old Testament." In *Nile Valley Civilizations,* edited by Ivan van Sertima, pp. 163-78. New Brunswick, N.J.: Journal of African Civilizations, 1985.

———. "3,000 years of Biblical Interpretation with Reference to Black Peoples." *The Journal of the Interdenominational Theological Center* 13, no. 2 (spring 1986): 225-46.

Coppes, Leonard J. "ḥāmam, et al." In *Theological Wordbook of the Old Testament,* edited by R. Laird Harris, Gleason L. Archer and Bruce K. Waltke, pp. 296-97. Chicago: Moody Press, 1980.

Corbon, Jean. "The Churches of the Middle East: Their Origins and Identity, from Their Roots in the Past to Their Openness to the Present." In *Christian Communities in the Arab Middle East: The Challenge of the Future,* edited by Andrea Pacini, pp. 92-110. Oxford: Clarendon, 1998.

Courbage, Youssef, and Philippe Fargues. *Christians and Jews Under Islam.* Translated by Judy Mabro. London: I. B. Tauris, 1997.

Cowles, C. S., Eugene H. Merrill, Daniel L. Gard and Tremper Longman III. *Show Them No Mercy: Four Views on God and Canaanite Genocide.* Grand Rapids: Zondervan, 2003.

Cragg, Kenneth. *The Arab Christian: A History in the Middle East.* Louisville, Ky.: Westminster John Knox, 1991.

Crowder, Stephanie Buckhanon. *Simon of Cyrene: A Case of Roman Conscription.* New York: Peter Lang, 2002.

Curtwright, Wesley. *The Hand of God in Ethiopia and Other Subjects.* New York: Vantage Press, 1974.

Denny, Frederick M. *Islam and the Muslim Community.* Prospect Heights, Ill.: Waveland Press, 1987, 1998.

Deutsch, Nathaniel. "The Proximate Other: The Nation of Islam and Judaism." In *Black Zion: African American Religious Encounters with Judaism,* edited by Yvonne Chireau and Nathaniel Deutsch, pp. 91-117. New York: Oxford University Press, 2000.

De Vries, S. J. "Chronology of the OT." In *The Interpreters Dictionary of the*

Bible, edited by George Arthur Buttrick 1:580-99. Nashville: Abingdon, 1962.

Diodorus Siculus. *Diodorus of Sicily in Twelve Volumes.* Cambridge, Mass.: Harvard University Press, 1970-1989.

Diop, Cheikh Anta. *The African Origin of Civilization: Myth or Reality.* Edited and translated by Mercer Cook. Chicago: Lawrence Hill Books, 1974.

Dowling, Archdeacon. *The Abyssinian Church.* London: Cope and Fenwick, 1909.

Dunn, James D. G. *The Partings of the Ways: Between Christianity and Judaism and Their Significance for the Character of Christianity.* Philadelphia: Trinity Press International, 1991.

Dunn, James D. G., ed. *Jews and Christians: The Parting of the Ways, A.D. 70-135.* Grand Rapids: Eerdmans, 1999.

Dunston, Alfred. *The Black Man in the Old Testament and Its World.* Philadelphia: Dorrance, 1974; Trenton, N.J.: Africa World Press, 1992.

Durant, Will. *The Age of Faith: A History of Medieval Civilization—Christian, Islamic, and Judaic—from Constantine to Dante: A.D. 325-1300.* New York: Simon & Schuster, 1950.

Ehrman, Bart D. *Lost Christianities: The Battles for Scripture and the Faiths We Never Knew.* Oxford: Oxford University Press, 2003.

Eisenman, Robert. *James the Brother of Jesus: The Key to Unlocking the Secrets of Early Christianity and the Dead Sea Scrolls.* New York: Viking, 1996.

Elazar, Daniel J. *The Other Jews: The Sephardim Today.* New York: Basic Books, 1989.

Emerton, J. A. "The Site of Salem, the City of Melchizedek (Genesis xiv 18)." In *Studies in the Pentateuch,* edited by J. A. Emerton, pp. 45-71. Leiden: Brill, 1990.

Equiano, Olaudah. "The Interesting Narrative of the Life of Olaudah Equiano, or, Gustavus Vassa, the African." In *The Classic Slave Narratives,* edited by Henry Louis Gates. New York: Penguin, 1987.

Erdmann, Carl. *The Origin of the Idea of Crusade.* Translated by Marshall W. Baldwin and Walter Goffart. Princeton, N.J.: Princeton University Press, 1977.

Erlich, Haggai. *The Cross and the River: Ethiopia, Egypt, and the Nile.* Boulder, Colo.: L. Rienner, 2002.

Felder, Cain Hope. *Troubling Biblical Waters.* Maryknoll, N.Y.: Orbis, 1989.

Felder, Cain Hope, ed. *Stony the Road We Trod: African-American Biblical Interpretation.* Minneapolis: Fortress, 1991.

Fenton, Steve. *Ethnicity.* Cambridge, England: Polity Press, 2003.

Ferguson, Everett. *Backgrounds of Early Christianity.* 2nd ed. Grand Rapids: Eerdmans, 1993.

Ferguson, John. *Clement of Alexandria.* New York: Twayne Publishers, 1974.

Finn, Thomas M. "Pash, Paschal Controversy." In *Encyclopedia of Early Christianity,* edited by Everett Ferguson, 1:876-77. 2nd ed. New York: Garland, 1997.

Firestone, Reuven. "The *Qur'ān* and the Bible: Some Modern Studies of Their Relationship." In *Bible and Qur'ān: Essays in Scriptural Intertextuality,* edited by John C. Reeves, pp. 1-22. Leiden: Brill, 2004.

Fitzmyer, Joseph A. "Melchizedek in the MT, LXX, and the New Testament." *Biblica* 81 (2000): 63-69.

Fitzsimmonds, F. S. "Simon." In *New Bible Dictionary,* edited by D. R. W. Wood, p. 1104. 3rd ed. Downers Grove, Ill.: InterVarsity Press, 1996.

Forey, Alan. "The Military Orders: 1120-1312." In *The Oxford Illustrated History of the Crusades,* edited by Jonathan Riley Smith, pp. 185-200. Oxford: Oxford University Press, 1995.

Franklin, John Hope. *From Slavery to Freedom: A History of Negro Americans.* 5th ed. New York: Alfred A Knopf, 1980.

Frend, W. H. C. *The Donatist Church.* Oxford: Clarendon, 1952.

———. *The Rise of the Monophysite Movement.* 2nd ed. Cambridge: Cambridge University Press, 1979.

Fretheim, Terrence E. "Genesis." In *New Interpreter's Bible,* edited by Leander E. Keck, 1:408. Nashville: Abingdon, 1994.

Fulcher of Chartres. *A History of the Expedition to Jerusalem: 1095-1127.* Translated by Frances Rita Ryan. Knoxville: University of Tennessee Press, 1969.

Funucane, Ronald C. *Soldiers of the Faith: Crusaders and Moslems at War.* New York: St. Martin's Press, 1983.

George, Timothy. *Is the Father of Jesus the God of Muhammad?* Grand Rapids: Zondervan, 2002.

Gibb, Hamilton A. R. "The Rise of Saladin, 1169-1189." In *A History of the Crusades,* edited by Marshall W. Baldwin, 1:563-89. Madison: University of Wisconsin Press, 1969.

Gil, Moshe. *A History of Palestine, 634-1099.* Translated by Ethel Broido. Cambridge: Cambridge University Press, 1992.

Goehring, James E. "Monasticism." In *Encyclopedia of Early Christianity,* edited by Everett Ferguson, 2:769-75. 2nd ed. New York: Garland, 1997.

Goldenberg, David M. *The Curse of Ham: Race and Slavery in Early Judaism, Christianity and Islam.* Princeton, N.J.: Princeton University Press, 2003.

Gordon, R. P. "Abimelech." In *New Bible Dictionary,* edited by D. R. W. Wood, p. 4. 3rd ed. Downers Grove, Ill.: InterVarsity Press, 1996.

Gottwald, Norman. *The Hebrew Bible: A Socio-Literary Introduction.* Philadelphia: Fortress, 1985.

Gregg, Robert C., and Dennis Groh. *Early Arianism: A View of Salvation.* Philadelphia: Fortress, 1981.

Grillmeier, Aloys, and Theresa Hainthaler. *Christ in Christian Tradition.* Vol. 2.4. Louisville, Ky.: Westminster John Knox, 1990.

Gurney, O. R. *The Hittites.* Baltimore: Penguin, 1962.

Halpern, Ben, and Jehuda Reinharz. *Zionism and the Creation of a New Society.* New York: Oxford University Press, 1998.

Hamilton, Victor P. *The Book of Genesis: Chapters 1—17.* Grand Rapids: Eerdmans, 1990.

———. *"misrayim."* In *Theological Wordbook of the Old Testament.* Edited by R. Laird Harris, Gleason L. Archer and Bruce K. Waltke, p. 523. Chicago: Moody Press, 1980.

Hansberry, William Leo. *Pillars in Ethiopian History.* Edited by Joseph E. Harris. Washington, D.C.: Howard University Press, 1974.

Harbeson, John W. *The Ethiopian Transformation: The Quest for the Post-Imperial State.* Boulder, Colo.: Westview Press, 1988.

Harrop, J. H. "Cyrene." In *New Bible Dictionary,* edited by D. R. W. Wood, p. 250. 3rd ed. Downers Grove, Ill.: InterVarsity Press, 1996.

Hartney, Aideen M. *John Chrysostom and the Transformation of the City.* London: Duckworth, 2004.

Harvey, Susan Ashbrook. "Nestorianism." In *Encyclopedia of Early Christianity,* edited by Everett Ferguson, 2:806-9. 2nd ed. New York: Garland, 1997.

———. "Nestorius (ca. 381-451)." In *Encyclopedia of Early Christianity,* edited by Everett Ferguson, 2:809-10. 2nd ed. New York: Garland, 1997.

Hastings, Adrian. *The Church in Africa: 1450-1950.* Oxford: Oxford University Press, 1996.

Hatch, Edwin. *The Influence of Greek Ideas on Christianity.* New York: Harper & Brothers, 1957.

Hays, J. Daniel. *From Every People and Nation: A Biblical Theology of Race.* Downers Grove, Ill.: InterVarsity Press, 2003.

————. "Zerah." In *Eerdmans Dictionary of the Bible,* edited by David Noel Freedman, pp. 1417-18, Grand Rapids: Eerdmans, 2000.

Herodotus. *The Histories of Herodotus of Halicarnassus.* Translated by Harry Carter. New York: Heritage Press, 1958.

Hill, Andrew E., and John H. Walton. *A Survey of the Old Testament.* Grand Rapids: Zondervan, 1991.

Hindson, Edward E. *The Philistines and the Old Testament.* Grand Rapids: Baker, 1971.

Hlatshwayo, Simphiwe A. *Education and Independence: Education in South Africa, 1658-1988.* Westport, Conn.: Greenwood Press, 2000.

Hoch, Martin. "The Price of Failure: The Second Crusade as a Turning-point in the History of the Latin East." In *The Second Crusade: Scope and Consequences,* edited by Jonathan Phillips and Martin Hoch, pp. 180-200. Manchester: Manchester University Press, 2001.

Hodgkin, Thomas. *Nigerian Perspectives: An Historical Anthology.* London: Oxford University Press, 1960.

Holden, Edith. *Blyden of Liberia: An Account of the Life and Labors of Edward Wilmot Blyden, LL.D. as recorded in letters and in print.* New York: Vantage Press, 1966.

Holter, Knut. "Africa in the Old Testament." In *The Bible in Africa: Transactions, Trajectories and Trends,* edited by Gerald O. West and Musa W. Dube, pp. 569-71. Boston/Leiden: Brill Academic, 2001.

Hopfe, Lewis M., and Mark R. Woodward. *Religions of the World.* 9th ed. Upper Saddle River, N.J.: Prentice Hall, 2005.

Hotaling, Ed. *Islam Without Illusions.* Syracuse, N.Y.: Syracuse University Press, 2003.

Hubbard, D. A. "Ethiopian Eunuch." In *New Bible Dictionary,* edited by D. R. W. Wood, p. 346. 3rd ed. Downers Grove, Ill.: InterVarsity Press, 1996.

————. "Queen of Sheba." In *New Bible Dictionary,* edited by D. R. W. Wood, p. 1088. 3rd ed. Downers Grove, Ill.: InterVarsity Press, 1996.

Isichei, Elizabeth. *A History of Christianity in Africa.* Grand Rapids: Eerdmans; Lawrenceville, N.J.: Africa World Press, 1995.

Jenkins, Philip. *The Next Christendom: The Coming of Global Christianity*. New York: Oxford University Press, 2002.

Jewett, Robert. *Christian Tolerance: Paul's Message to the Modern Church*. Philadelphia: Westminster Press, 1982.

Jomier, Jacques, ed. *The Bible and the Qur'an*. San Francisco: Ignatius Press, 2002.

Kahl, Hans-Dietrich. "Crusade Eschatology as Seen by St. Bernard in the Years 1146 to 1148." In *The Second Crusade and the Cistercians*, edited by Michael Gervers, pp. 35-47. New York: St. Martin's Press, 1992.

Kapteijns, Lidwien. "Ethiopia and the Horn of Africa." In *The History of Islam in Africa*, edited by Nehemia Letzvion and Randall L. Powels, pp. 227-50. Athens: Ohio University Press, 2002.

Karpat, Kemal H. "Millets and Nationality: The Roots of the Incongruity of Nation and State in the Post-Ottoman Era." In *Christians and Jews in the Ottoman Empire: The Functioning of a Plural Society*, edited by Benjamin Braude and Bernard Lewis, pp. 141-69. New York: Homes & Meier, 1982.

Kelly, J. N. D. *Golden Mouth: The Story of John Chrysostom: Ascetic, Preacher, Bishop*. Ithaca, N.Y.: Cornell University Press, 1996.

Killebrew, Ann E. *Biblical Peoples and Ethnicity: An Archeological Study of Egyptians, Canaanites, Philistines and Early Israel: 1300-1100 BCE*. Atlanta: Society of Biblical Literature, 2005.

Kitchen, K. A. "Eliezer." In *New Bible Dictionary*, edited by D. R. W. Wood, p. 310. 3rd ed. Downers Grove, Ill.: InterVarsity Press, 1996.

———. "Hophra." In *New Bible Dictionary*, edited by D. R. W. Wood, p. 480. 3rd ed. Downers Grove, Ill.: InterVarsity Press, 1996.

———. "Pharaoh." In *New Bible Dictionary*, edited by D. R. W. Wood, p. 913. 3rd ed. Downers Grove, Ill.: InterVarsity Press, 1996.

———. "Shishak." In *New Bible Dictionary*, edited by D. R. W. Wood, p. 1097. 3rd ed. Downers Grove, Ill.: InterVarsity Press, 1996.

Klengel, Horst. "Problems in Hittite History, Solved and Unsolved." In *Recent Developments in Hittite Archaeology and History: Papers in Memory of Hans G. Güterbock*, edited by K. Aslihan Yener and Harry A. Hoffner Jr., pp. 101-9. Winona Lake, Ind.: Eisenbrauns, 2002.

Larebo, Haile Mariam. "The Ethiopian Orthodox Church." In *Eastern*

Christianity and Politics in the Twentieth Century, edited by Pedro Ramet, 1:375-99. Durham, N.C.: Duke University Press, 1988.

Lascaratos, John, and Spyros Marketos. "Didymus the Blind: An Unknown Precursor of Louis Braille and Helen Keller." *Documenta Ophthalmologia* 86 (1994): 203-8.

Latourette, Kenneth Scott. *A History of the Expansion of Christianity*, vol. 1: *The First Five Centuries*. New York: Harper & Brothers, 1937.

Laudarji, Isaac. "Ritual as Quest for Well Being in the Religious Universe of the Tangale People of Nigeria." Ph.D. Dissertation, Northwestern University, 1994.

Leahy, Anthony. "Ethnic Diversity in Ancient Egypt." In *Civilizations of the Ancient Near East*, edited by Jack M. Sasson, pp. 225-34. Vols. 1-2 in 1 volume. Peabody, Mass.: Hendrickson, 2000.

Leeman, Bernard. *Queen of Sheba and Biblical Scholarship*. Queensland, Australia: Queensland Academic Press 2005.

Lefkowitz, Mary R., and Guy MacLean Rogers, eds. *Black Athena Revisited*. Chapel Hill: University of North Carolina Press, 1996.

Lewis, Bernard. *The Jews of Islam*. Princeton, N.J.: Princeton University Press, 1984.

Lieu, Samuel N. C. *Manichaeism in the Later Roman Empire and Medieval China: A Historical Survey*. Manchester: Manchester University Press, 1984.

Lipsky, George A. *Ethiopia: Its People, Its Society, Its Culture*. New Haven, Conn.: HRAF Press, 1962.

Maalouf, Amin. *The Crusades Through Arab Eyes*. Translated by Jon Rothschild. New York: Schocken Books, 1985.

Maccoby, Hyam. *The Mythmaker: Paul and the Invention of Christianity*. New York: Harper & Row, 1987.

MacGaffey, Wyatt. *Modern Kongo Prophets: Religion in a Plural Society*. Bloomington: Indiana University Press, 1983.

Mafico, Temba. "The Divine Name Yahweh 'Elōhîm from an African Perspective." In *Reading from this Place*, vol. 2: *Social Location and Biblical Interpretation in Global Perspective*, edited by Fernando F. Segovia and Mary Ann Tolbert, pp. 21-32. Minneapolis: Fortress, 1995.

Manley, Bill. *The Penguin Historical Atlas of Ancient Egypt*. London: Penguin, 1996.

Markschies, Christoph. *Gnosis: An Introduction*. London: T & T Clark, 2003.

Marlowe, W. Creighton. "Put." In *Eerdmans Dictionary of the Bible*, edited by David Noel Freedman, pp. 1100-1101. Grand Rapids: Eerdmans, 2000.

Maxwell, John Francis. *Slavery and the Catholic Church: The History of Catholic Teaching Concerning the Moral Legitimacy of the Institution of Slavery*. Chichester: Barry Rose Publishers, 1975.

Mayer, Hans Eberhard. *The Crusades*. Translated by John Gillingham. 2nd ed. Oxford: Oxford University Press, 1988.

McArthur, John F. *Galatians*. Chicago: Moody Press, 1987.

McAuliffe, Jane Dammen. "Followers of the *Qur'ānic* Jesus." In *Qur'ānic Christians: An Analysis of Classical and Modern Exegesis*. Cambridge: Cambridge University Press, 1991.

Metzger, Bruce M. "Survey of the Geography, History, and Archaeology of the Bible Lands." In *The New Oxford Annotated Bible: New Revised Standard Version*, edited by Bruce M. Metzger and Roland E. Murphy, pp. 407-23. New York: Oxford University Press, 1991.

Milton-Edwards, Beverly. *Islamic Fundamentalism Since 1945*. New York: Routledge, 2004.

Morkot, R. G. *Black Pharaohs: Egypt's Nubian Rulers*. London: David Brown, 2000.

Morrisey, R. A. *Colored People and Bible History*. Hammond, Ind.: W. B. Conkey, 1925.

Motyer, J. A. "Kenites." In *New Bible Dictionary*, edited by D. R. W. Wood, p. 643. 3rd ed. Downers Grove: InterVarsity Press, 1996.

Mourad, Suleiman A. "On the Qur'anic Stories about Mary and Jesus." *Bulletin of the Royal Institute for Inter-Faith Studies* 1 (1999): 13-24.

Murphy, Roland. "'Nation' in the Old Testament." In *Ethnicity*, edited by Andrew M. Greeley and Gregory Baum, pp. 71-77. New York: Seabury Press, 1977.

Nasr, Seyyed Hossein. *Islam: Religion, History, and Civilization*. New York: HarperSanFrancisco, 2003.

Nixon, R. E. "Apollos." In *New Bible Dictionary*, edited by D. R. W. Wood, p. 57. 3rd ed. Downers Grove, Ill.: InterVarsity Press, 1996.

———. "Simeon." In *New Bible Dictionary*, edited by D. R. W. Wood, p. 1104. 3rd ed. Downers Grove, Ill.: InterVarsity Press, 1996.

Nyaga, Daniel. *Customs and Traditions of the Meru*. Nairobi: East African Educational Publishers, 1997.

O'Connor, David. "The Hyksos Period in Egypt." In *The Hyksos: New Historical and Archaeological Perspectives*, edited by Eliezer D. Oren, pp. 45-67. Philadelphia: University of Pennsylvania Museum, 1997.

Oded, Bustenay. "The Table of Nations (Genesis 10): A Socio-Cultural Approach." *Zeitschrift für die alttestamentliche Wissenschaft* 98 (1986): 14-31.

O'Keefe, John J., and R. R. Reno. *Sanctified Vision: An Introduction to Early Christian Interpretation of the Bible*. Baltimore: Johns Hopkins University Press, 2005.

Oliver, Roland. *The Missionary Factor in East Africa*. London: Longmans Green, 1952.

Oussani, Gabriel. "Christianity in Arabia." In *The Catholic Encyclopedia*, 1:666-74. New York: Robert Appleton, 1907.

Owusu-Mensa, Kofi. *Saturday God and Adventism in Ghana*. Frankfurt: Peter Lang, 1993.

Pacini, Andrea. Introduction to *Christian Communities in the Arab Middle East: The Challenge of the Future*, edited by Andrea Pacini, pp. 1-24. Oxford: Clarendon, 1998.

Panzer, Joel S. *The Popes and Slavery*. New York: Alba House, 1996.

Paracka, Daniel J. *The Athens of West Africa: A History of International Education at Fourah Bay College, Freetown, Sierra Leone*. New York: Routledge, 2003.

Parfitt, Tudor. *Journey to the Vanished City: The Search for a Lost Tribe of Israel*. New York: Vantage Books, 2000.

Parrinder, Geoffrey. *Jesus in the Quran*. Oxford: One World, 1995.

Patterson, Sheila. *The Last Trek: A Study of the Boer People and the Afrikaner Nation*. London: Routledge, 1957.

Pelikan, Jaraslov. *The Christian Tradition: A History of the Development of Doctrine*, vol. 1: *The Emergence of the Catholic Tradition (100-600)*. Chicago: University of Chicago Press, 1971.

———. *Mary Through the Centuries: Her Place in the History of Culture*. New Haven, Conn.: Yale University Press, 1996.

Phillips, Wendell. *Qataban and Sheba: Exploring the Ancient Kingdoms on the Biblical Spice Routes of Arabia*. New York: Harcourt Brace, 1955.

Quasten, Johannes. *Patrology*, vol. 2: *The Ante-Nicene Literature after Irenaeus*. Vol. 3: *The Golden Age of Greek Patristic Literature from the Council of Nicaea to the Council of Chalcedon*. Utrecht: Spectrum Publishers, 1953, 1975.

Rainey, Anson F. "Palestine, Land of." In *Eerdmans Dictionary of the Bible*, edited by David Noel Freedman, pp. 998-1004. Grand Rapids: Eerdmans, 2000.

Redford, Donald B. *From Slave to Pharaoh: The Black Experience of Ancient Egypt*. Baltimore: Johns Hopkins University Press, 2004.

Rigby, Andrew. *Justice and Reconciliation: After the Violence*. Boulder, Colo.: Lynne Rienner, 2001.

Robinson, J. M. *The Nag Hammadi Library in English*. Rev. ed. San Francisco: Harper & Row, 1988.

Robinson, Neal. *Christ in Islam and Christianity*. Albany: State University of New York Press, 1991.

Rogers, Jeffrey S. "Table of Nations." In *Eerdmans Dictionary of the Bible*, edited by David Noel Freedman, p. 1271. Grand Rapids: Eerdmans, 2000.

Roukema, Reimer, and John Bowden. *Gnosis and Faith in Early Christianity: An Introduction to Gnosticism*. Harrisburg, Penn.: Trinity Press International, 1999.

Rubio, Gonzalo. "The Languages of the Ancient Near East." In *A Companion to the Ancient Near East*, edited by Daniel C. Snell, pp. 79-94. Malden, Mass.: Blackwell, 2005.

Rudolph, Kurt. *Gnosis: The Nature and History of Gnosticism*. San Francisco: Harper & Row, 1983.

Sack, Ronald H. "Evil-Merodach." In *Eerdmans Dictionary of the Bible*, edited by David Noel Freedman, p. 438. Grand Rapids: Eerdmans, 2000.

―――. *Images of Nebuchadnezzar: The Emergence of a Legend*. Selinsgrove, Penn.: Susquehanna University Press, 2004.

Salahi, Adil. *Muhammad: Man and Prophet*. Markfield, Leicestershire: The Islamic Foundation, 2002.

Sanneh, Lamin. *West African Christianity: The Religious Impact*. Maryknoll, N.Y.: Orbis, 1983.

Saunders, A. C. de C. M. *A Social History of Black Slaves and Freedmen in Portugal, 1441-1555*. Cambridge: Cambridge University Press, 1982.

Schaff, Philip. *History of the Christian Church*, vol. 3: *Nicene and Post Nicene Christianity from Constantine the Great to Gregory the Great, A.D. 311-600*. Grand Rapids: Eerdmans, 1910.

Schick, Robert. *The Christian Communities of Palestine from Byzantine to Islamic Rule*. Princeton, N.J.: Darwin Press, 1995.

Sellassie, Haile. *My Life and Ethiopia's Progress, 1892-1937: The Autobiography of Emperor Haile Sellassie I.* Translated by Edward Ullendorff. Chicago, Ill.: Frontline Distribution International, 1999.

Sharon, Moshe. "The Birth of Islam in the Holy Land." In *The Holy Land in History and Thought,* edited by Moshe Sharon, pp. 225-35. Leiden: Brill, 1988.

Shaw, Mark. *The Kingdom of God in Africa: A Short History of African Christianity.* Grand Rapids: Baker, 1996.

Shea, William. "The Murder of Sennacherib and Related Issues." *Near East Archaeological Society Bulletin* 46 (2001): 38.

Sheen, Fulton J. "Mary and the Moslems." In *The Bible and the Qur'an,* edited by Jacques Jomier, pp. 121-26. San Francisco: Ignatius Press, 2002.

Simons, J. "The 'Table of Nations': Its General Structure and Meaning." In *I Studied Inscriptions from Before the Flood: Ancient Near Eastern, Literary, and Linguistic Approaches to Genesis 1—11,* edited by Richard S. Hess and David Toshio Tsumura, pp. 234-53. Winona Lake, Ind.: Eisenbrauns, 1994.

Sinclair, Lawrence A. "Nile." In *Eerdmans Dictionary of the Bible,* edited by David Noel Freedman, p. 965. Grand Rapids: Eerdmans, 2000.

Sivers, Peter von. "Egypt and North Africa." In *The History of Islam in Africa,* edited by Nehemia Letzvion and Randall L. Powels, pp. 21-36. Athens: Ohio University Press, 2002.

Skinner, John. *A Critical and Exegetical Commentary on Genesis.* 2nd ed. Edinburgh: T & T Clark, 1930.

Snowden, Frank. *Blacks in Antiquity: Ethiopians in the Greco-Roman Experience.* Cambridge, Mass.: Belknap Press of Harvard University Press, 1970.

Sowell, Thomas. *Race and Culture: A World View.* New York: Basic Books, 1994.

Spaulding, Jay. "Precolonial Islam in the Eastern Sudan." In *The History of Islam in Africa,* edited by Nehemia Letzvion and Randall L. Powels, pp. 117-29. Athens: Ohio University Press, 2002.

Speiser, E. A. "In Search of Nimrod." In *I Studied Inscriptions from Before the Flood: Ancient Near Eastern, Literary, and Linguistic Approaches to Genesis 1—11,* edited by Richard S. Hess and David Toshio Tsumura, pp. 270-77. Winona Lake, Ind.: Eisenbrauns, 1994.

Steed, Christopher, and Bengt Sundkler. *A History of the Church in Africa.* Cambridge: Cambridge University Press, 2000.

Stillman, Norman A. *The Jews of Arab Lands: A History and Source Book.* Philadelphia: Jewish Publication Society of America, 1979.

Strabo. *The Geography of Strabo.* Translated by Horace Leonard Jones. 8 vols. Cambridge: Harvard University Press, 1982-1989.

Tafla, Bairu. "Ethiopian Orthodox Church." In *The Coptic Encyclopedia,* edited by Aziz S. Atiya, pp. 995-99. New York: Macmillan, 1991.

Tamrat, Taddesse. *Church and State in Ethiopia: 1270-1527.* Oxford: Clarendon, 1972.

Templin, J. Alton. *Ideology of a Frontier: The Theological Foundation of Afrikaner Nationalism, 1652-1910.* Westport, Conn.: Greenwood Press, 1984.

Thomas, Latta. *Biblical Faith and the Black American.* Valley Forge, Penn.: Judson Press, 1986.

Thompson, Leonard. *A History of South Africa.* New Haven, Conn.: Yale University Press, 1990.

Tilley, Maureen A. *The Bible in Christian North Africa: The Donatist World.* Minneapolis: Fortress, 1997.

Török, László. *The Kingdom of Kush: Handbook of the Napatan-Meroitic Civilization.* Leiden: Brill, 1997.

Trimingham, J. Spencer. *Islam in Ethiopia.* London: Oxford University Press, 1952.

Ullendorff, Edward. *The Ethiopians: An Introduction to Country and People.* 4th ed. Kingston, Jamaica: Headstart Printing and Publishing, 1998.

Usry, Glen, and Craig S. Keener. *Black Man's Religion: Can Christianity Be Afrocentric?* Downers Grove, Ill.: InterVarsity Press, 1996.

Van Fleteren, Frederick, and Joseph C. Schnaubelt, eds. *Augustine: Biblical Exegete.* New York: Peter Lang, 2001.

van Sertima, Ivan. *Black Women in Antiquity.* New Brunswick, N.J.: Transaction Books, 1984.

Walker, Eric Anderson. *The Great Trek.* London: A. & C. Black, 1934.

Walker, Sheila S. *The Religious Revolution in the Ivory Coast: The Prophet Harris and the Harrist Church.* Chapel Hill: University of North Carolina Press, 1983.

Wallace-Hadrill, D. S. *Eusebius of Caesarea.* Westminster: Canterbury Press, 1961.

Walton, John H., and Victor H. Matthews, eds. *The IVP Bible Background Commentary: Genesis—Deuteronomy.* Downers Grove, Ill.: InterVarsity Press, 1997.

Walton, John H., Victor H. Matthews and Mark W. Chavalas, eds. *The IVP Bible Background Commentary: Old Testament.* Downers Grove, Ill.: InterVarsity Press, 2000.

Wansbrough, John. *Quranic Studies: Sources and Methods of Scriptural Interpretation.* Oxford: Oxford University Press, 1977.

Weingarten, Michael A. *Changing Health and Changing Culture: The Yemenite Jews in Israel.* Westport, Conn.: Praeger, 1992.

Welsby, Derek A. *The Kingdom of Kush: The Napatan and Meroitic Empires.* London: British Museum Press, 1996.

Wenham, Gordon J. *Genesis 1—15; Genesis 16—50.* Word Biblical Commentary 1-2. Dallas: Word, 1987, 1994.

Williams, Joseph J. *Hebrewisms of West Africa: From Nile to Niger with the Jews.* New York: Dial Press, 1930.

Wills, Garry. *Saint Augustine.* New York: Penguin, 1999.

Wimbush, Vincent, and Rosamond Rodman, eds. *African Americans and the Bible: Sacred Texts and Social Textures.* New York: Continuum, 2000.

Wiseman, D. J. "Ashurbanipal." In *New Bible Dictionary,* edited by D. R. W. Wood, p. 94. 3rd ed. Downers Grove, Ill.: InterVarsity Press, 1996.

————. "Belshazzar." In *New Bible Dictionary,* edited by D. R. W. Wood, p. 127. 3rd ed. Downers Grove, Ill.: InterVarsity Press, 1996.

————. "Chedorlaomer." In *New Bible Dictionary,* edited by D. R. W. Wood, p. 182. 3rd ed. Downers Grove, Ill.: InterVarsity Press, 1996.

————. "Esarhaddon." In *New Bible Dictionary,* edited by D. R. W. Wood, p. 332. 3rd ed. Downers Grove, Ill.: InterVarsity Press, 1996.

————. "Evil Merodach." In *New Bible Dictionary,* edited by D. R. W. Wood, p. 349. 3rd ed. Downers Grove, Ill.: InterVarsity Press, 1996.

————. "Genesis 10: Some Archaeological Considerations." In *I Studied Inscriptions from Before the Flood: Ancient Near Eastern, Literary, and Linguistic Approaches to Genesis 1—11,* edited by Richard S. Hess and David Toshio Tsumura, pp. 254-65. Winona Lake, Ind.: Eisenbrauns, 1994.

————. "Nimrod." In *New Bible Dictionary,* edited by D. R. W. Wood, p. 825. 3rd ed. Downers Grove, Ill.: InterVarsity Press, 1996.

————. "Sargon." In *New Bible Dictionary,* edited by D. R. W. Wood, p. 1063. 3rd ed. Downers Grove, Ill.: InterVarsity Press, 1996.

————. "Sennacherib." In *New Bible Dictionary,* edited by D. R. W. Wood, pp. 1075-76. 3rd ed. Downers Grove, Ill.: InterVarsity Press, 1996.

————. "Shalmaneser." In *New Bible Dictionary*, edited by D. R. W. Wood, p. 1085. 3rd ed. Downers Grove, Ill.: InterVarsity Press, 1996.

————. "Tiglath-Pileser." In *New Bible Dictionary*, edited by D. R. W. Wood, pp. 1186-87. 3rd ed. Downers Grove, Ill.: InterVarsity Press, 1996.

Wit, C. de. "Neco, Necho." In *New Bible Dictionary*, edited by D. R. W. Wood, p. 811. 3rd ed. Downers Grove, Ill.: InterVarsity Press, 1996.

Worger, William H. "Historical Setting." In *South Africa: A Country Study*, edited by Rita M. Byrnes, pp. 1-86. Washington, D.C.: Library of Congress Federal Research Division, 1997.

Yamauchi, Edwin M. *Africa and the Bible*. Grand Rapids: Baker Academic, 2004.

Yurco, Frank J. "Were the Ancient Egyptians Black or White?" *Biblical Archaeology Review* 15 (Sept./Oct. 1989): 24-29, 58.

Zetterholm, Magus. *The Formation of Christianity in Antioch: A Social-Scientific Approach to the Separation Between Judaism and Christianity*. London: Routledge, 2003.

Name Index

Abd al-Malik, 166

Abdullah ibn Jahsh, 146

Abdul-Muttalib ibn Hashim, 142

Abeokuta, 228, 235-36

Abiathar, 105

Abimelech, 50-51, 91, 93-95

Abinadab, 84

Abishai, 85

Abraha, 141-42, 158

Abraham, 28, 33-34, 42, 44, 48-52, 54, 59, 74-76, 85-86, 91-95, 97, 101-4, 111-12, 134, 146-47, 150-51, 158, 166, 171, 204, 213, 234, 247-49, 251, 253, 257

Absalom, 70, 71, 84, 105

Abu Bakr, 142, 160

Achan, 37

Achbor, 251

Achish, 82-83

Achshaph, 97

Adah, 101

Adam, 17, 154

Adoni-bezek, 98

Adoni-zedek, 97

Adrammelech, 256

Aedesius, 136, 137

Aflaq, Michel, 212

Agag, 252

Agaw, 187, 188

Ahab, 100

Ahaz, 37, 255

Ahmad ibn Ibrahim, 192

Ahuzzah, 95

Alexander V, 198

Alexander, bishop of Alexandria, 89, 128, 198

Alexander, son of Simon, 89, 128, 198

Alexius, 176-78

Alfonso Mendez, 195

Al-Hakim, 175

Ali, 158, 165, 169

Ali bin Abi Talib, 165

al-Kahina, 169

Allah, 151-52, 155

Alwa, 138, 164

Alwan, 163

Amasis, 82

Ambrose, 133

Amda, 188

Amenemhat, 75

Amenhotep, 78, 79

Amhose, 82

Amin, Idi, 184, 242

Amlak, Yekuno, 188

Amos, 38-39, 53, 244, 246

Anah, 101

Ananias, 117

Anastasius, 141

Antony, 126

Apollos, 89-90

Aquila, 89, 131

Aramnaharaim, 98

Araunah, 106

Arius, 119, 128-29

Asa, 66

Asenath, 86

Ashkenazi, 213-14

Ashurbanipal, 257

Asshur, 25

Athanasius, 126, 128-29, 131, 137,

173

Augustine of Hippo, 133

Auxentius, 128

Baale-judah, 84

Baal-hanan, 251

Balaam, 68-70

Balfour, Arthur J., 214

Bani Hamuyah, 187

Barak, 99

Barbarossa, Frederick, 181

Barnabas, 89

Bartalomewos, 190

Bartholomew, 140, 178, 198

Basemath, 101

Basil the Great, 119

Basilides, 124, 125

Basilios, 218

Bathsheba, 105

Bathshua, 103

Beeri, 101

Bela, 92, 251

Belshazzar, 65

Beor, 251

Bera of Sodom, 92

Bermudez, 193

Bernard of Clairvaux, 179-80

Bilad al-Mahgrib, 168

Bilkis, 66

Blyden, Edward W., 235

Buthelezi, Mangosuthu, 241

Cain, 12, 18, 62

Candace, 67

Cardinal Biayenda, 241

Casluhim, 50

Cherdorlaomer, 92

Chrysostom, 119-21

Claudius, 193-94

Colchis, 73

Colenso, John Williams, 232

Constantine, 121, 128-29, 175

Constantius, 141

Cozbi, 253-54

Cushan-rishathaim, 98

Cyril II, 189

Cyrus, 167

Damietta, 183-84

Daniel, 17, 47, 61, 64-66, 97, 204, 215, 234

Darius, 65

Dawit, 189-90

Debir of Eglon, 97

Deborah, 99, 250

Decian, 133

Dedan, 25, 34, 36, 58, 244

Delilah, 86-87

Dhimmah, 210

Dhu Nuwas, 141

Didymus the Blind, 131

Diocletian, 126, 133

Diodore of Tarsus, 120

Diogo da Azambuja, 199

Doeg, 252

Donatus, 127

Dyani, 231

Ebedmelech, 71

Eglon, 97, 98

Elesbaan, 141, 162

Eliezer, 75, 103-4, 253

Elijah, 100, 106-7, 125, 150, 208
Elishah, 49
Elohim, 92
Elon, 101-2
Emesa, 179
Enaim, 103
Enoch, 62
Ephraim, 86
Ephron, 51, 94
Epiphanius, 116-17
Er, 102
Esarhaddon, 256
Esat (Judith), 187
Esau, 35-36, 39, 51, 59, 101-2, 247, 251-52
Esimephaeus, 141
Ethbaal, 100
Eugenius, 180
Euodius, 120
Eusebius Pamphili, 119
Euthymius, 139
Eve, 17
Evil-Merodach, 64
Ewostatewos, 190
Ezana, 14, 137, 162, 191
Filipos, 190
Freeman, Thomas Birch, 235-36
Frumentius, 137
Gabriel, 44, 139, 149, 158, 191, 238
Galawdewos, 193
Gedaliah, 43, 64
Genubath, 80
Gershom, 253
Ghazan, 161
Gideon, 250-51
Giyorgis, 191
Goliath, 50, 82-83, 85
Gomez, Diogo, 199
Gran, 192
Hadad, 80, 248,

251-52
Hadar, 251
Hagar, 33, 85-86, 101, 248-49
Haile Sellassie, 218, 221
Ham, 11-15, 17, 19, 21-24, 26-30, 32, 37, 41, 46-50, 54-55, 58-59, 61, 75, 90-91, 101-2, 108, 111-13, 143, 156, 170-71, 173-75, 177, 185-86, 188, 196-97, 201, 205-9, 215, 227, 230, 235, 237, 242, 244, 247, 254, 257
Hani, Chris, 241
Hannibal, 19
Hatshepsut, 78
Havilah, 25, 32-33, 36, 244, 249
Heber, 99, 250
Helena, 192
Herod, 44
Herodotus, 61, 73, 82
Herzl, Theodor, 214
Heth, 59, 88, 91
Hezekiah, 38, 45, 63, 71, 256
Hiram of Tyre, 99, 106
Hobab, 249
Hophra (Apries), 45, 81-82
Horam of Gezer, 97
Hosea, 38
Hoshea, 45, 80-81, 255
Ibn Hisham, 161
Ibn Ishaq, 158
Inyotef, 75
Irenaeus, 130
Isaac, 28, 51-52, 85, 94-95, 101-2, 104,

145, 204, 248-49, 251
Isaiah, 30, 40, 43, 45-46, 63, 135-36, 150, 256
Ishbak, 34, 101
Ishbi-benob, 85
Ishmael, 33-34, 43, 85-86, 101-2, 104, 158, 247-49
Iyasus I, 218
Jabin of Hazor, 98, 250
Jael, 99, 250
Jafar bin Abi Talin, 161
Japheth, 21-23, 28-29, 48-49, 54, 74, 178, 186, 236
Jehoahaz, 81
Jehoiachin, 64
Jehoiakim, 43, 81
Jehoshaphat, 35
Jehu, 100, 101
Jeremiah, 37, 43, 61, 71, 81, 82
Jeroboam, 43-44, 80-81, 136
Jerome, 117, 119, 131
Jesus, 14, 17, 39, 44, 65, 88-89, 93, 103-4, 107, 112-13, 115-18, 125-29, 136, 138, 145, 147, 150-56, 166, 171, 177-78, 204-5, 208, 232
Jethro, 99, 101, 249-50, 253
Jezebel, 91, 100-101, 106
Jones, William, 229
Judah, 35-39, 43-46, 63-64, 66, 71, 80-82, 102-4, 223, 255-57

Judith, 101
Julian, 138
Justinian, 138, 169
Karenga, Maulana, 207
Kaunda, Kenneth, 240-41
Kedar, 33, 248
Kenyatta, Jomo, 228
Keturah, 34, 59, 101, 104, 249, 253
Khadija, 146
Kimbangu, Simon, 238
Kimpa Vita, 238
Lalibala, 188
Lebna Dengel, 192-93
Lenisha, Alice, 239
Levi, 96, 222
Lij Iyasu, 218, 220-21
Livingstone, David, 230, 232
Mahalath, 102
Majorinus, 127
Makonnen, Ras Tafari, 221
Manasseh, 86
Mandela, Nelson, 240
Masrouq, 142
Mattaniah, 64
Mbeki, Thabo, 240
Melchizedek, 50, 91-93, 97, 101
Menelek, 66, 135, 217
Merodach-Baladan, 63
Micah, 44, 62
Mobutu, Sese Seko, 241
Montjuhotep, 75
Moses, 34, 36, 52, 77-79, 101, 140, 147, 150-52, 177,

188, 204, 208, 225,
249-50, 253-54
Muawiyah, 165
Muhammad, 14,
142, 145-47, 149-
68, 170-71, 181,
184, 188, 227, 242
Muhammad, Elijah,
125
Mweme Mutapa,
199-200
Nabonidus, 65
Naboth, 100
Nebuzaradan, 64
Neco, 81
Neriglissar, 64
Nestorius, 121, 130,
145, 152
Nimrod, 22, 25, 59,
62-63, 71, 82, 244,
247, 254
Nkomo, Joshua, 240
Nkrumah, Kwame,
240
Noah, 12, 21, 28, 48,
52-54, 62, 98, 147,
151, 171
Nyerere, Julius, 240
Obed-edom, 84
Oholibamah, 101
Onan, 102, 103
Origen, 118-19,
130-31, 139, 173
Osorkon, 66, 80-81
Othniel, 98
Pachomius, 126
Pakhom, 126
Pamphilus, 118-19
Pantaenus, 130, 140
Pekah, 255
Perez, 103
Pharaoh, 42-45, 50,
66-67, 73-77, 79-
82, 86, 93, 252-53
Phicol, 95
Philip Augustus, 181
Philippe, 142, 156

Philo, 123
Phineas, 254
Pierius, 118
Piram, 97
Plato, 123
Poitphar, 77
Potiphera, 77, 86
Prester John, 15,
186, 192
Ptah, 26
Pul, 255
Queen of Sheba, 65-
66, 141, 225
Rabshakeh, 45
Rachel, 51
Rahab, 39, 91, 104-5
Ramses, 43, 77
Rebekah, 51, 95,
101-2
Rehoboam, 44, 136
Rekem, 70
Reuel, 249
Saida, 188-89
Saladin, 181-83, 188
Salmon, 104
Samlah, 251
Samson, 86-87
Saph, 85
Sarah, 34, 42, 44,
50-51, 74-75, 85-
86, 93-95, 101,
248-49
Sargon, 62-63, 256
Sarsa Dengel, 194
Satan, 158
Saul, 35, 53, 80, 82-
83, 89, 201, 252-
53
Sennacherib, 38, 45,
63, 67, 256
Senusret, 75
Seretse, 240
Shabako, 67
Shadrach, 64
Shalmaneser, 255-56
Sharp, Granville,
202

Shaul, 251
Sheba, 25, 34, 36-
37, 58, 65-67, 135,
188, 220, 244
Shechem, 51, 95-96
Shelah, 102, 103
Shem, 21-23, 25,
28-29, 42, 47-49,
52-55, 58, 75, 88,
91, 104, 178, 244,
247
Shenuoda III, 225
Shenuote, 145
Shishak, 43-44, 80-
81
Shoshenk, 80
Shuah, 34, 101
Siamun, 80
Sihon, 53, 96-97
Silko, 138
Silvanus, 141
Silvera, 200
Simon of Cyrene,
17, 88
Sisera, 98-99, 250
Solomon, 36-37, 43-
44, 53, 64-66, 79-
80, 88, 99, 106,
135, 179, 188, 217,
220-21, 223, 225,
234, 252
Sozomenus, 139
Strabo, 61
Susenyos, 195
Symmachus, 117,
131
Taharka, 67
Tahpenes, 80
Tamar, 102-3
Tema, 248
Tertullian, 131-33,
168, 173
Tertullus, 117
Tewodros, 218-19
Theodora, 138
Theodore, 120-21
Theodosius, 119

Theodotion, 131
Theophilus, 141
Thutmose, 77-78
Tiglath-pileser, 37,
63, 254-55
Tirhaka, 256
Tukulti-Ninurta, 62
Tyrannius Rufinus,
131
Umar, 142, 160, 165
Uriah, 43, 91, 105
Uthmar, 165
Uzzah, 84
Valens, 140
Valentinus, 125-26
Weizmann, Chaim,
214
Wilberforce, Wil-
liam, 203
Yaksoum, 142
Yakub, 125
Zacharias, 153
Zadok, 105
Zalmunna, 251
Zara Yaqob, 190-92
Zarephath, 106
Zawditu, 221
Zebah, 251
Zedekiah, 45, 64, 71,
82
Zeeb, 251
Zephaniah, 39, 71,
135
Zerah, 66-67, 103,
251
Zetterholm, Magus,
119
Zibeon, 101
Zimran, 34, 101
Zimri, 254
Zipporah, 188, 253-
54
Zocum, 139
Zohar, 94

Subject Index

Abbasid Dynasty, 160

abolitionists, 203, 219, 227, 234-35

Abyssinia, 161-62, 171, 187-88

Achaia, 89

Achmimic, 123

Acre, 179, 182, 184

Addis Ababa, 225

Adessa, county of, 180

adoptionism, 195

Adowa, Battle of, 220

Adullamite, 103

adultery, 42, 76, 103

Africa, 11-19, 22, 24-25, 27-30, 32-33, 47-48, 54, 57-58, 61, 73-74, 102, 108, 111-12, 123-24, 126-28, 131, 133, 135-38, 144, 146-47, 157, 162-64, 166-71, 173-74, 184, 186, 188, 196, 198-204, 209, 217-19, 228-43, 246

African American, 18, 125

Afrikaner, 201, 231

Afrocentric, 12, 40, 108

AIDS, 102, 243

Akan, 204-5

Akkad, 25, 244

Akkadian, 47

Alexandria, 89, 112, 118, 120, 123, 128-31, 137, 140, 167

Algeria, 27, 133

Allah, 151-52, 155

allegory, 86, 249

Aleppo, 179-80

Amalek, 59, 83, 102, 252

Amalekite, 250, 252-53

Amarutu, 62

America, 47, 73, 126, 214, 234, 236, 239

American Colonization Society, 235

Amerindians, 202

Amhara, 163

Amharic, 222

Ammon, 34-35, 38, 40, 55, 58, 88, 105

Ammonite, 34, 47, 105

Amon, 80

Amorite, 47, 53, 96-97

Anamites, 27, 246

anarchy, 218

ancestry, 21, 57, 104, 247-48

Anglican, 234, 241

Angola, 19, 199-200

Annaba, 133

Antioch, 14, 89, 112, 118-21, 128, 176-78

anti-Semitism, 214

Antonian, 238

apartheid, 215, 232, 235

apocalyptic, 150, 239

apologists, 108, 124, 171

apostasy, 45, 53, 82, 98, 100, 143, 189, 221

Apostolic Canons, 190

apostolic succession, 117

Arabs, 25, 34, 37, 39, 139, 141, 146-47, 165-70, 184-85, 210-12, 214-16, 229

Arab nationalism, 212

Arabia, 14, 24-25, 32-34, 36-38, 46, 66, 139-42, 147, 156-58, 160-63, 197, 204, 247, 249, 253

Arabic, 47, 141, 149, 160-61, 168, 180, 189, 212

Arad, 96

Aram, 104, 255

Aramaic, 47

archaeology, 66

Archite, 105

Arianism, 128-30

ark of the covenant, 83

Arkites, 28, 246

Armenian, 210, 211, 212

art, 73, 179, 241

artisans, 99, 106

Arvad, 49

Arvadites, 28, 246

Ascalon, 179

ascension, 14, 112, 115, 154

Asia, 29, 65, 112, 236

Aspebaetos, 139

assassination, 43, 99-100, 105, 200

assimilation, 55, 169, 193, 213

Assyria, 13, 25, 32, 37-40, 45, 58-59, 62-63, 67, 71, 81, 135, 244, 247, 254-55

Augustinian, 199

Austria, 214

Axum, 138, 147, 157, 160-63, 186-87

Axumite, 137-38, 141-42, 158, 160-62, 187, 219

Babel, 62, 72

Babylon, 13, 25, 32, 35, 38-39, 53-54, 62-65, 81-82, 135, 140, 214, 225, 244, 256-57

Baghdad, 160, 244

Balfour Declaration, 214

Bantu, 23, 196-98, 205

baptism, 116, 136, 138, 195, 199, 201

Baptists, 89, 153, 236, 238

Bar Kokhba, 115

Bashan, 49, 96

Bedouins, 139

Beersheba, 51, 86, 94-95, 248

Beirut, 119, 179

Benin, 198, 200

Berber, 169-70

Berlin Conference, 229-30, 236

Beta Israel, 218, 224-25

Bethel, 50-51, 96

betrayal, 87

Bible translation, 227

Bilad al-Mahgrib, 168

bishops, 119-20, 126-30, 133, 137, 139-42, 156, 163-64, 181, 191, 193, 195, 223, 225, 232, 234, 241-42

Black Athena, 18, 73, 108

blasphemy, 129, 155

Boer, 19, 231, 233

Bohairic, 123

Botswana, 239-40

Brazilian, 236

Buganda, 230

Byzantine, 137, 156, 165-67, 173, 176, 183

Caaba, 141, 146, 158-59, 181

Caecilian, 127

Caesarea, 118-19

Caliphate, 160

Calneh, 25, 244

Cameroon, 236

Canaan, 12-15, 22, 24, 28-29, 33-37, 42, 44, 47-55, 59, 73-75, 82, 91, 95-96, 98-99, 101-2, 104, 107-9, 112, 115, 118-19, 122, 128, 135, 143, 147, 164, 166-67, 171, 175-78, 180-82, 184-85, 196, 201, 205-6, 208-10, 213-14, 216, 227, 231, 242, 246, 248, 250, 257

Canaanite, 35, 42, 47, 50, 53-54, 59,

91-93, 95, 97-98, 101-7, 227, 247

canon, 116-17, 131, 136, 166, 218

Cape Town, 204

Cape Verde, 198

Caphtor, 53

Capuchins, 238

Carthage, 127, 131, 133

Cassite, 32-33

Catholic, Catholicism, 116, 126, 132, 134, 136, 139, 147, 152, 176, 184, 186, 188, 191, 193-94, 197-99, 211, 213, 218, 225-26, 229-30, 235-36, 240-41

Chalcedon, 120, 130-31, 168, 195

Chalcedonian Creed, 210

Chaldean Catholics, 211

children, 14, 22, 37, 42, 77, 85-86, 93, 96, 98, 101, 103-4, 108, 143, 170, 183, 202-3, 205-6, 208, 214-15, 225, 229, 235, 243

Christ, 14, 89, 93, 119, 121, 125, 128, 130, 132, 137-39, 143, 146-47, 151-53, 155, 166, 176, 179, 183, 187, 195, 197, 200, 208, 239, 241

Christendom, 126, 164, 227, 237, 239, 241

Christian Missionary Society, 228-29

Christianity, 13-16,

22, 36, 40, 44, 48, 111, 113, 115-21, 124-26, 128-33, 135-41, 143-47, 152, 156-58, 160-71, 173-75, 183-84, 186-90, 193-95, 198-200, 203, 205-6, 211, 215, 217, 219, 224-25, 227-38, 240

Christology, 129, 147

Church of the Holy Sepulcher, 175, 178, 188

Cilicia-Syria, 90

Circumcellions, 127

circumcision, 96, 136, 147, 186, 248, 253

Cistercians, 179-80

civil wars, 15, 44, 46, 54, 70, 136, 194-95, 206

classical historians, 61

Clementine Homilies, 117

coalition, 97-98

colonialism, 15

commerce, 36, 159, 203, 228-29, 232

commerce and Christianity, 203

communism, 240

concubines, 13, 50, 85, 88, 101

Confessions of Claudius, 194

Congo, 198, 238, 241

conquistadors, 198-200

conservative movement, 169

conspiracy, 252

Constantinople, 119-21, 129-30, 177-78

constitution, 218, 221-23

contextualization, 232

conversion, 67, 130, 133, 136-37, 157, 168-70, 194, 198-99, 237, 239

Coptic, 123-24, 126, 167, 189-94, 211, 218, 225

Copts, 167-68, 171, 212, 223

Council of Clermont, 177

Council of Nicaea, 128, 139

coup d'etat, 105, 223

creation, 54, 150, 154, 207, 240

creeds, 142-44, 167, 171

Crete, 27, 53, 246

crucifixion, 54, 88, 153-54

crusades, 15, 176-77, 183, 197, 205, 215

cruzad, 176

curse of Ham, 11

Cush, 12-15, 22, 24-28, 30-41, 49, 54-55, 58, 61-63, 65-66, 70-73, 91, 109, 112, 135-36, 139, 143, 157, 174, 186, 193, 196, 205-6, 208-9, 227, 240, 242, 247-48, 250-51, 253-54

Cushite, 36, 38-40, 47, 53, 65, 67-68, 70-71, 99, 102, 158, 197, 257

Cyprian, 132-33,

168
Cyrene, 17, 88-89
Decapolis, 112
deception, 83, 171, 183
denominationalism, 194
denominations, 14, 115, 210-11, 225, 233, 236-37, 242
Derg, 224
dispersion, 213
Djibouti, 25
Donatism, 126-27
Dutch, 200, 201-2, 230-32. *See also* Holland.
Easter, 118
Eastern Orthodoxy, 15, 211
Ebionites, 116-17
economic reform, 221
ecumenical, 13-14, 117, 143, 218, 243
Eden, 13, 30-33, 55
Eder, 51
Edessa, county of, 178
Edom, 35, 36, 39, 46, 51, 55, 88, 102, 135, 251, 252
Egypt, 11, 13-15, 17-19, 25, 27-28, 34-55, 58, 63, 67, 73-82, 86, 89, 91, 93, 96, 109, 111-12, 123-24, 128-31, 135, 138, 143, 156, 160, 163-64, 166-68, 171, 181-82, 184, 186, 189-90, 192, 196, 204, 207, 210-12, 214, 216-17, 219, 223, 225, 246, 249, 252-57

Egyptian Coptic Church, 223
El Elyon, 92
Elam, 39, 63, 92
Elaphantine, 44
election, 217
El-roi, 85
emancipation, 99, 203, 206
England, 57, 181-82, 202-3, 211, 214, 222-23, 228, 230, 235
English, 30, 31, 66, 102, 124, 143, 182, 202-3, 230-32, 234-35, 240
Ephesus, 89, 121, 140
equality, 197, 203, 231
Eritrea, 25, 219-20, 223, 225, 242, 244
Ethiopia, 14-15, 17-19, 25, 30-33, 36-37, 39-42, 46-48, 61, 66-68, 71, 109, 111, 136-38, 141-43, 159, 161-63, 171, 186-97, 204-5, 217-25, 228-29, 236, 242, 244, 256
Ethiopian Eunuch, 68
Ethiopian Orthodox Church, 188-89, 194-95, 217-18
Ethiopic, 47, 136, 188
ethnicity, 12-13, 19, 24, 26, 47, 57-58, 71, 73, 91, 102, 209-10
etymology, 23
eunuchs, 14, 17, 40, 67-68, 100, 135-37

Euphrates, 32, 52-53, 55, 68
Eurocentric, 108, 203
Europe, 23, 29, 47, 108, 112, 171, 173-74, 176, 178-79, 181-86, 188, 196-97, 200-6, 209, 215, 219, 232, 234-36, 240
European, 15, 17, 30-31, 47, 49, 59, 74, 91, 108, 170, 173, 175, 177-78, 180-82, 184-87, 192-93, 195, 197-98, 200-201, 203-7, 211-14, 219, 222-24, 227, 229-30, 233, 234-37, 240-41
evangelism, 111, 157, 228, 231-32, 235-36
evangelists, 89, 120, 156, 158, 160, 199, 236,
evil, 38, 43, 71, 100, 125-27, 133, 155, 180, 242
Ewostathians, 190
excommunication, 119, 221
execution, 70, 97, 100, 251
exegesis, 153
exile, 35, 41, 84, 222, 256
Exodus, 28, 42-43, 224-25
Falasha, 187, 218, 224
famine, 42, 44, 51-52, 74-75, 95, 224, 257
fascists, 222

Fasilidas, 15, 195, 218
Fatamids, 176
Fayyumic, 123
Fetha Negast, 218
flood, 33, 150
Fort Hare University, 240
Fourah Bay College, 234
France, French, 19, 104, 176-78, 180-84, 201-2
Freetown, 234-35
Freretown, 228-29
Galilee, 99, 112, 115, 130
Galla, 193
Gama, 198-99
Ganges, 32
Gath, 82-84
Gaza, 97
Gebal, 49
Geez, 222
Genadendal, 201
genealogy, 21, 23, 71, 104, 196
General Act of the Berlin Conference, 229
Genoa, 179
genocide, 77, 170, 206, 212
Gentiles, 22, 112-13
Gerar, 34, 50-51, 93-95
Gerarite, 95
Germanic, 129, 169, 183, 236
Germans, Germany, 31, 180, 183, 229, 259
Gezer, 88, 97
Ghana, 199, 205, 236
Ghanaian, 240
giants, 84-85, 97

Gihon, 31-32, 33
Girgashites, 28, 246
Gittite, 84-85
Gnosticism, 124, 154
Gomorrah, 50, 92-93
Goshen, 42-43, 76, 96-97
government, 42, 44, 53, 64, 71, 94-95, 136, 163, 170, 202, 209, 212, 218, 220, 224-25, 227, 235-37, 239, 241, 243, 251
Graeco-Roman, 123
Great Trek, 231
Greece, 17, 31, 49
Greek, 14, 25, 31, 44, 54, 57, 67, 82, 90, 112, 117-18, 120, 130-31, 151, 154, 160-61, 210-12
hair texture, 13, 57, 58
Hamath, 39
Hamathites, 28, 246
Hamitic, 13, 15, 22, 33-34, 37, 39, 47, 49, 75, 88, 91, 99, 104, 108, 118, 126, 128, 130, 140, 145-47, 157, 159, 161-62, 166-67, 171, 176-78, 181-82, 184, 189, 197, 208, 210-14, 216, 223, 225, 227, 247
Hamo-Semitic, 25, 59, 62, 247, 251
Haran, 42, 50-51, 75, 247
harem, 42, 50, 74, 88, 93, 95
Harklensis, 122

Har-Psusennes, 80
Hattian, 59
Hausa, 235
health, 184, 249
Hebron, 50, 52, 94-95, 97
Herakleopolis, 75
heresy, 124, 128, 139, 171, 190, 195, 221
hermeneutics, 131, 134
Heshbon, 96
heterodoxy, 124
Heth, 59, 88, 91
Hexapla, 119, 131
Hijra, 159, 161
Himyar, 161
Himyarite, 140-42
Hippo, 133
Hira, 140
historical criticism, 232
Hittite, 51, 58-59, 90, 94, 101-2, 105
HIV, 102. *See also* AIDS
Hivite, 95, 101
holiness, 98, 127, 132-33, 169
Holland, 201-2. *See also* Dutch
Holy Spirit, 116, 151-52, 166
Horite, 51
Hormah, 96
Hospitaliers, 179
Hyksos, 75
idolatry, 39, 46, 141, 154, 254
immorality, 254
imperialism, 171, 185, 223
India, 130, 136, 200
Indo-European, 59, 91
injil, 147, 150-51,

209
inspiration, 147, 165, 189
interpretation, 12, 14, 19, 48, 76, 108, 119-21, 123-24, 131, 146-47, 156, 158, 160-61, 168, 187, 198, 205, 209, 227, 234, 238
Iran, 23, 160-61
Iraq, 19, 23, 25, 32, 160-61, 212, 244
Ishmaelite, 76
Islam, 14-15, 48, 129, 136, 140-42, 145-47, 151, 153, 155-57, 159-71, 173, 175-76, 178, 180-81, 183-84, 186-88, 192, 205, 208-11, 214-15, 218, 221-22, 230, 234
Islamic fundamentalism, 15, 212, 215
Israel, 11, 13, 19, 23, 31, 34-40, 42-48, 51-54, 58, 62-71, 76-77, 79-84, 86-88, 91-92, 96-100, 104-6, 111-12, 115, 128, 135, 143, 155, 160, 170, 174, 177, 179, 184, 205, 212-15, 218-19, 224-25, 246, 250-56
Israelite, Israeli, 14, 36-37, 40, 43, 53, 64-65, 67-70, 73, 77-78, 82-84, 86, 96, 98-99, 105-6, 135-36, 224-25, 250, 254-55, 257
Istanbul, 210

Italian, 19, 31, 131, 176, 178, 182, 219-20, 222-23
Italy, 17, 24, 183, 219-20
Jacobite, 130
Jaffa, 179, 182
Jamaica, 61, 163, 187, 236, 239
Japhetic, 23
jealousy, 80, 85, 236, 248
Jebusites, 28, 98, 106, 246
Jericho, 52, 97, 104, 109
Jerusalem, 14, 40, 43, 64-65, 68, 71, 83-84, 90, 92, 97-98, 105-6, 112, 115-18, 129, 135, 140, 159, 164-65, 175-84, 186, 188, 215, 217, 255-56
Jesuits, 193-94, 199-200
Jesus, divinity of, 116, 154-55, 195
jihad, 176
Jordan, 25, 34, 53, 240, 246
Judaism, 15, 48, 88, 113, 117, 119-20, 125, 146-47, 151, 157, 166, 168, 210, 218
Judea, 112, 115, 139, 186, 256
judgment, 38, 45-46, 53, 65, 71-72, 81, 106, 149, 153-56, 204, 213, 230
Kassite, 26
Kawaida, 207
Kebra Negast, 217
kemi, 26
Kenite, 250

Kenya, 19, 41, 196, 228-29
Kharijites, 169
Khoi, 231
Khoisan, 200
King James Version, 21, 30, 195
Kiriath-arba, 94
Kiriath-jearim, 84
Knights Templar, 179
Kongo, 238
Korahite, 39
kosher, 189
Kurd, 181
Kush, 25, 30, 61
Lachish, 97
Lake Tana, 41
League of Nations, 214
Lebanon, 19, 49, 246
Lehabim, 28
Lehabites, 27, 246
Lemba, 204
leprosy, 254
Levite, 84
liberal policies, 95, 211-13, 232
liberation, 127, 177, 193, 207-8, 221, 230, 235, 240, 242-43, 251
Liberia, 203, 235
Liberia College, 235
Libnah, 97
Libya, 17, 27-28, 37, 46, 196, 246
London Missionary Society, 229, 231
Lud, 46, 49
Ludites, 27, 246
Lugandan, 230
Machpelah, 51, 94
Magnesians, 120
Makkedah, 97
Makuria, 138, 163-

64
Malawi, 239
Malian, 199
Mamluk Turks, 164
martyrdom, martyrs, 119, 127, 130, 133, 230, 233, 238, 241
Marxism, 223-24
Matabeleland, 19
Mecca, 141-42, 146, 158-59, 161-62, 166, 175, 181
Mede, 65
Medina (Yathrib), 159, 165
Mediterranean, 27-28, 41, 46, 49, 52, 55, 74, 128
Melkites, 130
Meroe, 14, 25, 67, 136-38
Meru, 204
Mesopotamia, 24, 30-32, 61-62, 65, 160-61
Messiah, 13-14, 54, 88-89, 92, 112-13, 115-16, 118, 139, 143, 147, 151, 153-56, 159, 171, 176, 179, 183, 204, 212-13, 217
Methodists, 233, 235-36
Middle East, 12-13, 19, 25, 29, 54, 147, 210-11
Middle Egyptian, 123
Middle Egyptian Fayyumic, 123
Midian, 34, 55, 59, 69-70, 78, 101, 135, 249, 251, 253
Midianite, 34, 68-70, 76, 248-51,

253-54
Migdol, 43, 46
migration, 19, 159
Milan, 128, 133
millets, 210-11, 214
miracles, 14, 107, 139, 152, 207, 242
Misrayim, 12-15, 24, 26-28, 41, 50, 55, 59, 73-74, 82-83, 85-86, 88, 90-91, 101, 109, 123, 127, 135, 143, 147, 174, 196, 205-6, 208-9, 227, 240, 242, 257
missionaries, 15-16, 89, 111, 130, 137-39, 142-43, 146, 160, 169, 171, 187, 192, 194-95, 198-201, 204-5, 211, 218-19, 228-32, 234-38, 240
Mizrachi, 213
Moabites, 34-36, 39, 47, 68-69, 254
monasticism, 121, 126
Mongol, 161
monotheism, 147, 169
Montanists, 132
Mopsuestia, 121
Moravian, 201, 204
Morocco, 27, 215
Mosul, 178, 180, 244
Mozambique, 199
murder, 77
Muslims, 119, 130, 142, 145, 150-51, 153, 156-57, 159-66, 168-71, 173-84, 186-88, 192, 197, 200, 204-5, 210-15, 217, 219,

224, 229-30, 243, 249
Nag Hammadi, 124
Napata, 25
Naphtuhites, 27, 246
NASA, 33
Nation of Islam, 125
Native Americans, 235
Ndebele, 232
Neo-Babylonian Empire, 65
Nestorianism, 121
Nicaea, 119-20, 131
Nicene, 129, 147
Nigeria, 58, 204, 234
Nile, 18, 26, 32-33, 41, 44-46, 55, 77, 111, 126, 204, 219
Nineveh, 39, 71, 244, 256-57
Nobatia, 138, 163
nomads, 50-51, 53, 251
Nubia, 138, 157, 163-64
Nubian, 67, 138, 161, 163-64, 186
obedience, 39
Oman, 25, 142
Operation Moses, 225
Operation Queen of Sheba, 225
Operation Solomon, 225
original sin, 116, 134
Oromo, 193
Orthodox Christianity, 177
orthodoxy, 113, 121, 123, 131, 143, 145, 162, 166
Ottoman Empire, 15, 209-11
Paddan-aram, 101
padrao, 198-99, 227

padroado, 198
pagans, 15, 81, 88,
   128, 133, 137, 141,
   156, 163, 165, 179,
   186-87, 191, 206
Palestine, 15, 25, 44,
   88, 115, 118, 123,
   135, 143, 147, 156,
   159-60, 164-65,
   174, 176, 178-80,
   184, 186-87, 196,
   210-15, 217, 246
Palestinians, 14, 122,
   165, 179, 215, 259
papacy, 15, 192, 211
papal edicts, 197
Paras, 49
parousia, 153
Pathros, 39, 43, 46
Pathrusites, 27, 246
patriarchies, 210
patriarchs, 23, 41,
   52, 75, 117, 121,
   137, 140, 167, 186
peace treaty, 95, 140,
   250
Pelusium, 46
Pentecost, 14, 112,
   139
Peor, 69
Perizzites, 98
Persia, 165
Peshitta, 122
Pethor, 68
Philistia, 39, 50, 52-
   53, 59, 82, 85-87,
   115
Philistines, 27, 50-
   53, 55, 58-59, 73-
   74, 82-85, 87, 93,
   99, 105, 178, 246,
   253
philosophy, 67, 118,
   123, 130, 160
Philoxeniana, 122
pilgrimage, 175
Pisa, 179

Pishon, 32-33
plagues, 42, 75, 79,
   106, 254
political alliances, 46
politics, 31, 45, 179,
   199, 234
polygamy, 101, 238
polytheism, 146, 155
popes, 177, 180, 182,
   184, 197-98, 225
Portugal, 193, 197-
   98, 202
poverty, 224, 243
Presbyterians, 233,
   240
priesthood
   (Melchizedek,
   Aaron), 50, 92-93
prophecy, 28, 39, 48,
   52, 54, 63, 88, 100,
   127, 132, 136, 249
prophetess, 169
prostitute, 103-4
prostitution, 138
pseudepigrapha, 136
Punic Wars, 19
Punt, 28, 196
Put, 12-13, 15, 23-
   24, 27-28, 37, 41,
   46, 48-49, 174,
   196-206, 208, 215,
   227-29, 236-37,
   239-42
queen of heaven, 81
Quraish, 141-42,
   146, 158, 161
race, 11, 57, 68, 97,
   125, 177
racism, 19, 30, 102,
   229, 234, 236
rape, 51, 76, 96, 184,
   206
*Recognitions of Clem-
   ent*, 117
Red Sea, 17, 25, 33,
   52, 61, 66, 79, 139,
   158

redemption, 207
Rehoboth, 244, 251
religious tolerance,
   242
repatriation, 252
Rephaim, 97
resistance, 99, 127,
   161, 164, 167, 169,
   195, 222, 238
resurrection, 153-54,
   240
rhetoric, 90, 133,
   177
Robben Island, 233
Roman, 11, 18-19,
   25, 36, 55, 74, 88,
   90, 112, 115-16,
   119, 123, 127, 133,
   136, 138, 140, 152,
   161, 168, 173,
   175-76, 188, 193-
   94, 211, 241
Roman Catholi-
   cism, 152, 176,
   188, 194, 211, 241
Roman Empire, 25,
   112, 140, 161, 173,
   175
Rome, 17, 24-25, 31,
   137, 140, 169, 173,
   179, 183, 186-87,
   191-94, 197, 220
royalty, 67, 78-79,
   106, 112, 138, 217
Russia, 31
Rwanda, 203, 206,
   237
sabbath, 120, 136,
   147, 187, 189-91,
   194-95, 221, 238
Sabtah, 25, 244
Sabteca, 25, 244
sacrifice, 133, 249
Sahara, 15, 28, 227
Sahidic, 123
Salamis, 116
Salem, 50, 92

salvation, 14, 48, 72,
   125, 149, 227
Samaria, 112, 255-
   57
sanctuary (refuge),
   42-44, 51, 74, 80-
   83, 95, 99, 140,
   161, 214, 229, 249,
   250
São Salvador, 199
Sasanians, 165
Satanic verses, 158
Saudi Arabia, 19, 23,
   25, 32-33, 244
Scandinavian, 17
Scottish, 240
scramble for Africa,
   229
sea peoples, 50, 59
Seba, 25, 244
Seir, 35, 51
Seljuk Turks, 176
Semitic, 22-23, 25,
   32-33, 35, 37, 39,
   42, 47, 52, 55, 58,
   61, 66, 70, 75, 86,
   91-92, 101, 111,
   196, 247-48
Senegal, 19, 240
Senna, 204
Sephardim, 213, 215
Septuagint, 30, 131
settlement, 35, 96,
   104, 163
Shia, 210
Shiites, 169
Shinar, 39, 244
Shoa, 163, 228
Shona, 232
Shur, 33, 50, 249
Sidon, 49, 88, 107,
   109, 246
Sidonian, 100
Sierra Leone, 19,
   203, 234-35
sin, 42, 105
Sinites, 28, 246

Sion, 188

skin color, 26, 57, 254

slavery, 15, 26, 42-43, 86, 92, 102, 111, 197, 202-4, 206-7, 219, 223, 229-31

socialism, 240

Sodom, 50, 92-93

Somalia, 19, 28

Sotho Christians, 233

Soviet, 23, 223

Spain, 49, 176, 202

spouses, 13, 35, 74, 76, 101, 109

starvation, 106-7, 243

Sub-Achmimic, 123

Sudan, 25, 27, 163, 225, 244, 246

suffering, 161, 181

suicide, 127, 253

Sunna, 142

Sunni, 210

sura, 149-53

Swahili, 196, 228

synagogue, 111, 157, 166, 210

Syria, 14, 25, 44, 58, 104, 112, 115, 137, 140, 163, 165-66, 178, 181, 184, 212, 246

Syriac, 122

Table of Nations, 12, 21-24, 28, 54, 59

Tagaste, 133

Tahpanhes, 43

Talmud, 113, 218

Tanak, 131, 136, 150

Tanganyika, 229

Tanzania, 41, 196, 229, 240

Tarshish, 49

Tarsus, 90, 120-21

tawra, 147, 150-51, 209

Temanite, 251

Tembu National Church, 233

temple, 39, 44, 64-65, 80, 84, 90, 99, 106, 112, 115, 140, 166, 179, 255

Ten Commandments, 126

Tewahdo, 226

Tewahedo, 163

Thalia, 128

Thebes, 43, 46, 75, 80

theologians, 14, 66, 118, 122, 128, 130-31, 133, 135, 146, 156, 195, 202, 235, 240

theophany, 69

Tiber River, 25

Tigris River, 32, 55

Timnah, 87

Timnite, 87

tolerance, 113, 175, 180, 194, 215, 219

traditions, 101, 108, 135, 139, 140, 146, 153, 157, 161, 167, 169, 186-89, 218, 220

Transvaal, 231

treaties (Wichale),

181, 219

tribalism, 242-43

Trinidad, 235

Trinity, 116, 132, 147, 155

Tripoli, 178

Truth and Reconciliation Commission, 242

Tswana, 233

Tunis, 131

Tunisia, 27, 131, 184, 215

Turkey, 19, 23, 29, 49, 246

Tyre, 37-39, 49, 54, 99, 106-7, 179, 181

Uganda, 19, 240-41

Ugaritic, 47

Umma, 159

Ummayad Dynasty, 165, 169

Union Jack, 230

United Nations, 213, 215

unity, 118, 121, 123, 143, 181, 192, 219

University of Sierra Leone, 234

Venice, 179

virgin birth, 116-17, 152-53, 204

Vulgate, 131

covenant, 43, 50-52, 68, 86, 88, 91, 98, 103, 105, 111, 113, 151, 216, 247-48, 253, 257

Wadi Besor, 83

Wafd Nationalist

Party, 212

warfare, 179, 208

wedding, 87, 102

White Fathers, 230

widow, 102-3, 106-7, 137

women, 35, 51, 69, 85-87, 93, 98, 100-109, 115, 146, 151-53, 157, 170, 178, 180, 231, 248, 253-54

World War I, 211, 214, 223

World War II, 214, 223

Xhosa, 233, 237

Xhosan, 231

Yemen, 25, 66, 140-42, 244

Yoruba, 205, 234

Zagwe, 187-88, 217

Zaire, 241

zakat, 159

Zambesi, 198

Zambia, 239, 241

ZANU, 240

ZAPU, 240

Zarephite, 106-7

Zeboiim, 92

Zemarites, 28, 246

Zemer, 49

Ziglag, 83

Zimbabwe, 19, 199, 239, 241

Zoar, 50, 92

Zoroastrianism, 133

Zulus, 19, 58, 231-32

Scripture Index

Genesis
1—11, *22, 28, 62,*
    276, 278
1—15, *22, 32, 33,*
    278
2, *32*
2:10, *32*
2:10-14, *31, 32*
2:11, *32, 250*
2:11-12, *36*
2:13, *30, 32*
2:14, *32*
3:9-10, *72*
4, *22*
4:17, *62*
4:18, *21*
5, *21*
9:20-21, *48*
9:24, *48*
9:25-27, *35, 48*
9:26-27, *42*
9:27, *54, 178*
10, *7, 12, 22, 23, 25,*
    27, 29, 31, 54, 57,
    58, 59, 196, 274,
    278
10:1-4, *21*
10:2-5, *23*
10:5, *21*
10:6, *21*
10:6-8, *30*
10:6-20, *24, 250*
10:7, *21, 25, 34*
10:7-12, *250*
10:8, *21*
10:8-11, *25*
10:8-12, *32, 62*
10:9, *62*
10:10-11, *25*
10:11, *72*
10:13, *21, 50*
10:13-14, *50, 251*
10:14, *21*

10:15, *21*
10:15-19, *29, 251*
10:20, *21*
10:21-31, *23*
10:22, *25, 92*
10:22-23, *21*
10:31, *21*
11:1-9, *62*
11:8-9, *62*
11:27-28, *42*
12, *35*
12:1-3, *50*
12:1-8, *42*
12:2, *252*
12:4-5, *74*
12:4-9, *50*
12:10-20, *74, 93*
12:10—13:1, *42*
12:19, *74*
12:20, *91*
13:1, *50*
13:2-3, *50*
13:10, *41*
14:1-3, *92*
14:1-16, *50*
14:13-24, *92*
14:19-22, *92*
15:1-21, *103*
15:18-21, *254*
15:21, *251*
16—50, *85, 278*
16:1-15, *85*
16:2, *101*
16:10, *85*
16:11, *85*
16:13, *85*
17:5-8, *253*
17:18, *253*
17:20, *253, 254*
17:23-27, *253*
19:1-24, *50*
19:36-38, *34*
20:1, *50*

20:1-18, *51, 93*
20:4-5, *94*
20:6, *94*
20:7, *94*
20:9-10, *94*
20:11, *93*
20:17-18, *93*
21:1-3, *94*
21:8-16, *85*
21:9, *253*
21:11, *253*
21:15-16, *253*
21:17-19, *253*
21:17-21, *86*
21:22-34, *51, 94*
22:23, *21*
23:1-20, *51, 94*
23:3-20, *94*
24:2-10, *101*
24:3, *102*
25:1, *101*
25:1-2, *34, 254*
25:1-4, *101*
25:1-18, *146*
25:2, *34*
25:2-6, *34*
25:3, *21, 25, 250*
25:6, *34, 101*
25:9, *254*
25:13, *33, 253*
25:17, *254*
25:18, *33, 250, 254*
25:25, *256*
25:29-34, *256*
25:30, *256*
26:1, *51*
26:1-11, *51, 95*
26:7, *95*
26:9-11, *95*
26:10, *95*
26:12-16, *95*
26:12-23, *51*
26:26, *95*

26:34, *51, 101*
26:35, *101*
27:40, *35*
27:46, *102*
27:46—28:2, *101*
28:6-9, *102*
31—42, *36*
33:18-19, *95*
33:18-20, *51*
34:1-31, *96*
34:22-23, *96*
34:26, *96*
35:1, *96*
35:6, *51*
35:16-21, *51*
35:27, *52*
36:1-5, *35*
36:1-43, *51, 102*
36:2, *101*
36:6-8, *35*
36:9-19, *36*
36:16, *102*
36:31, *256*
36:31-39, *256*
37:14, *52*
37:36, *76*
38:1-5, *102*
38:6-11, *102*
38:9, *102*
38:12, *103*
38:13-23, *103*
38:24-30, *103*
39:1, *76*
39:1-6, *76*
39:7-10, *76*
39:21-23, *76*
40:1, *76*
40:4, *77*
41:1-24, *76*
41:25-36, *76*
41:38, *76*
41:45, *86*
41:50, *77*

41:50-52, *86*
42:7-32, *52*
45:7, *76*
45:16-20, *76*
46:26, *21*
46:28—47:12, *42*
47:1-6, *76*
47:7-10, *76*
47:11, *76*
49:29-33, *51*
50:20, *76*

Exodus
1:5, *21*
1:7, *42, 77*
1:8, *77*
1:8-22, *77*
1:11, *43*
2:5-10, *77*
2:11-15, *78*
2:15-22, *254*
2:15—4:19, *34*
2:16-22, *258*
2:22, *258*
2:23, *78*
3:1—4:20, *78*
4:18-20, *258*
4:24-26, *258*
5:1, *78*
5:2-21, *78*
8:8, *79*
8:15, *79*
8:25-28, *79*
9:27-28, *79*
10:12-20, *79*
10:24, *79*
10:25-29, *79*
12:29-32, *79*
12:37, *43*
12:40, *42*
14:5-9, *79*
14:21—15:21, *79*
17:8-16, *36*
18:1-27, *254*
18:3-4, *258*
18:5, *258*
18:10-12, *254*

18:18-22, *254*
23:31, *49, 50, 52*

Leviticus
21:9, *103*

Numbers
10:29-32, *255*
10:30, *255*
12:1, *258, 259*
12:10, *259*
12:12, *21*
13:29, *36*
14:25, *36*
20:14-21, *36, 96*
21:1-3, *96*
21:21-32, *96*
21:33-35, *96*
22:1—24:25, *35*
22:1—25:18, *34*
22:6, *68*
22:7-8, *68*
22:12, *68*
22:16-17, *68*
22:22, *69*
22:22-30, *69*
22:33, *69*
22:36-38, *69*
22:41—24:25, *69*
24:17, *70*
25:1-18, *69, 259*
25:4-9, *70*
25:6-9, *259*
25:7-8, *259*
25:14-15, *259*
25:16-18, *69*
25:17-18, *259*
26:59, *152*
31:1-11, *34*
31:8, *69, 70*
31:16, *69*

Deuteronomy
2:9-12, *34*
2:19, *34*
2:23, *251*
3:1-3, *97*

3:11, *97*
7:1, *251*
7:2, *49*
23:3-4, *35*
23:5, *69*
23:7-8, *36, 43*
25:5-10, *102*
29:7, *97*

Joshua
2:1, *104*
2:2-24, *104*
2:10, *97*
3:10, *251*
6:17, *104*
6:22-25, *104*
7:21, *37*
8:1-29, *97*
9:10, *97*
10:1, *97*
10:3-4, *97*
10:16-17, *97*
10:18-28, *97*
10:29-43, *97*
11:1-3, *98*
11:4, *97*
11:5-23, *98*
12:7-24, *53*
12:7—13:7, *52*
13:1-6, *49*
13:25, *34*
16:2, *251*
18:22, *251*
24:9-10, *69*
24:11, *251*

Judges
1:4-7, *98*
1:7, *98*
1:16, *255*
3:7-8, *98*
3:9-11, *98*
3:12-30, *35, 98*
4:1-3, *98, 255*
4:4-16, *99*
4:4-24, *255*
4:11, *255*

4:17, *255*
4:17-20, *99*
4:17-22, *255*
4:18, *255*
4:19-22, *255*
4:21-22, *99*
4:23-24, *99*
5:6, *255*
5:24-27, *255*
5:31—6:6, *255*
6:1—8:28, *34*
6:7—7:23, *255*
7:24-25, *256*
8:1-3, *256*
8:4-28, *256*
8:5, *256*
8:6-12, *256*
8:18-19, *256*
8:20-21, *256*
10:6-9, *35, 53*
10:11—11:33, *35*
11:14-18, *36*
13:1—16:31, *53*
14:1-9, *87*
14:4, *87*
14:10-14, *87*
14:15, *87*
14:16-18, *87*
14:19, *87*
14:20—15:2, *87*
15:3-17, *87*
16:1, *87*
16:4, *87*
16:5, *87*
16:6-19, *87*

Ruth
4:1-12, *102*

1 Samuel
2:11-19, *257*
4:1—7:14, *53*
5:1—7:1, *84*
5:8-9, *84*
9:16, *53*
11:1-15, *35*
14:47, *35*

15:1-8, *257*
15:7, *250*
15:8-9, *257*
15:17-21, *257*
15:32-33, *257*
17:4-11, *82*
17:42-44, *82*
17:48-53, *82*
21:1-6, *257*
21:6, *257*
21:10-15, *82*
22:3-4, *35*
22:6-10, *257*
22:9, *257*
27:1-4, *83*
27:5-7, *83*
28:1-2, *83*
29:1-11, *83*
30:1-6, *83*
30:7-20, *83*
31:1-5, *258*

2 Samuel
1:1-10, *258*
1:11-16, *258*
5:1-12, *99*
5:11, *99*
6:1-19, *84*
6:6-8, *84*
6:11-12, *84*
8:2, *35*
8:13-14, *36*
10:1—12:31, *35*
11:1-27, *105*
11:14-15, *105*
11:16-21, *105*
15:18, *84*
15:19-20, *84*
15:21-23, *84*
15:32, *251*
15:32-37, *105*
16:15-19, *105*
16:16, *251*
17:5, *251*
17:5-16, *105*
17:14, *251*
17:21-22, *105*

18:1-18, *105*
18:2, *84*
18:2-4, *70*
18:5, *70, 71*
18:14, *70*
18:19-21, *70*
18:19-23, *70*
18:21, *30*
18:21-32, *30*
18:22-31, *70*
18:32, *71*
21:15-17, *85*
21:18-22, *85*
23:39, *105*
24:1-25, *106*
24:16, *106*

1 Kings
3:1, *44, 79*
4:21, *44, 53*
4:25-28, *80*
4:30, *44*
5:1, *99*
5:1-12, *99*
7:8, *88*
7:13-14, *106*
7:15-47, *106*
9:10-14, *99*
9:13, *99*
9:14, *100*
9:16, *44, 88*
9:24, *88*
10:1, *65, 135*
10:1-13, *37, 65,*
  250
10:9, *135*
10:13, *66*
10:15, *37*
10:22, *100*
10:28-29, *44*
11:1, *88*
11:14-20, *36*
11:14-22, *80, 257*
11:21-22, *80*
11:25, *257*
11:26-40, *43, 80*
14:25-28, *44*

16:31, *100*
17:1, *106*
17:8-15, *106*
17:16-24, *107*
18:4, *100*
18:19, *100*
19:1-3, *100*
21:1-16, *100*
21:17-24, *100*

2 Kings
1:1, *35*
3:1-27, *36*
3:5-27, *35*
8:20-22, *36*
9:14-37, *100*
9:22, *100*
13:20, *35*
14:7-10, *36*
15:17-22, *37*
15:19-20, *260*
15:29, *260*
15:29—17:41, *38*
16:5-20, *260*
17:1-4, *45*
17:1-6, *260*
17:4, *81*
17:24-33, *38*
17:24-41, *260*
18:1—19:37, *261*
18:1—20:6, *38*
18:9-12, *260*
18:21, *45*
19:9, *45, 67*
19:31, *250*
19:36, *261*
20:1-11, *63*
20:12-19, *38, 63*
23:28-35, *45*
23:29-30, *81*
23:31-35, *81*
24:1-7, *81*
24:1-17, *63*
24:1—25:30, *38*
24:2, *35*
24:7, *45*
24:20, *64*

25:8-26, *64*
25:26, *43*
25:27-30, *64*

1 Chronicles
1:8-10, *30*
1:9, *250*
1:15, *251*
2:3, *102*
5:25-26, *38*
13:14, *84*
14:1, *99*
15:18-21, *84*
15:24, *84*
18:2, *35*
18:12-13, *36*
19:1—20:3, *35*
21:28—22:1, *106*
27:33, *251*

2 Chronicles
2:3-16, *99*
2:11-12, *99*
3:1, *106*
8:2, *100*
8:11, *88*
9:1-12, *37, 65,*
  250
9:14, *37*
10:2, *43*
12:1-12, *44*
12:2, *80*
13:4, *251*
14:9-15, *66*
14:12, *66*
20:1-30, *35*
21:8-10, *36*
25:14-19, *36*
28:16-17, *36*
28:16-21, *37*
28:16-27, *260*
32:1-33, *38*
32:31, *38*
35:20-24, *81*
35:20—36:4, *45*
36:1-4, *81*
36:5-21, *38*

Ezra
4:1-2, *261*
4:9, *250*
4:10, *262*
9:1—10:44, *35*

Nehemiah
9:8, *251*
13:23-30, *35*

Job
6:19, *37, 250*
28:19, *36*

Psalms
1, *92*
7:1, *30*
68:28-35, *40*
68:31, *40*
72:10, *37, 250*
72:15, *36, 250*
76:2, *92*
83:5-8, *35*
87:4, *39*
135:11, *97*
136:17-22, *97*

Song of Solomon
1:5, *33*

Isaiah
1, *156*
7:10—8:8, *37*
10:5-34, *39*
11:11, *30, 39, 251*
11:16, *40*
14:24-27, *39*
14:29-31, *54*
15:1—16:14, *39*
16:6, *39*
18:1, *32*
19:1-10, *46*
19:18-25, *46*
19:23-25, *40*
20:1, *261*
20:1-6, *37*
20:4, *46*

20:5, *37*
23:13, *37*
27:13, *39*
30:3, *45*
30:27-33, *39*
31:1-3, *45*
31:8-9, *39*
36:1—38:8, *38*
36:6, *45*
37:9, *45, 67*
37:37, *250*
37:38, *261*
39:1-8, *38*
43:3, *250*
45:14, *40, 46*
47:6, *38*
60:6, *36, 250*
60:7, *33*

Jeremiah
1:5, *21*
6:20, *36, 250*
13:23, *30, 61*
20:3-6, *38*
24:8, *43*
25:9, *38*
25:15-26, *38*
25:23, *250*
26:20-23, *43*
27:2-11, *39*
37:3-10, *45*
37:5-11, *82*
38:4-5, *71*
38:7-13, *71*
39:15-18, *71*
40:11, *35*
41:1—44:30, *43*
42, *39*
44:1, *251*
44:1-19, *81*
44:15, *251*
44:27-30, *43*
44:30, *82*
46:1-24, *46*
46:2, *81*
46:9, *37, 251*
47:1-7, *54*

47:4, *53, 251*
48:1-46, *39*
48:26-30, *39*
48:47, *40*
49:4, *38*
49:5, *39*
49:6, *40*
49:7-22, *39*
49:8, *250*
50:17, *38*
50:18, *39*
52:31-34, *64*

Lamentations
4:21-22, *39*

Ezekiel
9, *45*
17:11-15, *45*
17:11-21, *82*
21:20, *39*
23:5-10, *38*
23:11-23, *37*
25:1-7, *38*
25:4, *39*
25:8, *39*
25:8-11, *39*
25:12-14, *39*
25:13, *250*
25:15-17, *54*
26:4, *49*
26:7, *38*
26:7-14, *54*
26:12-13, *49*
26:15-17, *49*
27:3, *49*
27:4-11, *49*
27:8, *251*
27:11, *251*
27:12-25, *49*
27:20, *250*
27:20-22, *36*
27:21, *33, 37*
27:22, *36, 37, 250*
27:22-23, *250*
27:25, *49*
28:4-5, *49*

28:5-6, *54*
28:7-8, *54*
28:10, *54*
29:3, *45*
29:10, *37, 46*
29:12, *46*
29:13-14, *46*
29:14, *251*
29:14-15, *46*
29:17-20, *38*
29:20, *38*
30:4-5, *37, 38*
30:4-6, *46*
30:6, *46*
30:9, *37*
30:10, *38*
30:13, *46*
30:13-18, *46*
30:14, *251*
30:21, *45*
30:23, *46*
30:24, *38*
30:26, *46*
31, *45*
32:9, *46*
32:11, *38*
32:12, *45*
32:22-23, *39*
32:29-30, *39*
35:15, *39*
36:5, *39*
38:13, *36, 250*

Daniel
5:1-31, *65*
5:11-13, *65*
7:1, *65*
8:1, *65*

Joel
3:19, *39, 46*

Amos
1:11-12, *39*
1:13-15, *38*
6:2, *250*
9:7, *39, 53, 251*

Obadiah
1—21, *39*

Micah
5:6, *62, 250*
7:12, *44*

Nahum
1:1—3:19, *39*
3:8-10, *46*
3:9, *37, 251*

Habakkuk
3:7, *30*

Zephaniah
1:1, *30, 71*
2:5, *52*
2:8-9, *35*
2:12, *39, 72*
2:13, *71, 250*
2:13-15, *39*
3:8-13, *39*
3:10, *32, 39*

Zechariah
10:10, *44*
14:16-19, *46*

Malachi
1:2-5, *39*

Matthew
1, *153*
1—13, *104*
1:3, *103*

1:5, *104*
1:16, *103*
2, *117*
2:13-15, *44*
6:12, *242*
12:41, *39, 250*
12:42, *65*
13:24-30, *127*
15, *115*
15:21-28, *107*
15:22, *107*
19:21, *126*
24, *127*
27:32, *88*

Mark
7:24-30, *107*
7:26, *107*
15:21, *88, 89*

Luke
1, *153*
1:5-39, *150*
4:25-26, *107*
6:20-26, *249*
11:32, *39, 250*
23:26, *88*
23:27-31, *89*

John
3:16, *249*
17:12, *155*
17:15, *155*

Acts
1:8, *112*

2:10, *88*
2:11, *139*
3:10, *251*
8:26-39, *67, 136*
8:27, *40, 68*
10:9-16, *11*
10:34-35, *11*
11:26, *119*
13, *112*
13:1, *89*
15, *112*
15:13-21, *117*
18:24-28, *89*
18:27, *89*
21:17-26, *115*
21:27-36, *90*
21:37-38, *90*
24:5, *117*

Romans
11:1-6, *149*
16:13, *89*

1 Corinthians
1:12, *89*
4:6, *89*
8:6, *128*
16:12, *89*

Galatians
1:15-17, *34*
1:17-18, *139*
2:9, *117*
3:28, *249*
4:21-31, *86*

Ephesians
6:1, *120*

Philippians
3:4-6, *90*

Hebrews
7:1-22, *93*
7:2, *93*
7:3, *93*
7:7, *93*
7:9-10, *93*
11:24, *78*
11:31, *105*
11:35, *107*

James
2:25, *105*

2 Peter
2:15, *69*

Jude
11, *69*

Revelation
2:14, *69*
12:11, *241*
14:8, *38*
16:19, *38*
17:5, *38*
18:2, *38*
18:10, *38*
18:21, *38*
21:5, *249*